MONOGRAPH 38

Approaches to the Historical Archaeology of Mexico, Central & South America

Edited by Janine Gasco, Greg Charles Smith, and Patricia Fournier-García

The Institute of Archaeology
University of California, Los Angeles
1997

UCLA Institute of Archaeology Editorial Board
  Jeanne E. Arnold, Marilyn Beaudry-Corbett, Susan Downey, Ernestine S. Elster,
  Lothar von Falkenhausen, Richard M. Leventhal, Daniel C. Polz, Glenn Russell,
  James R. Sackett, and Stuart T. Smith.

UCLA Institute of Archaeology
  Richard M. Leventhal, Director
  Marilyn Beaudry-Corbett, Director of Publications

Edited by Jennifer Comeau, Rita Demsetz, Marilyn Gatto, Beverly Godwin,
Patricia Campbell Healy, and Brenda Johnson-Grau
Designed by Brenda Johnson-Grau
Production by Linda Tang and Michael Tang

Library of Congress Cataloging-in-Publication Data

Approaches to the historical archaeology of Mexico, Central & South America /
    edited by Janine Gasco, Greg Charles Smith, and Patricia Fournier-García.
        p.   cm. -- (Monograph ; 38)
    "The 1992 meetings of the Society of Historical Archaeology (SHA)
    held in Kingston, Jamaica"--P. v.
    English and Spanish.
    Includes bibliographical references.
    ISBN: 0-917956-89-3
    1. Latin America--History--To 1830. 2. Latin America--
History--1830-1898. 3. Indians--History. 4. Indians--Antiquities.
5. Latin America--Antiquities. I. Gasco, Janine. II. Smith, Greg
Charles. III. Fournier-García, Patricia. IV. Series: Monograph
(University of California, Los Angeles. Institute of Archaeology) ;
38.
F1412.A66   1997
980'.01--dc21   97-28890
                                                               CIP

Copyright © 1997 Regents of the University of California.
All rights reserved. Printed in the USA.

Contents

Chapter 1	Introduction *Janine Gasco, Greg Charles Smith, and Patricia Fournier-García*	1

MEXICO

Chapter 2	Indian Consumers on the Periphery of the Colonial Market System: Tracing Domestic Economic Behavior in a Tehuantepec Hamlet *Judith Francis Zeitlin and Lillian Thomas*	5
Chapter 3	Arqueología Histórica y Etnoarqueología de la Comunidad Alfarera Otomí de Santa María del Pino, México *Lourdes Mondragón, Patricia Fournier-García, y Nahúm Noguera*	17
Chapter 4	Settlement Patterns of the Late Colonial Period in Yaxcabá Parish, Yucatán, Mexico: Implications for the Distribution of Land and Population Before the Caste War *Rani T. Alexander*	29
Chapter 5	Survey and Excavation of Invisible Sites in the Mesoamerican Lowlands *Janine Gasco*	41
Chapter 6	Tendencias de Consumo en México durante los Períodos Colonial e Independiente *Patricia Fournier-García*	49

GUATEMALA

Chapter 7	Protohistoric to Colonial Settlement Transition in the Antigua Valley, Guatemala *Eugenia J. Robinson*	59
Chapter 8	La Arquitectura Industrial y Utilitaria de Santiago, Capital del Reino de Guatemala, y sus Alrededores *Rodrigo Aparicio*	71

HONDURAS

Chapter 9	The Mercedarians and the Missionization of the Lenca in Santa Bárbara de Tencoa, Honduras *Nancy Johnson Black*	83
Chapter 10	The Mercedarian Mission System in Santa Bárbara de Tencoa, Honduras *John M. Weeks*	91
Chapter 11	Setting an English Table: Black Carib Archaeology on the Caribbean Coast of Honduras *Charles D. Cheek*	101

ECUADOR

Chapter 12	Monumentos y Fragmentos: Arqueología Histórica en el Ecuador *Jozef Buys*	111
Chapter 13	Settlements and Ceramics of the Tambo River, Ecuador, from the Early Nineteenth Century *Karen E. Stothert, Kevin Gross, Anne Fox, and Amelia Sánchez Mosquera*	121

ARGENTINA

Chapter 14	Buenos Aires del Siglo XVI al XIX: Avances en Arqueología Histórica *Daniel Schávelzon*	133

URUGUAY

Chapter 15	La Arqueología Histórica en el Uruguay: Historia, Análisis, y Perspectivas *Nelsys Fusco Zambetogliris*	139

PERU

Chapter 16	Continuity or Change?: Vertical Archipelagos in Southern Peru During the Early Colonial Period *Mary Van Buren*	155
Chapter 17	Andean and European Contributions to Spanish Colonial Culture and Viticulture in Moquegua, Peru *Greg Charles Smith*	165
Chapter 18	Tin-Enameled Wares of Moquegua, Peru *Prudence M. Rice*	173

Glossary	181
Bibliography	185

Preface

THIS VOLUME BRINGS TOGETHER for the first time a collection of articles by scholars working in the field of historical archaeology throughout Latin America. Even though archaeologists have conducted investigations on historical sites in Latin America for many years, international borders have often limited interaction among researchers and the exchange of pertinent literature among interested readers. As a result, there has been little awareness or understanding of the breadth of research focused on the archaeology of post-contact Latin America, especially that performed outside the circum-Caribbean (Burger 1989; Schaedel 1992; Thomas 1991). Although it is premature to attempt to synthesize all the current research on historical sites in Latin America, this volume is meant to convey a sense of the work under way and the direction in which future research may be headed.

The 1992 meetings of the Society for Historical Archaeology (SHA), held in Kingston, Jamaica, presented a unique opportunity for historical archaeologists working in Latin America to participate in a single symposium. This gathering marked the first time that the SHA met outside the United States or Canada, and conference organizers expressed a specific interest in including papers from Latin America. Early in 1991, Janine Gasco and Greg Smith approached several of their colleagues to determine whether there was sufficient interest to warrant organizing a symposium. The initial response was overwhelmingly positive. An all-day symposium was held at the meetings in Jamaica in January 1992 where twenty-two papers were presented reporting on historical archaeology projects in seven countries. Symposium participants were in favor of publishing the symposium papers, and, with the addition of Patricia Fournier-García as a third editor of the volume, publication of the symposium papers became a truly pan-American effort. Fifteen of these papers appear in revised form in this volume (one of the original co-authored papers appears here as two separate chapters). In addition, a contribution from Uruguay, not included in the 1992 symposium, is included here to broaden the coverage. We would like to thank the other participants in the symposium who contributed greatly to its success: Thomas Charlton and Cynthia Otis Charlton, Fernando Cortés Brasdefer, Bernd Fahmel Beyer, Daniel Finamore, Craig Hanson, Fernando López Águilar, and Rebecca Orozco

Janine Gasco
Greg Charles Smith
Patricia Fournier-García

✝ Chapter 1

Introduction

Janine Gasco, Greg Charles Smith, and Patricia Fournier-García

THE DEVELOPMENT OF HISTORICAL ARCHAEOLOGY in Mexico, Central and South America has lagged behind North America for a variety of reasons: difficulties in the exchange of information, lack of financial support by local governments, and few opportunities for students to receive adequate training in the field. The situation has, however, improved markedly in the past few years. This and other recent publications are the result. If these trends continue, considerable progress in the field's development can be expected.

Exchange of Information

Growth in the field of historical archaeology in Latin America has been slow, in part because of a limited flow of information. Until recently, international borders created barriers that prevented the kind of interaction needed for a new and growing discipline. Related to this circumstance is the fact that no single organization has been able to create a forum for the exchange of ideas among scholars doing historical archaeology in Latin America.

Scholars working on historic sites in Latin America were always able to present papers at the annual meetings of the Society for Historical Archaeology (SHA), but in the past international participation has not been great. International travel is often not an option for historical archaeologists from Latin American countries. From time to time, papers that reported on historical archaeology projects in Latin America did appear on SHA meeting programs—usually a single paper in a session on Spanish Colonial California or Florida—or in the journal *Historical Archaeology* (see Andrews 1981; Lister and Lister 1974, 1978; Rice and Smith 1989).

In 1989, a session organized by Paul Farnsworth and Jack Williams at the SHA meetings in Baltimore entitled "The Archaeology of the Spanish Colonial and Mexican Republican Periods," several papers discussed work in Mexico. A number of papers from this session were subsequently published in a special volume of *Historical Archaeology* (vol. 26, no. 1, 1992), edited by Farnsworth and Williams. In 1990, a session at the Society for American Archaeology (SAA) meetings which focused on the native context of colonialism in Mesoamerica and Central America included papers from historical archaeologists. The papers from that symposium were published in the third volume of the *Colombian Consequences* series edited by David Hurst Thomas (1991). In 1992, Anita Cohen-Williams and Thomas H. Charlton chaired a session at the SHA meetings about the expansion of the Spanish Empire, which included two papers on historical archaeology in Central Mexico. By 1997 it has become routine for at least one symposium at the SHA meetings to feature papers that focus on Latin America.

In Mexico during the 1970s, papers dealing with field research in historical archaeology—generally based on salvage operations and restoration of historical monuments in Mexico City—were presented occasionally at meetings and conferences. By the 1980s and 1990s, however, growth in the field of historical archaeology has been reflected by an increase in the number of meetings and formal symposia.

A session at the 1981 Mesa Redonda de la Sociedad Mexicana de Antropología was devoted to historical archaeology in the Maya area. In 1985 a collection of these and other papers was published in the *Revista Mexicana de Estudios Antropológicos* (vol. XXXI, edited by Antonio Benavides and Anthony P. Andrews). The XIX Mesa Redonda de la Sociedad Mexicana de Antropología held in 1985 included one session about Colonial archaeology chaired by Patricia Fournier-García and another entitled "Archaeohistory in Mexico," organized by Eduardo Corona. The programs of the XXI and XXII Mesa Redonda de la Sociedad Mexicana de Antropología held in 1989 and 1991 included symposia dealing with historic sites archaeology and urban historical archaeology, the second chaired by Guillermo Pérez Castro. At the 1992 Congreso Internacional de Antropología e Historia, a symposium entitled "Archaeology of Colonial and Nineteenth Century Mexico" was presented, organized by Eduardo Corona. At the XIII International Congress of Anthropological and Ethnological Sciences held in Mexico City in 1993, a symposium organized by Eduardo Matos dealing with urban rescue archaeology included five papers about historical archaeology.

In South America, conferences and workshops have been organized recently with a focus on historical archaeology. For example, in 1983, the II Seminario de Arqueología-Histórica was held in Lima, Peru (Deagan 1984). In 1993 the II Workshop de Gerenciamento de Patrimonio Cultural was held in Brazil, and the Conferencia de Arqueología Histórica Americana was held in Colonia del Sacramento, Uruguay. These meetings, the first South American conferences to focus exclusively on historical archaeology, marked the beginning of a new era for the field in Latin America. At Colonia del Sacramento, Stanley South initiated a series of reports and papers published in English, Spanish, or Portuguese, entitled *Historical Archaeology in Latin America*. The series is funded by a grant from the Conference on Historic Site Archaeology (University of South Carolina). South also designated regional editorial coordinators from Brazil, Uruguay, Argentina, and Mexico. As of June 1995, eight volumes had been published in this series. A recent article (Schaedel 1992) provides a good bibliography of recent works on Spanish Colonial South America.

We can now see a clear trend toward much greater interaction among historical archaeologists in Latin America. The sheer number of symposia and conferences over the past few years is a very promising development. Moreover, a new trend—seen in such journals as *Latin American Antiquity* and *Ancient Mesoamerica* and in South's new series mentioned above—toward publishing in Spanish and English (and sometimes Portuguese) is also a positive step. For the first time publications that are widely read will be more accessible to a broader, multilingual audience.

Governmental Support for Historical Archaeology in Latin America

Historical archaeological research in Latin America has been limited in the past by a lack of governmental support for research and the scarcity of training programs for students. The spectacular prehistoric sites remain the primary drawing card for most archaeologists who work in these regions. Most scholars doing historical archaeology in Latin America (including the authors in this volume) have been trained as prehistoric archaeologists. There is a growing tendency in North America for some archaeologists to specialize exclusively in historical archaeology, but a similar trend is only beginning in Latin America. For example, in 1994 the Escuela Nacional de Antropología e Historia in Mexico City established a Master of Arts program specializing in documentary archaeology. For the first time, Latin American students will have the opportunity to receive the specialized training needed for working at historic sites.

The funding priorities of Latin American governments have contributed to the slow development of historical archaeology in the region. Many Latin American governments have provided resources for the excavation and restoration of numerous prehistoric sites (for example, Teotihuacan in Mexico, Tikal in Guatemala, and Machu Picchu in Peru) with the hope of luring tourist dollars. In contrast, the restoration of historical structures has been left, for the most part, to the private sector or the Catholic church. Government funds for historical archaeology are generally limited to restoring important buildings or salvage archaeology projects rather than to developing research programs or projects.

The growth of the field of historical archaeology in the United States and Canada is due, at least in part, to the growth of cultural resource management and to the environmental laws that give historic sites the same protection as prehistoric sites. Historical sites in Latin America generally have not been afforded the same protection. In some cases, an indifference toward historical archaeology might reflect a government's concern that new interpretations of the past could endanger the official history (see Fournier-García and Miranda-Flores 1992).

Throughout much of Latin America the archaeology of the Colonial period (circa 1520s–1530s to 1820s) and the post-Independence periods (1820s to the present) has been limited almost exclusively to the recovery of materials associated with the architectural conservation, stabilization, and restoration of such important buildings as religious structures, forts, and the homes of important historic figures. Notable exceptions to this general trend are the salvage archaeology projects sponsored by Mexico's Instituto Nacional de Antropología e Historia (see Fournier-García 1985a; Fournier-García and Miranda-Flores 1992). Similar projects have been undertaken in Peru under the auspices of the Instituto Nacional de Cultura (see G.C. Smith 1991). Archaeological research associated with architectural restoration and salvage archaeology projects has produced important studies of historic period architecture and artifacts, particularly technological and stylistic analyses of ceramics. Unfortunately, in many cases these studies are primarily descriptive reports that do not analyze the social context of material culture.

New Approaches

Over the past few years a growing number of archaeologists

working on the historic period in Latin America have begun to develop research designs that move beyond descriptions of artifacts and architecture. These archaeologists are focusing instead on such issues as ethnicity, acculturation, economic exploitation, changing patterns of socioeconomic inequality, exchange systems, and gender. This research was influenced by the processual, or "new," archaeology that had come to dominate the field of archaeology as a whole in North America, by intellectual trends in Latin America that tended to take a Marxist or historical materialist perspective, and by more interpretive approaches (see Besso-Oberto 1977; Charlton 1986; Charlton and Fournier-García 1993; Fossari 1992; Fusco 1990, 1995; Gasco 1993; Graham 1991; Graham, Pendergast, and Jones 1989; Mentz-Ribeiro, Torrano-Ribeiro, and da Silveira 1988; Pendergast 1991). Theoretical frameworks have been developed that are derived in part from political views of Latin American scholars facing the conditions of the Third World and living in underdeveloped countries. These views have led to a more critical interpretation of the recent past that is not so different from the present.

Marxist perspectives and the influence of French structuralism (itself partially based on Marxist analytical constructs) can be seen in some studies (see Fournier-García 1985a; Alvarez-Kern 1992a, b). Research by Cuban archaeologists has been influenced by Cuba's links to the former Soviet Union; yet, their contribution to the understanding of Colonial processes should not be ignored (Bernard-Bosch, Blanco-Conde, and Rives-Pantoja 1985; Dominguez 1978, 1980, 1984, 1989; Pratt-Puig 1980; Rives, Dominguez, and Pérez 1991).

Finally, we are beginning to see the influence of postprocessual archaeology (or archaeologies); historical archaeology is now considered by some as a way not only to study the past but also to understand the present and to modify cultural policies for the future (see Funari 1992). These more recent trends have resulted in some researchers questioning the use of the term "historical archaeology" and preferring instead the term "Colonial archaeology" (see Fournier-García 1993a). Proponents of this view argue that the effects of the socioeconomic, political, and ideological structures of Iberian colonialism are the essence of phenomena reflected in the archaeological record. In this view, the Third World forms a broad colony for developed countries even today.

More than fifty years ago Julian Steward (1943) pointed out a number of features inherent in Latin American research that remain as critical today as they were then, both for anthropology and archaeology. Because of the complexities involved in reconstructing cultural systems based on culture contact, Steward noted the necessity for integrating an anthropological viewpoint with an awareness of such features as rural economy, human geography, and history. Also, speaking specifically with regard to acculturation studies, he noted that in order to establish patterns and make generalizations about human behavior, it is necessary to look at a variety of contact situations in different places and at different periods. Latin America provides a vast laboratory within which historical archaeologists can address these concerns and provide a unified, yet diverse, body of literature based on the results of their work. Toward that end, it is hoped that this book makes a small contribution.

Contents of the Volume

The authors of the chapters in this volume are all indebted to the many scholars who have preceded them in their efforts to better understand Colonial and post-Colonial Spanish America. In some cases the research described here is an outgrowth of earlier work, and in others authors have investigated entirely new topics and regions.

As a whole, the research in this volume falls into the broad category of historical archaeology advocated by James Deetz as

> the archaeology of the spread of European societies worldwide, beginning in the fifteenth century, and their subsequent development and impact on native peoples in all parts of the world. (1991:1)

The chapters in this volume provide a sample of the various approaches currently being utilized by historical archaeologists working in Latin America. They range from descriptive reports on local developments to more analytical treatments of interactions among members of various groups within Colonial society. Some studies focus on architectural features while others rely on ceramic analysis. Archaeological data come from regional settlement surveys, from single excavated sites, and from individual structures. Some of the articles focus more heavily on the documentary record or on ethnoarchaeological approaches. While these studies represent diverse approaches to a wide variety of archaeological sites and problems, they all make some attempt to move beyond the historical particularism that once characterized much of research in historical archaeology. All authors place the topic of their own research—whether a single structure or an entire region—into a larger context and make comparisons whenever possible.

The volume is organized geographically, following a continuum from north to south, with chapters from each country grouped together. Chapters are presented in the language of the investigator, with abstracts in English and Spanish.

While the authors do not share a general theoretical perspective, all approach their research with a specific problem in mind and then proceed to collect empirical data that can be used to address the problem. Most chapters integrate historical background gleaned from either documentary or sec ondary sources that lend support to and strengthen their interpretations. In many cases, the research represents the collection of baseline data for an area in which no previous historical archaeological work has been done. Thus, some results are necessarily preliminary, but they represent a base upon which subsequent work can be built.

One theme that has become common within the field of historical archaeology is the analysis of the impact of Colonial or post-Colonial regimes on indigenous peoples and the African populations living in the Americas and the ways in which these societies adapted, modified, and rejected different elements of the dominant group. A number of the chapters (7, 10, 9, 16, 4, 2, 17, and 11) examine this process and the various strategies and contributions of different groups in the formation of Colonial and post-Colonial societies.

Seven of the chapters report more generally on local, regional, or national developments based on site survey and/or test excavations and ceramic analysis (chapters 8, 12, 18, 13, 14, 3, and 15). These chapters also discuss methodological strategies used in several different regions of Latin America from highland Guatemala (chapter 8) and Mexico (chapter 3) to coastal Ecuador (chapter 13), urban Buenos Aires (chapter 14), and several regions of Uruguay (chapter 15).

Chapters 12, 13, and 18 focus on ceramic analysis. Studies of such a specific nature are particularly necessary in certain regions of Latin America because of the newness of historical investigations. Additional work of this kind will provide the tools needed by future researchers to refine temporal controls through a better knowledge of material culture.

One chapter focuses more explicitly on methods used to locate historical sites (chapter 5). Finally, chapter 6 offers a theoretical treatment of a general phenomenon—consumption patterns (of ceramics) in Mexico during Colonial and Republican periods.

✝ Chapter 2

Indian Consumers on the Periphery of the Colonial Market System
Tracing Domestic Economic Behavior in a Tehuantepec Hamlet

Judith Francis Zeitlin and Lillian Thomas

Abstract

A preliminary survey of historic archaeological resources on the southern Isthmus of Tehuantepec in 1990 led to the location of Santa Cruz, an abandoned hamlet near the village of Chihuitán, Oaxaca. Documentary evidence of its disappearance long before the establishment of a nearby sugar mill gives us a mid-eighteenth-century terminus ad quem for this indigenous community, which appears to have weathered successfully the impact of an early Colonial physical relocation and economic reorientation. Changes in imported and local pottery styles, the roles of stone and metal artifacts, and food procurement habits are discussed as indicators of the community's growing participation in the Colonial market economy.

Resumen

Mediante un reconocimiento de superficie preliminar de sitios arqueológicos históricos en el sur del Istmo de Tehuantepec en 1990, se logró localizar el caserío abandonado de Santa Cruz, en las proximidades de la aldea de Chihuitán, Oaxaca. La evidencia documental de su desaparición mucho antes del establecimiento de un ingenio azucarero, brinda un terminus ad quem de mediados del siglo XVIII para esta comunidad, que aparentemente superó exitosamente el impacto de una reubicación física y una reorientación económica durante el periodo Colonial temprano. Se analizan los estilos de la cerámica importada y local, el papel de los artefactos de piedra y metal, además de los hábitos de obtención de alimentos como indicadores de la participación creciente de la comunidad en la economía colonial de mercado.

To what extent the postconquest transformation of rural Indian society can be attributed to the operation of specific Spanish Colonial economic institutions and policies is a topic of perennial interest but little agreement. For example, Chevalier's (1952) classic treatise on the role of the Mexican hacienda in converting indigenous communities into an impoverished, dependent labor force has been challenged by historical studies of more densely populated areas than the northern zone from which the model developed. In such areas, autonomous native communities persisted where Indians either retained more control over communal agricultural lands or sold their labor freely among competing Spanish landowners (Van Young 1983).

Yet the alternative model of a dual-sector economy operating in core areas of Spain's Colonial empire, wherein a culturally distinctive Indian peasantry contributed only its labor to a separate market-oriented economy, fails to capture colonialism's full impact on a changing native world (Grieshaber 1979; Taylor 1972). Whether one agrees with the perniciously oppressive character of the Colonial state system as portrayed by Spalding (1982) for highland Peruvian Indian society or with the more positive role Spores (1984) finds it playing in the economic expansion of the Mixteca Alta in Mexico, the many-armed reach of the Colonial political economy challenges the historical anthropologist to demonstrate precisely how native groups responded to its grip.

The documentary record lends itself to an examination of Colonial political institutions and the regional systems of land tenure and labor mobilization that fueled market production (see chapter 6), but these variables are often portrayed as forces extrinsic to the much less visible internal workings of native communities. Archaeology, on the other hand, with its dependence on the material goods found in specific places, more readily focuses on the actual behavior of Indian consumers—what they ate, how they sheltered their families, how they furnished their homes and workplaces. As Douglas and Isherwood (1979) reminds us, goods do more than serve bodily needs; they are the material vehicles by which individuals invest meaning in the world around them. By reflecting even a portion of these culturally and socially cir-

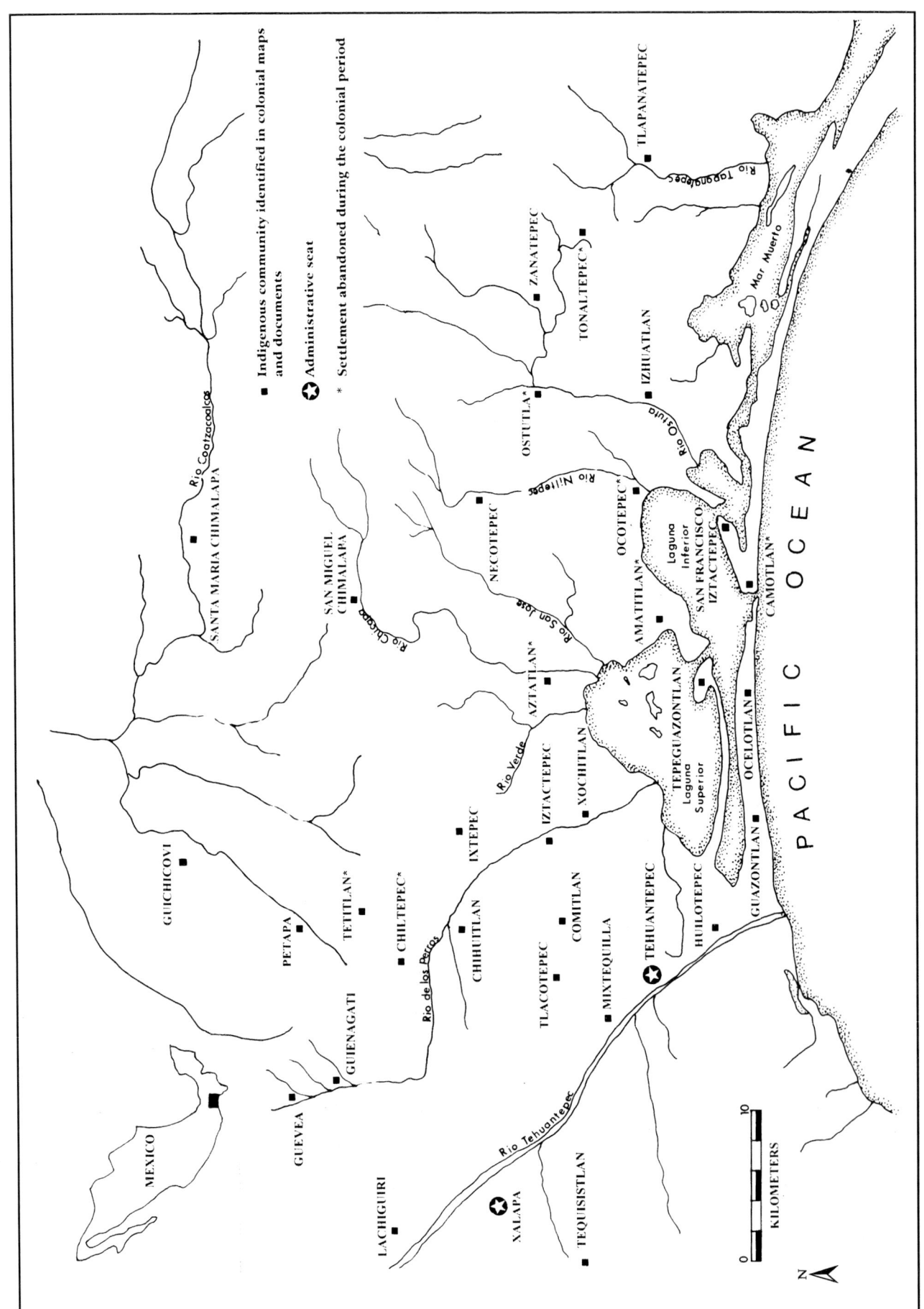

FIGURE 2.1 Colonial-period communities of Tehuantepec province and its environs. *Drawing by Judith Francis Zeitlin*

cumscribed values, the archaeological record has enormous potential to inform the historical study of indigenous peoples who may not have had a strong written voice of their own.

In the case study that follows, archaeological data from a Colonial-period Indian hamlet in provincial Tehuantepec are compared with information from documentary sources as part of a preliminary attempt to reconstruct the social dynamics of a rural economy. This study will take a closer look at the dual-sector model of the Mexican Colonial economy and examine whether this particular community of Indian "peasants" actively participated in market exchanges. The consumption choices made by households are examined in light of both local and interregional distribution networks for pottery and other durable goods to better understand how the community of Santa Cruz articulated with its Colonial social environment.

Historical Sketch of Colonial Tehuantepec

By the mid-seventeenth century, the lowland landscape of New Spain's Tehuantepec province had undergone a profound ecological transformation. Ravaged by the epidemic diseases that followed the conquerors into the New World, a once thriving Indian population had shrunk to under three thousand tributaries, approximately 10 percent of its estimated precontact total. Remnant communities became dislocated as ecclesiastical *congregaciónes* (centralized communities) rearranged the prevailing settlement configuration of dispersed rural hamlets and urban *barrios* (neighborhoods) into more easily monitored compact villages and towns (figure 2.1). Added to this climate of social change was the destabilizing impact of Tehuantepec's ranching revolution. Herds of cattle, horses, mules, sheep, and goats, first introduced into the province by Hernán Cortés himself, multiplied dramatically in the nearly 200 *estancia* (ranch) grants ceded by the Crown in the late sixteenth and early seventeenth centuries. With their destructive impact on cultivated fields and the region's xerophytic vegetation, domesticated animals and their Spanish owners and Afro-Mexican managers transformed the region permanently (Brockington 1989; J. Zeitlin 1989).

The impact of these changes within rural Indian society is difficult to gauge using conventional historical sources, despite an abundance of archival documentation for the province. Distance from the seat of royal authority, the Audiencia in Mexico City, did not deter the Isthmus Zapotec, Zoque, and Huave communities from making use of the Colonial courts to complain about negligent or abusive Spanish neighbors. The resulting litigation records rarely offer more than an offhand reference to household economies or agricultural practices, particularly outside the *villa* (small town) of Tehuantepec, in which a more cosmopolitan social environment prevailed. For the nearly three dozen villages identified on Colonial-period maps and tribute records for the province, we have difficulty penetrating the collective façade presented by these communities in their interaction with Spanish officialdom.

From the pretexts and protests offered on the Spanish side, it would appear that Tehuantepec rural communities stubbornly resisted new economic developments. Such arguments were the ostensible basis for prolonging the exercise of *repartimientos de efectos* (forced sales of goods) against Isthmus villages, by which they were compelled to produce specified quantities of cochineal, vanilla, salted fish, or other saleable commodities at a discounted price while purchasing manufactured goods at an inflated value. Rationalized as a means of drawing Indian communities into New Spain's commercial arena, the system more typically offered enormous opportunities for unchecked profiteering by the Crown-appointed *alcalde mayor* (district administrator), who benefited from exclusive repartimiento privileges.

This diverting of Indian production and consumption to the Spanish market had a broader economic impact on Isthmus communities than the direct appropriation of Indian labor by Colonial enterprises, practiced throughout New Spain. In their heyday, very large ranching establishments like the Tehuantepec Haciendas Marquesanas supplemented a permanent staff of slaves and free workers with draft Indian laborers. But the livestock orientation of Spanish land use on the Isthmus as a whole required little support from nearby villages (Brockington 1989; J. Zeitlin 1989). Greater disruption for most Isthmus communities was brought about by the costly, interminable boundary disputes that pitted Indians against Spanish *hacendados* (hacienda owners) and communities against one another in a hostile atmosphere of land scarcity.

Conflict with neighboring haciendas and aggravation from marauding cattle pushed many of the Zoque farmers of the eastern Isthmus either to flee or adopt a *vaquero* (cowboy) life-style, but there was remarkable cultural persistence and settlement continuity among the largely Zapotec-speaking communities of the western half of the coastal plain (J. Zeitlin 1989). Farming villages along the floodplains of the Tehuantepec and Perros rivers for the most part withstood Colonial period demographic and economic pressures, and many today hold considerably larger populations than they did before the Spanish conquest. In neighboring Soconusco province, just six of the twenty-five to thirty towns appearing on late sixteenth-century lists survived until Independence (chapter 5). Of the twenty-three coastal plain towns named on the 1580 *Relación Geográfica* map for Tehuantepec province, however, only six were lost. Several others from the Zapotec- and Mixe-speaking areas of the Sierra Atravesada may have disappeared as well, for they are not readily matched

FIGURE 2.2 Church of Santo Domingo Chihuitán. *Photograph by Judith Francis Zeitlin*

with modern communities in that mountainous zone.

Excavations at Rancho Santa Cruz

This strong pattern of community survival did not simplify the four-month program of archaeological reconnaissance and preliminary site testing undertaken in March 1990, a program aimed at addressing issues of socioeconomic change in the region's Colonial-period Indian communities. Reconnaissance strategy took advantage of Spanish settlement nucleation policies which, it was assumed, would have left exposed the archaeological remains of formerly dispersed hamlets and urban barrios. Such site-forming cultural processes are well illustrated at the city of Tehuantepec itself, the original late pre-Hispanic Zapotec capital of the province. One of the 1990 field operations involved excavation and survey at a 50-ha site 1 km south of the current barrio church of Santa Cruz Tagolaba, where the remains of a large pre-Hispanic settlement, with its own civic-ceremonial center, were identified. One of many constituent barrios of urban Tehuantepec, the depopulated Tagolaba community survived its relocation to a more nucleated site centered around the early-seventeenth-century church, leaving behind an extensive archaeological zone (J. Zeitlin 1994).

The investigation of similar effects of Spanish *congregación* (Spanish colonial institution of forcible removable of native peoples from dispersed settlements into a centralized community) policies on the rural Isthmus population revealed that maps from the sixteenth and seventeenth centuries drawn up to pinpoint estancia claims or to settle boundary disputes frequently illustrated separate hamlets that appear to have been typical components of presently more nucleated villages. The search for one of these abandoned hamlets led to Rancho Santa Cruz, a mixed livestock and agricultural establishment on the upper floodplain of the Río de los Perros, bordering the village of Santo Domingo Chihuitán. Although it is today one of the five smallest communities of the Isthmus, Chihuitán must have embraced a large and relatively prosperous early Colonial population— judging by the well-built seventeenth-century church in the village center (figure 2.2). Perennial piedmont streams feeding the Río de los Perros have made this sheltered area a productive zone for agriculture since late prehistoric times, when the Zapotec kings of Tehuantepec included irrigated orchards in Chihuitán and neighboring Laollaga among their patrimonial estates. Until recently, Spanish-introduced sugarcane was the area's major cash crop; the ruins of a sugar refinery from the late Colonial period dominate the buildings at Rancho Santa Cruz.

A descendent of a former owner of Rancho Santa Cruz, discovered in the rafters of the ranch house the original 1801 *merced* (land grant) granting the hacienda owner permission to construct this refinery. In response to the question whether the proposed project would harm any Indian households, the document stated that "...antes había un pueblo pero hace tiempo que se desapareció" (...there used to be a town, but it disappeared some time ago). Through surface survey, the abandoned hamlet was located about half a kilometer from the corrals of the modern ranch.

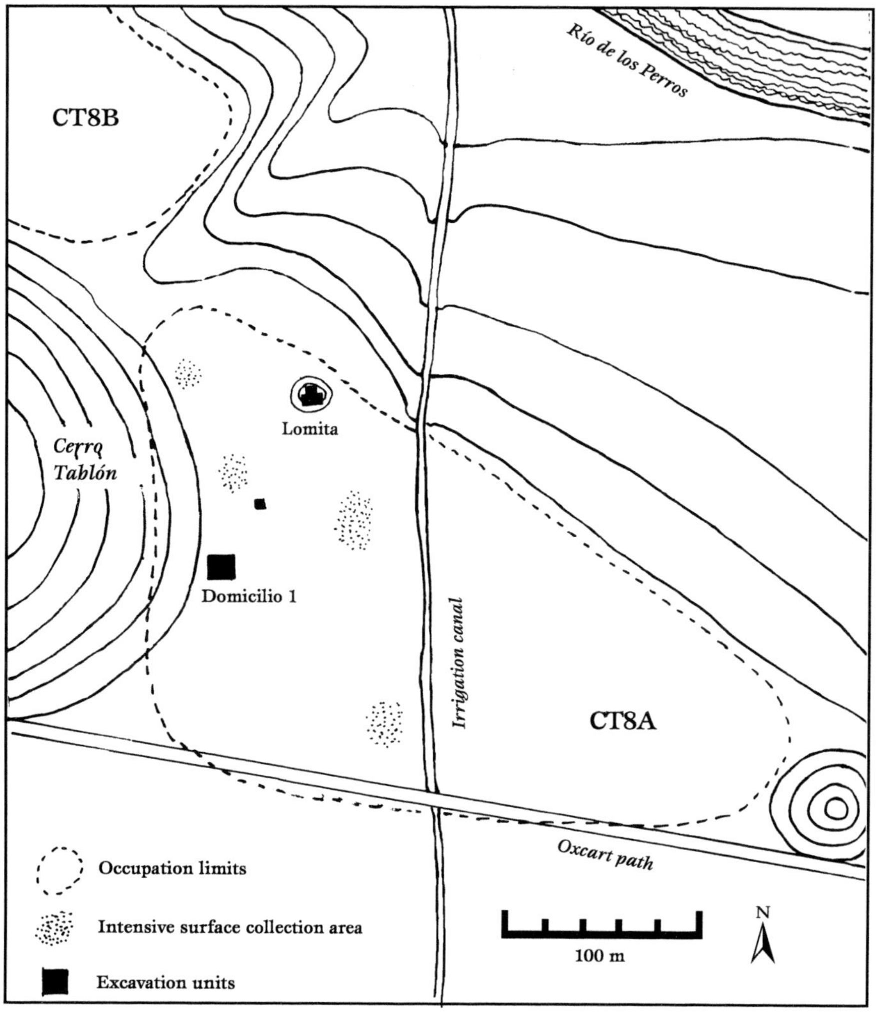

FIGURE 2.3 Rancho Santa Cruz archaeological zone. *Drawing by Judith Francis Zeitlin*

The archaeological site at Rancho Santa Cruz overlooks the river from a high terrace skirting the southeast slope of Cerro Tablón (figure 2.3). Two spatially distinct archaeological components are separated by a steep arroyo. The northernmost occupation area (CT8B) is scattered with Late Postclassic pottery and such an abundance of chert and quartzite cores and flakes as to suggest an economy based in part on stoneworking or the processing of some more perishable commodity using stone tools. South of the arroyo, the Colonial-period occupation area (CT8A) is distinguished by the presence of new pottery types, including glazed ceramics and fragments of fired brick and roof tile. Artifacts in this sector are scattered over an area of approximately 5 ha between Cerro Tablón and a small hill with a cross planted at its summit.

Excavation efforts focused on the cleared west side of the Colonial occupation zone where, despite extensive disturbance by modern farm equipment, two promising localities were found for subsurface testing. The first of these was a *lomita* (low mound) on the north side of the Colonial site; there, surface concentrations of broken roof tiles and brick fragments indicated the place where a house had once stood.

An area of 17 m² was opened in the course of stratigraphic excavations. The northernmost excavation squares revealed a floor of compacted earth 10 to 20 cm below the ground surface, south of which was a shallow east-west foundation wall (figure 2.4). Perhaps because this excavation area encompassed a habitation zone, the few potsherds found here were broken and badly eroded.

A richer zone of domestic refuse was found in the locality designated Domicilio 1, where eleven 1-m² test pits were dug. Stratigraphy suggested two distinct Colonial subcomponents. Subsequent artifact analysis has supported a chronological separation of the cultural materials, best regarded as tentative because of the small sample of households on which it is based. The more recent of these components has both indigenous-tradition pottery and Spanish trade wares; flaked-stone tools primarily made of local chert and quartzite; and a small number of metal artifacts, including some pieces of copper sheet metal and, more commonly, iron nails. A single iron fishhook was also found. The older component has less trade ware (although glazed pottery is found), there are no metal tools, and the flaked-stone artifacts more typically include broken obsidian blades. Fired brick fragments were found

FIGURE 2.4 View of the lomita excavations, looking west at an exposed stone foundation wall. *Photograph by Lillian Thomas*

FIGURE 2.5 Domicilio 1 excavation unit; north arrow points to the exposed posthole mold. *Photograph by Judith Francis Zeitlin*

in both strata. Although too few architectural elements were preserved to permit mapping any structure, two postholes were found associated with the older component, and a section of stone wall intersected the more recent component (figure 2.5).

Both strata yielded a large amount of animal bone. An initial sorting of faunal material from selected excavation units indicates that the Colonial occupants continued to rely on the deer, rabbit, armadillo, iguana, and other terrestrial game favored by the pre-Hispanic inhabitants of the southern Isth-

FIGURE 2.6 Sample of Mexico City commonware majolica recovered at Rancho Santa Cruz: sherds from Blue-on-Cream annular-based bowls. *Photograph by Judith Francis Zeitlin*

mus, with some consumption of domesticated animals, at least by the later residents (see J. Zeitlin 1978: Table 4.1). As our Chihuitán workers commented when they saw the quantities of animal bone being collected, "Comieron mejor que nosotros" (They ate better than we do). Although the diet may have been richer or perhaps just more diverse in its sources of animal protein, in many ways the Colonial community appears to have been composed of household groups outwardly very similar to those living in Chihuitán today—farming families living in wattle-and-daub, tile-roofed houses, who supplemented their diet with hunting.

Pottery of the Colonial Period

Dating of the Colonial-period occupation at Rancho Santa Cruz depends primarily on ceramic crossties among trade wares represented at the site; the only historic date is the 1801 merced. This terminus ad quem suggests that the hamlet had been abandoned by the mid-eighteenth century if not before ("...hace tiempo que se desapareció"). Estimating the beginning date of the relocation of the preexisting settlement to the south zone of the site is more difficult. Very likely, the Postclassic site continued to be occupied for some part of the sixteenth century, and the Colonial occupation zone may well have been first settled as the result of an early Dominican congregación.

An occupation of late-sixteenth through mid-eighteenth century would be compatible with the manufacturing time spans known for some of the more than twenty varieties of glazed earthenware and porcelain found at Rancho Santa Cruz. Although the 191 glazed sherds recovered during survey and excavation constitute less than 2 percent of the ceramic inventory, their appearance in any large number surprised us. Moreover, intensive, systematic surface collections made at four separate localities at the site indicated that use of glazed pottery was widespread across the community, although it may have been more abundant in some households than in others.

Typological analysis of the Chihuitán Spanish-style wares reveals some interesting procurement patterns. Very few examples (11 sherds) can be classed with the fine-grade majolica wares produced in important ceramic centers such as Puebla. None appears to have been manufactured in Guatemala, despite the existence of important trade networks linking Guatemala and the nearby Isthmus throughout the entire Colonial period. More than 80 percent of the Chihuitán sample matches the descriptions of what Lister and Lister term "common-grade wares" (1987:225), that is, majolica produced in or near Mexico City in imitation of the finer ware styles (figure 2.6). The common-grade ware

> superficially resembled the concurrent top grade, but...was made to sell at lower cost by certain modifications: it bore a less opaque glaze with reduced tin content and a careless patterning in a *contrahecho* (poor quality) blue derived from a mixture of copper oxide plus zinc, rather than cobalt, or, more commonly copper green and iron brown. (Lister and Lister 1987:225)

FIGURE 2.7 Major classes of Colonial-period indigenous pottery from Rancho Santa Cruz: *a–i*, Reu Silty fine grayware jars, ollas, and bowls; *j–m*, Barbacana whiteware types, including red-painted (l) and sgraffito-incised on red (m); *n–q*, Orozco coarse buff, burnished comales and brushed ollas; *r–u*, Tablón Orange bichrome painted types, including later cursive style, red and white on orange slip (r) and earlier orange and white on red (s–u). Color key: solid = red, stippled = orange, white = white. *Drawing by Judith Francis Zeitlin*

Typically, the low-tin glazes on such wares allow the paste to show through. The enamel is often unevenly applied and frequently stained with copper oxide (giving it a greenish cast). Decoration is haphazard or not well applied.

Most pottery used at Colonial Rancho Santa Cruz was of local manufacture, which in part continued the Isthmian Postclassic ceramic tradition based on fine-paste white and gray wares (figure 2.7). Unpainted Reu Silty open convex wall bowls dominate the Colonial grayware sample; initial findings indicate that tripod supports for these bowls, frequently adorned with moldmade serpent heads or other Postclassic images, were common only in the earlier Colonial assemblage. The Colonial inhabitants also used strap-handled jars; strainers; deep, straight-walled bowls; and large, thick bowls. From the lengthy Isthmus kaolin-pottery tradition, a small number of undecorated and red-painted or sgraffito-incised vessels with Postclassic antecedents were noted as well as a new brown-painted or brown-slipped whiteware type. Coarse buff paste ollas and *comales* (clay griddles) were the most common cooking vessels, as they had been in the Late Postclassic period.

What is most striking about the locally made Colonial pottery at Rancho Santa Cruz is the appearance of a new fine-paste ware we have designated Tablón Orange. This ware fits so comfortably within late pre-Columbian decorative and manufacturing norms as to be easily mistaken for a Postclassic pottery type, yet it has no direct Isthmian prehistoric antecedent. The reddish-yellow paste has been well fired and might, in fact, be an oxidized version of the same clay body used to make Reu Silty gray. The two wares differ, however, in vessel form, surface treatment, and mode of decoration. Typical Tablón Orange vessels are flat-bottomed convex or outslanting-wall bowls, ollas, and strainers. The most prominent surface is usually slipped and polished in either orange or red, but there are a few white-slipped examples as well. While surface erosion accounts for most unslipped sherds, a few vessel forms appear to have been plain originally. Curiously, three of these forms—a small bowl or cup with an annular base, a small-necked bottle, and some simple, palm-held *candeleros* (candlesticks)—imitate Spanish pottery forms and were crudely manufactured using a potter's wheel. By contrast, sherds from bowls and ollas seldom appear to have been wheelmade.

The slipped, outslanting-wall bowls (and some less common forms as well) were further decorated on the interior surface with white, orange, black, or red paint. Two design groups have been distinguished. The stratigraphically earlier of the two has fairly thick, bichrome- or trichrome-painted horizontal bands (4.5–6 mm) that define a field of pre-Columbian–style geometric designs, typically stepped frets and circles. The later "cursive" style has a thinner painted line (2–3 mm), usually executed in white or white and orange. The circles, zigzags, waves, and other geometric motifs are applied more fluidly, without being confined to bounded fields or zones of decoration.

Tablón Orange was the most popular ware used at Rancho Santa Cruz, and it may have been manufactured nearby. Although Gasco (1987:290f) includes identical pottery in her Fine Bichrome/Trichrome category from the Ocelocalco excavations, the small sample she collected (25 sherds) suggests that the pottery was traded into Soconusco. By contrast, its abundance in surface collections and test excavations at other postconquest sites makes Tablón Orange a good Colonial-period marker for the Isthmus. Later changes in the ware, seen in probable nineteenth-century contexts around Tehuantepec, include further simplification of the cursive style of decoration and, ultimately, a complete manufacturing transition as the controlled use of a potter's wheel became standard.

The evolution of this well-produced ware signals the presence of a vigorous local industry, responsive to indigenous tastes and domestic needs. Spanish-inspired forms remained on the periphery of Tablón Orange production, while decorative motifs and techniques continued to follow pre-Columbian models. Only late in the history of this ware did the European potter's wheel become important, although local potters did make occasional earlier use of it. This technological change probably followed important socioeconomic changes in production and distribution patterns, rather than resulting from unspecified acculturative pressures.

Majolica Usage and Procurement Patterns in Other Communities

While the local pottery industry built on traditional styles and techniques during the sixteenth and seventeenth centuries, Spanish-style glazed earthenware bowls and rare pieces of Chinese porcelain also found their way into Indian homes at Rancho Santa Cruz. The fact that Spanish-style pottery, especially majolica, even reached this Chihuitán hamlet contradicts many scholarly assumptions. None of the sherds come from large vessels of a type that might have been used to transport other goods along established commercial routes; the pottery must itself have been an object of trade. It is generally thought, however, that early Colonial-era Mexico City common-grade wares were produced exclusively for local use in the Valley of Mexico. Although certain types of top-grade majolica were traded widely, there is little evidence for widespread distribution of common-grade wares. According to Lister and Lister, friable common-grade wares did not "reach distant users" (1987:229).

Scholars have assumed that glazed wares, even those of low quality, were manufactured for Spaniards and were very rare among indigenous communities (see chapter 6). Goggin, who studied New World majolica extensively, found that its use was associated with higher-status households and that it

> ...does not seem to have been a trade item to Indians, at least until late in the eighteenth century, and while found in 'pure' Indian sites, it is never common. (Goggin 1968:211)

Carvajal and Valencia (1989:244) similarly conclude that majolica was restricted to "las clases pudientes de la Nueva España" (the upper classes of New Spain).

In his excavations of rural Colonial communities much closer to Mexico City, Charlton (1972) found only small quantities of majolica before the eighteenth century at long-occupied indigenous sites like Santa María Tilmatlan. A numerical distribution and typological analysis of the majolica from these excavations led Seifert to propose a kind of majolica frequency indicator for socioeconomic status. She finds that low status, as was historically equated with Indian communities, is indicated by majolica frequencies under 1 percent, while high status, associated with Spaniards and some wealthy Indian nobles, is exhibited by majolica frequencies of 4 to 5 percent (Seifert 1977:116). Applying this status index more widely, however, would require more rigorous parameters defining the inclusiveness of the ceramic assemblage to which these rather small majolica frequency differences pertain. Even in the Teotihuacan samples, a much more obvious indicator of status is the distribution of less expensive lead-glazed earthenwares. These earthenwares comprise less than 5 percent of the ceramics in low-status sites and between 30 and 50 percent in high-status sites (Seifert 1977:116).

Far away from the Mexico City and Puebla production centers, the relative importance of lead-glazed and majolica pottery is reversed at the late-sixteenth- to mid-eighteenth-century site of Ocelocalco, located in the Soconusco region of Chiapas, Mexico. Excavating at what Colonial census records indicate was a predominantly Indian community, Gasco (1992) found lead-glazed earthenware comprising only 2 percent of the ceramic corpus, while majolica represented a surprisingly high 12 percent. Although excavations at a few structures had particularly high majolica frequencies (exceeding 20 percent), most areas tested yielded pottery samples with at least 5 percent majolica (Gasco 1992:70).

Such a high usage of majolica in an Indian community stands in strong contrast to typical socioeconomic patterns in the Valley of Mexico, but here, too, the procurement of expensive majolica pottery is a reasonable indicator of Ocelocalco's relative wealth. Soconusco's Indian communities, unlike their poorer Teotihuacan contemporaries, profited greatly from the Colonial expansion of cacao production, which remained largely under native control. While Spanish middlemen certainly took unfair price advantage of their Indian suppliers, on the whole cacao farmers benefited both from an increase in the size of their individual orchards and the higher value placed on Soconusco's quality product (Gasco 1989a). As traditional sociopolitical hierarchies and patterns of land tenure changed in these communities, the Colonial cacao market acted to increase wealth and spread its distribution among households. Consumption of costly trade items, in fact, was more evenly distributed across the community later in Ocelocalco's Colonial period occupation than in its early phase (Gasco 1993).

Gasco infers that the largely Mexico City–produced range of majolica types represented at Ocelocalco entered Soconusco through the same trade network that extracted cacao. While the Tehuantepec province, long important for its own mule-train traffic with Guatemala, would have been a logical node on this transport route, it is still unclear how a hamlet like Rancho Santa Cruz acquired the wealth to enter into the majolica commerce, albeit on a modest scale. No obvious commercial product from Colonial Chihuitán is known to have been especially valued in interregional trade, although Isthmian products like salt and salted fish from the coast or cochineal and vanilla from the mountains north of Chihuitán figured significantly in New Spain's market economy.

If it is difficult to picture the Rancho Santa Cruz population as prosperous cash-crop farmers for whom majolica was one of perhaps many expensive new luxuries, there is also little to support the alternative proposition that majolica was a commodity forced on Isthmian communities through the entrenched system of repartimientos de efectos. For example, a highly charged 1720 dispute against Tehuantepec's alcalde mayor, Don Pedro de Saravía, cited onerous repartimientos of cochineal, vanilla, and mules, but neither majolica nor any kind of pottery figures among the community account records from Saravía's store which entered into the Indian complainants' brief.[1]

Isthmus villages purchased machetes, wax, soap, cacao, tobacco, paper, gunpowder, and cloth for pants and skirts from this *tienda* (store), goods typically sold in Spanish-owned stores located among Oaxaca's Indian communities. As Carmagnani (1988:161) observes, Spanish stores played the positive economic role of providing communities with goods that Indians themselves could not produce but which were necessary for their own social and economic "reproduction." The commodities purchased from Saravía's store represent both practical household aids (machetes, soap) and items required for a community's political and ceremonial sustenance (paper, wax, cacao, gunpowder). The purchase of manufactured cloth indicates a significant transition from exclusive reliance on home-woven textiles, but it appears, by its absence from this and most Oaxaca store lists, that glazed pottery in general had not attained the same intensity of demand.

The complaint against Saravía's store was not that it forced unwanted goods upon the Indians but that the alcalde mayor prohibited the free movement of other traders into the province. Isthmian communities were thus denied an outlet for the sale of their own products, including *huipiles* (Indian women's blouses), local fruits, poultry, eggs, tortillas, and especially salt, and were forced to pay the higher prices charged by Saravía for the goods they needed (see note 1). Direct evidence is lacking as to the ethnicity or home base of these merchants.

In her extensive examination of Colonial tax records, wills, contracts, and other documents from the Mixteca Alta, Romero (1990:105–108) found that Spanish and mestizo itinerant traders made heavy commercial inroads among Indian villages in that area beginning in the latter half of the sixteenth century. Gradually, they supplanted indigenous long-distance traders whose lack of credit access ultimately confined them to the regional market system (Romero 1990:186). Economic conditions may have been more favorable to Zapotec traders from Tehuantepec, whom the mid-seventeenth-century chronicler Burgoa (1989:389) observed leading mule trains of forty to fifty animals, looking for all the world like well-appointed Spaniards riding their finely saddled mules.

The bulk of merchandise traded into Oaxaca communities consisted of wine, cloth, wax, and articles of clothing, but a diverse range of other goods—both items produced in

New Spain and imported from Spain and China—was traded as well. In the Mixteca, sixteenth-century Spanish traders marketed leather shoes, horse tackle, knives, scales, and candlesticks, among other things (Romero 1990:144f). Burgoa described a similarly practical inventory transported over long distances by the Tehuantepec traders:

> que trajinan estos reinos de México, Veracruz, Chiapa y Guatemala, fletando sus bestias, para llevar las haciendas de unas a otras partes, con grande puntualidad y confianza y ellos hacen sus empleos en Soconusco en cacao y en la Puebla de paños surtidos, jabón y herramientas de machetes, hachas, arados, rejas, frenos, estribos y corazas... (Burgoa 1989:389)

> they move back and forth across the kingdoms of Mexico, Veracruz, Chiapa, and Guatemala, using pack animals to carry goods from one place to another promptly and confidently, investing in cacao in Soconusco, and in assorted textiles, soap, machetes, axes, plows, plow blades, bridles, stirrups, and armor in Puebla.

Although majolica or other glazed pottery does not appear in this list and is seldom included in sales tax records or merchants' contracts (Romero 1991), both Spanish and Indian traders dealing in goods from Mexico City or Puebla might have carried glazed pottery with them from time to time, if there was a sufficient market for it.

Whatever the ethnicity of these traders, it was a different commercial network marketing majolica and other Spanish goods to Indian communities on the Isthmus than that supplying the Dominican convent at Tehuantepec, for which we also have a small archaeological collection. The mid-sixteenth-century structure, after suffering a century of abuse, first as a military barracks, then as a prison, now serves as the city's Casa de la Cultura. During the 1990 field season, pottery and other artifacts salvaged from the courtyard during the building's restoration were examined and a separate collection was made from a small stratigraphic trench dug in the convent kitchen patio. Although both convent collections included examples of indigenous tradition pottery, only one of the majolica sherds could be classified with the same Mexico City common-grade wares that prevailed at Rancho Santa Cruz. Of twelve classes of glazed earthenwares distinguished in the convent sample, there were just two other correspondences. That these differences reflect different procurement networks, rather than just ethnic differences of taste, cost, or utility, is indicated by the strong presence of two majolicas of likely Antigua manufacture in the convent collections. No Guatemalan majolicas were recognized in the pottery from Rancho Santa Cruz. The Dominicans of Tehuantepec may have relied on exchange relationships with the order's Guatemalan province to acquire needed nonlocal goods rather than depending on itinerant traders from Mexico City or Oaxaca.

Cultural and Economic Implications of Spanish Trade Goods at Rancho Santa Cruz

Our archaeological inventory from Rancho Santa Cruz contains a list of introduced European goods and habits that portrays a more acculturated community than might be suggested by the Isthmus documentary record alone. These Indian villagers of the late-sixteenth and seventeenth centuries lived in tile-roofed houses, used metal tools, raised and consumed domesticated animals, and displayed small quantities of prestigious majolica and other imported pottery in their homes. At the same time, long-standing uses for flaked-stone tools persisted, a wide variety of terrestrial game contributed to household diets as before, and local potters created new styles of vessels from traditional patterns widely marketed on the Pacific coast.

How is this taste for things Spanish reconciled with an otherwise conservative life-style, at least as it is represented in the archaeological record? The pragmatic appeal of some goods, like more durable iron tools and kiln-fired roof tiles, is intuitively plausible, but technological replacement by itself is not an adequate explanation for what seem to be more complex underlying cultural processes. In many cases, the substitution of an imported or introduced item for a locally produced traditional good in itself carried serious socioeconomic implications concerning the distribution of wealth within the community or the organization of labor. Such implications are at odds with a dual-sector model of the Colonial Indian economy.

Some introduced goods may have been used in ways that reinforced traditional community values and principles of economic reciprocity. Late-sixteenth- and early-seventeenth-century mercedes for Indian sheep and goat estancias on the Isthmus, for example, were requested by communities as collective entities, while individuals making similar requests are almost invariably identified as *caciques* (Indian chiefs) or *principales* (Indian nobles). Our archaeological samples of domesticated animal bone may very well represent household shares of meat from community feasts rather than privately raised and consumed foods. Some such intracommunity redistribution mechanism for trade goods is implicit in the early-eighteenth-century tienda records kept by Don Pedro de Saravía, the Tehuantepec alcalde mayor. These records show that village officials were held responsible for payments on the machetes, clothing, cacao, and so forth, charged to their community accounts.

Could such a community-wide redistribution system also have allocated expensive imported pottery to individual households, among other goods brought to Isthmus communities by itinerant traders, or did these households enter into private transactions with the traders? Without more specific historical information concerning the Isthmus merchants, that question can only be approached through more detailed archaeological and documentary data on household property than we have available for Rancho Santa Cruz. The situation in other parts of Oaxaca indicates that any such intracommunity redistributive mechanisms would have needed compelling institutional support to counteract the powerful forces of individuation that permeated the Colonial market economy. As Romero points out for the early Colonial Mixteca, the volume of mercantile activity directed at Indian communities was itself a product of socioeconomic change:

> Todas estas alteraciones en el seno de la sociedad mixteca: cambios en el consumo individual, cambios en el consumo colectivo y nuevos canales de ascenso, facilitaron y posibilitaron el trabajo de los comerciantes españoles. (Romero 1990:141)

> All these changes in the heart of Mixtec society: changes in individual consumption, changes in community consumption, and new means for social mobility, made the work of Spanish merchants easier.

In the Tehuantepec province, similar changes are reflected archaeologically in the record of durable goods. Long-distance commerce, which had been an important strategic component of the pre-Hispanic political economy as well, witnessed significant changes both in the volume and social target of its Isthmus market under Spanish colonialism. While iron machetes, knives, and nails had their pre-Columbian counterparts in imported tools made from obsidian and other nonlocal stone, what is known of the much more limited consumption of nonutilitarian goods (like fancy imported pottery) in pre-Hispanic times indicates that high-status households were the primary beneficiaries of such trade (R. Zeitlin 1993; J. Zeitlin 1978).

Throughout ancient Mesoamerica, restrictive sumptuary laws reinforced a rigid traditional social hierarchy. Not surprisingly, the postconquest documentary record is replete with petitions from native caciques and principales to wear Spanish dress, ride horseback, and bear arms, all newly imported markers of high status used to further traditional social distinctions. But as Colonial political and cultural pressures eroded customary boundaries, access to elite goods widened. Little by little, new income opportunities for Isthmus villagers rooted in the Colonial cash economy fostered a more broadly based demand for luxuries once denied commoners.

The presence of majolica pottery in this remote hamlet signals an unanticipated level of voluntary engagement with the Colonial market economy on the part of Tehuantepec's indigenous population as it rebounded from the devastation of epidemic disease and the institutionalized economic exploitation of Spanish rule. The small quantity of expensive, high-status, imported pottery recorded at Rancho Santa Cruz does not challenge the point Fournier-García (chapter 6) makes: vastly different consumption patterns persisted between Spanish/creole and Indian populations throughout the Colonial period, differences maintained by an exploitative political economy.

Regionally distinct outcomes in the postconquest survival of Mexico's indigenous communities challenge researchers to look beyond the socioeconomic chasm that structured interethnic relations generally in New Spain and to examine more closely the internal dynamics of native societies. The pre-Columbian roots of a demand for exotic pottery make native tastes for European-style goods more understandable, but the contrasting distribution patterns for pre-Hispanic and Colonial period exotica underscore the structural changes experienced by Isthmus Zapotec society. Our task is to document the novel institutional adaptations that helped maintain native community integration in the wake of the market economy's centripetal pull.

Acknowledgments. The 1990 survey and excavations were supported by a grant to the senior author from the Wenner-Gren Foundation for Anthropological Research. Our investigations at Rancho Santa Cruz were facilitated by the cooperation and assistance of many individuals from Chihuitán, especially Sr. José Santos Ibaños, owner of the ranch, and Sr. Solomón Jiménez, Presidente Municipal. Sr. Fernando Lavin Mier of Ixtepec kindly showed us the 1801 merced for the sugar refinery. In Tehuantepec, permission to examine collections and excavate a test trench at the former Dominican convent was generously extended by the Director of the Casa de la Cultura, Contador Cesar Rojas Petris. Jan Gasco, Carlos Manzo, Angeles Romero, and Robert Zeitlin read earlier drafts of this paper, and their thoughtful comments are greatly appreciated.

Notes
1. Archivo General de la Nación, Mexico City, Civil 599, exp. 4–5.

Chapter 3

Arqueología Histórica y Etnoarqueología de la Comunidad Alfarera Otomí de Santa María del Pino, México

Lourdes Mondragón, Patricia Fournier-García, y Nahúm Noguera

Resumen

A través del análisis de arqueología histórica y etnoarqueológico de la comunidad alfarera de Santa María del Pino, se logra una aproximación al modo de vida de los indígenas otomíes de la región del Valle del Mezquital, México. El desarrollo del grupo étnico desde la época Prehispánica se basa en la explotación del maguey y es a partir de esta base económica que se generan concepciones ideológicas particulares, manteniéndose durante los períodos Colonial y Republicano.

Abstract

Through historical archaeological and ethnoarchaeological analysis of the potting community of Santa María del Pino we can gain a better understanding of the lifeways of the indigenous Otomí people of the Mezquital Valley, Mexico. Since the pre-Hispanic era, development within this ethnic group has been based on the exploitation of maguey. From this economic base, Otomí ideological concepts were maintained during the Colonial and Republican periods.

ESTE ESTUDIO tiene como objetivo la reconstrucción histórico-social de procesos de desarrollo y conformación del modo de vida en una comunidad indígena otomí del centro de México, Santa María del Pino, ubicada en la región conocida como Valle del Mezquital (figura 3.1). El complejo económico del agave permite caracterizar a los otomíes que habitan zonas semidesérticas como el Valle del Mezquital, y las estrategias de supervivencia así como los aspectos ideológicos asociados los diferencian de otros grupos étnicos. Destaca en la región la ingesta de la savia del maguey (*Agave* sp.; figura 3.2), que a su vez implica la demanda de recipientes para su transporte, almacenamiento o consumo y, por ende, la producción de alfarería. Dentro del ámbito religioso, durante los siglos XVII y XVIII hay una proliferación de oratorios domésticos en la localidad, al parecer gracias a un relativo auge económico y a prácticas mágicas vinculadas con la manufactura de cerámica.

Estos procesos económico-ideológicos históricos tienen sus raíces en la época Prehispánica; no obstante el énfasis se da al período Colonial durante el cual se generan transformaciones y adecuaciones del modo de vida otomí debidas al impacto del sistema intrusivo europeo (véase Charlton y Fournier-García 1993). Por otra parte, con base en el análisis de los elementos actuales de la sociedad indígena se identifican cambios radicales que emanan de la cultura nacional moderna, con los consecuentes procesos de conformación de un nuevo modo de vida que aún se está consolidando.

De acuerdo con la problemática de estudio, la perspectiva de investigación tiene que ser integral, conjuntando correlatos de diversa naturaleza, sean arqueológicos, documentales o etnográficos.

Los Otomíes del Valle del Mezquital

El estudio de caso se refiere al poblado de José María Pino Suárez o Santa María del Pino, que se ubica en la región geocultural del Valle del Mezquital (figura 3.1), la que se caracteriza por sus precarios recursos naturales y clima semidesértico, con una superficie total de 7,206 km². Se localiza en el altiplano central mexicano y está conformada por una serie de subcuencas hidrológicas (López Águilar, Fournier-García, y Paz 1988), con limitados recursos acuíferos permanentes. El Mezquital ha sido el escenario donde el grupo otomí, o hñähñú como ellos se autodenominan tal vez desde épocas Prehispánicas,[1] ha desarrollado un modo de vida propio desde el siglo IX de nuestra era de acuerdo con datos etnohistóricos (Códice Chimalpopoca 1975), o incluso desde el siglo VII según hipótesis basadas en evidencias arqueológicas (López Águilar y Fournier-García 1992).

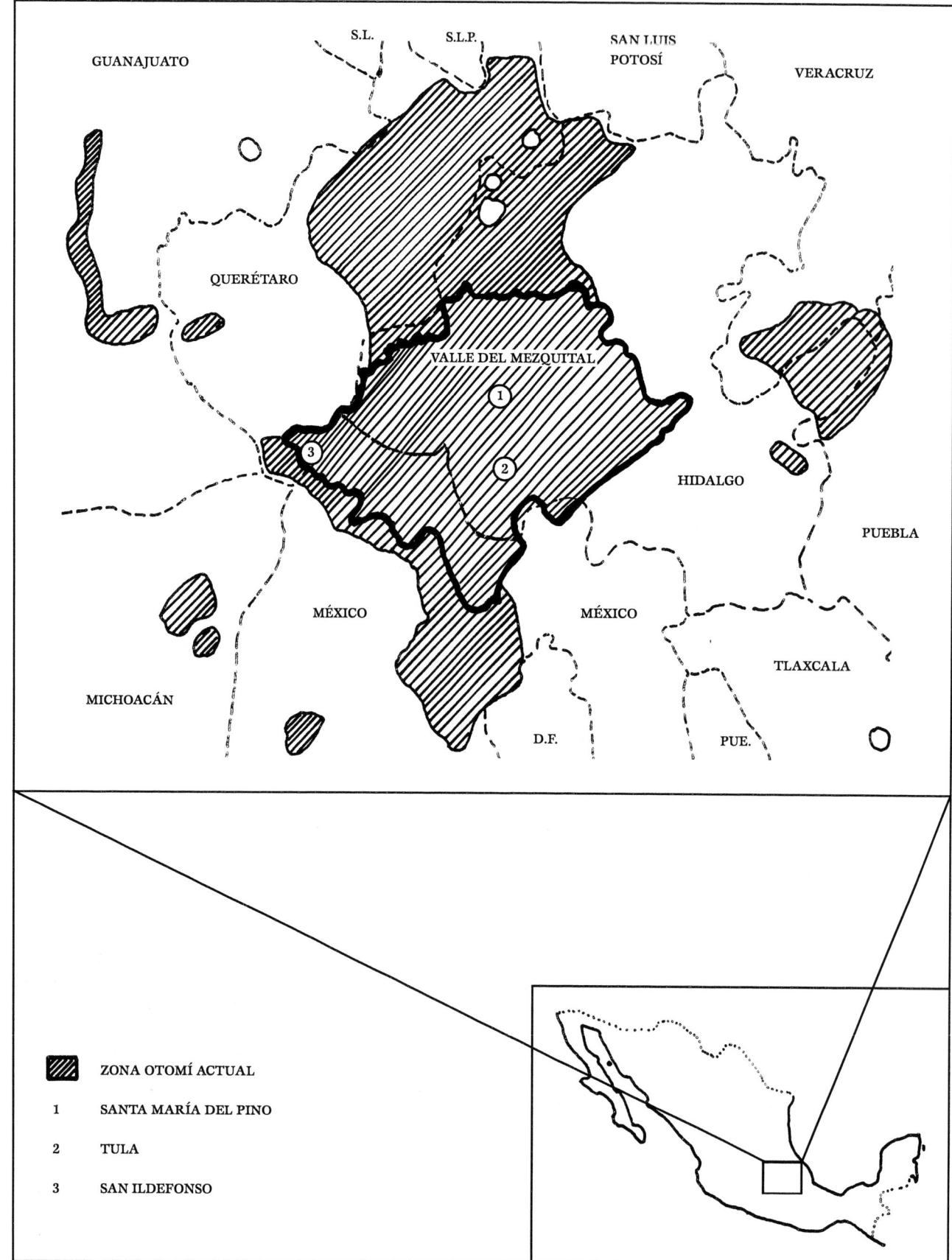

FIGURA 3.1 Localización del Valle del Mezquital y de las principales comunidades alfareras actuales

Figura 3.2 Maguey pulquero (*Agave* sp.). *Todas las fotografías son por las autoras*

En la literatura antropológica, etnográfica, histórica y etnohistórica, los otomíes comúnmente se conceptualizan como un grupo marginado por parte de los grupos dominantes, quienes los han sojuzgado mediante diversos mecanismos, como la guerra y el tributo antes de la conquista, su explotación en encomiendas, minas y haciendas en períodos históricos o su integración actual al estado nacional (véase Johnson 1982; López Aguilar y Fournier-García 1991; Sahagún 1989; Tranfo 1974).

El ambiente ha sido importante en la organización y desarrollo de las poblaciones del Mezquital y, según las evidencias disponibles, no ha habido modificaciones drásticas del medio durante casi un milenio. La región presenta bajos regímenes de precipitación, con vegetación semidesértica, predominando matorral inerme y subinerme, mezquites, cactáceas del género Opuntia entre las que destacan la choya y el nopal, así como diversas especies de maguey, como *Agave salmiana*, *Agave atrovirens*, *Agave* sp. y *Agave lechuguilla*. La zona está fuertemente erosionada y los suelos son delgados, provocando la degradación de la roca madre, sea ígnea, sedimentaria o metamórfica (González Quintero 1968).

Como respuesta a este agreste paisaje, el grupo otomí generó un sistema socioeconómico fundamentado en una estrategia de uso múltiple de los recursos con un patrón de asentamiento de tipo disperso, que le permitió no depender del agua como recurso estratégico para su subsistencia. Excepto en las actuales zonas de riego, la agricultura es de temporal con siembra de productos básicos, donde es importante el cultivo del agave, y la recolección de frutos, plantas e insectos así como la caza de fauna menor (González Quintero 1968). Considerando como región social al Valle del Mezquital, resalta el complejo económico del agave para caracterizar un modo de vida propio de sus habitantes.

El Complejo del Agave

En las *Relaciones geográficas* del siglo XVI (Acuña 1985, 1986a, 1986b) se presenta una lista detallada de todos los artículos que los otomíes obtenían de la explotación del agave, para satisfacer la mayoría de sus necesidades de subsistencia e intercambio, al igual que para el pago de tributos. Entre ellos destaca la savia del agave, fresca o aguamiel, fermentada o pulque, así como miel y azúcar de maguey, material de construcción, y combustible, además de fibras para la elaboración de textiles y diversos artefactos.

La escasez de agua en gran parte de la región se ha visto solucionada gracias al consumo de los líquidos obtenidos del agave, y para la extracción, transporte, fermentación y consumo de la savia se han requerido y empleado recipientes de diversas clases, fundamentalmente de cerámica (figura 3.3).

En diversas fuentes etnohistóricas hay representaciones de vasijas asociadas con el transporte y consumo de la savia de maguey (Gonçalvez de Lima 1986), las cuales son idénticas o en extremo semejantes a las que se producen hoy día en el Valle del Mezquital. Por ejemplo, en el Códice Mendocino y la Matrícula de Tributos se muestran pictogramas de cántaros (figura 3.4), forma que se empleaba como recipiente para la miel espesa de maguey que dos de las provincias del Valle del Mezquital tributaban en el Posclásico Tardío (circa 1150–1521 d.C.) a la Triple Alianza dominada por los mexica (Castillo F. 1978; Paso y Troncoso 1979:fs. 27, 29).

La sustitución de vasijas cerámicas por recipientes de otros materiales ha sido paulatina desde la conquista hispana. Así, durante el período Colonial, muchos *tlachiqueros*—los raspadores de maguey que extraen la savia fresca— abandonaron el uso de cántaros de cerámica y adoptaron odres de cerdo o barriles de madera para transportar con burros el aguamiel o el pulque. A mediados del siglo XVIII en las haciendas se empleaban cueros de res fijados en marcos de madera para la fermentación hasta de mil litros de savia por tina. A fines del siglo XIX las redes ferroviarias conectaron las haciendas con los principales centros de consumo y diariamente se distribuía el pulque en barriles a la Ciudad de México, y en las pulquerías frecuentemente se servía en

FIGURA 3.3 Ollas de cerámica para fermentar pulque y recipientes de plástico para el transporte de la savia fresca del maguey, los cuales han sustituido a los tradicionales cántaros de cerámica.

FIGURA 3.4 Pictograma que representa un cántaro empleado para tributar miel de maguey en el Posclásico Tardío. *Matrícula de Tributos, Castillo F. 1978:541*

vasos de vidrio en lugar de *cajetes* o jarros de cerámica (véase Guerrero 1985). Es factible que durante los períodos Colonial y Republicano en el ámbito rural se mantuviera el uso de alfarería para el acarreo del aguamiel y la fermentación del pulque, tanto a nivel doméstico como para su venta comunitaria, costumbre que perdura hoy día en algunas zonas del Valle del Mezquital (Fournier-García 1993b; Fournier-García y Cedeño 1993).

La evidencia arqueológica es fundamental para inferir el papel que ha tenido la savia del maguey en la vida cotidiana de los hñähñü. A partir del análisis de colecciones de superficie recuperadas en más de setecientos sitios detectados en el Valle del Mezquital, se ha determinado que los materiales históricos más abundantes corresponden a lo que hemos denominado el "complejo cerámico del pulque" (López Águilar, Fournier-García, y Paz 1988). En términos formales se caracteriza por cántaros, ollas, cajetes y *apiloles* o jarros. En la actualidad es limitado el número de centros productores

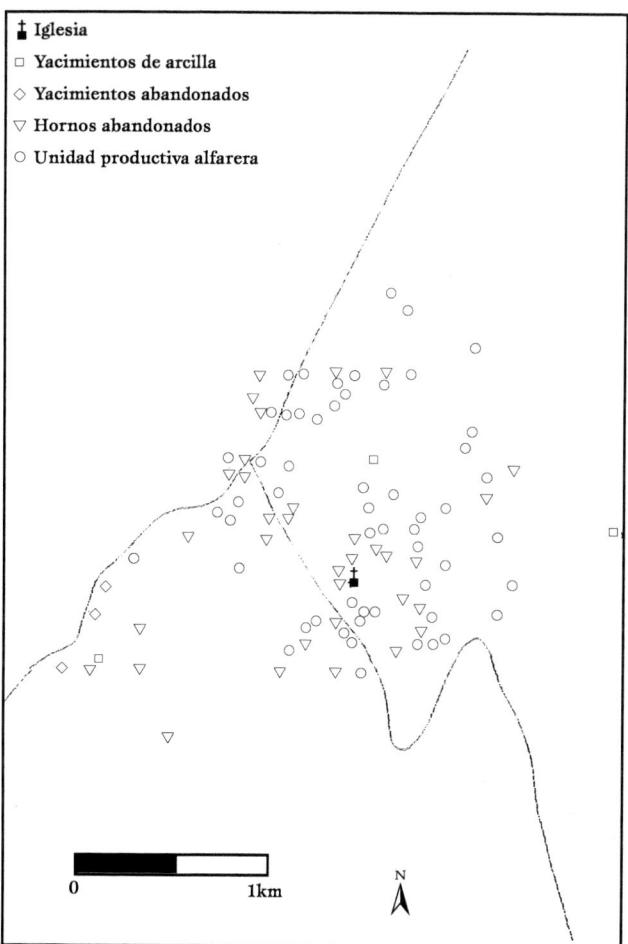

FIGURA 3.5 La localidad de Santa María del Pino

de estas vasijas, aunque es posible que con anterioridad en la región y otras zonas ocupadas por grupos otomíes existieran más comunidades especializadas en la manufactura de alfarería.

La evidencia etnoarqueológica, combinada con el análisis documental y la historia oral, es fundamental para determinar el desarrollo histórico-social de los otomíes del Mezquital, en particular de las comunidades alfareras, así como la importancia económica de la savia del maguey entre los hñähñü de la región en su conjunto.

La Comunidad Otomí de Santa María del Pino
Aspectos Etnoarqueológicos

San Ildefonso Tultepec (Estado de Querétaro) y José María Pino Suárez o Santa María del Pino (Estado de Hidalgo) destacan entre los pocos centros alfareros que perduran en el Valle del Mezquital hoy día (figura 3.1), dedicados a la producción del complejo cerámico del pulque (Fournier-García 1993c). En esta investigación nos centraremos en el pueblo de Santa María del Pino, que se localiza aproximadamente a 23 km al nornoroeste de la ciudad de Tula de Allende; desde 1990 se han realizado estudios intensivos etnoarqueológicos e históricos en la localidad.

El área del poblado, de aproximadamente 22 km², está delimitada de las comunidades vecinas por un conjunto de cerros y lomeríos. El paisaje se caracteriza por cañadas y cauces intermitentes, pequeñas mesetas y lomeríos y es drenada por dos arroyos de temporal.

En la localidad son abundantes las rocas de origen ígneo así como arcillas montmoriloníticas (formadas a partir de vertisoles pélicos combinados con feozem háplico de textura fina), cuyas características son óptimas para la producción de cerámica con una tecnología tradicional; esta clase de depósitos existen principalmente en el sur del Valle del Mezquital. En Santa María del Pino y sus alrededores, los suelos son delgados y tepetatosos, con vegetación predominantemente crasicaule y de matorral rosetófilo. Los habitantes del poblado reconocen su incidencia en la desforestación de la zona, quedando actualmente únicamente relictos de encino y pino, debido a la explotación desmedida de recursos maderables como combustible para la manufactura de la loza (Fournier-García 1990).

En la actualidad la comunidad tiene una población aproximada de 875 habitantes y en el sur del Mezquital es una de las pocas en donde todavía hay un porcentaje relativamente alto de hablantes de otomí. En 1990 entre los 7,430 habitantes del Municipio de Tepetitlán únicamente había 127 hablantes de lengua indígena, concentrándose 99 de ellos en José María Pino Suárez.[2] A partir de un censo preliminar en el poblado, realizado como parte de nuestros estudios etnoarqueológicos, se han identificado ochenta unidades productivas autónomas dedicadas a la manufactura de loza y hay aproximadamente cincuenta alfareros retirados (figura 3.5, y véase Fournier-García 1993c).

La población es cruzada por una de las carreteras que conectan el noroeste y suroeste del Valle del Mezquital, construida en la década de los años setenta siguiendo parcialmente el trazo de un camino real Colonial. Hace aproximadamente veinticinco años se instalaron los servicios de agua potable y alumbrado eléctrico, además de que se adoptó el uso de estufas de gas en lugar de braseros de cerámica con carbón como combustible. Estos factores han incidido en la modificación de las costumbres y el modo de vida en Santa María del Pino (Aronson y Fournier-García 1993).

La tenencia de la tierra es de dos tipos, pequeña propiedad privada y comunal; las actividades económicas primarias son la agricultura de temporal (con maíz y frijol como cultígenos) de tradición prehispánica, y el pastoreo de ganado menor (ovejas y cabras fundamentalmente) que cobró importancia entre los otomíes durante el período Colonial (véase Mendizabal 1947), así como la crianza de aves de corral. A principios del siglo XX la mayoría de los miembros de la comunidad carecían de terrenos de cultivo, por lo que básicamente se dedicaban a la produccion alfarera.[3] Gracias

Figura 3.6 Comerciante de loza del mercado de Ixmiquilpan. Nótese en primer plano los dos cántaros producidos en Santa María del Pino.

Figura 3.7 Alfarero otomí de Santa María del Pino, mostrando una olla con capacidad de 80 litros que él produjo

Figura 3.8 Preparación de arcillas empleadas en la producción de loza en Santa María del Pino

Figura 3.9 Etapa final en el moldeado de macetas

a la reforma agraria y al reparto de parcelas efectivo en la década de los años veinte, se dio mayor énfasis a las actividades agrícolas y la alfarería se convirtió en un medio para complementar los ingresos familiares. Por ende, esta actividad ha pasado a un segundo plano económico y se desempeña cuando las labores de cultivo y cosecha lo permiten, durante años de sequía, o bien se asocia con las familias que carecen de tierras o que cuentan con terrenos insuficientes para el sustento de sus integrantes. Según los informantes, antes todos los miembros de la comunidad eran loceros y muchos eran especialistas de tiempo completo.

En Santa María del Pino las principales formas que se han producido en su mayoría corresponden al complejo cerámico del pulque, incluyendo cántaros para el transporte de agua y aguamiel (figura 3.6), ollas para el almacenamiento de estos líquidos y la fermentación de pulque (figura 3.7), cajetes, jarros o apiloles para su consumo y cantimploras para su acarreo, además de *apaxtles* o lebrillos. Entre las formas no tradicionales se cuentan macetas, tejas y ollas para piñatas, así como la loza vidriada cuya manufactura se introdujo en 1985, al igual que el uso del torno. Cada clase de vasija se produce en distintos tamaños y capacidades, siendo su volumen la manera común de designarlas entre los productores y consumidores. Es interesante observar que una evidencia que apoya el que consideremos como tradicionales a diversas clases de vasijas, tanto las que corresponden al complejo cerámico del pulque como las destinadas a otras funciones, es que cuentan con nombre tanto en otomí como en castellano, mientras que los alfareros únicamente designan en español a las formas de introducción reciente (Fournier-García 1993c).

Formalmente los cántaros manufacturados en el Pino son prácticamente idénticos a los pictogramas de los recipientes para miel espesa de maguey, que las provincias tributarias del Mezquital entregaban a la Triple Alianza, controlada por los aztecas durante el Posclásico Tardío (figura 3.4). Además, las ollas contemporáneas son sumamente semejantes, incluso en cuanto a la localización de zonas decoradas, a representaciones en códices (Gonçalves de Lima 1986).

El proceso de trabajo de la actividad alfarera incluye las etapas de extracción de materias primas, preparación de arcillas (figura 3.8), moldeado (figura 3.9), decorado, secado, aplicación del acabado de la superficie y horneado. La mayoría de los aspectos técnicos del proceso de trabajo tienen antecedentes prehispánicos, que representan el resultado de una tradición cerámica otomiana que tal vez se remonte al período Epiclásico (650–900 d.C.; Fournier-García 1993b).

Hace tres décadas los alfareros colocaban directamente sus productos en diversos mercados del Estado de Hidalgo, algunos localizados a más de 100 km de la localidad, donde los "cantareros" intercambiaban sus vasijas, transportándolas con *mecapal* o en burro, mientras que sólo en ocasiones llegaban intermediarios a Santa María del Pino a adquirir las vasijas para revenderlas en el Mezquital o fuera de la región. Es probable que durante el período Colonial la mayor parte de la producción de loza del Pino se destinara a satisfacer la demanda regional,[4] básicamente de formas de vasija del complejo cerámico del pulque. En la actualidad los mecanismos de distribución han cambiado de manera radical y el papel fundamental lo tienen los acaparadores.

Aspectos Históricos

La información documental disponible es escasa para reconstruir los antecedentes históricos del lugar en el período Colonial, en parte debido a que su nombre se ha modificado a través del tiempo, así como a la dispersión y escasez de acervos relevantes.

En 1553 la comunidad de Santa María del Pino estaba conformada por indios viejos agregados cristianos[5] y en 1698 se registró bajo el nombre supuestamente otomí de Tehcli (Vetancurt 1971)—tal vez una corrupción del vocablo nahuatl *teuhtli* (polvo)—mientras que para el siglo XVIII se le denominaba María Asunción del Pino (Feldman y Mastache 1990:404–405).[6]

En la actualidad los habitantes del lugar se dicen ser del Pino, además de llamar a su pueblo Santa María Pino Suárez o El Pino, creando el sincretismo de las diferentes designaciones. El nombre de José María Pino Suárez, tal como aparece en las cartas geográficas actuales, pudo ser utilizado después de la construcción de la carretera federal que cruza al poblado, o bien asignado durante el período del presidente Plutarco Elías Calles (1924–1928).

Respecto a la evangelización de los naturales otomíes, en 1553 el poblado era una dependencia de la Provincia de Xilotepec, jurisdicción franciscana (véase nota 5), visita de Tula en la Provincia del Santo Evangelio (Vetancurt 1971:64). Por otra parte, en 1613 se registró como sujeto a la cabecera de Tula, siendo doctrina de Tepetitlán fundado como monasterio en 1571 y también a cargo de los franciscanos (Gerhard 1986:342). La zona del Mezquital donde se ubica Santa María del Pino fue secularizada entre 1754 y 1768 (Gerhard 1986:394).

En esta región originalmente evangelizada por los franciscanos de Tula (Kubler 1990:611), en 1566 se fundó la vicaría de Santiago Chapantongo de la Orden Agustina, que pasó a ser priorato en 1569 (Gerhard 1986:342). Después de 1572 los franciscanos cedieron a los agustinos varios conventos (Ricard 1986:142), al parecer incluso el de Tula. Actualmente, la iglesia de Santa María del Pino está dedicada a San Nicolás de Tolentino, normalmente asociado con los agustinos. Por tanto, la información es ambigua para determinar la jurisdicción de alguna de estas dos órdenes mendicantes durante el período Colonial Temprano en la comunidad, aunque como se expondrá más adelante, parece haber una predominancia de elementos iconográficos tal vez agustinos en la arquitectura histórica de Santa María del Pino.

Antes de 1927 éste era un pueblo de especialistas en la producción alfarera (véase nota 3), actividad que según los registros existentes caracteriza a sus habitantes al menos desde el siglo XVIII. No obstante, en un documento de 1614 referente a una de las poblaciones indígenas más importantes del Mezquital, se registra el uso de cántaros para aguamiel[7] que es factible hubieran sido producidos en El Pino o algún otro centro alfarero del sur de la región.

No hay datos sobre las actividades productivas desempeñadas por los hñähñü de este pueblo en el período Colonial Temprano, a excepción de que se dedicaban al cultivo de temporal en 1613.[8] Para el siglo XVIII es posible inferir, a partir de los litigios de tierras con comunidades, haciendas y ranchos vecinos, además de la Cofradía del Santísimo, que requerían terrenos donde existieran recursos maderables, probablemente necesarios para la manufactura de loza, pues sus parcelas eran pocas, de suelos delgados y tepetatosos (véase nota 5).

Incluso desde el siglo XVI el Virrey don Antonio de Mendoza (1535–1550) había ordenado que se respetaran las tierras de los naturales de Santa María del Pino. En un documento del siglo XVIII también se hace referencia a la mala calidad de los terrenos, la cual parece ser la justificación para la expansión de los límites de la comunidad, como ocurrió en la invasión a la Hacienda Endóo y algunos ranchos aledaños.[9] Sin embargo, muchas de las tierras usurpadas eran impropias para la agricultura, y quizá únicamente eran adecuadas para obtener madera, empleada como leña, así como para el pastoreo de ganado menor. Un ejemplo adicional es la renta de tierras pertenecientes a la Hacienda Endóo a los naturales de El Pino para que obtuvieran dichos recursos maderables, en quince pesos anuales.[10]

Por otra parte, en 1750 se registró la manufactura de cántaros y ollas (véase nota 4), presumiblemente para la contención de savia del agave, reiterándose la pobreza de los indios y la insuficiencia de las tierras de cultivo a las que tenían acceso.[11]

Lo anterior también es evidente para 1809, momento en que el pueblo cubría una extensión de 600 varas, con algunas porciones de tierras tepetatosas en donde se sembraban maíz y otras semillas de temporal.[12]

La referencia de mayor importancia existente es un padrón de 1823,[13] en el cual se registró que la mayoría de los indígenas varones económicamente activos de El Pino se dedicaban a la manufactura de loza (véase el cuadro 3.1); el hecho de que para ese momento la producción alfarera era la principal actividad de los habitantes del poblado, implica que necesariamente con anterioridad se habían generado las bases de esta especialización comunal.

Cuadro 3.1 Padrón de los ciudadanos de Santa María del Pino, 1823

EDAD (años)	SEXO	ESTADO CIVIL	OCUPACIÓN	NUMERO	%
20–80	M	Casado	Locero	54	21.09
49	M	Casado	Fiscal	1	0.39
16–65	F	Casada	-	54	21.09
26–56	M	Viudo	Locero	5	1.95
28–70	F	Viuda	-	15	5.86
12–19	M	Soltero	-	12	4.69
15–28	M	Soltero	Locero	4	1.56
17	M	Soltero	Colegial	1	0.39
10–15	F	Donceya	-	10	3.91
12–28	M	Soltera	-	6	2.34
1–12	M			50	19.53
1–10	F			44	17.19
TOTAL				256	99.99
Hombres*				77	30.08
Mujeres				85	33.20
Niños (ambos sexos)				94	36.72
*Hombres adultos (todos estados) dedicados a la alfarería				63	24.61

Historia Oral

Entre los hñähñü de Santa María del Pino la producción de loza es una parte integral de los mitos transmitidos oralmente de generación en generación. Sus ancestros, conocidos como gentiles o *wema* (gigantes en otomí), les enseñaron a producir loza antes del diluvio—o "antes de que se volteara la tierra," según manifestara una informante—y en la localidad los hallazgos casuales de restos óseos de megafauna se asocian con los gentiles, dado que se dice que su estatura era de al menos 2.5 m.

El mito de los gigantes o wema es común entre los hñähñü de diversas regiones (Galinier 1990), pero en El Pino adquiere un carácter único. Así, se relata que los wema eran hábiles alfareros, producían vasijas de paredes delgadas y con superficies lustrosas, sin usar vidriado y, según los atributos que describen los informantes, esta cerámica corresponde a lozas prehispánicas que datan de 650 a 1521 d.C.

La interpretación de la historia oral indica que los gentiles vivían en casas de piedras amontonadas o hechas con pencas de maguey y pasto, con un patrón de asentamiento disperso, sin que el cultivo de maíz fuera la base de subsistencia ya que la economía se centraba en la caza-recolección. Es interesante observar que estos datos coinciden con la información arqueológica, histórica y etnográfica acerca de los otomíes del Valle del Mezquital (Acuña 1985, 1986a, 1986b; Guerrero 1983; Mendizabal 1947; Soustelle 1937). Por ejemplo, la arquitectura vernácula con piedras sueltas y pencas de maguey, o únicamente con pencas, seguía siendo común incluso a fines del siglo XIX en el sur de la región[14] y hay escasos remanentes contemporáneos en Santa María del Pino (figura 3.10).

FIGURA 3.10 **Arquitectura doméstica tradicional con muros de piedras superpuestas. El uso de tejas en las techumbres es de introducción Colonial en el Valle del Mezquital. Nótese la acumulación de pencas de maguey, empleadas como combustible, en el extremo inferior izquierdo.**

FIGURA 3.11 **Oratorio doméstico con cubierta de bóveda, posiblemente del siglo XVIII**

Arquitectura Doméstica Devocional

Las capillas domésticas indígenas en la Nueva España fueron el resultado del sincretismo religioso prehispánico y europeo. Del siglo XVI al XVIII hay testimonios documentales de que estas estructuras se encontraban separadas de las unidades residenciales de los naturales y, en la medida de sus posibilidades económicas, eran de mejor calidad constructiva que éstas, además de que era común la colocación de cruces en los patios de las casas frente al oratorio (Ajofrín 1986:195; Grijalva 1985:162, 168; Moreno 1985:80, 98, 139; Vetancurt 1971:6). La costumbre de edificarlos se asocia con comunidades de distintas filiaciones étnicas del centro de México y del Bajío, incluyendo a los mazahuas y otomíes (Cortés 1972; Dow 1974).

En Santa María del Pino los oratorios se consideraban los lugares más sagrados del hogar y algunos todavía se destinan al culto, además de que en su interior presentan esculturas e imágenes religiosas, así como óleos sobre tela o madera con la representación de los ancestros de las familias; los primordiales aparecen como ánimas en el purgatorio con sus nombres pintados (Mondragón, Noguera, y Fournier-García 1991). Algunos autores proponen que entre los otomíes estas

FIGURA 3.12 Oratorio doméstico con humilladero en el exterior

estructuras constituyen emblemas de linajes patrilineales, destinadas al culto a los ancestros (Galinier 1990).

En Pino Suárez existen hoy día treinta y seis oratorios domésticos (véase figura 3.11), observándose dos tipos, de bóveda y de techo de una sola pendiente. Generalmente miden de 4 a 5 m de largo, 3 a 4 m de ancho, con una altura de 2 a 3.5 m, construidos con materiales de la región, por ejemplo tezontle, pómez y tobas compactadas (Mondragón y Noguera 1992). Algunos oratorios presentan platos de mayólica ornamental y los tipos cerámicos datan de fines del siglo XVIII a principios del XIX (por ejemplo, Aranama Policromo, San Elizario Policromo, Puebla Azul/Blanco); no obstante, la colocación de estas vasijas quizá es posterior a su construcción (véase Mondragón, Noguera, y Fournier-García 1991).

Los oratorios de bóveda presentan planta basilical, bóveda de cañón, acceso frontal o lateral, adintelado o de arco. En algunos casos tienen contrafuertes y peldaños en el acceso, gárgolas de cantera o cerámica en cada costado a la altura del desplante de la cubierta y rosetas en los paños; en el interior cuentan con altar escalonado con nichos y pintura mural. En relación con su iconografía y ornamentación se observan relieves en dinteles (IHS, corazón con cruz o cruces sobre pedestal) y motivos fitomorfos o estrellas estilizadas en las jambas. Estos iconos, al igual que otros observables en la iglesia del poblado (posiblemente construida en el siglo XVII), evidencian la probable influencia agustina en la localidad.

Las capillas de techo de una sola pendiente presentan los mismos atributos arquitectónicos que los anteriores, diferenciándose por la techumbre y el acceso adintelado con la abreviatura de IHS. Quizá muchas de estas estructuras tuvieron bóveda de cañón que se reemplazó al colapsarse por cubierta de una sola pendiente.

Los pequeños altares (figura 3.12), que se ubican aproximadamente de 2 a 4 m del acceso de los oratorios, se dividen en baldaquinos y nichos abovedados por sus características arquitectónicas. Todos estos humilladeros presentan basamento para cruz, y ocasionalmente se observa pintura mural en su interior; al igual que los oratorios algunos muestran platos de mayólica incrustados en el interior del techo.

En lo referente al uso de estas estructuras, posiblemente sus antecedentes fueron los humilladeros con cruces que abundan por los caminos del norte de España, del siglo XIII en adelante (Rojas 1981:32). Otra hipótesis sobre su localización frente a las capillas domésticas se basa en una analogía con las cruces atriales del siglo XVI, relacionadas con el proceso de evangelización de los naturales. Es decir, en menor escala en el ámbito rural, la asociación espacial de los oratorios con humilladeros que presentan cruces es reminiscente de los atrios del período Colonial Temprano (Mondragón, Noguera, y Fournier-García 1991).

Es probable que a principios del siglo XVIII o incluso fines del siglo XVII, el decremento acelerado de la población indígena que se diera a partir de la conquista se frenara relativamente, hasta alcanzarse cierta estabilidad y, finalmente, a principios del siglo XIX se iniciaran tendencias al aumento demográfico que se continúan hasta la actualidad (Cook 1989; Gerhard 1986; Mendizabal 1947). Aunque son limitados e imprecisos los datos poblacionales para el período Colonial, podría suponerse que la demanda regional de consumo de vasijas llegó también a adquirir un carácter estable tal vez desde fines del siglo XVII, con lo cual los alfareros de Santa María del Pino pudieron colocar sus productos en los mercados del Mezquital.

De esta manera, la producción y venta de alfarería durante el período Colonial de El Pino permitieron no sólo que los hñähñü de El Pino lograran satisfacer sus necesidades básicas de subsistencia, sino que además se canalizaran recursos, tiempo y energía en la construcción de oratorios domésticos, fenómeno común desde el siglo XVI entre indígenas y mestizos. Así, puede inferirse cierta bonanza económica durante los siglos XVII y XVIII, que se plasma en estas edificaciones como reflejo ideológico de elementos de identificación étnica entre los naturales loceros y, paralelamente, tal vez inclusive de carácter mágico; cabe señalar que en la actualidad los alfareros otomíes de la región de las tierras altas al occidente del Mezquital realizan ritos propiciatorios en los oratorios, como parte del culto a la tierra, que junto con los cultos generalizados al fuego, la fecundidad y los ancestros, constituyen remanentes de concepciones religiosas precortesianas (véase Galinier 1976).

Conclusiones

A partir del estudio interdisciplinario de la comunidad alfarera de Santa María del Pino, es factible generar inferencias analógicas para comprender el modo de vida otomí con una perspectiva diacrónica. Aunque algunos de sus elementos esenciales han desaparecido o están en proceso de transformación, se cuenta con datos relevantes a partir de correlatos materiales y documentales.

Mediante la reconstrucción histórica de procesos socioeconómicos en la comunidad, se puede observar que actualmente la explotación del maguey, que durante mucho tiempo constituyó la base de subsistencia de los otomíes del Valle del Mezquital, ha perdido importancia frente a la introducción de nuevos cultígenos, además de que el consumo del pulque ha disminuido radicalmente. Las raíces de estos cambios se gestan a partir de la conquista hispana, aunque los factores causales de mayor peso se vinculan de manera directa con el proceso de modernización de México y la integración de las comunidades indígenas a la nación.

Así, a pesar de la importancia del agave como componente de un modo de vida propio de los hñähñü del Mezquital, en las últimas décadas se ha dado un decremento en la producción y consumo del complejo cerámico del pulque, debido al uso de recipientes de plástico (figura 3.3), a la introducción de redes de agua potable en la región y a la ingesta generalizada de bebidas comerciales, sobre todo cerveza y refrescos embotellados. Sin embargo, la producción alfarera no ha desaparecido totalmente, sino que se ha adaptado y transformado ante las necesidades de demanda y consumo actual, elaborándose formas cerámicas nuevas, como macetas y piñatas, además de cerámica vidriada. De cualquier manera, es limitado el número de alfareros activos, y los jóvenes, que han tenido la oportunidad de cursar estudios primarios y secundarios, tienden a emigrar de la comunidad en busca de mejores oportunidades de trabajo (véase Fournier-García 1993c).

Asimismo, se ha dado un proceso de transformación de la comunidad, antes organizada con base en lazos de parentesco, a raíz de tensiones políticas, las modificaciones en los sistemas de tenencia de la tierra y el acaparamiento de nuevos conocimientos tecnológicos en la manufactura de loza, en particular el uso del torno y de vidriado (Fournier-García 1993c).

Los procesos de cambio e integración de los otomíes a la nación mexicana también han afectado los valores ideológicos tradicionales, incluyendo el uso de oratorios familiares. En la actualidad en Santa María del Pino se ha perdido su simbolismo mágico-religioso, y es común que estas edificaciones se encuentren abandonadas o se utilicen como habitaciones o áreas de almacenamiento. Sólo en casos excepcionales se colocan ofrendas para la celebración anual del día de muertos, reminiscencia de su uso anterior asociado con el culto a los ancestros, el cual se mantiene, por ejemplo, entre los otomíes del límite suroeste del Mezquital (Fliert 1988). Las causas de su desuso en Santa María del Pino son inciertas, aunque parecen vincularse con cambios en los elementos de identificación étnica, cuyo análisis servirá de base a futuras investigaciones.

Desde el punto de vista arqueológico, se requiere realizar reconocimientos de área que permitan la detección de asentamientos abandonados o en uso, que estén relacionados con la producción alfarera y sirvan de base para conocer la profundidad histórica del proceso, incluyendo excavaciones controladas en contextos no alterados. De esta manera, se espera contar con elementos para desarrollar un modelo para predecir los indicadores arqueológicos que permitan el reconocimiento de la existencia de la actividad alfarera en el pasado, y determinar si las técnicas de su producción son análogas a las modernas.

Dentro del ámbito etnoarqueológico hay temáticas de investigación que aún falta explorar en detalle, como la estacionalidad del proceso alfarero en términos de variaciones técnicas adecuadas a las condiciones fluctuantes ambientales, o de la demanda de formas de vasija específicas en temporadas particulares y de la manufactura realizada sobre pedido. También es importante estudiar el patrón de asentamiento y área de captación en la localidad, registrando la distribución espacial de las unidades productivas alfareras, además de aquéllas relacionadas con otras actividades del grupo, tanto económicas como religiosas, políticas, jurídicas y sociales.

Dado que se cuenta con información referente a la organización de la fuerza de trabajo comunitaria en torno al proceso alfarero a partir de archivos documentales, información etnohistórica, e historia oral, en la medida en que se disponga de más datos arqueológicos y etnoarqueológicos se espera definir si lo que actualmente se observa es análogo con procesos pretéritos, así como tendencias subregionales demográficas y de especialización productiva.

El estudio etnoarqueológico y sobre arqueología histórica de la comunidad alfarera de Santa María del Pino, permite aproximarse a aspectos estructurales y superestructurales de la sociedad otomí contemporánea y Colonial para, de esta manera, acceder al conocimiento de diversas clases de procesos presentes y pasados. Aún no ha sido posible reconocer los correlatos materiales para caracterizar étnicamente a las poblaciones prehispánicas del Valle del Mezquital, pero la explotación del agave en definitiva es un marcador de un modo de vida regional que está a punto de desaparecer.

Agradecimientos. El Proyecto Etnoarqueología Cerámica Otomí se inició en 1991 en la Escuela Nacional de Antropología e Historia, sobre la base de estudios previos realizados en el Estado de Hidalgo dentro del marco del Proyecto Valle del Mezquital; para la consecución de las investigaciones se ha contado con apoyo presupuestal del INAH y del Consejo Nacional de Ciencia y Tecnología (Proyecto 0251-H9107). Deseamos hacer patente nuestro más profundo agradecimiento a la comunidad de Santa María del Pino por su hospitalidad, paciencia, desinteresada colaboración y amistad, así como al Padre Victor M. Castillo, Párroco de Tepetitlán, por permitir el acceso al Archivo Parroquial, además de al Sr. Manuel Pacheco, Presidente Municipal de Tepetitlán, y al Sr. Lara, Secretario Particular, quienes posibilitaron la investigación documental en los archivos municipales. Los dibujos fueron realizados por Francisco C. Ramírez Quintero y Felix Domínguez Acosta.

Notas

1. En documentos del siglo XVII, en particular de 1622 sobre registros matrimoniales, aparece el término *aniñani-nu*, que seguramente se utilizaba para designar a los indios otomíes desde épocas precortesianas.
2. *XI censo general de población y vivienda. Hidalgo, resultados definitivos*, 86.
3. Carpeta básica, 1972. Documentos básicos que amparan la propiedad y posesión de la tierra de Pino Suárez. Mpo. de Tepetitlán, Hidalgo. Departamento de Asuntos Agrarios y Colonización.
4. Archivo Parroquial de Tepetitlán, Hidalgo (APT). Sección Disciplinar, Serie Jurídico-Eclesiástica, Caja 8, Folder 1. Carta de Miguel de Arce Samozano dirigida al Sr. Cristóbal Martínez, Cura Mayor de esta Doctrina de San Bartolomé Tepetitlán, Jurisdicción de Tula, 1750.
5. Archivo General de la Nación, México, D.F. (AGN) Tierras, v. 1708, exp. 2. Diligencias y vista de ojos practicada a favor de los naturales de Santa María del Pino, de la jurisdicción de Tula, 1760, f. 3v.
6. Véase nota 5, s.f.
7. Instituto Nacional de Antropología e Historia, México, D.F. Serie Hidalgo, rollo 23, miscelánea diversa.
8. AGN. Tierras, vol. 1708, cuad. 1, f. 6–8.
9. La lucha por tierras y agua que entablaron los indígenas despojados por los españoles, en particular los hacendados, es un fenómeno generalizado durante el siglo XVIII en la Nueva España (véase Wobeser 1983:67).
10. Véase nota 5, fs. 1–307.
11. "en este pueblo, el de San Pedro Nextlalpa, Sta. María de el Pino y sus barrios...[que] caen en esta Jurisdicción de Tula, se ha experimentado...por no haberse cosechado ningún maíz en el año próximo pasado [1749]...notoria falta y carestía de él...los indios, tributarios de dichos Pueblos y sus Barrios...aun en tiempos abundantes de semillas, las tienen...muy escasas por las pocas tierras que tienen que sembrar, siendo tan notoriamente pobres, que no sólo no tienen facultades, ni grangerías, tratos, ni comercios, de que poder mantenerse...aunque muy pocos indios del Pueblo de Sta. María de el Pino se aplican a hacer ollas y cántaros para vender" (APT 1750) (véase nota 4).
12. AGN. Indios, vol. 80, exp. 10, fs. 244–245, 247; Indios, vol. 79, exp. 3, fs. 49–64v.
13. APT. Sección Disciplinar, Serie Status Animarum, Caja 7. Padrón de los Ciudadanos del Pueblo de Santa María del Pino para el Derecho Auxiliar Nacional, Febrero 12 de 1823.
14. Archivo Municipal de Tepetitlán, Hidalgo. México Independiente, Recaudación de Rentas, Caja 1, Folder 6, fs. 90, 160, s.f; folder 9, s.f.

Chapter 4

Settlement Patterns of the Late Colonial Period in Yaxcabá Parish, Yucatán, Mexico
Implications for the Distribution of Land and Population Before the Caste War

Rani T. Alexander

Abstract

A regional archaeological survey of sites from the late-eighteenth and early-nineteenth centuries in the parish of Yaxcabá, Yucatán, Mexico, reveals several discrepancies between the archaeological model of the settlement hierarchy and the historical view of Colonial community typology. Analysis of the distribution of population among the cabecera, pueblos, haciendas, and independent ranchos demonstrates that most of the population growth occurred in settlements integrated with the tributary sector of the economy rather than in the haciendas comprising the commercial economic sector. Furthermore, although the number of haciendas increased, the estates did not support a corresponding proportion of the region's population. The archaeological and historical evidence suggest an imbalance of land and population within Yaxcabá parish prior to the Caste War.

Resumen

Un reconocimiento regional arqueológico de los sitios pertenecientes a los siglos dieciocho tardío y diecinueve temprano de la Parroquia de Yaxcabá, Yucatán, México, revela varios discrepancias entre el modelo arqueológico y la vista histórica de la tipología de comunidades coloniales. El análisis de la distribución de población entre la cabecera, los pueblos, las haciendas, y los ranchos independientes muestra que la mayoría de la crecensia en la población ocurrió en los sitios más integrados con la sección tributario de la economía más bien que en las haciendas que comprendían la sección comercial de la economía. Además, aunque el número de haciendas se aumentó, las propiedades no sostenía una proporción correspondiente de la población de la región. La evidencia arqueológica y histórica sugiere una falta de equilibrio de tierra y población en la Parroquia de Yaxcabá antes de la Guerra de Castas.

DURING THE YEARS 1847 THROUGH 1855, Yaxcabá parish in central Yucatán (figure 4.1) was caught in the middle of some of the most violent fighting of the Caste War. As the rebel Maya and the Spanish American armies battled back and forth, Yaxcabá changed hands four times (Reed 1964). Virtually all the haciendas were destroyed, and massacres took place at several pueblos and ranchos. Bullet holes in the walls of haciendas and churches, pillboxes constructed at the corners of the churchyard in Yaxcabá, and blockaded streets of abandoned settlements are archaeological evidence of the conflict. The 1862 census records the total population of Yaxcabá parish as 673 persons (Rejón 1862). The census totals for the parish before the Caste War range between ten and twelve thousand persons. Thus, the 1862 figure represents a loss of approximately 90 percent of the population (figure 4.2).[1] Only seven of an original twenty-nine settlements within the Yaxcabá region retained minimal populations; the rest were abandoned.

Analysis of archaeological settlement patterns and historical population figures reveals a schism in the settlement hierarchy that corresponds to a transformation of the economic structure in the years leading to the Caste War. The division among settlement types corresponds to the development of a dual economy (see Geertz 1963; Wolf 1982) in Yaxcabá parish in the late eighteenth and early nineteenth centuries. The expansion of cattle haciendas corresponds to the development of a commercial economic sector, whereas the pueblos and independent ranchos remained entrenched in subsistence production, the basis for the tributary sector of the economy. The *cabecera* (administrative seat) represents the point of articulation between the two sectors. Although the number of haciendas increased, most of the population growth occurred in the cabecera, pueblos, and independent ranchos. While the commercial sector gained control of more land, the critical resource over which the cattle-raising estates and the subsistence agriculturalists were competing, it did not support a corresponding proportion of the region's population. This severe imbalance of land and population culminated in the Caste War of 1847.

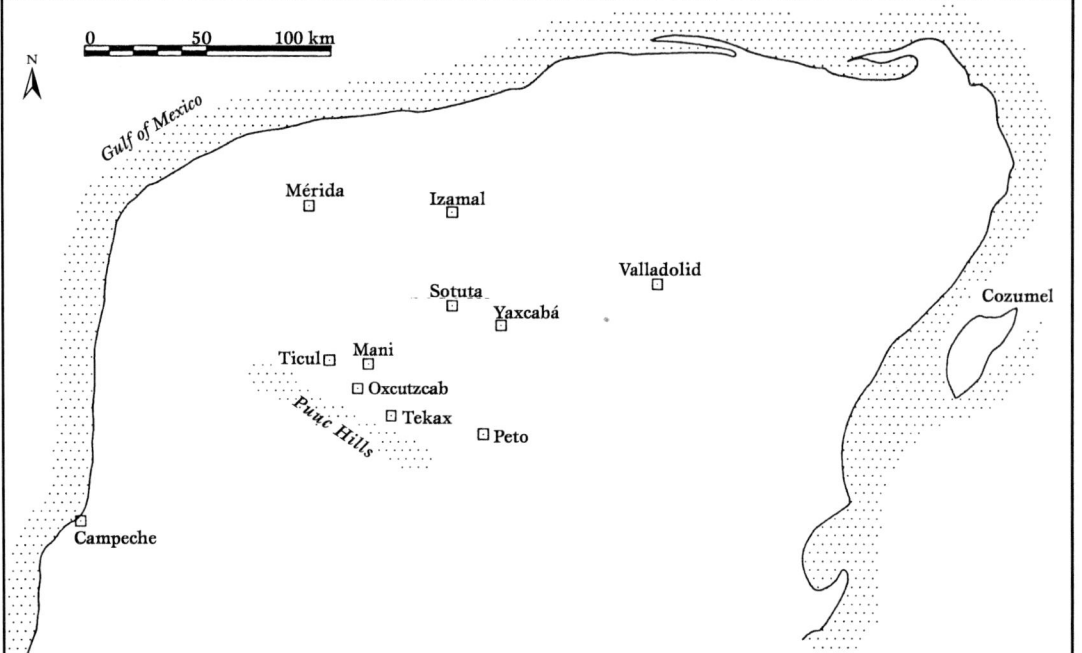

FIGURE 4.1 Yaxcabá, Yucatán, Mexico. *All drawings by Rani T. Alexander*

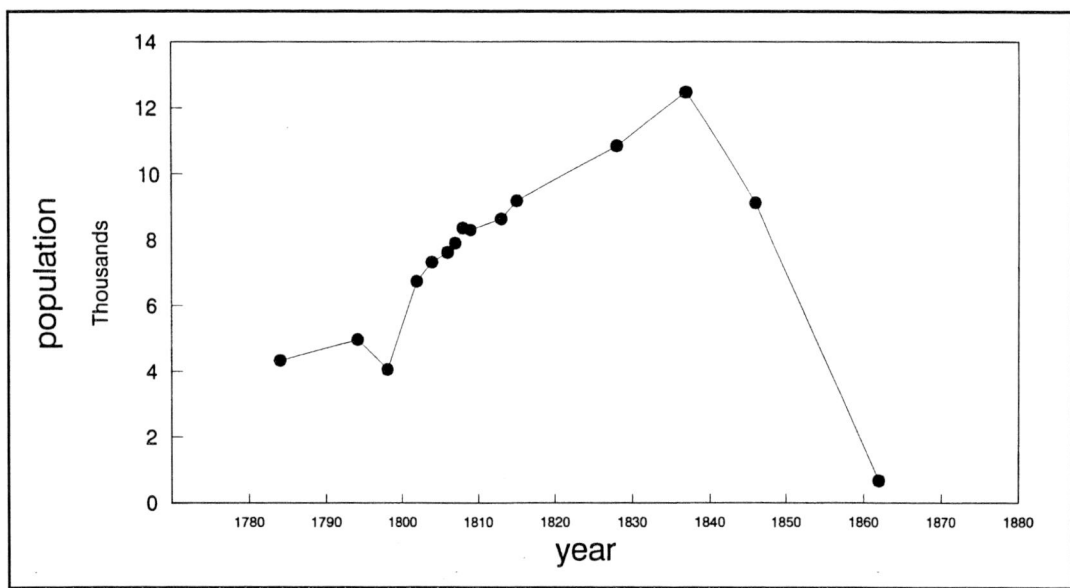

FIGURE 4.2 Total population in Yaxcabá parish, 1784–1862

The lack of correspondence between the archaeological evidence and the historic model of settlement organization has been identified elsewhere in Colonial Mesoamerica, most notably in Central Mexico, Oaxaca, and Guatemala (Charlton 1986; MacLeod 1973; Taylor 1972). The archaeological survey of Yaxcabá parish provides further evidence that the development of the Colonial market economy and transformation in the structure of urban-rural relations occurred considerably later than indicated by interpretations based exclusively on documentary data.

Economy of Yaxcabá Parish

During the late eighteenth and early nineteenth centuries, the economy of Yucatán began to shift from a tribute-based mode of production to a production system dominated by entrepreneurs and commercial pressures (Farriss 1984; Patch 1979, 1993). In the northwest and southern regions of the province where production focused on henequen and sugar cane, respectively, much of the indigenous population was incorporated into the commercial sector of the economy through aggregation on the haciendas. The northeast and central regions of Yucatán, including Yaxcabá parish, were dominated by cattle raising, which unlike henequen and sugar production is not labor intensive (Bracamonte 1984, 1985; Patch 1985; Strickon 1965). The incorporation of indigenous laborers onto the haciendas in these areas was accordingly less than in the northwest and southern regions of Yucatán (Bracamonte 1984; Cline 1950). Many historians

(Cline 1950; Farriss 1984, 1986; Patch 1979, 1985) view the expansion of haciendas and the process of labor incorporation on the estates as a marker for the transition from a tribute-based to a market-based economy. Much of the historical evidence from Yaxcabá indicates, however, that the transition was never completed in this area. Instead, a protracted series of conflicts arose over land and resources between those involved in the tributary and commercial sectors of the economy.

During the late eighteenth and early nineteenth centuries, settlements within the Yaxcabá region belonged to one of two vastly different economic sectors. The cattle haciendas of the commercial sector acquired large amounts of land, while the cabecera, pueblos, and independent ranchos of the tributary sector absorbed the majority of the indigenous population principally engaged in subsistence agriculture, horticulture, and apiculture.[2] This imbalance was exacerbated by the drastic increase in the population of the parish during this period (figure 4.2). The indigenous population was displaced and increasingly relegated to the tributary sector of the economy. As the church and the state extracted tribute payments in various forms, the burden of tribute became heavier for the indigenous residents of the region.

At the same time, land and resources were appropriated by the hacienda owners of the commercial sector.[3] As the haciendas absorbed more land, stress was placed on the tributary sector of the economy as fewer resources were available to the tribute-paying population. This situation led to a severe land shortage, especially after Independence (1821) when laws permitting the sale of *terreno baldío* (vacant land) came into effect (Cline 1950; Reed 1964).

Historical Classification of Communities

The historical classification of each settlement within Yaxcabá parish was identified in the *visitas pastorales* (pastoral visits) of 1784, 1804, and 1828.[4] These records list all settlements within the parish, their population, their distance from the cabecera, and their classification as pueblo, rancho, or hacienda. Additional community-type categories frequently discussed in the historical literature differentiate privately owned ranchos, independent ranchos, and *cofradía* (religious cofraternity) estates, but primary sources are often unspecific with reference to these latter three categories. Notarial documents of the Archivo Notarial del Estado de Yucatán (ANEY) were used to distinguish between privately owned ranchos and independent rancho communities, as well as settlements associated with cofradías. The documentary classification of each settlement and its population for each year of a visita pastoral are listed in table 4.1.

Historians have reported six different types of communities for Yaxcabá in the eighteenth and nineteenth centuries: cabeceras, pueblos, haciendas, privately owned ranchos, independent ranchos, and cofradía estates.

Cabecera

A cabecera is defined as the administrative seat of a parish, usually with a large population, a church, and a resident curate.

Pueblo

A pueblo is a town, also known as a *visita* or auxiliary town, smaller than and subordinate to the cabecera, with a church and, in some cases, a resident priest.

Hacienda

A privately owned livestock-producing and/or agricultural estate, a hacienda is characterized by permanent structures and a large number of workers. Haciendas constitute a social as well as an economic unit (Patch 1979). In Yaxcabá, haciendas are principally cattle-raising establishments that conduct subsidiary maize cultivation (see note 2; Bacamonte 1988, 1989, 1990; Patch 1985).

Privately owned rancho

A privately owned parcel of land, usually smaller than a hacienda, is characterized by a small number of resident workers. Bracamonte (1989, 1990) suggests that the major difference between a privately owned rancho and a hacienda is the total value and amount of capital invested in its *planta* (the buildings and facilities that form the core of the estate). In historical documents, a privately owned rancho may be referred to as either a hacienda or a rancho.

Independent rancho

A small settlement, an independent rancho may consist of a single household or as many as several hundred people engaged in farming or other extractive endeavors on communal lands. Dumond and Dumond (1982) state that, in some cases, ranchos may have been satellites of haciendas and that the inhabitants of smaller ranchos were fairly mobile. Some independent ranchos are organized as cofradía estates.

Cofradía estate

Defined as the property of a religious co-fraternity, a cofradía estate may be classified in historical documents as either a hacienda or an independent rancho. The produce of these communities, usually cattle and agricultural commodities, supports the cofradía and is used for the annual celebration of the cofradía's patron saint (Farriss 1984). Cline (1950) refers to them as "church haciendas."

According to the documentary sources, whose classifications varied over time, Yaxcabá parish consisted of one cabecera, one to four pueblos, thirteen to fifteen hacien-

Table 4.1 Historical classification and population of settlements

	ARCH. CLASSIFICATION	1784 CLASS.	1784 POP.	1804 CLASS.	1804 POP.	1828 CLASS.	1828 POP.
Yaxcabá	Cabecera	Cabecera	1491	Cabecera	3292	Cabecera	3128
Mopila	Pueblo	Pueblo	155	Pueblo	284	Pueblo	342
Santa María	Pueblo	Rancho	379	Pueblo	592	Pueblo	1290
Kancabdzonot*	Pueblo	Rancho	680	Hacienda*	1008	Pueblo	2097
Yaxuná	Pueblo	Rancho	205	Rancho	357	Pueblo	896
Cabalkom	Independent rancho	Rancho	254				
Santa Lucía	Independent rancho	Rancho	151				
Xkeken	Independent rancho	Rancho	8				
Xiat*	Independent rancho	Rancho	67	Hacienda*	87	Rancho	167
Canakom	Independent rancho	Rancho	248	Rancho	325	Rancho	560
Chimay	Independent rancho	Rancho	64	Rancho	124	Rancho	178
Cacalchen	Independent rancho	Rancho	184	Rancho	327	Rancho	634
Kulimché*	Independent rancho	Rancho	173	Rancho	294	Rancho	322
Santa Cruz	Independent rancho					Rancho	380
Cetelac	Hacienda	Hacienda	8	Hacienda	25	Hacienda	51
Popolá	Hacienda	Hacienda	16	Hacienda	65	Hacienda	138
Nohitzá	Hacienda	Hacienda	52	Hacienda	87	Hacienda	220
Kambul	Hacienda	Hacienda	63	Hacienda	95	Hacienda	169
Chacxul**	Hacienda	Rancho	61	Hacienda	125	Rancho	121
Xbac**	Hacienda	Rancho	143	Rancho	206	Hacienda	19
Holop	Hacienda			Hacienda	29	Hacienda	107
Yaxleulá	Hacienda					Hacienda	27
Xuul	Hacienda					Hacienda	39
Xkopteil	Hacienda					Hacienda	13
Cacalchen	Hacienda					Hacienda	20
San José	Hacienda					Hacienda	58
Yximché	Hacienda					Hacienda	16
San Lorenzo	Hacienda					Hacienda	23
Oxolá	Hacienda					Hacienda	37

Note: * Cofradía estate; ** Privately owned rancho. Sources: Archivo de la Mitra Emeritense, Cathedral Archive, Mérida, Yucatán (AME). Visita a Yaxcabá, 1784, Visitas Pastorales 1783–1784, vol. 2, exp. 42; Visita a Yaxcabá, 1804, Visitas Pastorales 1803–1805, vol. 5, exp. 43; Yaxcabá, 1828, Selección Joaquin Arrigunaga Peon, caja 5, Ticul-Yotholin; Sotuta, 1829, Selección Joaquin Arrigunaga Peon, caja 4, Pencuyut-Teya.

das, between six and eleven independent ranchos, two privately owned ranchos, and as many as three cofradía estates. Pueblos were subordinate to the cabecera, and haciendas and privately owned ranchos were linked to the cabecera or to individual pueblos, depending on where the owner lived. Independent ranchos were considered subordinate to the cabecera or the pueblos. Independent ranchos organized as cofradía estates were an extension of religious co-fraternities attached to a particular church either in the cabecera or in a pueblo.

Archaeological Classification of Settlements

An extensive archaeological survey of Colonial sites in the Yaxcabá region was conducted to compare the views held by historians of the Colonial community typology with an archaeological assessment of settlement types. The twenty-nine communities of the Yaxcabá parish listed in the visitas pastorales were located and surveyed (figure 4.3). Information collected for each settlement includes a basic description of structures and features present at the site, its ecological setting, an estimate of site size, the amount and stylistic characteristics of standing architecture, and any evidence for specialized functions within sites.

The attributes that permit the division of these settlements into classes are site size, area of masonry structures, and site layout. With regard to the area of masonry structures, two subcategories—religious and residential—were considered which further distinguish the settlement classes. Site layout is a categorical variable having two states: house-lot enclosures aligned along streets focused on a central plaza and a *noria* (pump well) surrounded by livestock corrals often associated with a masonry residential structure with smaller masonry ancillary features such as stables and water troughs. The archaeological survey demonstrates that there were four settlement types within the region; one cabecera (Yaxcabá), four pueblos, nine independent ranchos, and fifteen haciendas (table 4.1).

Cabecera and the pueblos

Two archaeological characteristics differentiate the cabecera, Yaxcabá, from its four pueblos: site size and amount of Colonial masonry architecture. The cabecera and the auxiliary towns have the same basic layout consisting of *solares* (house lots) arranged on a square grid centered on the church and the main plaza. All settlements have either a *cenote* (natural well; sinkhole that reaches the underground aquifer) or a

Settlement Patterns of the Late Colonial Period in Yaxcabá Parish, Yucatán, Mexico

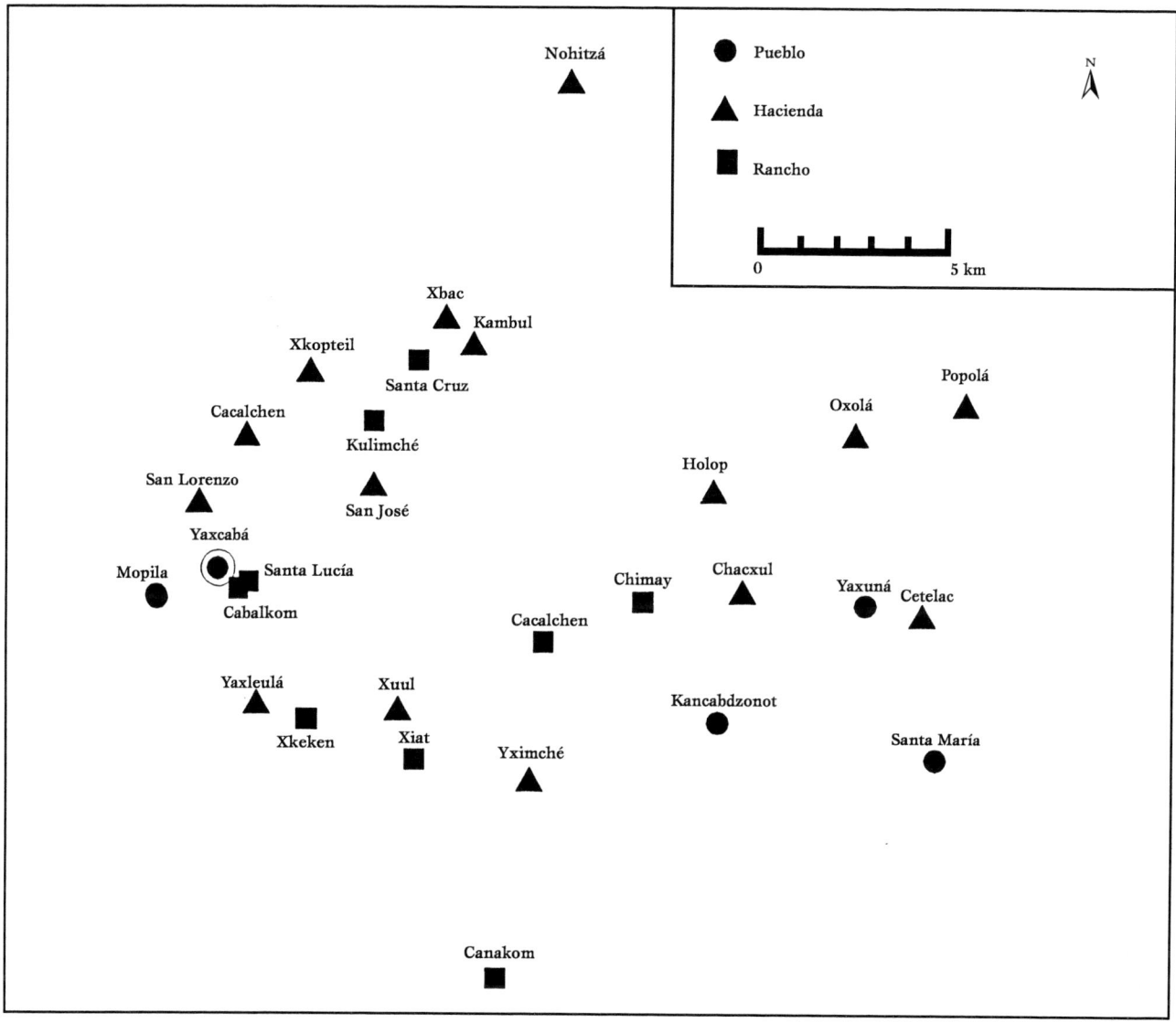

FIGURE 4.3 Settlements in Yaxcabá parish

well located next to the main plaza near the church. Additional wells are located either in solares or in small public spaces along streets throughout each community. Taking into account the modern occupation of the towns, as well as abandoned house lots around the periphery of the communities, Yaxcabá covers about 1 km²; auxiliary towns vary in area between 30 and 60 ha.

Auxiliary towns are smaller than the cabecera; they also lack substantial amounts of Colonial masonry architecture. Yaxcabá possesses two Colonial churches and an elaborate curate's residence adjacent to the larger church. The smaller church (La Hermita) bears a date of 1803. The larger church was completed around 1757[5]; the entrance to the attached cemetery bears the date 1789. Yaxcabá also contains more than twelve standing *quintas* (large, elaborately decorated, rectangular masonry houses) whose architecture is similar in style to the surrounding haciendas of the late eighteenth and early nineteenth centuries.

Each pueblo has a church with an adjacent cemetery but lacks separate formal residences for clergy. The church at Mopila was constructed earlier than 1757, and the thick walls that characterize its construction suggest it probably dates to the seventeenth century. The churches in Yaxuná, Kancabdzonot, and Santa María bear dates of 1817, 1813, and 1816, respectively; the church cemetery in Kancabdzonot is dated 1808. These dates correspond approximately to the dates of the visitas pastorales in which these communities were classified for the first time as pueblos instead of ranchos (table 4.1). Yaxuná and Kancabdzonot each have one standing quinta in Colonial architectural style, while Mopila and Santa María lack Colonial masonry architecture except for their churches (see figure 4.4). Pueblos may also contain additional shrines and cemeteries located at the edge of the settlement.

Independent ranchos

The Yaxcabá region contains nine settlements (not including the three pueblos that originated as independent ranchos)

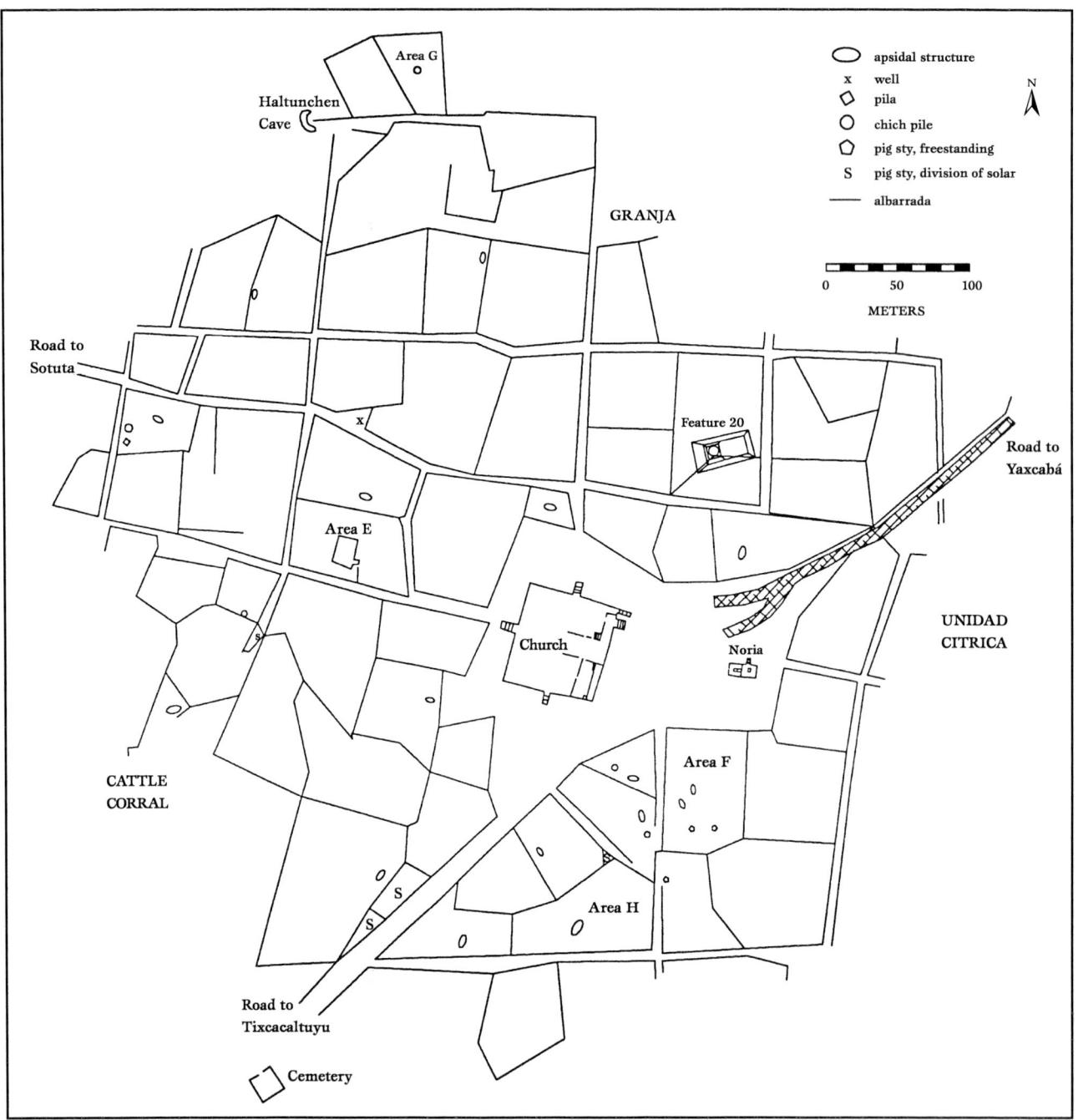

FIGURE 4.4 Site plan of the pueblo Mopila

that can be archaeologically classified as independent ranchos (table 4.1). All the settlements, except Rancho Santa Cruz, were founded prior to the visita pastoral of 1784. Two of the communities, Kulimché and Xiat, were associated with cofradías. None of these settlements appears on the 1862 census following the Caste War (Rejón 1862).

As in the case of the pueblos, independent ranchos consist of house lots aligned along streets, although the grid pattern is generally less rigidly laid out. All have a central water source, either a well, noria, or cenote. The streets of these communities also widen at intervals, creating small plazas. They may also have *adoratorios* (shrines), additional wells, and cemeteries. One of the independent ranchos in the survey, Cacalchen, covers about 35 ha and possesses three adoratorios, a cemetery, a cenote, and six other wells (figure 4.5). Xiat and Santa Cruz each have an adoratorio and a cemetery. Xiat and Kulimché have central norias as their principal water source. Unlike the pueblos, however, ranchos lack formal churches and quintas.

Table 4.2 compares the maximum population, size, and population density among pueblos and independent ranchos in Yaxcabá parish. Values for size and density are approximate because of the cursory nature of the extensive survey and refer to the maximum size and density reached by each

Settlement Patterns of the Late Colonial Period in Yaxcabá Parish, Yucatán, Mexico

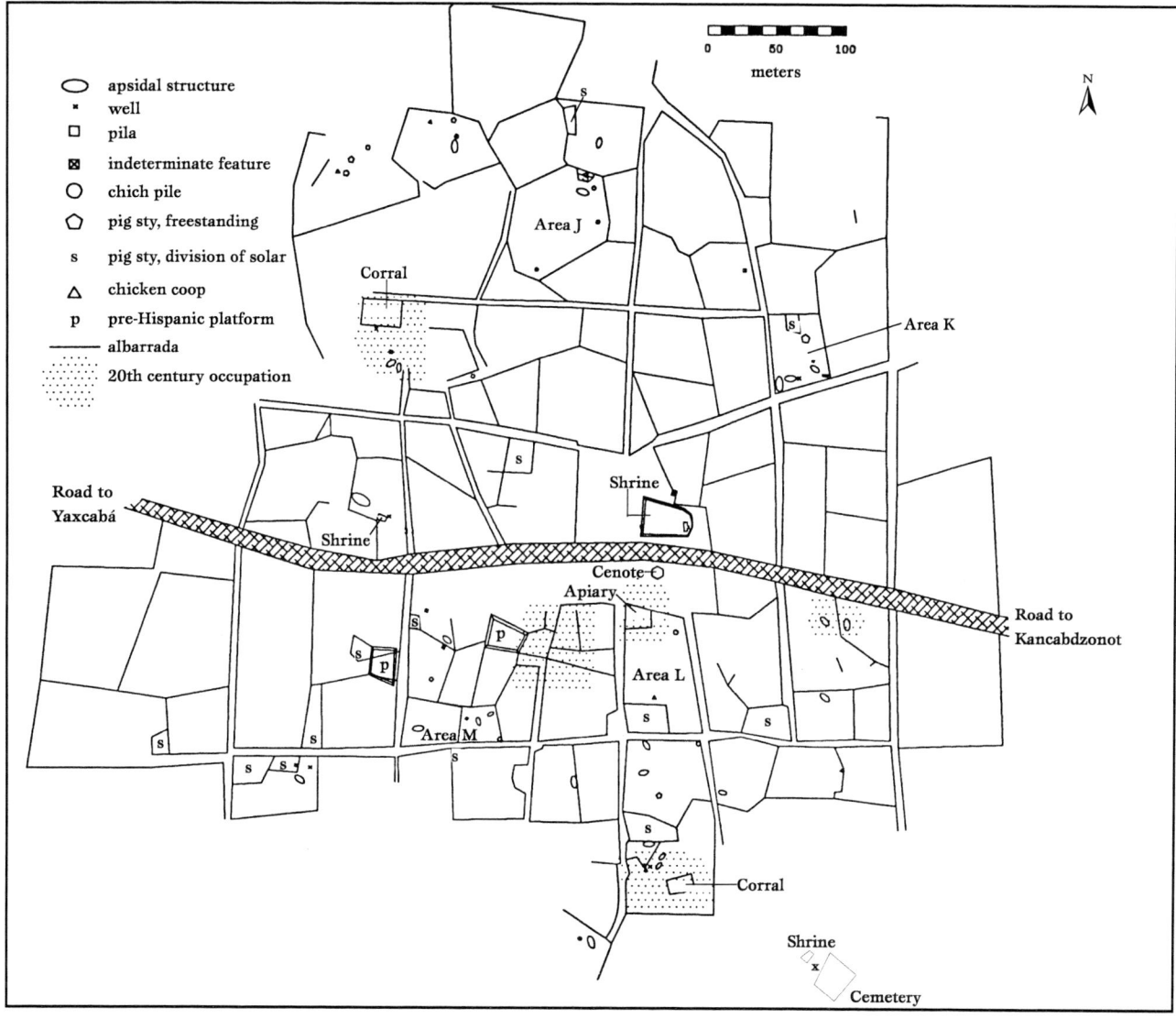

FIGURE 4.5 Site plan of the rancho Cacalchen

settlement in the six decades prior to the Caste War. The size of independent ranchos ranges from 1 to 61 ha, which overlaps with the size range for pueblos (30–60 ha). According to the visitas pastorales, independent rancho populations range from 8 to 634 inhabitants. The population density of the independent ranchos ranges from 5 to 28 persons per hectare. With the exception of Mopila, which has a population density of 6 persons per hectare in the decades immediately preceding the Caste War, the density for the pueblos and the cabecera ranges from 30 to 35 persons per hectare, considerably higher than the values for the independent ranchos. The two independent ranchos associated with cofradías, Xiat and Kulimché, show no physical differences from the other independent ranchos in the survey.[6] Kancabdzonot, before it was designated a pueblo, was also an independent rancho organized as a cofradía estate[7]; it likewise shows no differences from other pueblos in the region. An examination of the maximum density in persons per hectare for Xiat and Kulimché, however, shows these communities to have the lowest population densities of independent ranchos in the region (table 4.2). Cofradía estates may exhibit many other differences from ordinary settlements, but these features are not visible in surface surveys.

In general, the independent ranchos in Yaxcabá parish are not radically different from the pueblos, either in their layout and facilities or their size and population. The principal difference between the two types of communities is the scale of religious architecture: towns have churches, and ranchos have shrines. Significant disparity in population density between towns and ranchos did not exist until the early nineteenth century. Physical and functional variation between the two types of communities appears to be minimal, with the exception of the differences in scale of religious architecture.

Haciendas

The most variable archaeological settlement category within the Yaxcabá region is the hacienda. Historical documents show that production on the estates consisted mostly of cattle, maize and subsistence agricultural products, and small livestock (see note 2). Although the mixture of productive activities did not differ greatly among the haciendas of the region, the amount of wealth invested in the buildings and facilities forming the core of the hacienda varied considerably. Of the fifteen sites archaeologically classified as haciendas in Yaxcabá parish, six estates (Cetelac, Popolá, Nohitzá, Kambul, Chacxul, and Xbac) are considerably older than the others and existed prior to the visita pastoral of 1784 (table 4.1). The remaining nine estates were established in the early nineteenth century. Of these fifteen estates, only two (Yaxleulá and Nohitzá) were listed on the first census following the Caste War in 1862 (Rejón 1862).

Haciendas in the Yaxcabá region generally consist of a main house, sometimes with two stories, a noria, water troughs for livestock, two to four central corrals, and sometimes a small stable (Roys 1939; figure 4.6). Most of the large haciendas also have an extensive area of surrounding *albarradas* (dry stone wall) and solares containing the remains of residential structures. Some also possess *pilas* (small water tanks), *eras* (irrigation channels), *palomares* (dovecotes), ovens, apsidal masonry structures, and other wells. The smallest haciendas in the area lack most of these features, however. Three of the haciendas (San Lorenzo, Oxolá, and Yximché) consist of a noria or a well, a water trough, and a main corral, but lack a main house. Although many of the estates are architecturally well appointed, the haciendas of the Yaxcabá region do not begin to compare with the architectural elaboration, scale, and grandeur of the mid- to late-nineteenth-century henequen and sugar haciendas in the northwest and southern regions in Yucatán.

The two estates classified as privately owned ranchos in the historical documents, Chacxul and Xbac, illustrate a discrepancy between archaeological data and the historical community typology. On the basis of their archaeological characteristics, they would be categorized as two of the largest haciendas of the region. Rancho Chacxul has a two-story main house, a large noria and water troughs, several corrals, and an elaborate network of pilas and eras. Rancho Xbac has a very large and elaborately decorated main house, two norias, a large stable with a dovecote, and an extensive network of corrals and solares. Although it is possible that Xbac and Chacxul survived the Caste War and their plantas were elaborated at a later date, the architectural style of the buildings is not different from that of other haciendas in the region, nor do they appear in the first census following the Caste War in 1862. On the basis of archaeological characteristics, the privately owned ranchos of the Yaxcabá region are indistinguishable from estates historically classified as haciendas.

Comparison of Classifications

The historical classification of several communities listed in

Table 4.2 Maximum population (1828), size (in hectares), and population density (persons per hectare) for pueblos and independent ranchos in Yaxcabá parish

	ARCH. CLASS.	MAX. POP.	SIZE	POP. DENSITY
Yaxcabá	Cabecera	3292	100	33
Mopila	Pueblo	342	55	6
Santa María	Pueblo	1290	43	30
Kancabdzonot	Pueblo	2097	60	35
Yaxuná	Pueblo	896	30	30
Kulimché*	Rancho	322	61	5
Santa Cruz	Rancho	380	43	9
Cacalchen	Rancho	634	35	18
Xiat*	Rancho	167	30	6
Chimay	Rancho	178	21	8
Canakom	Rancho	560	20	28
Cabalkom**	Rancho	254	17	15
Santa Lucía**	Rancho	151	14	11
Xkeken**	Rancho	8	1	8

Note: *Cofradía estate. **Population in 1784.

table 4.1 does not jibe with the archaeological classification in three specific situations. First, the privately owned ranchos, Chacxul and Xbac, are described in the visitas pastorales as either haciendas or ranchos, whereas their archaeological classification places them clearly within the hacienda settlement type. To analyze the role of these settlements in the regional economy, it is critical to be able to distinguish between haciendas on the one hand and independent ranchos on the other. The historical records for the privately owned ranchos blur this distinction.

A second inconsistency between documentary and archaeological classification involves the cofradía estates of Xiat, Kulimché, and Kancabdzonot (prior to 1828). These settlements are described in the visitas pastorales as ranchos or haciendas, while archaeologically they correspond to the independent rancho or pueblo (in the case of Kancabdzonot) settlement type. The confusion of cofradía estates with the term hacienda is reminiscent of Cline's (1950) description of these communities as "church haciendas." Again, to understand the position of these communities in the region, it is important that they not be confused with haciendas.

Finally, in a third case, the inconsistencies between archaeological and historical classification reflect the changing status of communities through time. Three settlements classified as ranchos in 1784, Yaxuná, Santa María, and Kancabdzonot, are classified as pueblos in subsequent visitas pastorales. This reclassification probably represents an actual change in the hierarchical status of these communities from independent rancho to pueblo. In the case of Kancabdzonot, the change in classification from independent rancho to church hacienda/cofradía estate to pueblo corresponds to the sale of the cofradía estate which appears to have been disputed in the late eighteenth century (Farriss 1984:537, N82).[8] Following the sale, the settlement became a pueblo. In this case, the archaeological classification is consistent with the latest historical classification.

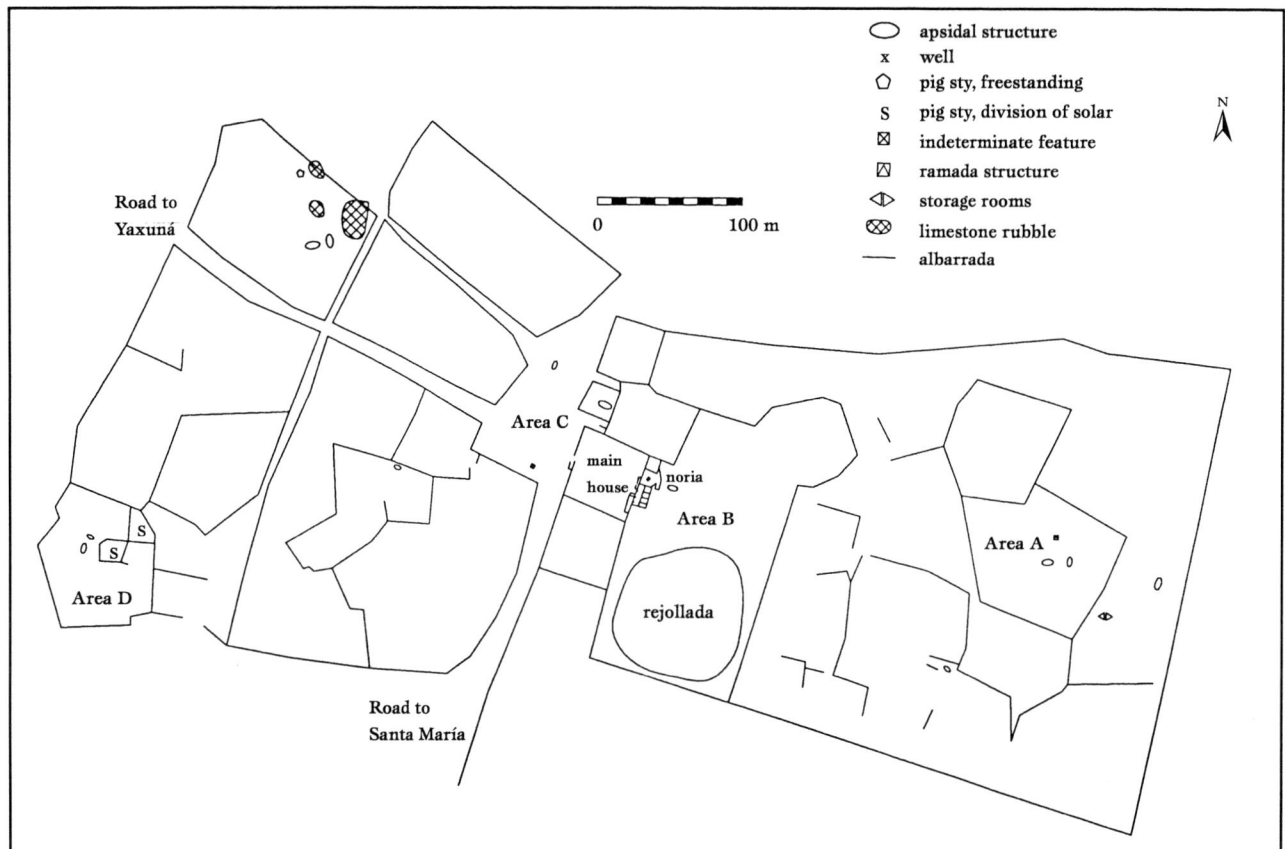

FIGURE 4.6 Site plan of the hacienda Cetelac

Distribution of Land and Population in Yaxcabá Parish

Further examination of the differences between the archaeological and the historical settlement typologies and analysis of population figures for Yaxcabá parish reveal several interrelated patterns in the distribution of land and population in the region. To determine whether a community's population provided the basis for its classification, difference-of-means tests were performed to evaluate whether the mean population size of each archaeologically defined settlement type could have been drawn from the same statistical population. Settlements historically classified as privately owned ranchos and cofradía estates were not included in the calculations.

For pueblos and independent ranchos, no significant difference in the population distribution of the two types of communities was found ($p<0.089$). Between independent ranchos and haciendas and between pueblos and haciendas, however, the population distributions of the settlement types were found to differ significantly ($p<0.0001$ for both tests). For the cabecera and the pueblos, the population distributions of the settlement types were also found to be significantly different ($p<0.009$). These results suggest that the populations on haciendas were significantly smaller than the population sizes of either pueblos or independent ranchos. Also, the population figures for the cabecera are significantly larger than those of the other settlement types. The values for population size of pueblos and independent ranchos, however, tended to be more similar to each other. It would appear that the population of a community was not the principal criterion by which a settlement was designated as a pueblo or an independent rancho, and that some other factor, probably the presence or absence of a church, was the deciding factor in the curate's classification system.

Two important processes were at work between 1784 and 1828, the period bracketed by the three visitas pastorales. First, several independent rancho communities were formally incorporated into the formal Colonial civil and ecclesiastical systems. Of the original eleven independent ranchos listed in 1784, three had been reclassified as pueblos by 1828 (table 4.1). The communities of Cabalkom and Santa Lucía, classified as independent ranchos in 1784, do not appear in later documents. Because these two communities were located on the outskirts of the cabecera, Yaxcabá (figure 4.3), it is likely that their inhabitants were counted as part of the cabecera population in subsequent years. Another rancho, Xkeken, disappeared after 1784. Rancho Santa Cruz was added to the inventory in 1828. The result was that more people were brought "into the fold," making them subject to church and civil jurisdiction and increasing the number of taxpayers within the parish.

Second, by 1828 the number of haciendas and privately owned ranchos had increased from six to fifteen (table 4.3).

Table 4.3 Quantity and population of settlement types in Yaxcabá parish, 1784–1828

	1784			1804			1828		
	QTY	POP.	%	QTY	POP.	%	QTY	POP.	%
Cabecera	1	1,491	34	1	3,292	45	1	3,128	28
Pueblos	1	155	4	2	876	12	4	4,625	42
Independent ranchos	11	2,413	55	5	2,522	34	6	2,241	20
Haciendas/privately owned ranchos	6	343	8	7	632	9	15	1,058	10
TOTAL	19	4,402	100	15	7,322	100	26	11,052	100

Sources: Archivo de la Mitra Emeritense, Cathedral Archive, Mérida, Yucatán (AME). Visita a Yaxcabá, 1784, Visitas Pastorales 1783–1784, vol. 2, exp. 42; Visita a Yaxcabá, 1804, Visitas Pastorales 1803–1805, vol. 5, exp. 43; Yaxcabá, 1828, Selección Joaquin Arrigunaga Peon, caja 5, Ticul-Yotholin; Sotuta, 1829, Selección Joaquin Arrigunaga Peon, caja 4, Pencuyut-Teya.

This situation indicates that there was both an increase in the proportion of privately held lands, as opposed to *ejidos* (communal lands), and an increase in the number of large livestock, especially cattle, supported on those lands within the region. The result of this process was that a greater proportion of land within the parish was used to support livestock by 1828 and less land was available for cultivation. Examination of the distribution of population between 1784 and 1828 according to the archaeologically defined settlement types shows that while the number of haciendas increased in comparison to pueblos and independent ranchos, haciendas did not support a correspondingly larger proportion of inhabitants (table 4.3). During the late-eighteenth and early-nineteenth centuries, population growth in Yaxcabá parish was concentrated in the cabecera and the pueblos. Haciendas supported a relatively small share of the population. Fewer than 1100 people, or less than 10 percent of the parish's inhabitants, were resident on haciendas during this period.

Taken together, the population data and the information regarding settlement distribution indicate that there was increasing competition for land in Yaxcabá parish prior to the Caste War. According to the visitas pastorales and other census information, the population of the region almost tripled in the sixty years (1780–1840) preceding the Caste War (figure 4.2). Several documents in the Archivo Notarial del Estado de Yucatán (ANEY) also provide evidence for direct conflict over land between the *hacendado* (hacienda owner) of Cetelac and the Indians of the neighboring rancho/pueblo Yaxuná.[9] The *Registro de denuncias de terrenos baldíos* in the Biblioteca Cresencio Carrillo y Ancona (BCCA) for the years 1845 through 1847 and the documents of land sales in the ANEY demonstrate that many Spanish Americans in the Yaxcabá region, as well as a few individuals with Maya surnames, were claiming and buying vacant land from the government[10] (Patch 1988). Many of the claims were intended to enlarge the holdings of existing haciendas. At least nineteen claims of terreno baldío were recorded for Yaxcabá parish[3], including 150 km^2 of land, one cenote, and six claims of unspecified size. Yaxcabá parish, as defined by the area that incorporates all the settlements in the parish, comprises about 713 km^2. Therefore, the amount of land claimed as terreno baldío during the period immediately prior to the Caste War represents approximately 21 percent of the total land within the region. Because many of the parcels declared as terreno baldío bordered the communal lands held by pueblos and independent ranchos, this entire process contributed to the loss of cultivable lands available to the Maya communities and an increase in the amount of land held by haciendas.

Summary and Conclusions

The archaeological settlement survey of Yaxcabá parish departs from the historical community typology on three major points:

‡ Variation within the hacienda category is much broader than suggested by historical sources. The physical characteristics of settlements historically classified as privately owned ranchos could not be distinguished from those of haciendas, and some settlements historically classified as haciendas demonstrated very little architectural elaboration of buildings at the core of the estate.

‡ Differences between pueblos and independent rancho communities are minimal, and neither population nor settlement size are significantly different for these two archaeological classes. Only the presence of a church within the pueblos distinguishes them from the independent ranchos. This pattern suggests that while the political or administrative functions of the pueblos may have been more integrated in the formal Colonial civil and ecclesiastical systems, the basic economic organization of pueblos was quite similar to that of independent ranchos.

‡ Cofradía estates are indistinguishable from independent ranchos at the level of the regional archaeological survey. Although some evidence suggests a lower population density at cofradía estates than at independent ranchos, this evidence is not conclusive. In terms of population size, site size, and site form, cofradía estates show no evidence of specialized features or facilities that would distinguish them from independent ranchos.

An important advantage of the archaeological classification system is that it allows us to remove the ambiguity that surrounds the classification of certain kinds of settlements in the historical documents.

The division between the commercial and tributary sectors of Yaxcabá's economy is evident from the distribution of settlements at the regional level. The pueblos and independent ranchos, representing the tributary sector, consist of aggregations of house lots. They share a morphological similarity that varies only with reference to the scale of religious architecture within the settlement. In contrast, haciendas, representing the commercial sector, are formally and functionally distinct from pueblos and independent ranchos. Haciendas are composed of an architecturally elaborate planta surrounded by corrals interspersed with house lots. The cabecera combines elements from both types of settlements and represents the point of articulation between the two economic sectors. On the one hand, Yaxcabá is characterized by large-scale religious architecture surrounded by solares, yet it also contains architecturally elaborate residences, quintas, that are formally similar to the plantas of the haciendas. Settlements composed of house lots correspond to communities whose residents are engaged in subsistence agriculture entrenched within the tribute-based economic sector. Settlements containing architecturally elaborate plantas (which would include quintas) correspond to communities or households engaged in cattle raising articulated with the commercial economic sector.

Competition between the commercial and tributary sectors of Yaxcabá's dual economy intensified in the early nineteenth century. The rapid rate of population growth and the division of population among the different settlement types indicate, however, that land, rather than labor, was the critical resource limiting the transition to a market-based economy. Ninety percent of the parish population was concentrated in the cabecera, pueblos, and independent ranchos. As a consequence, the basic social and economic unit of the tributary sector, the Indian community engaged in subsistence agriculture, appears to have remained intact and did not undergo a significant transformation with the introduction of the hacienda. The low proportion of the population resident on haciendas suggests that these estates used *luneros* (day laborers) from surrounding settlements to provide the necessary labor, like the earlier *estancias* (cattle ranches; Hunt 1974, 1976). The haciendas in Yaxcabá parish did not supplant the Indian communities as the basic social unit within the region. Instead, the expansion of cattle raising exacerbated land stress for a rapidly growing indigenous population. Because the potential for agricultural intensification is limited in Yucatán because of environmental constraints, the subsistence agriculturalists and the hacienda owners reached an impasse over the distribution of land which coincided with the beginning of the Caste War.

This situation occurred at different times in other regions in Colonial Mesoamerica. In Central Mexico, according to Gibson (1964), the hacienda system using hired Indian labor on agricultural estates developed between 1580 and 1620. Recent archaeological studies suggest, however, that the archetypical hacienda, a grandiose estate with a large number of resident workers, developed only after 1750 (Charlton 1986; Jones 1980). Not only were the archaeological remains of these estates indicative of rather modest plantas (Jones 1980) but most of the labor force also remained in Indian communities (Konrad 1980; Tutino 1976). Charlton (1986:130-132) argues that although the large and elaborate haciendas began to develop after 1750 corresponding to the demographic recovery of the Indian population (Gibson 1964:141,148), evidence is lacking that these estates incorporated a significant proportion of the population as residents or that the haciendas functioned as social units. He suggests that the hacienda as a social unit and the concomitant transformation in urban-rural relations in Central Mexico occurred after 1850 (Charlton 1986:132). Furthermore, the outcome of the development of the hacienda system in Central Mexico is remarkably similar to conditions in Yucatán. The acquisition of lands by haciendas, combined with a growing Indian population, created a disenfranchised rural population that provided a stimulus for the Mexican Revolution (Charlton 1986:132).

In Oaxaca and Guatemala, similar conditions prevailed. Taylor (1972:8, 121-135) demonstrates that haciendas in the Valley of Oaxaca were considerably smaller than estates in Northern Mexico, and hacienda expansion was not characterized by the incorporation of the majority of the rural population onto the estates. Although the labor supply of the haciendas did consist of resident workers bound to the estate through debt peonage, the development of haciendas did not result in the disintegration of Indian towns. Unlike Central Mexico and Yucatán, however, land stress and disenfranchisement of the Indian population was minimal (Taylor 1972:8). In Guatemala, the first haciendas were relatively small, and the impact of mercantile capitalism on native communities varied from one region to another (MacLeod 1973, 1983). Carmack (1986) makes the distinction between the hacienda system, which permitted the cultural survival of Indian communities, and the plantation system, which promoted acculturation and ladinoization of the indigenous population in coastal areas where plantations were most numerous. In areas dominated by haciendas, Indians competed with Spaniards over land, but Indian communities survived relatively intact and in some cases were able to regain lands appropriated by haciendas (Carmack 1986).

The data from the Yaxcabá region, as well as the comparative studies mentioned above, suggest that the development and expansion of the hacienda system was not always the catalyst for transition from a tribute-based to a market-based economy. Archaeological evidence from Yaxcabá indicates that often the scale and amount of capital investment in the estates was much smaller than that conveyed by historical generalizations and that Indian communities were numerous, surprisingly large, and complex. The data suggest that the indigenous social unit was not in the process of disintegration nor being replaced by the haciendas.

Evaluation of the historical evidence in light of archaeological data on settlement pattern demonstrates a protracted conflict over critical resources between Indian communities entrenched in a tributary economy and the haciendas of the commercial sector. In Yaxcabá parish, the imbalance of land and population culminated in the Caste War; in other areas of Colonial Mesoamerica, similar imbalances were also resolved through conflict, often in favor of the Indian communities. The data from Yaxcabá demonstrate the importance of integrating archaeological and documentary information to understand the roles of haciendas and rural Indian communities in the development of the Colonial market economy.

Acknowledgments. The archaeological fieldwork and archival research for this project were funded by grants from the National Science Foundation (BNS-8813858), the Wenner Gren Foundation for Anthropological Research (Gr 5089), the Organization of American States, Tinker-Mellon Field Research Grants of the Latin American Institute, University of New Mexico, Sigma Xi Grants-in-Aid of Research, and the Student Research Allocations Committee of the University of New Mexico. Permission to conduct the research was granted by the Instituto Nacional de Antropología e Historia, Centro Regional de Yucatán. I wish to express my appreciation to Arqlgos. Rubén Maldonado Cárdenas, Fernando Robles Castellanos, and Alfredo Barrera Rubio for their support of these investigations. I gratefully acknowledge the assistance of several scholars in locating historical materials, including Anthony Andrews, Pedro Bracamonte, Robert Patch, and Sergio Quezada. The contributions of my field assistants, Eunice Uc González and Elena Canché Manzanero, were invaluable. Thomas Charlton and Robert Santley provided helpful comments on early drafts of this paper, though any errors of fact or interpretation are my own.

Notes

1. Archivo de la Mitra Emeritense, Cathedral Archive, Merida, Yucatán (AME). Yaxcabá, 1828, Selección Joaquin Arriguanaga Peon, caja 5, Ticul-Yotholin. University of Pennsylvania, Berendt Collection, 1837. Trabajos hechos por la comision de la H. junta departamental, Auxiliada de Facultativos sobre la division provisional de este departamento que previene la constitucion, Mérida, Yucatán. Oficina de Espinosa. *Documentos Politicos de Yucatán*, vol. 1. Rejón C., Antonio G. 1846, Memoria Leida ante el agusto Congreso extraordinario de Yucatán por el Secretario General de Gobierno, 18 septiembre de 1846, SPI.
2. Biblioteca Cresencio Carrillo y Ancona, Mérida, Yucatán (BCCA). Declaraciones de diezmos en el Partiod de Beneficios Altos y Bajos, son frutas de setenta y siete colectados en 1778 años. B. Granado Baeza. Informe dado por el cura de Yazcaba. In Registro Yucateco, vol. 1. Colección Alfredo Barrera Vásquez, Centro Regional de Yucatán, Instituto Nacional de Antropología e Historia, Merida, Yucatán, 1845.
3. BCCA. Registro de las denuncias de terrenos baldíos, 1845–1847.
4. Archivo de la Mitra Emeritense, Cathedral Archive, Mérida, Yucatán (AME). Visita a Yaxcabá, 1784, Visitas Pastorales 1783–1784, vol. 2, exp. 42; Visita a Yaxcabá, 1804, Visitas Pastorales 1803–1805, vol. 5, exp. 43; Yaxcabá, 1828, Selección Joaquin Arrigunaga Peon, caja 5, Ticul-Yotholin; Sotuta, 1829, Selección Joaquin Arriguanaga Peon, caja 4, Pencuyut-Teya.
5. British Library, Dept. of Manuscripts, London. Visita a su obispado pr el Yllmo So Fr Dn Ygnacio Padilla, BM Add. 17569.
6. Archivo Notarial del Estado de Yucatán, Mérida, Yucatán (ANEY). Peniche 1830–1831:232–238; N. del Castillo 1828:223–229.
7. AME. Pueblo de Yaxcabá, Libro de Cofradías Generales de 1797. Biblioteca Cresencio Carrillo y Ancona, Mérida, Yucatán (BCCA). Declaraciones de diezmos en el Partiod de Beneficios Altos y Bajos, son frutas de setenta y siete colectados en 1778 años.
8. AME. Pueblo de Yaxcabá, Libro de Cofradías Generales de 1797.
9. ANEY. N. del Castillo 1818:251–253; Peniche 1818:83.
10. ANEY. Barbosa 1845:119; Barbosa 1845–1846:26–27, 57–58; F. del Rio 1845–1846:103–104; Barbosa 1847–1849:23; BCCA. Registro de las denuncias de terrenos baldíos, 1845–1847.

Chapter 5

Survey and Excavation of Invisible Sites in the Mesoamerican Lowlands

Janine Gasco

Abstract

The survey and excavation of sites of the Colonial period in many parts of the lowlands of Mesoamerica present archaeologists with a difficult set of problems because many sites are virtually invisible on the surface. This chapter examines these problems and discusses strategies used in survey and excavation in the lowland region of Soconusco in Chiapas, Mexico. In Soconusco, environmental conditions have been largely responsible for the destruction of perishable Colonial structures. A brief comparison with the neighboring lowland region of Suchitepéquez illustrates that other factors such as native population size and density and the role of Spanish clergy also affect the visibility of Colonial remains.

Resumen

La prospección y excavación de sitios del periodo Colonial en diversas zonas de las tierras bajas mesoamericanas presentan una difícil serie de problemas a resolver por parte del arqueólogo debido a que muchos sitios son prácticamente invisibles en superficie. En este capítulo se examinan estos problemas y se discuten estrategias que se emplean en la prospección y excavación en la región de tierras bajas del Soconusco, Chiapas, México. En gran medida en el Soconusco las condiciones ambientales han provocado la destrucción de estructuras coloniales hechas con materiales perecederos. A partir de una somera comparación con la región vecina de las tierras bajas de Suchitepéquez, se ilustra que otros factores como el tamaño y densidad de la población autóctona asi como el papel del clero español, también afectan la visibilidad de los restos coloniales.

HISTORICAL ARCHAEOLOGISTS who work in certain lowland regions of Mesoamerica face a fundamental problem. How do we find historical sites that are virtually invisible? Within Mesoamerica, invisible sites are most problematic in the humid lowland zones, although certain kinds of remains may be difficult to find in highland zones as well. Unlike prehistoric archaeologists who design surveys using a wide range of sampling strategies, those looking for sites of the Colonial period often know what they are looking for, but not where it is. In many cases, no survey strategy short of 100 percent coverage will allow archaeologists to find these sites. In some cases, nothing short of subsurface testing will enable them to conclusively identify Colonial remains (Pendergast, Jones, and Graham 1993). In the Soconusco region of southeastern Mexico and a small portion of southwestern Guatemala (figure 5.1), entire townsites are buried beneath dense vegetation. Even when standing right on top of an abandoned Colonial town, it is quite possible to be unaware of what lies just below your feet. The high rates of depopulation in the Colonial province of Soconusco (Gasco 1989c, 1991; Gerhard 1993; MacLeod 1973) resulted in the abandonment of over twenty communities, approximately half the estimated forty towns that existed in the region at the time of the conquest (figure 5.2; table 5.1). Finding the remains of these numerous abandoned towns has proved extremely difficult. In the Soconusco, not only are there often no surface remains of structures, but there are few, if any, artifacts on the surface.

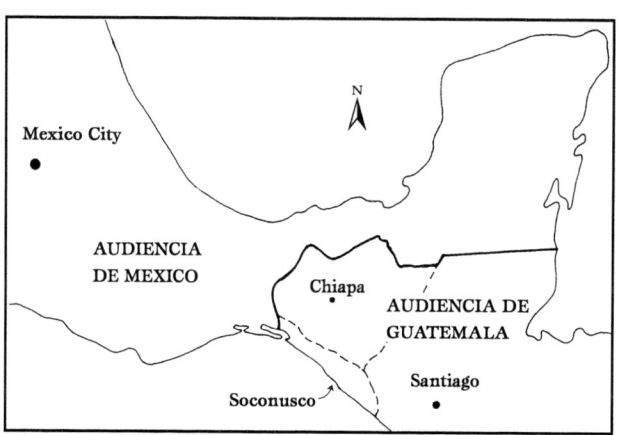

FIGURE 5.1 Province of Soconusco

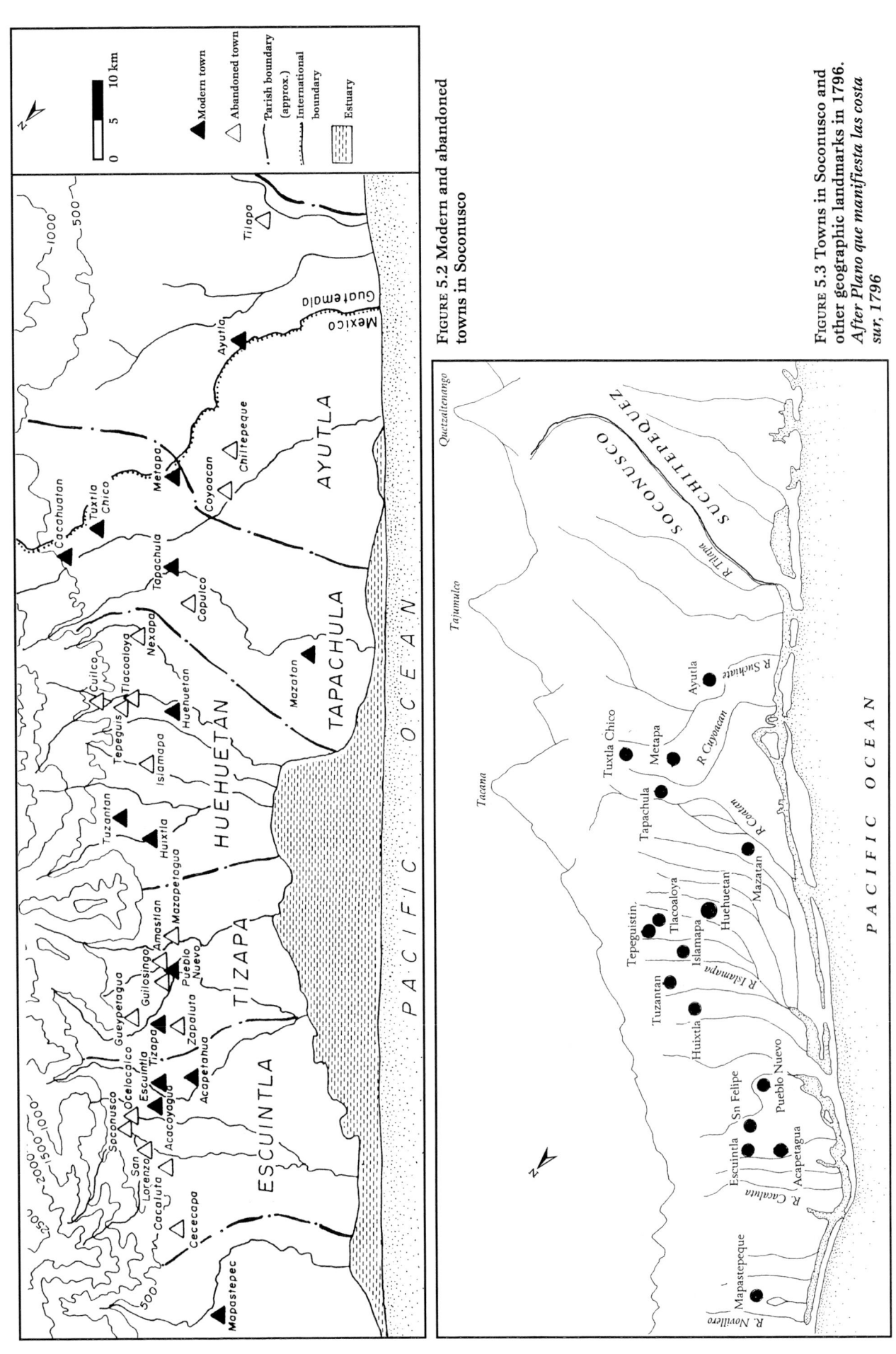

FIGURE 5.2 Modern and abandoned towns in Soconusco

FIGURE 5.3 Towns in Soconusco and other geographic landmarks in 1796. After *Plano que manifiesta las costa sur*, 1796

Table 5.1 Soconusco towns with approximate dates of occupation

PARISH	TOWN	OCCUPATION
AYUTLA	Ayutla**	Postclassic–present
	Coyoacan	Postclassic–1575
	Chiltepeque	??–1778
	Chacalapa*,**	??–1726
	Tilapa**	??–1684
	Naguatan*,**	Postclassic–present
	Apazapa*,**	??–1664
	Tonalapa*,**	??–1684
TAPACHULA	Tapachula	Postclassic–present
	Cacahuatan	??–present
	Mazatan	Postclassic–present
	Tuxtla Chico	Postclassic–present
	Copulco	??–1684
	Metapa	1778–present
HUEHUETAN	Huehuetan	Postclassic–present
	Tuzantan	??–present
	Huixtla	Postclassic–present
	Talibe*	??–1684
	Nejapa	??–1735
	Cuilco	??–1684
	Tlacoaloya	??–1857
	Ilamapa	??–1857
	Tepeguis	??–1857
TIZAPA	Tizapa	??–present
	Tianguistlan*	??–1735
	Gueypetagua	??–1735
	Caguala*	??–1684
	Amastlan	??–1684
	Guilocingo	??–1735
	Mazapetagua	??–1735
	Zapaluta	??–1735
	Pueblo Nuevo (now Villa Comaltitlan)	1778–present
ESCUINTLA	Escuintla	??–present
	Soconusco***	Postclassic–1797
	Ocelocalco	Postclassic–1767
	Acapetahua	Postclassic–present
	Acacoyagua	Postclassic–present
	San Lorenzo	??–1735
	Cacaluta	??–1611
	Cececapa	??–1582
	Zacapulco*	??–1684

* No information regarding location except for parish affiliation
** May be (or is) in modern Guatemala
*** Modern town of Soconusco was founded in the twentieth century

It is likely that most, if not all, Colonial Soconusco towns were located near Late Postclassic–period communities, but in Soconusco the identification of Late Postclassic sites has also been problematic. Apparently in Late Postclassic period Soconusco, as in other areas of Mesoamerica, there was less emphasis on mound building and an increased reliance on ground-level structures which, like the Colonial townsites, are virtually invisible.

This chapter explores strategies used to locate abandoned Colonial townsites in the Soconusco region. The physical remains of sites located during survey and excavations at the abandoned Colonial town of Ocelocalco are described. The situation in Soconusco is contrasted with that in other neighboring regions, and possible explanations for differences are discussed.

Documentary Evidence for Town Locations

Several strategies can be used to locate Colonial townsites in areas like the Soconusco. An obvious source of information is the documentary record, which includes both descriptions of town locations and maps. The earliest known map showing the location of Soconusco towns is an undated fragment showing only a portion of the region. It probably dates to around the middle of the sixteenth century (Navarrete 1978:78). While this map illustrates relative locations of several communities, given the difficulty of finding remains on the ground, it is of limited use in locating specific towns.

A map (figure 5.3) that dates to 1796[1] is more useful, except that many Soconusco communities had already been abandoned by that time. The map provides a relatively detailed and accurate view of the province. It has been very useful in narrowing the possibilities of town locations, making it possible to determine in which river drainage and even on which side of a river a community was located. River names have not changed in Soconusco since at least the eighteenth century. No Colonial map, however, is ever going to allow archaeologists to pinpoint town locations in the Soconusco.

In addition to maps, there are written descriptions of town locations. In the case of Soconusco, these are often provided by parish priests who explain their rare visits to a particular town by describing just how difficult it is to get there. The earliest accounts, like the sixteenth-century map mentioned above, provide only relative locations of towns; typically town A is described as so many leagues to the east of town B. A 1586 account of the trip of Franciscan friar and Comisary General for New Spain, Fray Alonso Ponce, is an example:

> ...Sabado doce de abril salió de Xoconusco...y andadas seis leguas no largas en que se pasan cuatro rios y mucha y muy espesa montaña entre muchas cuestas pedregosas y llenas de peñas, que no poco penoso hacen el camino, llegó al salir del sol a un razonable pueblo...llamado Metzapetláuac.... (Ciudad Real 1976:185–186)

> ...Saturday, April 12, he left Soconusco...and walking six short leagues in which he passed four rivers and a very dense mountainous area with steep, rocky grades full of boulders which make the road difficult, he arrived at sunset at a reasonably [sized] town...called Metzapetláuac [Mazapetahua]...

Later in the Colonial period, descriptions become more detailed, although not necessarily more helpful. A 1748 description of the parish of Huehuetan describes the location of all towns in the parish.[2] The community of Santa María Magdalena Nexapa is described as three leagues to the east

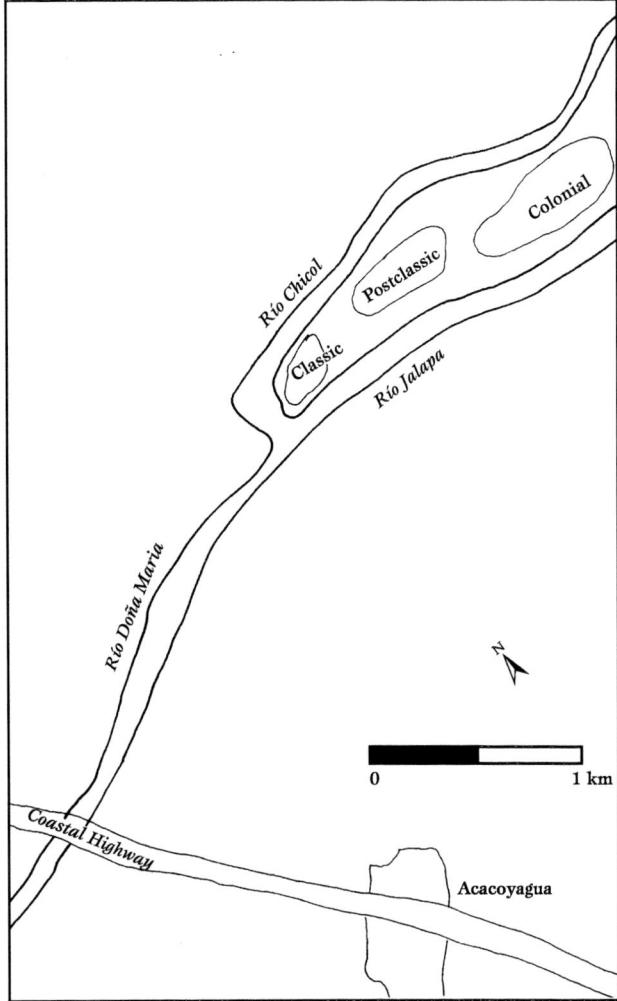

FIGURE 5.4 Map of Ocelocalco

of Huehuetan:

> ...con el transito de dos ríos grandes peligrosos...el primero río es de este pueblo de Huehuetan y dos arroyos, caminos malos peligrosos...

> ...crossing two large dangerous rivers...the first river is the Huehuetan, and two arroyos, the road is very bad and dangerous...

In the same document, we are told that San Blas Tlaqualoya was three leagues to the north of Huehuetan:

> ...de camino mui fragoso por ser todo serranias, cuestas peligrosas, pues en partes no se puede andar a mula por el peligro que hay.

> ...a very rough road because it is mountainous with dangerous slopes, in some places not even a mule can pass because of the danger.

In the case of the Soconusco town of Ocelocalco, a mid-eighteenth-century document describes it as lying on a flat area between two rivers.[3] A Colonial townsite, which according to local oral tradition is the site of Ocelocalco, is located in just such a position—on a flat area between the Río Jalapa and the Río Chicol (figure 5.4). The written record in this case helped to confirm that the site was indeed Ocelocalco, but the information alone would not necessarily have led to the site because many other locations also fit this description. In sum, written reports and maps must, of course, be consulted, and they are useful in narrowing down possible locations of towns. They may make it possible to estimate within a few kilometers where a community might be found, but documentary evidence alone does not normally provide enough detailed information to actually find abandoned townsites on the ground.

Identifying Patron Saints

Another strategy for pinpointing the locations of abandoned communities involves the images of patron saints. In Soconusco and presumably in other regions, when a town was abandoned, the last inhabitants typically took the image of their patron saint, as well as other valuables from the church, with them. This practice is mentioned in an eighteenth-century document in which the Bishop of Chiapas was making inquiries about several abandoned Soconusco towns.[4] The Bishop was concerned about what had happened to the valuables in the churches—candlesticks, other silver objects, and the church bells. Indian leaders of the community of Acacoyagua responded that, in the case of Ocelocalco, the last residents had brought their patron saint, San Mateo, to the Acacoyagua church when they resettled there. During the course of fieldwork, an image of San Mateo was found in the Acacoyagua church, and local residents reported that this image had been brought to Acacoyagua from the site of Ocelocalco.

Another image in the Acacoyagua church is the Virgin of the Assumption, and when what is thought to be the Colonial town of Soconusco was located in 1989, local residents reported that this image had been brought to Acacoyagua from that site. From Colonial documents it is known that the patron saint of Colonial Soconusco was indeed the Virgin of the Assumption. At least in these two instances it was possible to elicit from people the original locations of the images of certain saints in their churches. Although the identification occurred after the fact, it was hoped that the same situation might present itself in other towns. Consequently, part of a 1989 survey included an attempt to inventory saints in existing churches with the expectation that local residents might know the original locations. Unfortunately, this did not prove to be as easy as it had been in Acacoyagua.

In one community, the old images of saints have been relegated to a storage area behind the modern church. They had been replaced in a newly remodeled church with plaster and plastic saints having a more modern look. Similarly, in another town, the old images of many of the saints had been

Figure 5.5 Sculpted stone from façade of Ocelocalco church

deposited in the choir loft, and it was not possible during a short visit to the community to locate anyone who had any information about them. While these attempts to trace town locations through the statuary of saints have not been spectacularly successful so far, this approach has potential. It may require considerable time, however, to find the right people within a community, long-time residents who have been involved in church activities and are willing to talk to outsiders.

Oral Tradition

The best way to locate abandoned Colonial townsites is to find local residents who are familiar enough with the land to know where the sites are located, but this approach is difficult in places like Soconusco because it is difficult to describe adequately what Colonial sites look like. Soconuscans are very much aware of the pre-Columbian archaeological remains that are common throughout the region—the typical mound sites in which people find large quantities of figurine fragments, potsherds, obsidian, and so on. But in the case of Colonial remains, only the landowner may be aware of their existence because they are so difficult to see. The Colonial sites do not yield any valuable artifacts, and even when artifacts are found, these items—glazed pottery, metal fragments—are not easily distinguished from modern household refuse. There is little public awareness that such artifacts may have historical value.

Archaeological Evidence for Colonial Townsites in Soconusco
Locating Colonial Townsites During Survey

Ocelocalco was the first abandoned Colonial townsite in Soconusco to be studied. Its remains had been reported in the literature (Culebro 1975; Navarrete 1978:79), and Barbara Voorhies visited the site during her 1981 Proyecto Soconusco survey. In the case of Ocelocalco, a road cutting through the site exposed the foundation stones of several structures. A small number of majolica potsherds that appeared to date to the Colonial period also were observed on the surface, making it possible to identify the site as a Colonial town. In addition, a few pieces of sculpted stone, presumably from the façade of the church (figure 5.5), were located at the site and at the nearby ranch house. The remains of the church consisted of a long, low mound approximately 1 m high and barely noticeable in the grass. Excavations conducted at this site are described below (see also Gasco 1989b, 1992).

Subsequently, a survey was carried out in 1989 (Gasco 1990) to locate additional abandoned Colonial townsites. Using documentary evidence, approximate town locations were plotted on topographic maps. Once in the field, the previously described strategies were employed in an attempt to pinpoint the location. During the survey, one new Colonial townsite was located conclusively, and the locations of three others were identified tentatively. Only with subsurface testing will these identifications become certain.

What is thought to be the Colonial town of Soconusco was located during the 1989 survey. This identification is based on local oral tradition and Colonial descriptions of the community's location relative to neighboring towns. Like Ocelocalco, this site is characterized by a long, low mound, presumably the church, surrounded by the remains of residential structures, identified by the presence of foundation stones (figure 5.6). Colonial potsherds, including majolica, lead-glazed earthenware, and unglazed wares, were observed on the surface, confirming that this site dates to the Colonial period. Adjacent to the Colonial remains is a large Late Postclassic site. As was the case at Ocelocalco, this site had no visible mounds and was identified solely by an extensive and dense sherd scatter.

Near the location where the remains of the town of Cacaluta were expected to be found, a number of carved stones were discovered in the yard of a ranch house (figure 5.7). These stones were undoubtedly part of a Colonial church. In the location where the stones reportedly had been found, however, there was virtually no evidence on the surface that a town once stood there. No Late Postclassic materials were visible either.

The town of Tlacoaloya is reported to have been located on a ranch a few kilometers north of Huehuetan (Culebro 1975). The rim of an olive jar that appeared to be of the "Middle" period (1580–1780; Goggin 1960) was found at this location, but, again, there was no other visible evidence on the ground for the existence of any structures. In an adjacent cattle pasture where ground visibility was somewhat better, nondiagnostic potsherds that appeared to date to the pre-Hispanic period were observed.

A third community, Cuilco, was reportedly located northwest of Tapachula near the coffee *fincas* (plantations) of Las Maravillas and Argovia (Culebro 1975:28; Helbig 1964:27).

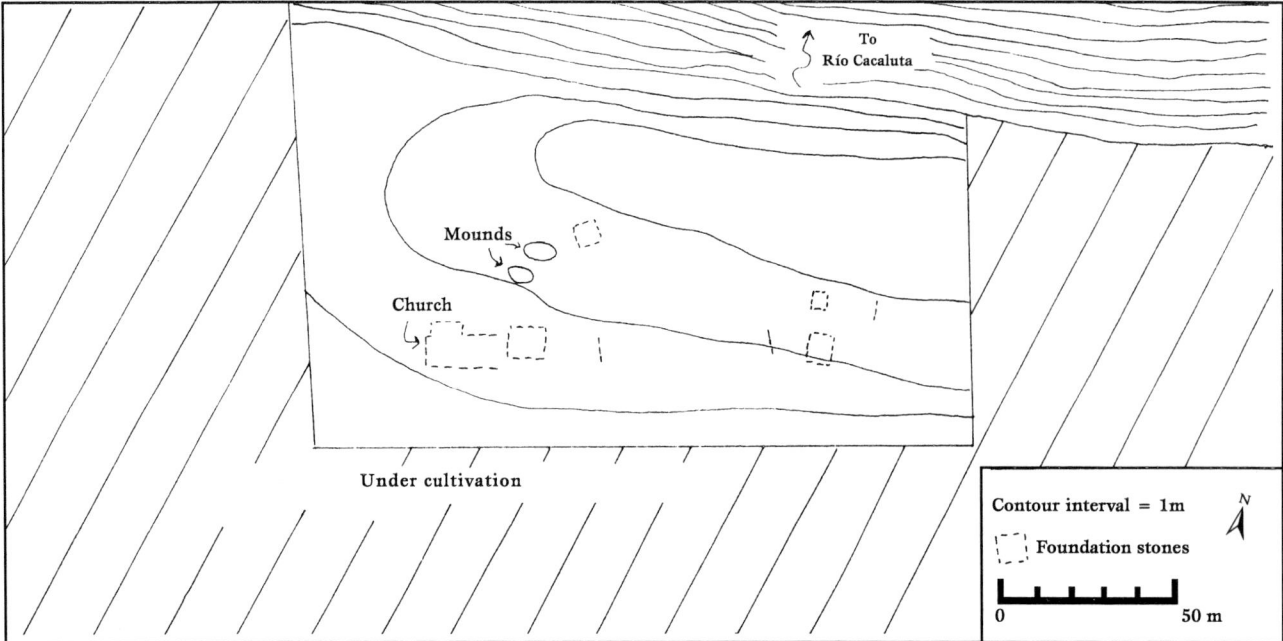

FIGURE 5.6 Plan of Colonial site of Soconusco

At the Colonia Zaragoza, a community established earlier this century adjacent to the Cuilco River, local residents reported that when they excavated in their yards they frequently found glazed pottery and lines of stone. Unfortunately, it was not possible to look at any of the pottery, and there was no other evidence of Colonial structures on the surface. One resident did report, however, that his grandmother had told him that an ancient town had once existed where Zaragoza now stands. Pre-Hispanic potsherds are abundant throughout the community and on the nearby coffee fincas.

Finally, what was initially identified as a fourth possible site is located on the small island of Los Cerritos in the estuary zone where a single piece of sculpted stone was found very much like a piece found at Ocelocalco. The island was visited during the survey because potsherds that looked as if they might date to the Colonial period had been collected there by Voorhies during her 1978 survey of the estuary system. During the 1989 visit no evidence was seen, other than the sculpted stone, that a town had once been located there. Subsequently, another archaeologist reported that the sculpted stone was brought to Los Cerritos from Ocelocalco in 1963; an enterprising individual had attempted to sell the stone to archaeologists working in the area at the time (Navarrete 1994).

Excavating Ocelocalco

As mentioned previously, the remains of Ocelocalco were found because a road cut had exposed several structures. Once work began in earnest at the site, the remains became more visible. The situation improved when the landowner allowed the burning of much of the pasture in which the site

FIGURE 5.7 Sculpted stone, possibly from façade of Cacaluta church

was located. With vegetation reduced, some topographic relief became apparent in what previously had seemed to be a perfectly flat field. Very low mounds (10–30) cm were present, and a few stones could be seen poking through the surface. Subsurface probing with machetes exposed the foundation stones of many structures with a minimum of disturbance. Over the course of about three weeks more than 50 structures were located (figure 5.8). The ability to locate foundation stones was hampered in some portions of the site by disturbance associated with ranching activities. North of the road, for example, considerable subsurface disturbance had occurred in an orchard and a corral (figure 5.8). The area south of the road had always been used as a pasture; it had never been plowed nor sustained any other significant subsurface disturbance. Thus, even within a single site, postdepositional history varies (Gasco 1989b, 1992).

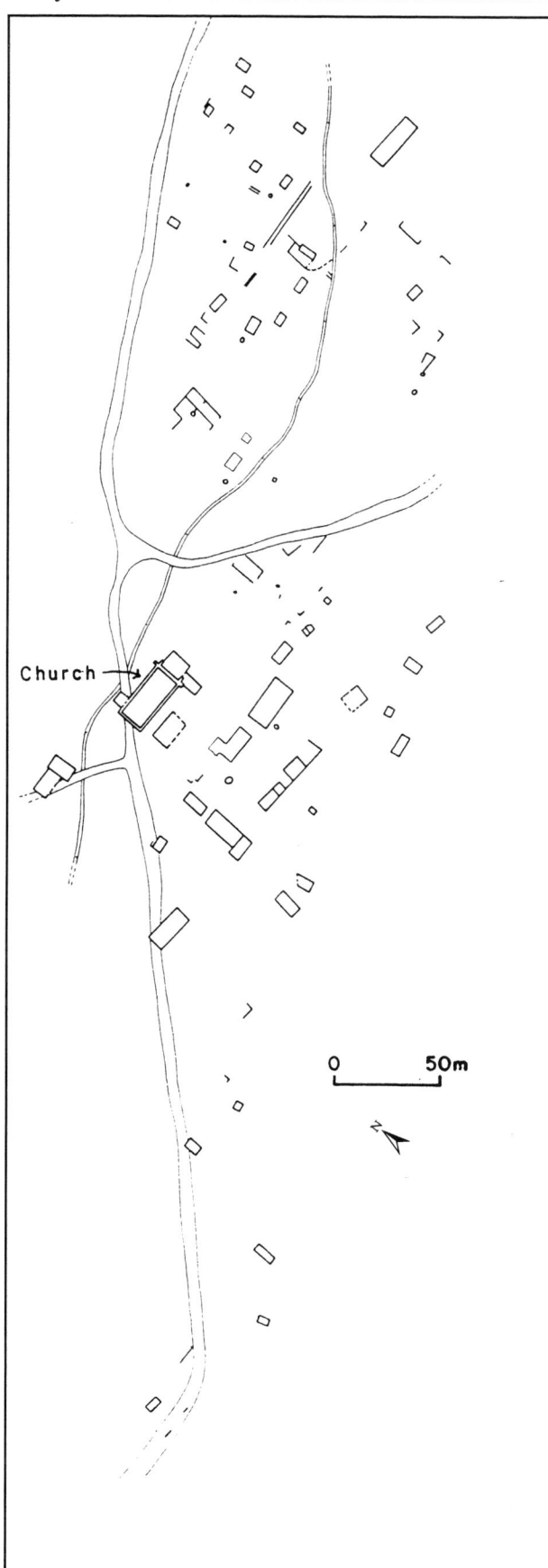

FIGURE 5.8 Plan of Ocelocalco

FIGURE 5.9 Excavation of Colonial house at Ocelocalco

Preservation was quite good in undisturbed portions of the site. Small artifacts were not always in their original places because of rodent and root activity, and sherds from the same vessels were found in different parts of the same house and in different levels, but foundations and features were found intact. Archaeological deposits were very shallow, with sterile soil encountered at 50 cm or less, making it possible to excavate large horizontal units (figure 5.9)

If Ocelocalco is at all representative of Colonial sites in Soconusco and other lowland areas of Mesoamerica, then standard excavation procedures can be followed once a site has been found. That is, unlike survey strategies, excavation strategies for Colonial period sites are no different from those used to excavate prehistoric sites. Precise excavation strategies will vary, of course, depending on the problem under investigation and on the specific postdepositional history of a site.

Comparison of Soconusco and Suchitepéquez

The situation in Soconusco differs quite dramatically from that of the neighboring region of Suchitepéquez (figure 5.1), also a lowland region with an environment very similar to Soconusco. Archival research carried out on Suchitepéquez in 1990 provided the same kinds of documentary evidence available for Soconusco—that is, maps and descriptions in historical documents. With this information the locations of several abandoned Colonial towns were hypothesized. In sharp contrast to Soconusco, the Colonial churches in Suchitepéquez, substantial structures built of stone, are still standing centuries after being abandoned. As a result, abandoned Colonial townsites are much easier to find. In a three-day casual visit to the Suchitepéquez region, the remains of three abandoned Colonial towns were located. This number compares to the possible four towns found in Soconusco during three months of intensive survey.

Why is there such a difference in two neighboring regions? Although an extensive analysis of this issue must await additional research, briefly, the most obvious differences between Soconusco and Suchitepéquez have to do primarily with the size of the native population. Even after the severe depopulation of the sixteenth century, the native population of Suchitepéquez was several times larger and the population density much greater than in Soconusco. This served to attract members of the religious orders; in Suchitepéquez, the Franciscans established convents in several towns (Van Oss 1984). The Franciscans not only had a long-term commitment to the region they also had control over large native populations who could be called upon to build substantial stone structures. Soconusco, with a much smaller Indian population, was administered after the 1540s by the secular clergy. Parish priests generally served for short periods of time, and, judging from their correspondence, they were anxious to leave. They did not put their energies into church construction, and churches in Soconusco were built of pole-and-thatch or adobe, neither of which fares very well in a tropical climate, particularly after years of neglect.

This brief comparison illustrates that not all Colonial sites in lowland regions of Mesoamerica are invisible. In many areas like Suchitepéquez, Tehuantepec (see chapter 2) and Yucatán (see chapter 4), Colonial remains are easily identifiable. In others they are not.

There are important historical and cultural reasons for the differential development of Colonial Indian communities. The specific aspect of community development that is perhaps most critical for locating sites during archaeological survey is the nature of the church buildings themselves. Colonial church building activity was not a random process. In regions that had either small indigenous populations and/or little commitment on the part of religious authorities, substantial churches and other buildings were never constructed.

In these regions Colonial townsites are always going to be difficult to find, particularly if they are in humid lowland zones. From the point of view of the historical archaeologist, the easiest solution to this problem is simply to avoid such areas, but understanding the full range of indigenous societies during the Colonial period in Mesoamerica hinges on the ability to identify the diverse situations that existed across the region. As a result, it is necessary to continue to examine the full range of community types, including communities that, for a combination of cultural historical and environmental reasons, are virtually invisible today. Work in areas like Soconusco is challenging, but as methods for finding these sites are refined, the task will become easier.

Acknowledgments. Excavations at Ocelocalco and the survey of additional Colonial sites in Soconusco were conducted with the permission of the Instituto Nacional de Antropología e Historia, with funding provided by the National Science Foundation and the Wenner-Gren Foundation for Anthropological Research. I also want to thank don Rito Takemura, owner of the property on which Ocelocalco is located, for allowing us to excavate. Archival research on Suchitepéquez was supported through a Fulbright Research Grant.

Notes

1. British Library, Department of Manuscripts, London. Add 17654, Plano que manifiesta la costa sur, 1796.
2. Archivo Histórico Diocesano de San Cristóbal de las Casas, Chiapas, Mexico (AHDSC). Report by Manuel Cansino Barba, 26 August, 1748.
3. AHDSC. Report by Antonio de Villatoro, 3 September, 1748.
4. Archivo General de Centroamérica, Guatemala City. A3.16 362 4693, Sobre la estinción de los pueblos de Oselocalco, Guipetagua y Masapetagua...año 1779.

✝ Chapter 6

Tendencias de Consumo en México durante los Períodos Colonial e Independiente

Patricia Fournier-García

Resumen

En este capítulo se examinan las tendencias de consumo que imperaron en México en los ámbitos urbano y rural durante los períodos Colonial e Independiente, a través de una perspectiva materialista. Se analiza la estructura de clases y étnica de la población, considerando la posición de los integrantes de los diversos segmentos, su poder adquisitivo así como sus necesidades sociales e individuales. Resulta de interés tomar en cuenta el precio de los bienes en el mercado con base en evidencias documentales, en particular de artefactos cerámicos. El análisis propiamente arqueológico se basa en muestras de excavación y superficie recuperadas en la Ciudad de México, Cuernavaca, Veracruz y Mérida, y dos regiones con predominio poblacional indígena, el Valle del Mezquital, Hidalgo, y Sonora.

Abstract

In this chapter consumer trends that dominated in urban and rural settings in Mexico during the Colonial and Independence periods are examined from a materialist perspective. Class and ethnic structures are analyzed, taking into account the position of diverse segments of the population, acquisition power, and social and individual necessities. Also taken into account are the prices of goods in the market, particularly ceramic artifacts, based on documentary records. The archaeological analysis is based on samples from excavations and from surface collections from Mexico City, Cuernavaca, Veracruz, and Mérida, and from two predominantly indigenous regions, the Valle del Mezquital in Hidalgo and Sonora.

EN LA ARQUEOLOGÍA HISTÓRICA es fundamental el estudio de los procesos sociales asociados con el surgimiento y consolidación del modo de producción capitalista y el desarrollo de formaciones socioeconómicas bajo este marco (Fournier-García y Miranda-Flores 1992:78–79). Así, aquí empleamos correlatos materiales como base para inferir las relaciones de dependencia comercial de la formación socioeconómica mexicana, dominada por las fuerzas externas a ella que emanan del capitalismo mercantil, el industrial y el imperialista, así como las contradicciones internas asociadas; los períodos de interés son el Colonial (1521–1821) y el Republicano (1821–1910).

Entre las características inferibles de los datos arqueológicos están la temporalidad, las singularidades culturales y los contenidos sociales. Con base en la información arqueológica que se ordena y analiza, se infieren e identifican las asociaciones y recurrencias de las formas culturales, con el fin de conocer sus contenidos sociales y, así, identificar y reconstruir los procesos económicos—de la producción, distribución, cambio y consumo—que integran el modo de producción (Bate 1989:12). Para interpretar los correlatos materiales del consumo, es necesario considerar la relación dialéctica entre estos cuatro procesos que son partes diferentes de un todo en la concepción materialista:

> en la producción, los miembros de la sociedad se apropian (producen, crean) los productos de la naturaleza para las necesidades humanas; la distribución determina la proporción en que el individuo participa de estos productos; el cambio le trae los productos particulares en los cuales quiere convertir la cuota que le ha correspondido por la distribución; finalmente, en el consumo los productos se convierten en objeto de disfrute, de apropiación individual.... Entre el productor y los productos se coloca la distribución, la cual, mediante leyes sociales, determina su parte en el mundo de los productos y se interpone, por tanto, entre la producción y el consumo. (Marx 1974a:242, 243, 250)

La circulación es parte del cambio, el cual

> es un momento mediador entre la producción y la distribución que ella determina con el consumo... no existe cambio sin división del trabajo.... La producción da lugar...al consumo.... Produce...el objeto de consumo. El consumo produce también la disposición del productor, colocándolo

como finalidad y solicitando su necesidad. (Marx 1974a:248, 256)

Por otra parte, las relaciones sociales de producción determinan la organización de la distribución y, asimismo, la intensidad, extensión y género del cambio (Marx 1974a:250, 251).

Dado que en el registro arqueológico están presentes evidencias materiales de actividades pretéritas llevadas a cabo por los integrantes de unidades sociales que participaron en una formación socioeconómica, para explicar el consumo a través de sus correlatos materiales, en este estudio es indispensable remitirse a las esferas de la distribución y cambio en el México Colonial y Republicano. De hecho, el estudio de esta clase de procesos económicos y de la organización social en términos de relaciones dialécticas con un enfoque marxista, ha sido tema de investigaciones tanto en México como en los Estados Unidos de América, aun cuando en este último país se trata de un área poco explorada (véase Deagan 1982:164).

La Formación Socioeconómica Mexicana

La conquista española de México en 1521, como parte de la política expansionista y colonialista del capitalismo mercantil ibérico, llevó a la modificación de la estructura económica y social prehispánica y a la imposición de formas ideológicas, jurídicas y políticas, así como a cambios ambientales desastrosos y a la depresión demográfica de la población indígena (véase Charlton 1986; Charlton y Fournier-García 1993).

La formación socioeconómica mexicana se desarrolló a partir de una estructura feudal-capitalista (Semo 1981:46) gestada con base en la combinación de elementos de origen indígena y español, dominando estos últimos, para culminar en una capitalista industrial (Peña 1979:233–236). A lo largo de los períodos Colonial y Republicano la tierra fue propiedad no de los productores directos, sino de las minorías españolas y criollas que controlaron todas las ramas productivas y extractivas. Este sector minoritario controló y explotó la fuerza de trabajo de los indígenas, los mestizos y la mayoría de las *castas* (Israel 1980:273). La clase dominante quedó conformada por los funcionarios, los criollos descendientes de los conquistadores, y la nobleza española y criolla, así como el clero. Muchos de ellos se dedicaron a la minería, el comercio, la agricultura y ganadería a gran escala, controlando las ramas productivas más lucrativas (Brading 1975).

La colonia de Nueva España estuvo dividida en dos sectores antagónicos, la República de Indios y la República Española, que al mismo tiempo reflejaban divisiones rurales/suburbanas y urbanas para la concentración geográfica, la explotación económica y la conversión católica de la población indígena (Broda 1979:75; Moreno Toscano 1976:63). Paralelamente, esta división representó el origen de la contradicción entre la ciudad y el campo que prevalece hasta la actualidad y que, al mismo tiempo y en gran medida, es un reflejo de diferencias étnicas y de clase.

En la República de Indios el número de colonos españoles era reducido, relacionándose con el cumplimiento de funciones específicas, es decir, para el gobierno, la religión, la encomienda, sistema fundamental como mecanismo político para la jurisdicción privada de las comunidades indígenas (Charlton 1986:125), ranchos agropecuarios, y la minería (véase capítulo 2). Las estructuras hispanas asociadas con estas actividades continuamente se disputaban el control y monopolio de la fuerza de trabajo indígena, además de requerir la producción de alimentos, ya fuera cultígenos autóctonos o de origen europeo, la explotación ganadera basada en la cría de animales domésticos traídos del viejo mundo, diversos bienes de consumo y aun dinero. Muchos de estos artículos llegaban a manos de los españoles mediante relaciones de tributación (véase Broda 1979; Gibson 1980; Moreno Toscano 1976; Palerm 1979; Ricard 1986; *Libro de las tasaciones* 1952).

Los sistemas Coloniales intrusivos produjeron cambios radicales en el modo de vida de las comunidades indígenas al privarlas de los medios de producción básicos para su supervivencia y reproducción (Charlton y Fournier-García 1993). Las élites indígenas y mestizas pronto asimilaron el modo de vida europeo y, en este proceso de aculturación, rechazaron muchas de las prácticas prehispánicas, mientras que entre los campesinos prevalecieron costumbres tradicionales (Broda 1979:67–69), en el nivel tanto de la base económica como de la superestructura; esta situación se continúa incluso hasta la actualidad.

Durante el siglo XVI en el ámbito urbano, la clase dominante estuvo conformada por peninsulares, es decir la aristocracia de los conquistadores, la nobleza, los funcionarios y los encomenderos (Valero de García Lascuráin 1991:245–251), aunque un porcentaje mínimo de las élites indígenas mantuvieron parcialmente estructuras de control pero siempre subordinadas a los conquistadores.

Se conformaron distintos sistemas de producción y cambio en los ámbitos urbanos y rurales, generándose relaciones desiguales en dichos ámbitos respecto a la distribución, así como en la realización de la acumulación a través del consumo. En la escala urbana, los sistemas productivos incluyeron gremios artesanales, en donde los productores eran propietarios de los medios de producción, controlando el proceso de trabajo y la venta de los artículos (Castro 1986:11). Los obrajes, que se originaron a fines del siglo XVI aun cuando su auge fue a fines del período Colonial, tenían un carácter capitalista dada su base en el trabajo asalariado y la explotación de la fuerza de trabajo (véase Viqueira y Urquiola 1990). De hecho, estas instancias productivas fueron la base para el desarrollo fabril de México a fines del siglo XIX.

En el ámbito rural, se generaron sistemas de producción con una presencia mínima de españoles y criollos, quienes únicamente se hacían cargo del control de actividades agropecuarias y extractivas. Así, en el siglo XVI se conformaron encomiendas, repartimientos y mercedes, para ser sucedidos en épocas posteriores por ranchos y haciendas, estas últimas prevaleciendo desde mediados del siglo XVII (Mörner 1975:19–21) hasta después del movimiento revolucionario de 1910. En los territorios del norte las misiones constituyeron sistemas semejantes, mientras que los reales de minas se caracterizaron por ser entidades productivas con un carácter peculiar, dada su especialización en la explotación de metales sin la producción de insumos básicos, con población de diversas filiaciones que en su mayoría ponía en circulación cantidades considerables de dinero. Por otra parte, los presidios eran parte del sistema defensivo Colonial, con concentraciones relativamente altas tanto de militares como de población civil, española o criolla, mestiza e indígena, cuyo poder adquisitivo era por lo general limitado (Fournier-García y L. Fournier 1992:927; Palerm 1979).

El Proceso Económico del Cambio en la Sociedad Colonial y Republicana

A lo largo del desarrollo histórico de México ciertas capas de la sociedad se dedicaron a la lucrativa actividad del comercio, controlando la circulación de bienes de producción y de consumo, nacionales e importados, básicos y suntuarios. Este comercio permitió que, por lo menos en cuanto a los bienes de consumo, se satisficieran las demandas de la población que tenía acceso a artículos de alto costo dado su nivel socioeconómico privilegiado.

Los sistemas de cambio y la circulación asociada, con su centro en la capital del virreinato y a fines del siglo XVIII en otras ciudades de importancia, se fundamentaron en los consulados de comerciantes que tuvieron a su cargo el tráfico de productos sobre todo de importación que llegaban tanto desde Europa como desde el Lejano Oriente (Smith, Ramírez Flores, y Pasquel 1976).

Por las características del colonialismo monopolista ibérico, en el virreinato de Nueva España los comerciantes peninsulares controlaron muchas de las operaciones mercantiles sobre todo de bienes de alto costo. Dado el bajo desarrollo de las fuerzas productivas en España, estos comerciantes redistribuían artículos producidos en los países europeos donde comenzaban a proliferar industrias, fundamentalmente Inglaterra y Holanda (Wallerstein 1979:397–398). Así, la plata americana contribuyó al proceso de acumulación originaria sobre todo en Gran Bretaña, aunque muchos caudales se dilapidaron o salieron de la circulación por destinarse a guerras, al enriquecimiento del clero y al consumo suntuario de la nobleza hispana (véase Fournier-García 1990:30, 270; Frank 1979:230–232).

Las mercancías europeas llegaban a Nueva España, desde 1561 hasta 1778, en una flota que arribaba a Veracruz desde donde se enviaban a la capital para su venta y circulación en todos los territorios del virreinato. Por otra parte, de 1576 a 1821 grandes volúmenes de artículos asiáticos, muchos de ellos objetos de consumo de las clases acomodadas, llegaron a la colonia cruzando el Océano Pacífico a través de una compleja ruta comercial que unía China, Filipinas y Acapulco. En esta población costera se celebraba una feria prácticamente cada año, con la finalidad de poner a la venta el cargamento de la Nao de Manila, aunque además en el puerto de San Blas llegaba a desembarcarse contrabando (Fournier-García 1990:30; Fournier-García y L. Fournier 1992:957–959).

En las colonias hispanas las severas limitaciones comerciales impuestas por la metrópoli, que persistieron inclusive después del establecimiento del libre comercio vigente en Nueva España desde 1789, propiciaron el contrabando a gran escala, que era una vía ilegal común para el arribo de mercancías extranjeras (Fournier-García 1990:32).

Una vez que México se independizó de España, la importación de bienes europeos cobró gran importancia, al introducirse a los mercados nacionales toda clase de mercancías manufacturadas en las potencias capitalistas. Los principales países industrializados que mantuvieron vínculos comerciales con México fueron, en orden de importancia, Inglaterra, Francia, Alemania y España. Desde 1825 Estados Unidos fungió como reexportador de mercancías europeas, con lo cual logró injerencia en la vida económica mexicana (Herrera Canales 1977:79–91, 108).

Puesto que muchos de los puertos abiertos al comercio exterior estaban alejados de bastantes zonas con alta densidad de población hispana, surgieron subcentros de redistribución interna. Ahí se celebraban periódicamente ferias, según el modelo europeo del medioevo, a donde acudían acaparadores intermediarios para la compraventa de mercancías, tanto nacionales como europeas y asiáticas (Carrera Stampa 1959).

En suma, en lo que concierne a las esferas de la distribución y el consumo, desde la época Colonial Temprana la circulación de artículos importados benefició únicamente a un sector mínimo de la población en México, puesto que los excedentes se concentraron en pocas manos dadas las relaciones sociales de producción y dado que las masas no tenían acceso a productos europeos y orientales, e incluso a muchos de los de factura local dado su bajo poder adquisitivo (Fournier-García 1990:33). Debido tanto al acaparamiento como a la acumulación de bienes y capitales producto de la explotación de la clase sojuzgada, la clase dominante tuvo la posibilidad de adquirir bienes de alto costo, sobre todo importados. Así, hay diferencias en cuanto a tendencias de consumo según la posición de clase o socioétnica al interior de la formación socioeconómica Colonial y Republicana.

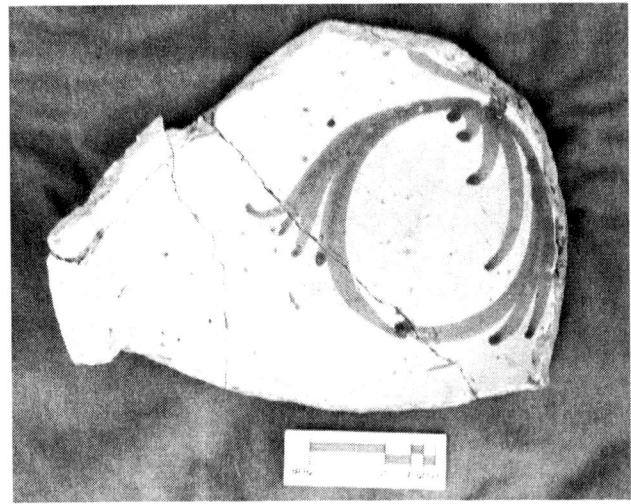
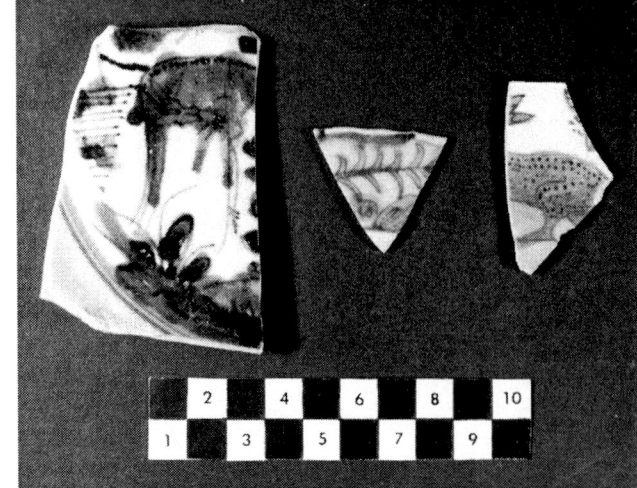

SUPERIOR, IZQUIERDA: FIGURA 6.1 Mayólica española del siglo XVI, tipo Santo Domingo Azul sobre Blanco. *Todas las fotografías por la autora*

SUPERIOR, DERECHA: FIGURA 6.2 Porcelana china azul sobre blanco del período Wan Li (ca. 1575–1619)

IZQUIERDA: FIGURA 6.3 Mayólica novohispana y mexicana, azul sobre blanco o policromo sobre blanco; tipos característicos de los períodos Colonial y Republicano

Además, tanto durante el período Virreinal como el Republicano, el precio de las mercancías era alto, sobre todo las extranjeras, dado que pasaban por múltiples intermediarios quienes aprovechaban la oportunidad de lucro encareciéndolas (Fournier-García 1990:33), amén de los costos intrínsecos al transporte de los artículos; por ejemplo, en 1785 en las operaciones comerciales de una tienda de Sonora, zona alejada de los principales centros de producción y circulación de bienes, el costo de los fletes se calculaba en 21 por ciento sobre el valor original de las mercancías.[1]

Diferencias Socioétnicas y Consumo de Bienes

Respecto al consumo, cabe señalar que el costo de los artículos determina en parte que se asocien con estatus socioeconómico; es decir, mientras más elevado es el precio de una mercancía simboliza una posición económica más alta (Deagan 1983:237–242; Miller 1980:3; Spencer-Wood y Heberling 1983:33). Lo anterior es equivalente en términos interpretativos a la propuesta de South (1990) de que mientras mayor sea el gasto energético involucrado en la producción y transporte de un artículo, mayor será su relación con un estatus socioeconómico alto del consumidor. Complementariamente, deben tomarse en cuenta aspectos asociados con la conducta de los consumidores, quienes eligen el uso de determinados bienes de acuerdo con, por ejemplo, su posición étnica (Heberling 1985:139). Así, en el México Colonial y Republicano tanto la mayólica como las cerámicas de importación constituyeron bienes asociados con estatus socioétnico (Fournier-García 1990:33).

De acuerdo con la evidencia documental, entre las clases alta y media las tendencias de consumo durante los períodos Colonial y Republicano variaron según la disponibilidad de bienes importados provenientes tanto del Lejano Oriente como de Europa, además de los producidos en México

Figura 6.4 Loza fina blanca británica pintada a mano, rosa lustre sobre blanco; fábrica de Davenport, año de 1836

(Calderón de la Barca 1976:89, 158; Fournier-García 1990:33; González Obregón 1983:285–286; Kolonitz 1984:130; Obregón s.f.:61–63; Toussaint 1974:96).

Las clases acomodadas adquirían durante los siglos XVI y XVII mayólica europea (figura 6.1), que a partir de 1575 empezaría a ser desplazada del mercado por la porcelana china (figura 6.2) y, en menor medida, la mayólica novohispana (figura 6.3), además de que para las grandes ocasiones y entre los individuos pertenecientes a la nobleza novohispana, se utilizaban diversos objetos de plata. A partir de fines del siglo XVIII entre los integrantes del estamento alto, se inició un proceso de sustitución de la porcelana china por la europea, básicamente francesa, mientras que para el siglo XIX, sobre todo después de consumada la independencia en 1821, las facturas orientales prácticamente desaparecieron del mercado mexicano ante la introducción masiva de mercancías europeas. La loza fina predominantemente inglesa (figura 6.4) y en menor proporción francesa y holandesa se convirtieron, junto con la porcelana francesa, en los principales símbolos de estatus socioeconómico, aun cuando su consumo se amplió hacia la clase media, por lo cual desplazaron inclusive a la mayólica mexicana.

Correlatos Materiales del Consumo de Cerámica en México

En términos tecnológicos la cerámica histórica incluye las lozas alisada, bruñida (ambas de tradición prehispánica), vidriada con barniz plúmbeo, mayólica (tanto europea como producida en Nueva España), porcelana y gres (orientales y europeos), y loza fina europea. Para estas lozas en términos funcionales hay cuatro clases de vajillas cerámicas que predominan:

- Vajilla utilitaria asociada con la preparación y almacenamiento de alimentos, sean sólidos o líquidos. Corresponde a las lozas alisada, vidriada y bruñida, con formas como ollas, cazuelas, cántaros, jarras, comales, *molcajetes* y anafres. Los tibores de mayólica y porcelana también se relacionan con funciones de almacenamiento.

- Vajilla de servicio vinculada con el consumo de alimentos. Se identifica para todas las lozas históricas, siendo las formas más comunes platos y platones tanto extendidos como hondos, tazas y tazones, además de formas con funciones especializadas como copas, tarros, soperas, ensaladeras, fruteros, teteras, cafeteras, azucareras, salseras, saleros y cucharones.

- Vajilla de higiene tanto corporal como de elementos de cultura material de uso cotidiano. Corresponde a todas las lozas para las formas de palangana y bacín, mientras que las jofainas, escupideras y bacías se asocian con la mayólica y la cerámica de importación.

- Vajilla ornamental. Corresponde a todas las lozas con formas como floreros, jarrones, macetas, miniaturas y figuras.

Podrían definirse otras vajillas con funciones especializadas y de consumo por lo general restringido, a excepción de la de iluminación, asociada con todas las lozas, con candeleros y candelabros como únicas formas; además puede mencionarse la vajilla relacionada con el adorno personal, incluyendo formas como cajas de rapé, tarros y cajas para cremas, ungüentos y joyas, así como porta pelucas; también puede considerarse la vajilla de farmacia destacando los albarelos para el almacenaje de medicamentos; asimismo se identifica la vajilla vinculada con diversas ramas productivas y extractivas, como la minería con formas como crisoles, las vasijas empleadas en ingenios azucareros o las usadas para la producción de sal.

Aun cuando la vajilla utilitaria es de amplio consumo, por lo general de manera independiente a la clase social a la que pertenezcan los individuos, cuando las diversas lozas y formas presentan decoración, dada la mayor inversión requerida en su producción debe asumirse que su costo es mayor y, por tanto, su consumo potencialmente se asociaría con estamentos sociales o segmentos étnicos intermedios y altos.

Las otras vajillas resultan ser las más adecuadas para inferencias sobre el estatus socioeconómico o socioétnico de los agentes sociales (Shephard 1983:88, 98), sobre todo en el caso de la mayólica y las lozas de importación. Inclusive las formas empleadas como envases, como las oliveras o botijas españolas, tinteros, botellas de gres y especieros de mayólica europeos, se asocian con la posición socioétnica de los individuos. En el caso específico de la mayólica, la misma

Cuadro 6.1 Precios unitarios (en reales o pesos) de distintas formas de vasijas de diferentes lozas entre 1730 y 1821

	PLATOS	PLATÓN	TAZAS O JARROS	POZUELO	OLLITAS	TIBORES O TINAJAS	JARRAS
Mayólica	.08 – 2 reales	6 reales	.33 –2 reales	.08 – .50 reales	.16 reales		
Porcelana china	.50 –6 reales	1 – 2 pesos	1.8 r – 4 pesos	.50 –6 reales	3.50 reales	3 reales – 1 pesos	
Ordinaria	1.25 r –1 pesos						
Fina	1 –1.03 pesos			3 reales			
Superior	1 pesos						
Bruñida de Tonalá	.33 reales		.33 – .66 reales			2 reales – 1.50 pesos	
Loza Vidriada	.16 – 1 reales		.16 – 1.25 reales	.25 reales	.33 reales	1 pesos	
Cerámica Indígena	.20 reales				.50 reales	2 reales –3 pesos	.25 r
Loza fina europea	5 reales	1 pesos					1.50 p

Fuentes: Archivo General de la Nación, México, D.F. Consulado, vols. 228 y 120, exp. 2; Archivo General de la Nación, México, D.F. Consulado, vols. 228 y 120, exp. 2, y Archivo Municipal de Hidalgo del Parral, Chihuahua. Causas Civiles, Años de 1730 a 1821.

gradación de la loza (grado fino o común), puede ser un indicio de su costo en el mercado (Fournier-García, Charlton, y Aronson 1993; Lister y Lister 1982a).

Otros elementos de cultura material, rara vez representados en contextos arqueológicos históricos en México, son indicadores de la posición social de los individuos debido a su precio en el mercado. Aquí deben considerarse la vestimenta, de hecho, el mayor volumen de las importaciones desde inicios de la colonia estuvo constituida por textiles, los recipientes y demás artefactos de cobre y hierro empleados en la preparación de alimentos, así como todos los objetos de plata, quintada o sin quintar, cuyo costo se tasaba según el peso del metal. El vidrio, en su mayoría conformado por envases de diversos licores, así como el cristal con artefactos asociados con distintas funciones, también se asocia con la posición socioétnica de los consumidores (Hernández 1980).

Con base en avalúos testamentarios e inventarios de tiendas del norte de México[2] es posible apreciar las diferencias de precios de las lozas mexicanas en relación con las de factura oriental y europea. Resultan de interés las piezas correspondientes a la vajilla de servicio, platos, platones, tazas y pozuelos, especie de tazones, así como de la vajilla utilitaria, es decir ollitas, tibores o tinajas, y jarras. Cabe señalar que en los registros el precio de las vasijas depende de la calidad o grado de la loza, así como de los atributos decorativos de las piezas.

Así, según lo que se enlista en el cuadro 6.1, puede apreciarse que el precio de la porcelana china y de la loza fina europea (registrada en los documentos como "loza pedernal") es aproximadamente equivalente, aunque la loza europea parece ser ligeramente más costosa. La mayólica poblana tiene un precio menor al de la porcelana china y mayor en términos generales a la loza bruñida de Tonalá (producida en Jalisco), mientras que las lozas vidriadas y de tradición indígena tienden a ser las de más bajo costo.

Por otra parte, según los registros de importaciones y exportaciones durante los siglos XVIII y XIX (Lerdo de Tejada 1967), el precio por cajón de la mayólica española es de dos a tres veces la de Puebla, y el cajón de porcelana china es aproximadamente diez veces mayor que el de mayólica poblana, mientras que el cajón de porcelana europea tiene un costo de tres y media a nueve veces el de la mayólica de Puebla.

Evidencias Arqueológicas del Consumo de Cerámica en México

Los correlatos materiales del consumo proceden de diversos sitios de México, predominantemente recuperados en rellenos arquitectónicos o en operaciones de superficie, sin que haya sido posible identificar áreas de actividad específicas.

Se cuenta con datos arqueológicos de numerosas excavaciones realizadas en la Ciudad de México, entre los que destacan los del Templo Mayor de Tenochtitlan (con una muestra de más de 120,000 tiestos), de Tlatelolco (Proyecto SRE [Secretaría de Relaciones Exteriores] de la Subdirección de Salvamento Arqueológico del INAH, con colecciones de aproximadamente 95,000 tiestos) y el antiguo convento de San Jerónimo. Este convento se fundó en 1585, situado en el límite sur de la traza original para el asentamiento europeo sobre las ruinas de la ciudad azteca. Todos los artefactos que se encontraron en las excavaciones se catalogaron y estudiaron. La colección de más de 400,000 fragmentos de cerámica (véase el cuadro 6.2) y vidrio que cronológicamente abarcan desde el período Colonial Temprano hasta el siglo XX, constituye una de las mayores muestras para estos períodos que se hayan estudiado hasta la fecha en Latinoamérica (Fournier-García 1990:13).

En Cuernavaca los estudios arqueológicos se han enfocado fundamentalmente al Palacio de Cortés, construido en 1535 (Ángulo y Ángulo 1979) por el conquistador español. El edificio fue remodelado constantemente a través de su historia. También se realizaron excavaciones en las calles adyacentes y en el zócalo. Los materiales incluyen porcelana china, loza blanca inglesa, porcelana francesa, botijas, mayólica tanto española como mexicana, loza roja Colonial, loza bruñida de Tonalá, y una tradición local de loza roja (Charlton et al. 1987), así como cerámica vidriada, contándose con una muestra de más de 2,500 tiestos (véase el cuadro 6.3).

Cuadro 6.2 Cuantificación de lozas identificada en el exconvento de San Jerónimo

	FRECUENCIA ABSOLUTA	FRECUENCIA RELATIVA
Azteca III*	17,153	4.04
Azteca III/IV*	1,779	0.42
Azteca IV	1,853	0.44
Bruñida Colonial	27,448	6.47
Alisada	144,512	34.06
Bruñida de Tonalá	565	0.13
Vidriada	76,547	18.04
Mayólica**	88,365	20.83
Azulejos	5,416	1.27
Porcelana china	12,461	2.94
Lozas europeas	48,188	11.36
TOTAL	424,287	100.00

Fuente: Fournier-García 1990
* Cerámica indígena prehispánica
** En el análisis no se cuantifican de manera separada la mayólica española y la producida en México.

Cuadro 6.3 Cuantificación de lozas asociadas con estatus socioeconómico en Cuernavaca*

	FRECUENCIA ABSOLUTA	FRECUENCIA RELATIVA
Bruñida Colonial	5	0.19
Roja Colonial Local	139	5.31
Bruñida de Tonalá	8	0.30
Mayólica europea	8	0.30
Mayólica novohispana y mexicana	2,169	82.91
Porcelana china	8	0.30
Lozas europeas	279	10.67
TOTAL	2,616	99.98

Fuente: Charlton et al. 1987
* No se incluyen en el análisis las lozas alisada y vidriada.

Cuadro 6.4 Cuantificación de lozas identificada en Sonora

	FRECUENCIA ABSOLUTA	FRECUENCIA RELATIVA
Pima Rojo*	14	1.43
Bruñida Colonial	6	0.61
Bruñida de Tonalá	5	0.51
Vidriada	183	18.67
Mayólica novohispana y mexicana	341	34.80
Porcelana china	82	8.37
Lozas europeas	349	35.61
TOTAL	980	100.00

Fuente: Fournier y Fournier 1992
* En este análisis sólo se incluyeron pocas muestras de esta loza, la cual es la predominante en todos los sitios históricos de la región Pima-Opata de Sonora (Braniff 1992), contándose con más de 1,000 tiestos.

Las colecciones procedentes de Veracruz del sitio de las atarazanas (aproximadamente 700 tiestos), en donde se realizaron reparaciones de navíos durante los períodos Colonial y Republicano, son en extremo semejantes a las de Cuernavaca, a excepción de la abundancia de tejas producidas en Francia y España que llegaron al puerto como lastre en los barcos (Hernández 1992).

En Sonora el área cubierta ha sido definida como la frontera protohistórica Pima-Opata (Braniff 1992). Se recolectaron materiales de superficie en veintisiete asentamientos, algunos con evidencias de ocupación prehistórica. Estos sitios incluyen misiones, visitas, presidios, reales de minas y haciendas. La muestra consta de materiales locales como mayólica, loza pulida Colonial, loza fina blanca mexicana, loza vidriada, loza bruñida de Tonalá, y cerámica Pápago Roja, así como productos de importación, es decir porcelana china, botijas, loza perla y loza blanca europeas, gres y porcelana francesa (Fournier-García y L. Fournier 1992); existen cerca de dos mil tiestos en la muestra (véase el cuadro 6.4).

Las colecciones arqueológicas de la Península de Yucatán se limitan al centro de la ciudad de Mérida. La principal muestra de excavación proviene de la Casa Montejo, construida en 1549 por Francisco de Montejo, capitán general de la conquista de la Provincia de Yucatán. El edificio fue remodelado drásticamente en 1880 (Barrera Rubio 1983; Peniche 1983; Siller y Abundis 1984). Los materiales consisten básicamente de loza fina blanca inglesa y francesa, tiestos de una tradición local de loza roja, y unos cuantos ejemplos de porcelana china y francesa, así como mayólica española, novohispana y botijas; se trata de una colección de aproximadamente 250 tiestos.

Las muestras de superficie de regiones rurales con predominio de población indígena corresponden al Valle del Mezquital y al Valle de Otumba. En el primer caso, se recuperaron colecciones en más de 350 sitios, predominando una loza de tradición local otomí (aproximadamente 2,500 tiestos), siendo sumamente reducido el porcentaje de otras lozas como mayólica, loza vidriada, y porcelana china y francesa, así como oliveras y loza fina europea (cerca de 500 tiestos). La escasez de lozas no indígenas se relaciona con la mínima presencia de población española y criolla en la región, siendo semejante el caso para el Valle de Otumba (Charlton y Fournier-García 1993).

En todas las colecciones estudiadas, para las lozas que consideramos marcadoras de estatus socioétnico—mayólica española y novohispana, porcelana china y francesa, y loza fina europea (véase el cuadro 6.5)—las formas predominantes corresponden a la vajilla de servicio (véase el cuadro 6.6). Resulta relevante señalar que en el caso de la mayólica novohispana, en todas las regiones estudiadas se identifican tipos cerámicos que corresponden tanto al grado común como al fino. En los centros urbanos predomina la mayólica de mejor calidad así como la de un grado intermedio que identificáramos nosotros (Fournier-García y Charlton 1993), no definido en análisis previos (por ejemplo, véase Lister y Lister 1982a). Por otra parte, en zonas rurales los porcentajes de mayólica de grado común suelen ser más altos, lo cual indica que la redistribución de esta clase de loza de baja calidad circuló sobre todo hacia regiones donde habitaban

Cuadro 6.5 Proporción de lozas identificadas en diversos sitios y regiones de Mexico

	CD. MÉXICO*	CUERNAVACA*	MÉRIDA*	VERACRUZ*	SONORA**	MEZQUITAL**
Lozas importadas						
Mayólica europea	Alta	Baja	Baja	Baja	–	-
Porcelana china	Alta	Media	Baja	Baja	Baja	Baja
Loza crema	Alta	Baja	Baja	Baja	Baja	-
Loza perla	Alta	Baja	Baja	Baja	Baja	-
Loza blanca	Alta	Media	Media	Alta	Media	Baja
Porcelana francesa	Alta	Media	Baja	Baja	Baja	Baja
Gres europeo	Alta	Baja	Baja	Baja	Baja	Baja
Botijas españolas	Alta	Media	Baja	Media	Baja	Baja
Lozas coloniales						
Mayólica novohispana	Alta	Alta	Media	Media	Media	Baja
Mayólica republicana	Alta	Media	Baja	Baja	Baja	Baja
Loza indígena local	Media	Baja	Baja	Baja	Alta	Muy alta
Loza alisada	Muy alta	Alta	Media	Baja	Alta	Baja
Loza Bruñida de Tonalá	Alta	Baja	–	–	Baja	Baja
Loza Bruñida de la Cuenca	Alta	Baja	-	Baja	Baja	Baja
Loza vidriada	Muy alta	Alta	Baja	Media	Media	Media

Proveniencia de las colecciones: * Rellenos arquitectónicos ** Superficie

consumidores con una menor capacidad económica de compra (véase capítulo 2).

Comparando estas muestras de materiales, pueden observarse distribuciones arqueológicas diferenciales, básicamente de la cerámica de importación y la mayólica, las cuales se asocian con las características socioétnicas de los consumidores que habitaban en los sitios y regiones mencionados con anterioridad.

En primer lugar, en el caso de la Ciudad de México, Cuernavaca, Veracruz y, parcialmente a nivel regional, Sonora, en los centros urbanos se encontraba una alta concentración de población con alto poder adquisitivo, es decir españoles y criollos. En Sonora es en los reales de mina donde predomina cerámica costosa, dado que sus habitantes contaban con los recursos económicos necesarios para su adquisición.

En segundo lugar, se dio una modificación a través del tiempo en la composición de la población con alto poder adquisitivo y una transformación económica de los sitios, caso de algunas misiones y haciendas de Sonora, al igual que de Yucatán. A pesar de que es limitado el volumen de mayólica novohispana en las colecciones arqueológicas de Mérida, resalta la abundancia relativa de lozas europeas. Debe, además, considerarse que en estos dos casos se trata de zonas relativamente alejadas de los principales centros de redistribución de bienes de alto costo, tratándose en consecuencia de un problema de potencial falta de accesibilidad debido a factores vinculados con la circunscripción geográfica de las regiones en cuestión.

Así, respecto a la problemática del consumo hay sitios como la Ciudad de México y Cuernavaca donde son tajantes las diferencias. El fenómeno urbano, asociado con marcadas divisiones socioétnicas, de poder adquisitivo y, en consecuencia, de capacidad de consumo, se refleja en el registro arqueológico. Para las vajillas de servicio, de higiene y ornamental, no son las lozas más costosas las de mayor representatividad en comparación con las locales (véanse los cuadros 6.2 y 6.3), que eran objeto de consumo por parte de las clases bajas, cuya participación en la distribución de capitales era mínima debido a los sistemas de explotación de la fuerza de trabajo. En estos sitios es patente la abundancia relativa de integrantes de la clase dominante y durante el período Colonial de las castas ubicadas en la cúspide de la pirámide socioétnica, quienes estuvieron en la capacidad de adquirir artículos de costo elevado.

Por otra parte, al tratar con sitios con distinta función a nivel regional, como en el caso de Sonora, en definitiva son abundantes los materiales de alto costo en los asentamientos como reales de mina y presidios (véase el cuadro 6.4). Ahí se concentró la población española y criolla, cuyo consumo no se restringía a artículos de producción regional, como sucedía con la población indígena y mestiza.

Además, las crisis socioeconómicas relacionadas con el control de la fuerza de trabajo y la extracción de recursos en zonas alejadas de los grandes centros nacionales de producción y redistribución, inciden en la posibilidad de acceso a bienes de alto costo inclusive entre las clases acomodadas, según se infiere en el caso de Yucatán.

Con la información disponible generada a través de estudios de arqueología histórica en México, los correlatos materiales indican el carácter cosmopolita del consumo de las clases media y alta logrado por el capitalismo mediante la explotación del mercado mundial (Marx y Engels s.f.). Es decir, con el modo de producción capitalista surgen esferas cerámicas a nivel mundial inferibles a partir de la distribución espacial de lozas europeas, en particular británicas. La presencia de materiales orientales se relaciona con el sistema redistributivo, por vías legales o el contrabando, dominado por Nueva España, ya que era la única colonia autorizada por la metrópoli para el tráfico con Oriente a través de

Cuadro 6.6 Proporción de formas predominates según vajilla y loza

	M. EUROPEA	M. MEXICANA	P. CHINA	P. FRANCESA	L. FINA EUROPEA	L. VIDRIADA	L. ALISADA	L. BRUÑIDA
Vajilla de servicio								
Escudilla	Muy alta	Media	–	–	–	–	–	–
Plato	Baja	Muy alta	Media	Muy alta	Muy alta	Alta	–	Media
Lebrillo	–	–	–	–	–	–	Muy alta	–
Mancerina	–	Baja	Baja	–	–	–	–	–
Platito	–	Baja	Baja	Media	Alta	Baja	–	–
Platón	Baja	Baja	Baja	Baja	Baja	Baja	–	–
Taza	Baja	Media	Media	Alta	Alta	–	–	–
Tazón	–	Media	Alta	Baja	Media	–	–	–
Tarro	–	–	–	–	Baja	–	–	–
Copa	–	Baja	Baja	–	Baja	–	–	–
Jarro	–	–	–	–	–	Alta	Baja	Baja
Cuenco	–	–	–	–	–	Media	Alta	Media
Cajete	–	–	–	–	–	Baja	Media muy alta	
Tetera	–	Baja	Baja	Baja	Baja	–	–	–
Cafetera	–	–	–	Baja	–	–	–	–
Jarra	–	Baja	–	–	–	Media	Media	Alta
Sopera	–	Baja	Baja	Baja	Baja	–	–	–
Ensaladera	–	–	–	Baja	Baja	–	–	–
Frutero	–	–	–	Baja	Baja	–	–	–
Azucarera	–	–	–	Baja	Baja	–	–	–
Cremera	–	–	–	–	Baja	–	–	–
Salero	–	–	–	–	Baja	–	–	–
Cucharón	–	–	–	–	Baja	–	Baja	Baja
Vajilla de higiene								
Bacín	–	Media	–	Baja	Baja	Alta	–	–
Palangana	–	Baja	–	–	Baja	Media	Baja	Alta
Jofaina	–	–	–	Baja	Baja	–	–	–
Escupidera	–	–	–	–	Baja	–	–	–
Vajilla ornamental								
Maceta	–	Media	–	–	Baja	Baja	Media	Baja
Jarrón	–	Baja	Baja	Baja	Baja	–	–	–
Florero	–	Baja	–	–	Baja	–	–	–
Tibor	–	Media	Media	–	–	–	–	–
Frasco o botella	–	Baja	Baja	–	–	–	–	Baja
Miniatura	Baja	Baja	Baja	Baja	Baja	Baja	Baja	Baja
Figura	–	Baja	Baja	Baja	–	Baja	Media	–
Benditera	–	Baja	–	–	–	–	–	–
Vajilla utilitaria								
Olla	–	–	–	–	–	Alta	Alta	Muy alta
Cántaro	–	–	–	–	–	Baja	Muy alta	Muy alta
Cazuela	–	–	–	–	–	Muy alta	Baja	Media
Comal	–	–	–	–	–	–	Media	Media
Molcajete	–	–	–	–	–	Media	Media	Media
Anafre	–	–	–	–	–	Baja	Alta	Media
Tibor	–	Media	Media	–	–	–	–	–
Tinaja	–	–	–	–	–	Baja	Baja	Media
Veilleuse	–	–	–	Baja	–	–	–	–

M. = mayólica, P. = porcelana, L. = loza

Filipinas (Fournier-García 1985b:322–323). Por otra parte, la presencia de mayólica en zonas alejadas del centro de México en donde se producía esta loza que constituía la de mayor estima por su alta calidad, responde a la eficacia de los sistemas redistributivos regionales y a la homogeneización del consumo de la población hispana y criolla en México.

Consideraciones Finales

Hasta la fecha rara vez se han identificado a partir de intervenciones en sitios históricos urbanos en México contextos primarios, dada la predominancia de exploraciones en monumentos destinados a su restauración, o bien a raíz de salvamentos arqueológicos, que han producido abundantes contextos secundarios. Por otra parte, aun cuando las colecciones de superficie son indicio de pautas generales de consumo, los factores que afectan el registro arqueológico y la representatividad de esta clase de muestras presentan limitaciones.

En esta investigación hemos propuesto tendencias de consumo que se vinculan con el acceso diferencial de distintos segmentos poblacionales a elementos de cultura material, con base en el análisis de abundantes colecciones (más de 600,000 tiestos) recuperadas en depósitos secundarios o en reconocimientos de superficie en centros urbanos o asentamientos rurales, además de apoyar parte de las inferencias en el registro documental. Sin embargo, se requiere estudiar a futuro muestras provenientes de unidades residenciales que habitaran individuos pertenecientes a las diversas castas, clases y estamentos sociales en distintos momentos del desarrollo de la formación económico-social mexicana, realizando además estudios de áreas de actividad y uso diferencial del espacio.

Asimismo, a futuro es importante en el manejo estadístico de las entidades tipológicas definidas, considerar no sólo el número de tiestos, sino calcular el número mínimo de vasijas representadas en las muestras estudiadas, en forma tal que se cuente con parámetros adecuados para la evaluación de la cantidad de material representado en los depósitos estudiados (Miller 1986:59). Puede darse el caso de que al tratar con muestras muy reducidas, el uso exclusivamente del número de fragmentos o su porcentaje (véase capítulo 2), llegue en realidad a representar un bajo número de piezas completas, por lo que las inferencias que se deriven a partir del estudio de colecciones de esta naturaleza no necesariamente son certeras.

Por otra parte, se requiere realizar minuciosos estudios documentales de testamentos e inventarios de tiendas para distintos períodos y diferentes zonas del actual territorio de la República Mexicana, además de recabar información referente a registros de cargamentos de buques. Sólo así será factible generar índices de precios (Miller 1980) y fluctuaciones de éstos a través del tiempo para las diversas lozas, grupos, tipos y formas cerámicas que están representadas en contexto arqueológico en sitios históricos, además de precisar la posición socioétnica de los consumidores que tuvieron acceso a bienes de diferente precio. Aquí únicamente hemos presentado una primera aproximación al problema, con datos limitados al norte de México y los disponibles sobre importaciones-exportaciones.

Por último, cabe señalar que la conquista española de México implicó el surgimiento de relaciones de dependencia económica hacia el exterior. Los arqueólogos del futuro manejarán como correlatos materiales de fines del segundo milenio los envases de los artículos producidos en las altamente industrializadas potencias capitalistas, que llegaron al país incluso antes de la formalización política del Tratado del Libre Comercio o NAFTA. Sus efectos sobre la industria mexicana ya se han dejado sentir y muchos productos mexicanos tienden a desaparecer al no ser competitivos ante los extranjeros que los sustituyen, creándose incluso nuevas necesidades de consumo entre la burguesía nacional, mientras que las masas históricamente desposeídas se mantienen al margen de esta clase de tendencias consumistas.

Al igual que hemos inferido para los períodos Colonial y Republicano con base en correlatos documentales y materiales, las posibilidades del desarrollo de las fuerzas productivas en México quedarán limitadas y a merced de las imposiciones de las potencias capitalistas del Primer Mundo que, aunadas a las contradicciones internas del sistema sociopolítico mexicano, irremediablemente mantienen al país como parte del Tercer Mundo.

Notas

1. Archivo General de la Nación, México, D.F. Consulado, vols. 228 y 120, exp. 2.
2. Archivo General de la Nación, México, D.F. Consulado, vols. 228 y 120, exp. 2, y Archivo Municipal de Hidalgo del Parral, Chihuahua. Causas Civiles, Años de 1730 a 1821.

✝ Chapter 7

Protohistoric to Colonial Settlement Transition in the Antigua Valley, Guatemala

Eugenia J. Robinson

Abstract

In central highland Guatemala, after the Spanish conquest, a presumed settlement change occurred: Colonial towns were created by *congregación* in which dispersed Indian households were brought together in a single community. Investigations by the Proyecto Arqueológico del Area Kaqchikel in the Antigua Valley have demonstrated that there are unexpected continuities in the settlement patterns of the Protohistoric and Colonial periods. Many Colonial towns are situated on top of pre-Columbian remains, and others are located within a short distance of Protohistoric communities. In the highlands, different cultural groups have selected the same environmental zones for settlement for nearly three thousand years.

Resumen

Se asume que en la porción central de las tierras altas de Guatemala hubo un cambio en el patrón de asentamiento después de la conquista española: se crearon pueblos a través del sistema de congregación, mediante el cual las unidades residenciales indígenas que se encontraban dispersas se aglutinaron en una misma comunidad. Las investigaciones realizadas en el marco del Proyecto Arqueológico del Area Kaqchikel en el Valle de Antigua han demostrado que hay continuidades enesperadas en los patrones de asentamiento de los periodos Protohistórico y Colonial. Muchos pueblos coloniales se sitúan sobre los restos precolombinos, y otros se localizan a poca distancia de las comunidades protohistóricas. En las tierras altas distintos grupos culturales han elegido las mismas zonas ambientales para asentarse durante casi 3,000 años.

THIS CHAPTER examines the Protohistoric to Colonial settlement transition in the Antigua Valley, Department of Sacatepéquez, Guatemala, a portion of the Kaqchikel-speaking zone of the Central Highlands of Guatemala (figure 7.1). Two sixteenth-century Colonial capitals of the "Kingdom" (*Reino*) of Guatemala were located in the valley, making it one of the most important regions of Colonial Latin America. Numerous Spanish ruins in the area identify the location of early Colonial towns and industries (see chapter 8), but until the current study, little information was available regarding the location of Kaqchikel settlements prior to the Spanish conquest (Borhegyi 1950; Kramer 1988; Lutz 1984; Shook 1952). Pottery of the pre-Columbian period had been found at some locations, but the spatial distribution of the Protohistoric (ca. 1400–1520) sites, the site hierarchies, and spatial relationships between the Protohistoric and Spanish settlements could not be assessed. Since 1988, archaeological survey in the Antigua Valley has filled the void in our knowledge about this critical transitional period.

Physical Description of the Antigua Valley

The Antigua Valley is situated 1,524 m above sea level and is surrounded by steep mountains that ascend to elevations over 2,000 m (figure 7.2). Two rivers cross the 20 km² valley floor. The larger, the Guacalate River, cuts a deep gorge in the northwestern passage to the valley, traverses the western part of the valley, and exits through the southwestern passage that lies between the Agua and Fuego volcanos. The Pensativo River enters the valley on the northeastern side. It once joined the Guacalate on the west side of the valley but was rechanneled to the south by the Spanish. The valley soils are alluvial, and today much of the valley floor is used for coffee cultivation. In the past, the bottomlands were swampy, making the edges of the valley preferable for settlement.

At the southwestern entrance to the valley is the 3-km–long shallow lake bed of what was formerly Lake Quilisimate (figure 7.2). A remnant lagoon lies about 2 km west of the entrance to the valley. Before being drained in the 1920s, the lake provided important lacustrine resources such as small fish (Lutz 1981). The reeds that grow there were used for matmaking in the towns of San Antonio Aguas Calientes and Santa Catarina Barahona (Gall 1978–1983, vol. III:213, 554); the same craft continues today in Santiago Zamora.

There are other desirable natural resources in the Antigua

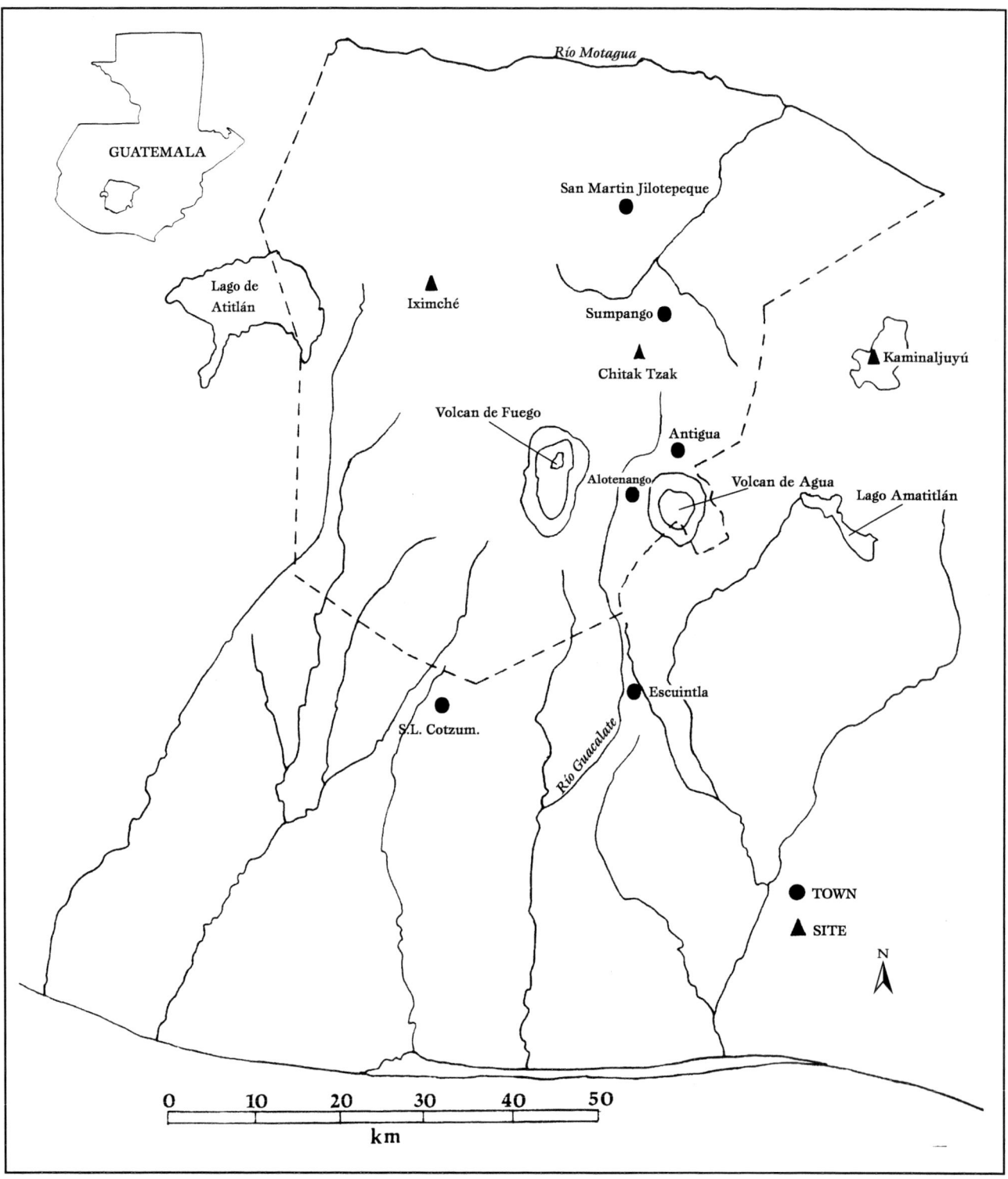

Figure 7.1 Kaqchikel-speaking zone (indicated by broken line) of the Central Highlands of Guatemala showing important towns and archaeological sites

Valley. Wood comes from the surrounding hillsides, and pumice and ash strata are found in natural exposures. Hot springs exist in various locations at the edges of the valley, including San Antonio Aguas Calientes and San Lorenzo el Cubo in the south and Pastores and San Lorenzo el Tejar in the north. Andesite and granite stone outcrops on the hills surrounding the valley provide excellent building stone. Within the last century, cochineal was grown in households in Antigua and San Juan del Obispo (Shook 1993; Gall 1978–1983, vol. III:362), and both corn and wheat have been grown in the valley.

Archaeological Data

This study focuses on seventy Protohistoric and Colonial

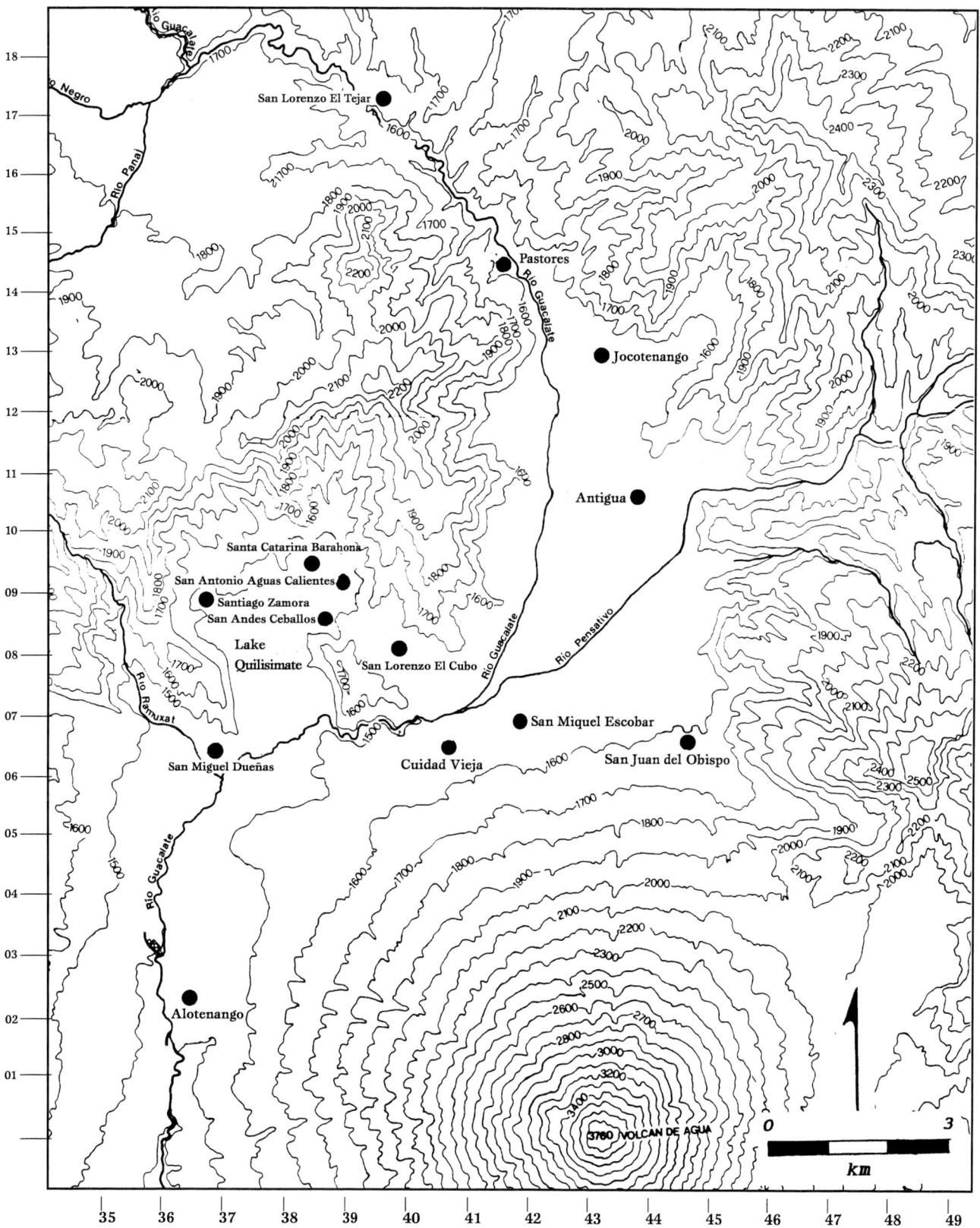

Figure 7.2 Towns and environmental features of the Antigua Valley and surrounding region

period sites recorded in the Antigua Valley during the 1990–1991 field season by the Proyecto Arqueológico del Area Kaqchikel (PAAK). The project's goal was to survey the strategic northwest and southwest passageways into the valley and the Lake Quilisimate area. An almost 100 percent survey of *municipios* (political divisions similar to counties) of Ciudad Vieja, San Antonio Aguas Calientes, San Miguel Dueñas, Santa Catarina Barahona, Antigua, Jocotenango, and Pastores has been completed (table 7.1). Data from the more distant municipios of Sumpango and Alotenango (figure 7.1) were also collected during an earlier survey phase in 1988–1989 with the project Encuesta Arqueológica Kaqchikel (Robinson 1990), sponsored by the Centro de Investigaciones Regionales de Mesoamerica (CIRMA). Both surveys have located 250 sites so far. The database also includes three sites in the southern Almolonga arm of the valley (Borhegyi 1950).

The PAAK survey included both foot survey and interviews. Small parties of two or three people first discussed the project's objectives with local authorities and landowners. Site records consisted of a map and descriptive site form. The surveyors avoided extremely steep mountain slopes because these areas were often heavily wooded and so precipitous that settlement would have been impossible. Site locations and, in many municipios where Kaqchikel is still spoken, their Kaqchikel names were determined through interviews with municipal authorities and local residents. Systematic surface collections were made during the 1990–1991 season. Survey within towns was not pursued intensively because it was relatively unproductive. Sometimes surface artifacts were found, or residents reported buried sites.

Ceramic cross-dating, based on a few standard references for the highlands (Hatch 1987; Rands and Smith 1965; Wetherington 1978), provides dates for the archaeological sites. For the Protohistoric and Colonial periods, we have relied on the work of Sharer, Ashmore, and Hill (1970), which defined eleven ceramic type-varieties for their Early Facet of the Panchoy Ceramic complex (the Protohistoric period) and nine type-varieties for the Late Facet (the Early Colonial period). Our project has defined one other micaceous Protohistoric type, El Pilar (Benítez and Chinchilla 1990).

Ceramic continuity from Protohistoric to Colonial periods is exhibited by the maintenance of nine of the eleven Early Facet types into the Late Facet (Sharer, Ashmore, and Hill 1970). Only two ceramic types ceased in the Late Facet, making them important diagnostics of Protohistoric sites that were not occupied later. These two types are Alotenango Crema: Alotenango Variety and Patzaj Unslipped: Patzaj Variety. In our collections, we have identified only one of the exclusively Early Facet types, Alotenango Crema, a white-slipped, fine red-paste ceramic that most commonly occurs as a bowl and less frequently as a jar. The slip is burnished, hard and enduring. Sherds in surface collections are distinctive but rare. The presence of Alotenango Crema indicates conclusively a Protohistoric date, but because it occurs in such low frequencies, its absence does not necessarily indicate an exclusively Colonial date. Based on the ceramic data, sites fall into one of three categories (table 7.1[1]):

‡ Sites with the characteristic Protohistoric pottery and Alotenango Crema are classified as Protohistoric

‡ Sites with only Colonial pottery are classified as Colonial

‡ Sites with Protohistoric pottery, but lacking Alotenango Crema, constitute a dubious class; they could be Protohistoric or Colonial (sites in this category do not appear on figures 7.3 or 7.7).

Indigenous Populations Before and During the Conquest Period

Lutz concludes (1984), based on documentary and archaeological sources, that the northern and southern ends of the Antigua Valley had low populations at the time of the Spanish conquest. San Miguel Escobar, the second capital of Guatemala, and its Indian barrio, Ciudad Vieja (figure 7.2), were established by the Spaniards at reportedly abandoned locations (Lutz 1984:39). Only one Kaqchikel place name, Bulbux-ya, exists in documentary sources for the Antigua Valley; this citation has been interpreted to mean that only a small Kaqchikel population existed when the Spaniards arrived. Bulbux-ya, or *chorro de agua* (rapids), was a small pueblo used to maintain vigilance over the surrounding cornfields that became part of Ciudad Vieja (Lutz 1984:49). During the Indian rebellion of 1524–1530 (Polo Sifontes 1986), the Kaqchikel fought in various locations, and it is possible that during this disruptive period populations were low and there was some discontinuity in settlement locations.

Lutz (1981) also notes that in the Early Colonial period some Colonial towns were peopled with Indians from other regions; the immigration or forced relocation of Indians from outside the valley is interpreted to mean that local Indian populations were low. One Colonial town, Santa Catarina Barahona, in the area of Lake Quilisimate at the southwestern entrance to the Antigua Valley, was settled with foreign Indians. The Indians' ethnicity or origin included Chamelco (Alta Verapaz), Utlatecas (Utlatán), Atitlán, Chontales (Tabasco or Oaxaca), and Pipil of the Pacific coast (Lutz 1981). Mexicans, Tlaxcalans, and Cholultecans accompanied Pedro de Alvarado to the new capital at San Miguel Escobar and became residents of the adjacent service community at Ciudad Vieja.

After the 1524–1530 rebellion, some Kaqchikel were placed in *encomiendas* (grants of Indians and their tribute to a Spaniard), some were enslaved, and others worked in the corn-

Table 7.1 Protohistoric and Colonial sites located during PAAK survey listed by municipio and time period. Site coordinates refer to coordinates noted on figures 7.3 and 7.7

	PROTOHISTORIC W/ ALOTENANGO CREMA	PROTOHISTORIC	COLONIAL
Muncipio of Antigua			
El Pilar 478089		x	
Cerro de los Dolores 450115		x	x
San Cristobal El Alto 457081		x	
El Hato 467132		x	
Carmona 461058		x	x
Pompeya 432067		x	x
Terrenos 418057		x	x
Finca Primavera and Angostura 435076		x	
Muncipio of Ciudad Vieja			
397067	x	x	x
399069	x	x	x
399062		x	x
398068		x	x
398062		x	x
397061	x	x	x
399066	x	x	x
399057		x	
395044	x	x	x
397054		x	x
Rucal 403055	x	x	x
407058		x	x
402063	x	x	x
402067		x	x
402042		x	
404052		x	x
398052		x	x
398047		x	
398043		x	
397069		x	x
392067		x	
397083		x	x
396076		x	x
395073	x	x	
402088		x	
396082		x	x
398077		x	
402089		x	
401085	x	x	x
403087		x	
406087		x	x
401087		x	x
398077		x	
Vista Alegre 380064	x	x	x
Muncipio of San Antonio Aguas Calientes			
389106	x		x
398113	x	x	
385108		x	
402115	x		x
402113	x		x
423179			
Las Verapaces 392108		x	
388108		x	
394112		x	
Terminal de Sanjon de Verapas		x	
394083		x	
Muncipio of Santa Catarina Barahona			
375096	x	x	
382099	x	x	
375099	x	x	x

continued

Table 7.1, continued			
	PROTOHISTORIC W/ ALOTENANGO CREMA	PROTOHISTORIC	COLONIAL
Muncipio of Pastores			
431160	x	x	x
428162	x	x	
426152			x
409148		x	
415142		x	
423158	x		x
412143	x	x	x
Santa Rosa			
427148		x	
416156		x	
406130		x	
427158		x	
Muncipio of Jocotenango			
463145		x	
Las Victorias 437128	x	x	x
Vejucales 447148	x	x	x
Vejucales 446143	x	x	x

fields and mines. Many were brought to the Antigua Valley as early as 1541, and Kaqchikel slaves were present in the town of San Juan del Obispo (Gall 1978–1983, Vol III:363). Lutz (1984:83) concludes that after Indian slavery was abolished in 1542, the "Indian" populations in the Antigua Valley were very heterogeneous, coming from various areas of Guatemala and Mexico.

Protohistoric Settlement Patterns

Different Maya ethnic groups controlled the Central Highlands of Guatemala in the Protohistoric period and were based at primary centers (figure 7.1). Iximché was the capital of the Kaqchikel people. According to ethnohistoric sources, it was founded between 1470 and 1490 (Guillemin 1977; Wauchope 1949). The distribution of the Kaqchikeles from the Motagua River on the north to the Pacific Piedmont on the south, and from Lake Atitlán on the west to Cerro Alux on the east, was about as great as it is today, covering approximately 3,500 km².

The mountain topography of the Central Guatemalan Highlands is characterized by small expanses of level land cut by deep ravines. To control this varied landscape, the Kaqchikeles established regional centers housed by nobles (Polo Sifontes 1986). At the time of the conquest the Kaqchikel were expanding southward and battled the Pipil for control of Escuintla, and they held land near the southern corridor into the Antigua Valley (Polo Sifontes 1981).

Within the Antigua Valley, we have identified a three-tiered settlement hierarchy consisting of a regional center (type-1 site); smaller, less complex sites (type 2); and even smaller sites with no architecture (type 3). It is likely that this settlement pattern was established around the time of the founding of Iximché (ca. 1470–1490).

Type 1 Sites

The type-1 site is the most complex discovered in the survey zone. A single example, Chitak Tzak, is located a few kilometers southwest of Sumpango (figures 7.1, 7.3). This site is a regional center with stone architecture, plaster floorings and façade facings, and multiple plazas (figure 7.4). Stone walls define the limits of the site and divide it into three sections. The southern and largest plaza is bounded by platforms; Str. D4-1, the largest (3 m tall), is located on the north side of the southern plaza. The site is about 250 m long. Protohistoric pottery exists around its perimeter, indicating there was residential settlement in this area (Robinson 1993a, 1993b).

Chitak Tzak, which means "destroyed houses" in Kaqchikel, is now known as "Old Sumpango." Oral tradition states that the site was abandoned after an earthquake destroyed its houses and the population moved during the Protohistoric period to the current location of Sumpango only a few kilometers to the northeast. Chitak Tzak is one of the thirty-eight or forty pueblos listed in the sixteenth-century *Crónica Franciscana* as one of Iximché's subjects (Carmack 1973).

The site is not a miniature Iximché but does have some elements in common with the capital. While it lacks the opposing temples and grand palaces of the Kaqchikel capital, it has similar plaza proportions and the same construction techniques of rubble fill and calcium cement floorings. Clay and andesite slab floorings are regional features.

This site is the only Protohistoric regional center found during the survey; it probably was preserved because it was not destroyed by superimposed Colonial construction. Based on oral tradition, it can be concluded that the Colonial town of Sumpango was located upon the Protohistoric town established after the destruction of Chitak Tzak. Protohistoric pottery from the town of Sumpango indicates a pre-Hispanic occupation.

No other sites of comparable complexity have been discovered in the Antigua Valley or the surrounding area. It is possible that sites could have been destroyed by Colonial construction or buried by alluvium and wind-blown and eroded soils from the mountain sides. Within the entire Kaqchikel region, there may be four or five other sites of comparable complexity (Garcia, Hill, and Shook 1991).

Type 2 Sites

Four type-2 sites are smaller in size and less complex than Chitak Tzak. Casa Roja, Vista Alegre, Las Verapaces, and Vejucales (figure 7.3) each has a large mound as much as 10 m high. These were probably elite residences, perhaps where the heads of a social unit resided. All of these sites, except Vista Alegre, are located in very remote areas on steep mountain slopes. Vista Alegre is an exception because it is situated on a broad slope of the Guacalate River, east of San Miguel Dueñas and facing the former Lake Quilisimate.

Las Verapaces, a typical type-2 site, is located in a ravine and is known as "Old San Antonio Aguas Calientes." This site, located 2 km above the town of the same name, has a single platform 10 m tall faced with *talpetate* (volcanic ash) on the downslope. The base of the structure is 10 x 15 m. The upper 1.5 m is made of stone and has smaller platform dimensions of only a few meters.

The second level sites, although they consist of only single stone mounds, may have been centers of importance in the Protohistoric period. They are all within a few kilometers of Colonial towns, suggesting they may have been the Protohistoric counterpart of the Colonial town.

Type 3 Sites

Type 3 sites are identified by surface scatters of pottery and other materials; there is no standing architecture. Sites usually measure less than 200 m in diameter. Interpreted to be the remains of single family residences, they are found in all topographic situations, including flat, low terrain; slopes; and level spurs of land in the mountains. Type 3 sites are located on the flat plains of Sumpango, on the edges of the Antigua Valley, and on the steep mountain slopes surrounding the former Lake Quilisimate and Pastores to the northwest (figure 7.3).

Summary of Protohistoric Settlement

Borhegyi's (1965) hypothesis that Late Postclassic (ca. AD 1200–1520) sites in the highlands were located exclusively in defensive positions—such as Iximché, located on a constricted peninsula of land with steep encircling ravines—is not supported by our data. Although three of four type-2 sites and some of the type-3 sites have these highly defensive situations (figure 7.3), the type-1 site, Chitak Tzak, confounds the rules of the predicted settlement pattern because it is located on the east side of a flat plain, an open location. The site does have protective ravines to the south and mountains to the north, however, and the site itself is surrounded by walls.

Modern Sumpango, the location to which the Protohistoric population of Chitak Tzak apparently moved, is also in an open, undefensive position. It seems probable that access to good agricultural land and transport routes were the determining factors in the location of the type-1 site, Chitak Tzak, and its probable successor, Sumpango. Vista Alegre, a type-2 site, and several type-3 sites also occur on flat, open terrain, as well as in defensive locations.

Continuities and Discontinuities: Protohistoric and Colonial Town Placement

In spite of the reported settlement discontinuity that occurred with the indigenous populations in the Antigua Valley in the early 1500s (Lutz 1981, 1984), archaeological data suggest that there was cultural continuity from the Protohistoric through the Early Colonial period in this area. The ceramic study by Sharer, Ashmore, and Hill (1970) indicates that the domestic pottery of Antigua did not change very much from Protohistoric to Colonial periods; all but two types continue into the Colonial period. Indeed, some types seem to be related to the pottery still produced in Santa Apolonia (Yepocapa Ceramic group), Chinautla (Chinautla Ceramic group) and Antigua (the Almolonga group; see Reina and Hill 1978; Sharer, Ashmore, and Hill 1970).

Data confirm that there was settlement continuity in the Antigua Valley and surrounding areas; certain locations were occupied in both the Protohistoric and Colonial periods. The Spanish located their towns on relatively flat land, large enough to accommodate a plaza and grid town layout, with adequate natural resources and sufficient land for crops and herds. In many instances, these centers were either near or superimposed upon Protohistoric sites. Locations outside but near these Spanish towns also show continuity of occupation. The major settlement discontinuity occurred with Indian settlements on steep mountain slopes; Protohistoric sites in remote locations were abandoned.

The Spanish institution of congregación was, in some cases, responsible for the continued use of a single location. Congregación brought scattered Indian households into Colonial towns; sometimes existing Indian towns were used as the Colonial center, or the Spanish established a new Colonial town within a few kilometers of a Protohistoric center. Local officials were consulted about the locations of the new towns. Spanish and native authorities (*principales* and *caciques*) looked at and tested a new site, and if the old people

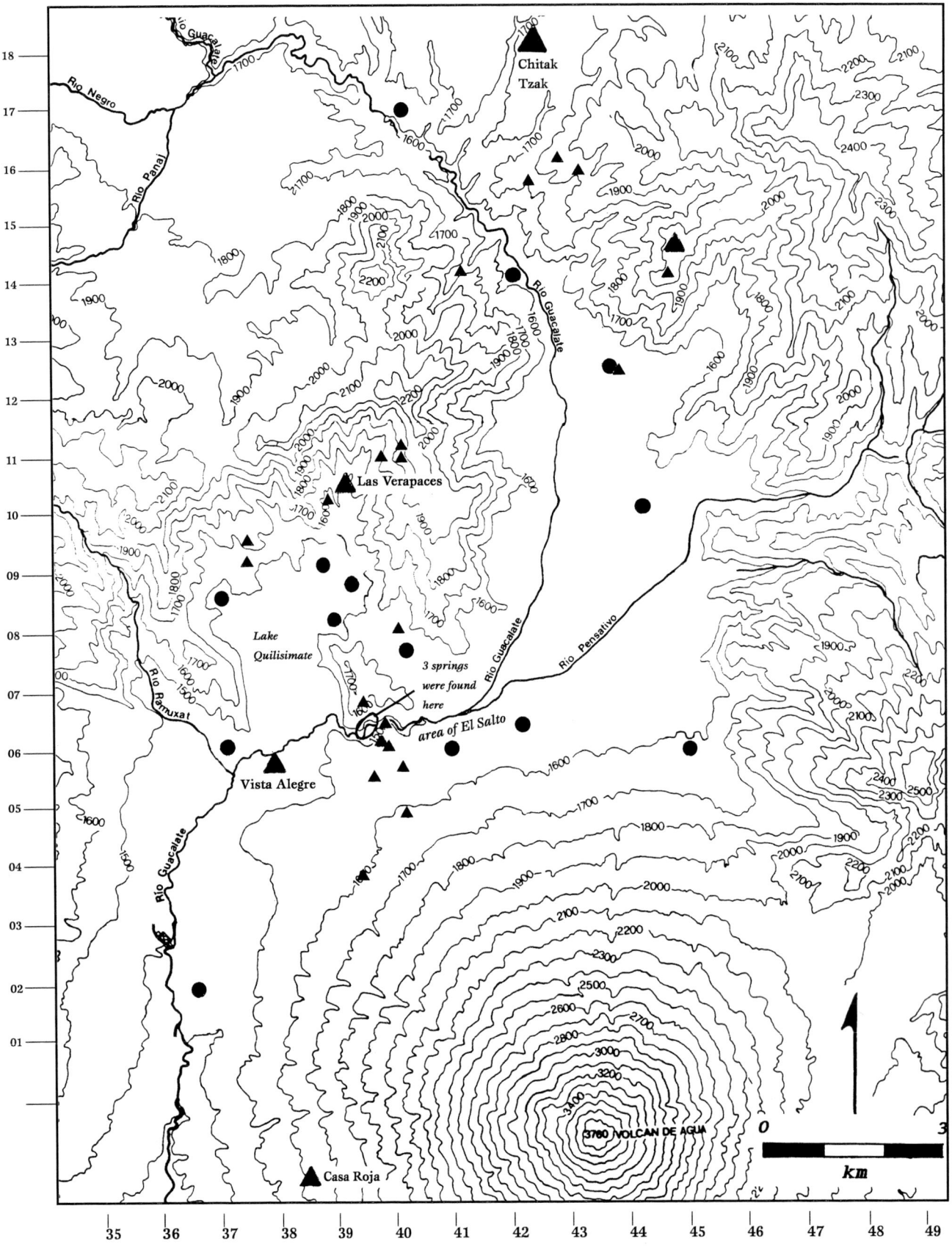

Figure 7.3 Protohistoric-period sites in the Antigua Valley: ▲ = type 1; ▲ = type 2; ▲ = type 3. Solid circles indicate modern towns (see figure 7.2).

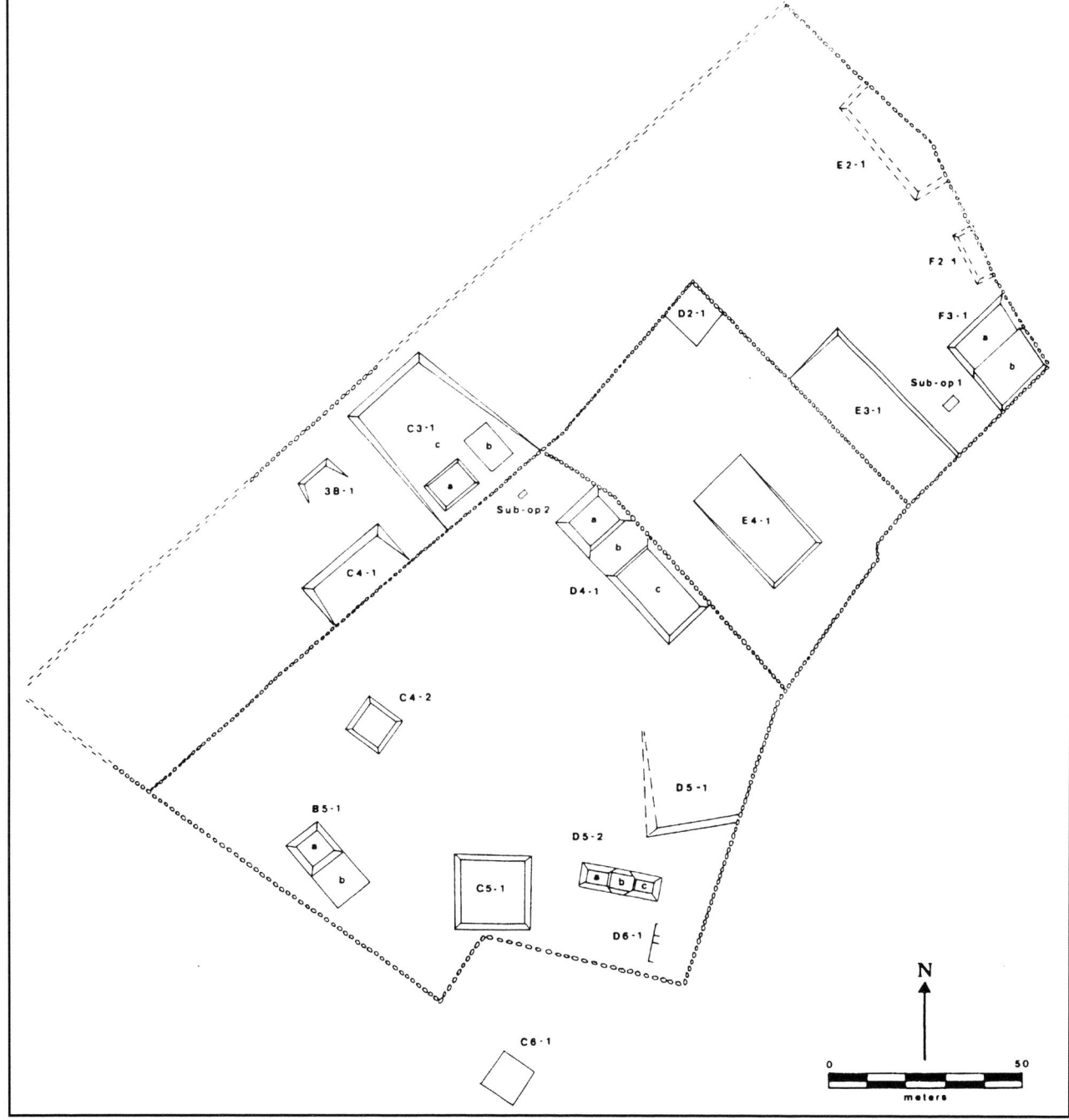

Figure 7.4 Chitak Tzak

liked the place, they ordered it to be used (Villacorta 1942). A 1602 document states that the natives of Santa Lucia Milpas Altas, to the east of the Antigua Valley, had lived there since before the conquest.

Examples of this early colonization process exist within and outside the Kaqchikel region. Tecpan, the first capital of Guatemala, was established in 1524 only a few kilometers to the northeast of Iximché, the Protohistoric capital of the Kaqchikel state. Closer to Antigua, the Protohistoric town of Sumpango became the seat of a Spanish encomienda in the early 1500s. There are other examples outside the Kaqchikel region. On the Pacific coast, the Protohistoric Pipil site Itzcuintepec was destroyed by Pedro de Alvarado in 1524 (Polo Sifontes 1986) and the Spanish town of Escuintla was settled near this pre-Columbian town (Polo Sifontes 1981). Similarly, in the Quiché zone to the west, the population of the Protohistoric site of Gumarcaah was resettled at nearby Santa Cruz del Quiché, and people from Protohistoric Zaculeu were resettled at Huehuetenango (Polo Sifontes 1981).

San Miguel Escobar, known as San Miguel Tzacualpa during the Colonial period, is another example of a Spanish town located near an Indian settlement, Bulbux-ya. In this case, the indigenous site near Ciudad Vieja was small (Lutz

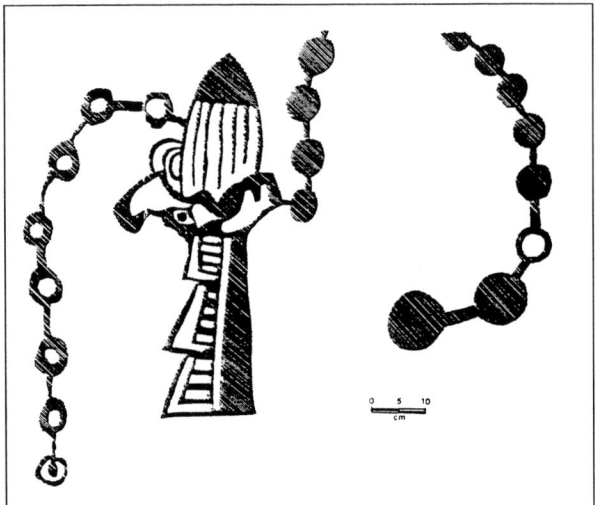

Figure 7.5 Rock painting of serpent

1984), but it had a long history. In fact, the entire zone between the Guacalate River and the base of the Agua Volcano around Ciudad Vieja is unusual because of the age and frequency of occupations. Three springs located on the banks of the Guacalate River approximately 1 km west of Ciudad Vieja were almost certainly part of Bulbux-ya and explain how the site got its name (figure 7.3). One of these springs still provides ample water and is used today. In this area known as El Salto (waterfall), on a cliff above the springs, are the ruins of an electrical plant. Nearby are pre-Columbian rock paintings—rare features in Guatemala. These red paintings lie on 500 m of rock cliffs above the Guacalate River about three-quarters of a kilometer west of Ciudad Vieja. At the base of the cliffs is a small surface site with Early Classic (AD 300–600) and Protohistoric pottery. The first painting, 70 cm tall, has several typically Mesoamerican features (figure 7.5). It depicts a serpent with an ear of corn coming out of its mouth and dots surrounding the motif. The second painting is 1.5 m tall and has several animals, including monkeys, alligators, birds, and turtles (figure 7.6). Several other small paintings on the rock cliffs are of butterflies and abstract designs, including squares.

San Miguel Escobar was said to be located near a pre-Hispanic settlement with structures and other ruins nearby, which had been abandoned sometime before the conquest (Lutz 1984). Borhegyi (1950) investigated the slopes of the Agua Volcano north of San Miguel Escobar and Ciudad Vieja to find the Protohistoric site and discovered two Late Classic (AD 600–900) archaeological sites, Los Terrenos and Pompeya. The architecture at these sites is Late Classic, but surface ceramics show they were occupied during the Preclassic, Classic, and Postclassic periods (700 BC–AD 1500; Shook 1952). Thus, the precise location of the Protohistoric site of Bulbux-ya remains unknown, but it certainly was located

Figure 7.6 Rock painting of animals

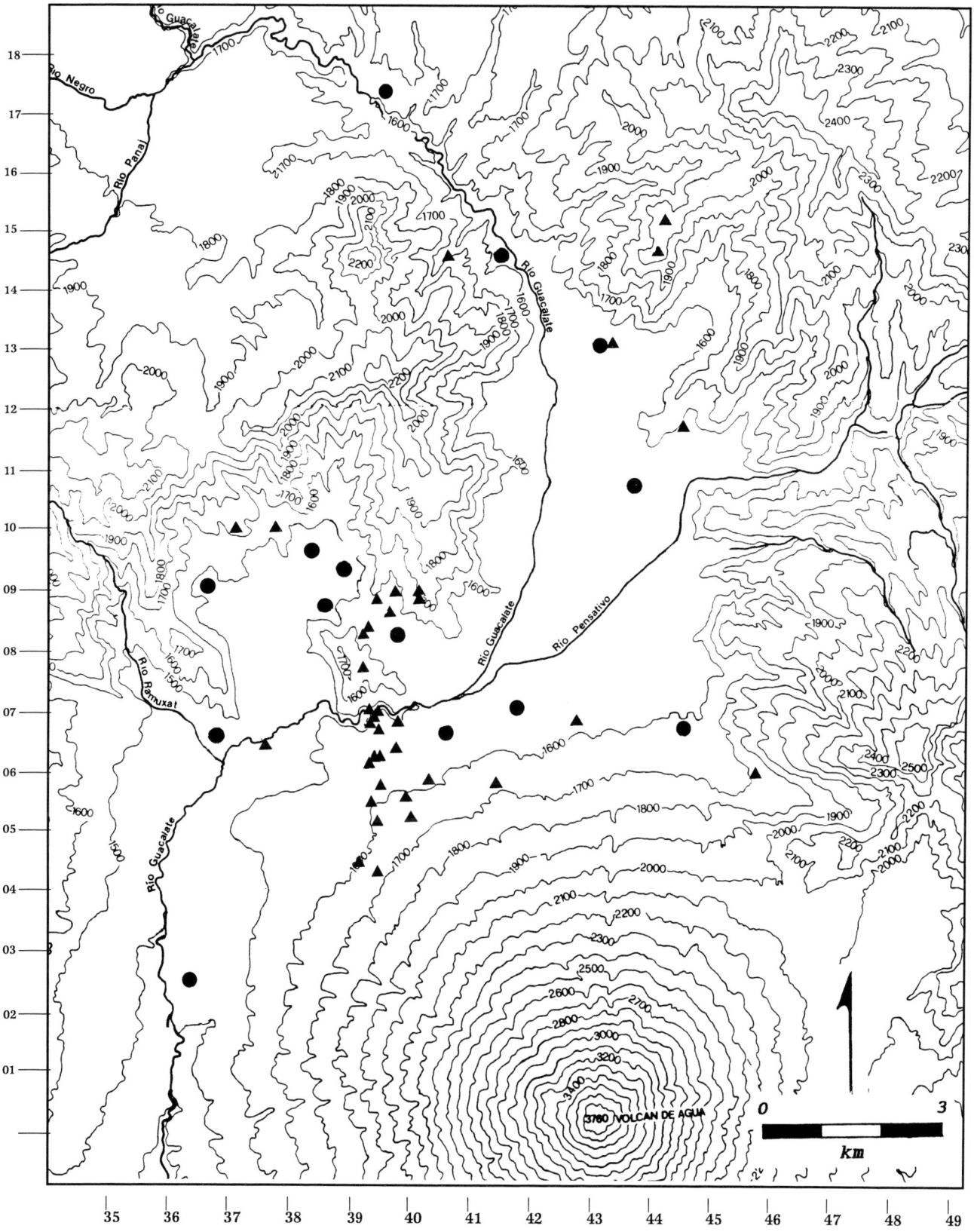

Figure 7.7 Colonial-period sites in the Antigua Valley. Solid circles indicate modern towns (see figure 7.2).

in the vicinity of Ciudad Vieja, possibly near the springs at El Salto.

The location of San Miguel Escobar was probably favorable to the Spanish for the same reasons that the inhabitants of earlier settlements chose to locate their centers in the area. The terrain is relatively flat and fertile, lying at the base of the Agua Volcano but in an area high enough not to flood. Water was plentiful, with springs, mountain streams, a major river, and access to Lake Quilisimate only a few kilometers away. The location was also strategic because it was situated on the southern entrance to the Antigua Valley, atop the Alotenango north-south–trending passageway to the south coast. Lutz argues that the location, because of its elevation above the valley floor, was defensive (1984:39).

Another important example of settlement continuity is the location of Antigua, formerly Santiago de los Caballeros. After the destruction of San Miguel Escobar in 1541 by a mud slide, the *cabildo* (municipal council) decided to move the capital a few kilometers to the northeast arm of the Valley (figure 7.2). This decision was made because many residents had established corn fields, stables, and slave residences outside the town and did not wish to change them. There were abundant water sources and building supplies, both stone and wood, in the area (Lutz 1984:59-60). This location had been occupied in Protohistoric and earlier times (Sharer, Ashmore, and Hill 1970; Valencia 1991; Shook 1991), as was the Cerro de los Dolores just outside the northeast corner of the original town (Robinson 1990).

In addition to these examples of settlement continuity, there is also evidence for discontinuity in settlement location from Protohistoric to Colonial periods. Three of the four type-2 sites (Vejucales, Las Verapaces, and Casa Roja) are located on steep mountain slopes. Colonial towns (Jocotenango, San Antonio Aguas Calientes, and Alotenango) were established at lower elevations and on flatter ground within 2 to 3.5 km of the Protohistoric sites (figure 7.3). It seems likely that people from the Protohistoric settlements were moved to these new locations.

Several type-3 sites also lie on steep, elevated mountain terrain. The survey data indicate that many of these sites were abandoned by the Colonial period (compare figures 7.3 and 7.7; Robinson 1990). Presumably, these locations were not deemed desirable by the Spaniards, and Indian residents had either abandoned the location during the Protohistoric period or were forced to relocate under the policy of congregación.

Conclusions

The data presented here enable us to reevaluate certain notions about Protohistoric and Colonial settlement patterns in the Antigua Valley. First, what has been cited as a common pattern of Protohistoric sites being located in defensive locations (Borhegyi 1965) is not supported by our survey data. Protohistoric sites at all three levels of the settlement hierarchy have been found on flat terrain and in open locations, although some type-2 and type-3 sites were located in defensible positions.

Second, historical documents have led researchers to conclude that the Antigua Valley was sparsely settled in the early 1500s (Lutz 1981, 1984). Archaeological data provide an alternative interpretation, although the imprecision of ceramic cross-dating does not allow for the documentation of Kaqchikel populations in the critical 1520s. A large number of sites can be definitively dated to the Protohistoric period, suggesting that the native population was larger than that indicated in the documents. In addition, the continued use of Protohistoric ceramic types into the Colonial period suggests continuity within the native population.

Finally, with regard to continuity and discontinuity of settlements from Protohistoric to Colonial periods, the archaeological data indicate that sites with low, open areas with easy access tended to be occupied in both the Protohistoric and Colonial periods. Colonial settlement was particularly dense in the area of Ciudad Vieja and San Lorenzo el Cubo (compare figures 7.3 and 7.7). Archaeological data also show that elevated sites with difficult access were generally abandoned at the end of the Protohistoric period.

Acknowledgments. The majority of the fieldwork for this paper was supported by the Wenner-Gren Foundation and the Organization of American States. The Centro de Investigaciones Regionales de Mesoamérica and a Fulbright grant supported the first phase of the investigation. I would like to thank the Instituto de Antropología e Historia and Vanderbilt University and Tulane University for their institutional support of the research.

Notes

1. The sites listed in table 7.1 were located during the PAAK survey of the municipios of Ciudad Vieja, San Antonio Aguas Calientes, San Miguel Dueñas, Santa Catarina Barahona, Antigua, Jocotenango, and Pastores. Sites mentioned in the text which are in other municipios (such as Chitak Tzak and Casa Roja) are not listed in table 7.1.
2. Archivo General de Centroamérica, Guatemala City. Legajo 5936, exp. 51921, f. 45; Robert Hill, personal communication, 1992.

✝ Chapter 8

La Arquitectura Industrial y Utilitaria de Santiago, Capital del Reino de Guatemala, y sus Alrededores

Rodrigo Aparicio

Resumen

A partir de investigaciones realizadas en Antigua Guatemala y zonas circunvecinas, se han descubierto más de cincuenta estructuras arquitectónicas industriales y utilitarias del periódo Colonial. Su localización se logró con base en distintas líneas de evidencia, sean fuentes históricas, testimonios orales o recorridos de campo. Muchas de ellas se han ubicado en planos. También se han hecho levantamientos y croquis, además de registros fotográficos así como recabación de notas acerca de los métodos constructivos empleados. Algunas estructuras y complejos han sobrevivido al paso del tiempo y en algunos casos aún se utilizan para su función original, mientras que otras se encuentran en un estado precario. Algunas han desaparecido, ya sea por su demolición o al quedar cubiertas por sedimentos de ríos cercanos o bajo cenizas de volcanes, abandonándose al olvido después de que se trasladara la capital de Guatemala tras el terremoto de 1773. En este capítulo se incluye un catálogo acerca de estas construcciones, el cual facilitará a futuro realizar estudios sistemáticos al respecto.

Abstract

Based on research carried out in Antigua Guatemala and the surrounding area, more than fifty industrial and utilitarian structures from the Colonial period have been discovered. The architectural features were located through various lines of evidence including historical sources, oral history, and field survey. Many of the structures have been located on maps. They have also been drawn, and notes and photographs have been taken to record construction methods. Some structures and complexes have survived the passage of time, and in some cases they are still used for their original purpose, whereas others were found in a precarious state. Some structures have disappeared, either demolished or covered by river sediments or volcanic ash, abandoned when the new capital of Guatemala was established elsewhere after the earthquake of 1773. This chapter includes a portion of a catalog of these constructions, which will facilitate future research on this topic.

LA INVESTIGACIÓN de las estructuras arquitectónicas industriales y utilitarias ubicadas en y alrededor de Santiago, capital del Reino de Guatemala, hoy día La Antigua Guatemala, abre nuevas oportunidades para analizar la presencia española en el campo de la industria en el nuevo mundo. Con él conoceremos gran parte de su desarrollo económico durante la época Colonial. Este estudio puede constituir la base para conocer construcciones de interés histórico-arquitectónico, partiendo de la época Colonial, además de proporcionar elementos para incrementar su apreciación y ayudar a garantizar su conservación para el futuro.

La historia única de Santiago, que se ha conservado como una ciudad del siglo XVIII, brinda un caso espectacular con magníficas posibilidades en el sentido de su potencial histórico-arquitectónico, arqueológico, y educativo para aprender sobre las técnicas constructivas y la industria del periódo Colonial. Para el campo de arqueología histórica este estudio puede proveer datos importantes sobre la arquitectura industrial y utilitaria española, hasta ahora no bien estudiada.

En este capítulo se encuentran un resumen de la historia de Santiago y una descripción y resultados de la investigación de la arquitectura industrial de la ciudad. Además, información específica sobre varias industrias Coloniales aparece en el apéndice a este capítulo y en las figuras 8.1 a 8.9.

Antecedentes Históricos

El Reino de Guatemala abarcó el actual territorio de Centroamérica, incluyendo parte de México y una porción de Panamá; su capital estuvo localizada en la actual República de Guatemala. Santiago, en el Valle de Panchoy, ramo del Valle de Antigua, se fundó en 1543. Fue la tercera capital del reino, ubicada a escasos tres kilómetros de distancia del Valle

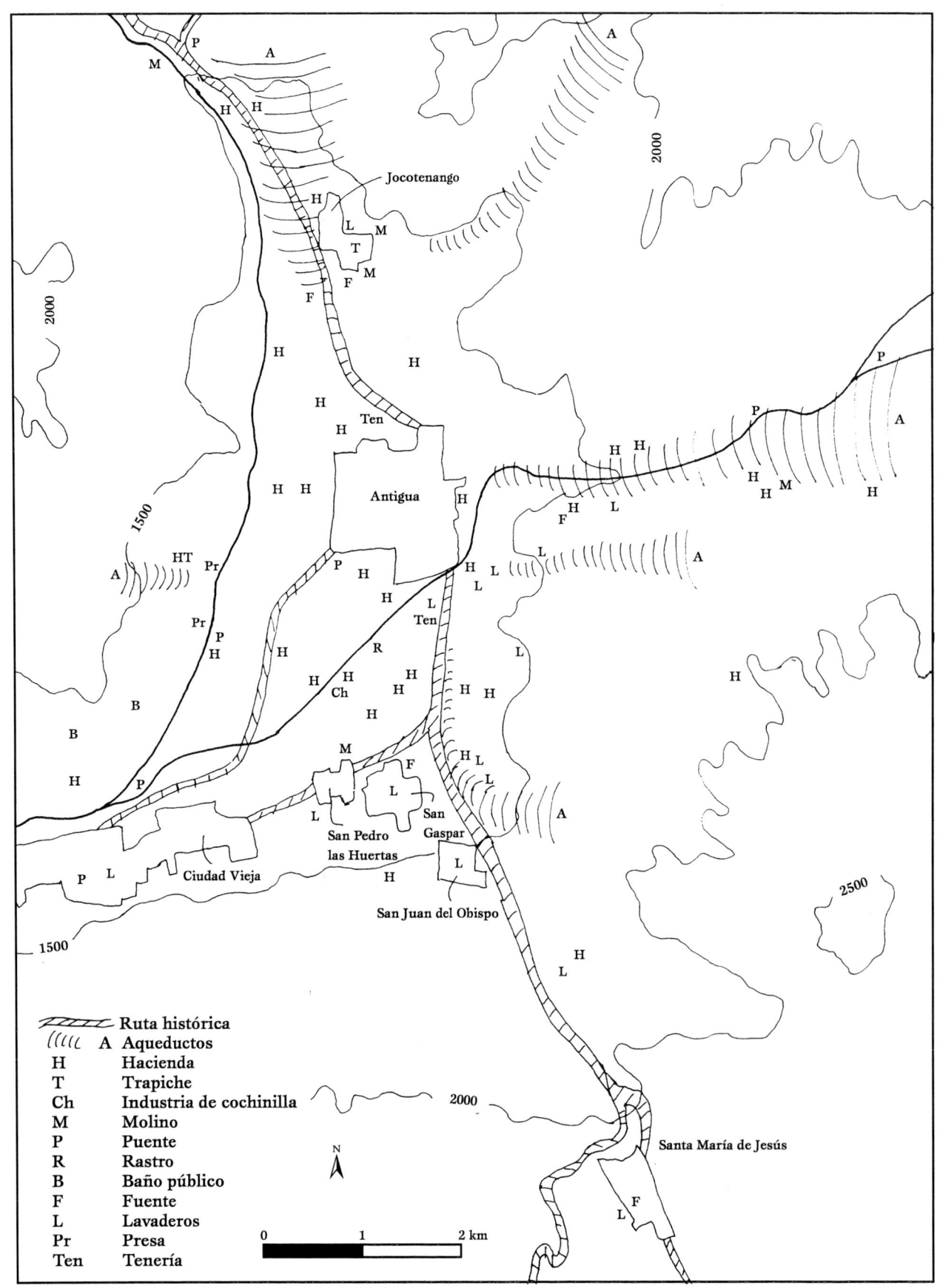

FIGURA 8.1 Localización de conjuntos y estructuras arquitectónicas industriales y utilitarias mencionadas en el texto. *Dibujos por el autor*

de Almolonga, otro ramo del Valle de Antigua, sitio donde estuvo localizada la segunda capital Santiago en Almolonga. Este asentamiento estuvo ocupado durante escasos catorce años debido a que fue destruido por un aluvión que bajó de las faldas del Volcán de Agua, ubicado en la actual población de San Miguel Escobar.

Santiago de Panchoy tuvo en cierto sentido una escabrosa historia debido a los periódicos terremotos (1565, 1577, 1586, 1606, 1651, 1663, 1689, 1715, 1717, 1751, 1773) así como las frecuentes amenazas del Volcán de Fuego entre 1520 y la última parte del siglo XIX, registrándose más de cincuenta erupciones; asimismo, sufrió por las constantes inundaciones (1566, 1652, 1689, 1762) provenientes de los cerros y desbordamientos de ríos vecinos, y las erupciones de 1581, 1932, 1945 y 1983 (Annis 1968:11; Rubio Sánchez 1989:9). A pesar de ello en sus 230 años de vida Santiago llegó a adquirir fama de ser una de las ciudades más bellas de los dominios españoles en América (Rubio Sánchez 1989:9). Según registra Gall, en el siglo XVIII, al momento de su destrucción Santiago era

> suntuosa y magnífica por sus edificios; numerosa por su vecindario; frecuentada por su floreciente comercio; respetuosa por sus tribunales y acomodada por su apacible templado clima y cercanía de pueblos, haciendas y labores de sus contornos; constituyéndola este agregado de apreciables cualidades, la segunda Ciudad de estas Américas después de México y haciéndola competir con las más célebres de España. (1978–1983, 1:121)

Era metrópoli y capital—en jurisdicción eclesiástica y jurisdicción real—de un vasto reino que se extendía por más de 600 leguas, comprendiendo en su extensión muchas villas y más de 900 pueblos y diecisiete reales de minas de oro y plata.

Santiago tuvo veinticinco templos y ocho ermitas pequeñas, todos de costosa simétrica arquitectura y adornados por dentro de retablos, pinturas y otras preciosas alhajas. Las ocho comunidades de religiosos, cinco de religiosas, y tres beatarios habitaban conventos y casas espaciosas. Habían casas consistoriales de ayuntamiento y de moneda, universidad, dos seminarios de niños y uno de niñas, y real aduana. Las plazas tenían hermosas fuentes, fuertes y seguros acueductos, dos hospitales y otros públicos edificios. Había más de ocho mil casas de particulares.

El hecho de su parcial destrucción por los terremotos de Santa Marta en el mes de julio de 1773 y el forzado traslado de la capital por orden superior al Valle de la Virgen, la actual Guatemala de la Asunción, provocó el casi total abandono de la ciudad. Muchas de sus construcciones fueron desmanteladas para utilizar la cantera en la edificación de la nueva capital; esta depredación ha continuado a través del tiempo, ya que hoy día siguen siendo muy apetecidas para construir "nuevas casas Coloniales" las piedras de sus banquetas, de los marcos de las casas señoriales, las repisas que forman el sillar de ventanas, y en general la piedra.

El congelamiento en el tiempo de Santiago, su casi abandono por cerca de cien años y luego su lenta repoblación iniciada con el auge del cultivo del café, la llevaron a adquirir características muy especiales. Así, se ha conservado como una ciudad del siglo XVIII, sin los cambios producidos por construcciones, desarrollos urbanos y arquitectónicos contemporáneos, y en general alteraciones de los siglos sucesivos. Esta situación la ha hecho famosa y se le han otorgado diversos títulos en las últimas cinco décadas, como el de Monumento Nacional en 1944 y Ciudad Emérita en 1958. Además, el gobierno de Guatemala en 1989 emitió un decreto para su protección (Luján 1974:31), y la UNESCO ha incluido a La Antigua Guatemala como patrimonio mundial (UNESCO 1979:12).

Todas estas circunstancias brindan una oportunidad magnífica para estudiar la organización y estructura de la industria del período Colonial en las comunidades y ciudades españolas.

Resumen de Investigaciones Previas

Académicos, estudiosos e instituciones encargadas que tratan con la conservación, desarrollo urbanístico y arquitectura en la capital del Reino, actualmente La Antigua Guatemala, en su mayoría han investigado los patrones de asentamiento, los complejos religiosos e iglesias, o bien se han circunscrito a documentar los conjuntos y edificios religiosos del lugar.

En este campo, el Consejo Nacional para la Protección de La Antigua Guatemala, ha elaborado una lista inicial con los nombres de las fincas, algunos puentes, y los acueductos principales que abastecían a Santiago; recientemente se ha efectuado un inventario de las cajas de agua, que servían para lograr la distribución del preciado líquido a través de la ciudad, ya que muchas de ellas aún existen dispersas dentro del tejido urbano. La Facultad de Arquitectura de la Universidad de San Carlos de Guatemala ha efectuado un reconocimiento de los tres principales acueductos; por otra parte, en la Municipalidad de Antigua se han localizado tres acuarelas hechas por el artista José Muñoz entre 1840 y 1843, las cuales son un reconocimiento visual de los acueductos citados.

Hay una serie de publicaciones recientes acerca de temas diversos asociados con Antigua Guatemala. Por ejemplo, el Dr. Luis Luján Muñoz ha publicado estudios acerca de las fuentes de la ciudad (1977) y las obras del Maestro Mayor de Arquitectura Diego de Porres (1982a) y un corto artículo sobre la fabricación de la cerámica vidriada o mayólica (1981). El Dr. Stephen Webre realizó un estudio de los tres principales abastecimientos de agua alrededor de Antigua (1990); el Lic. Manuel Rubio Sánchez analizó la producción de añil,

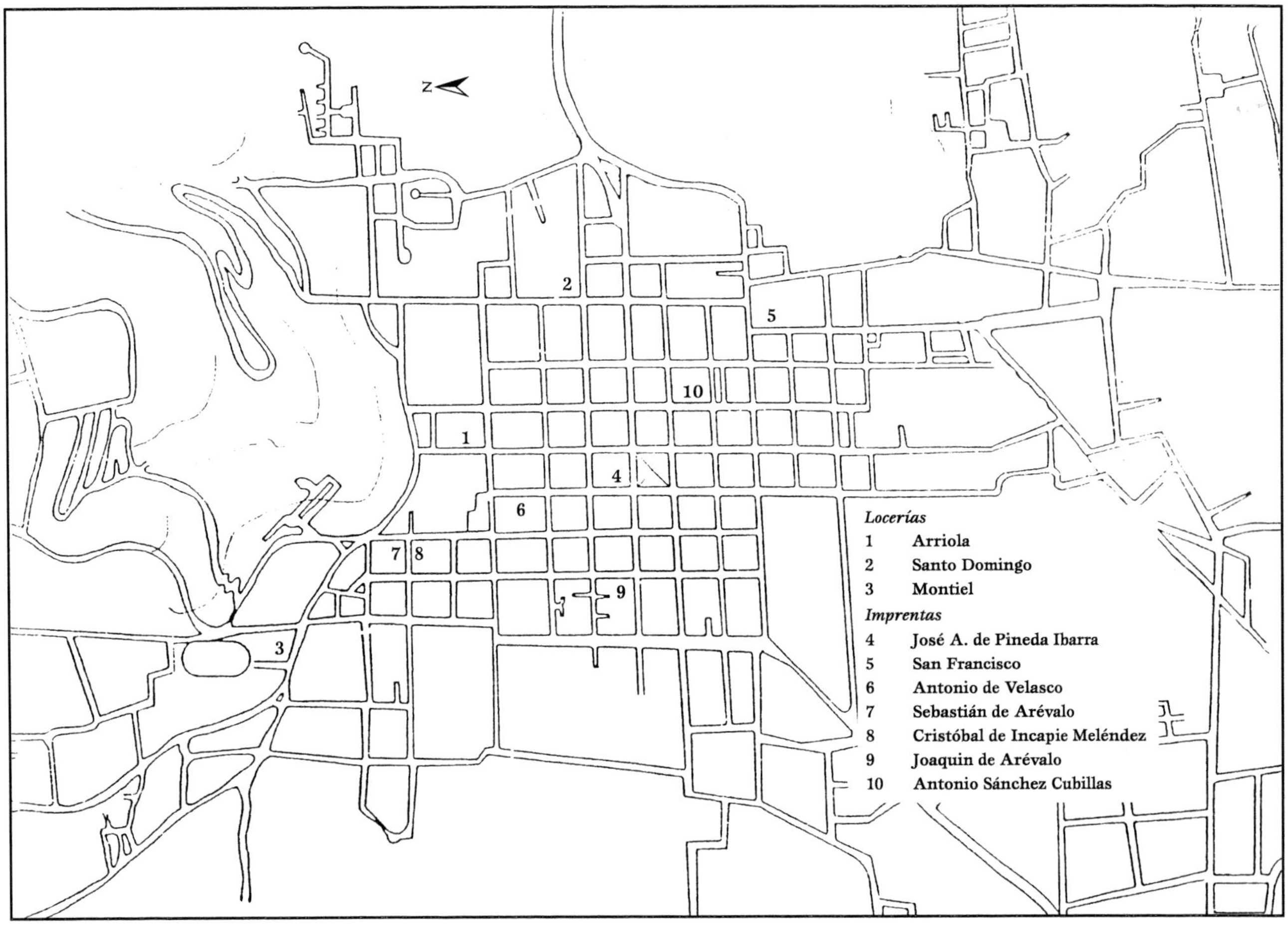
N
1
2
3
4
5
6
7
8
9
10
Locerías
1 Arriola
2 Santo Domingo
3 Montiel
Imprentas
4 José A. de Pineda Ibarra
5 San Francisco
6 Antonio de Velasco
7 Sebastián de Arévalo
8 Cristóbal de Incapie Meléndez
9 Joaquin de Arévalo
10 Antonio Sánchez Cubillas

FIGURA 8.2 Locerías e imprentas en Antigua Guatemala

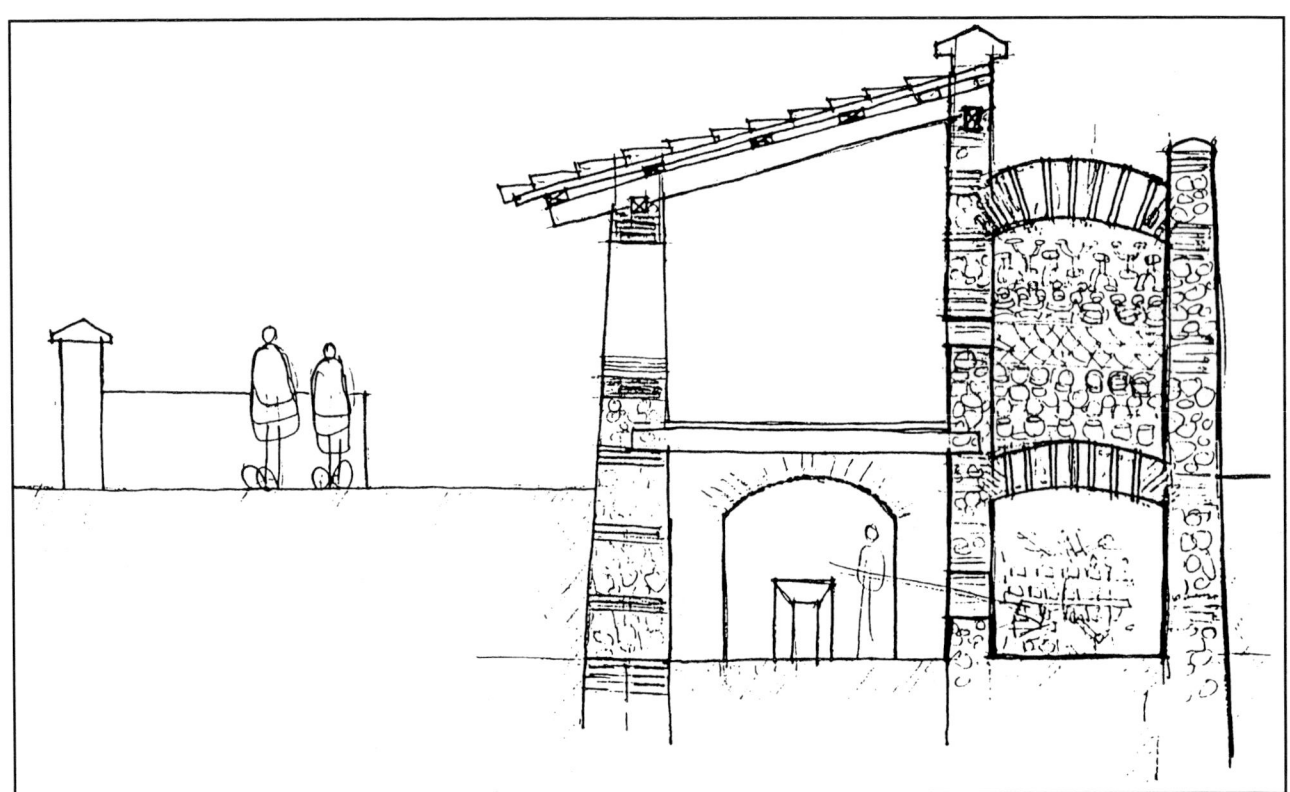

FIGURA 8.3 Un horno en Antigua Guatemala

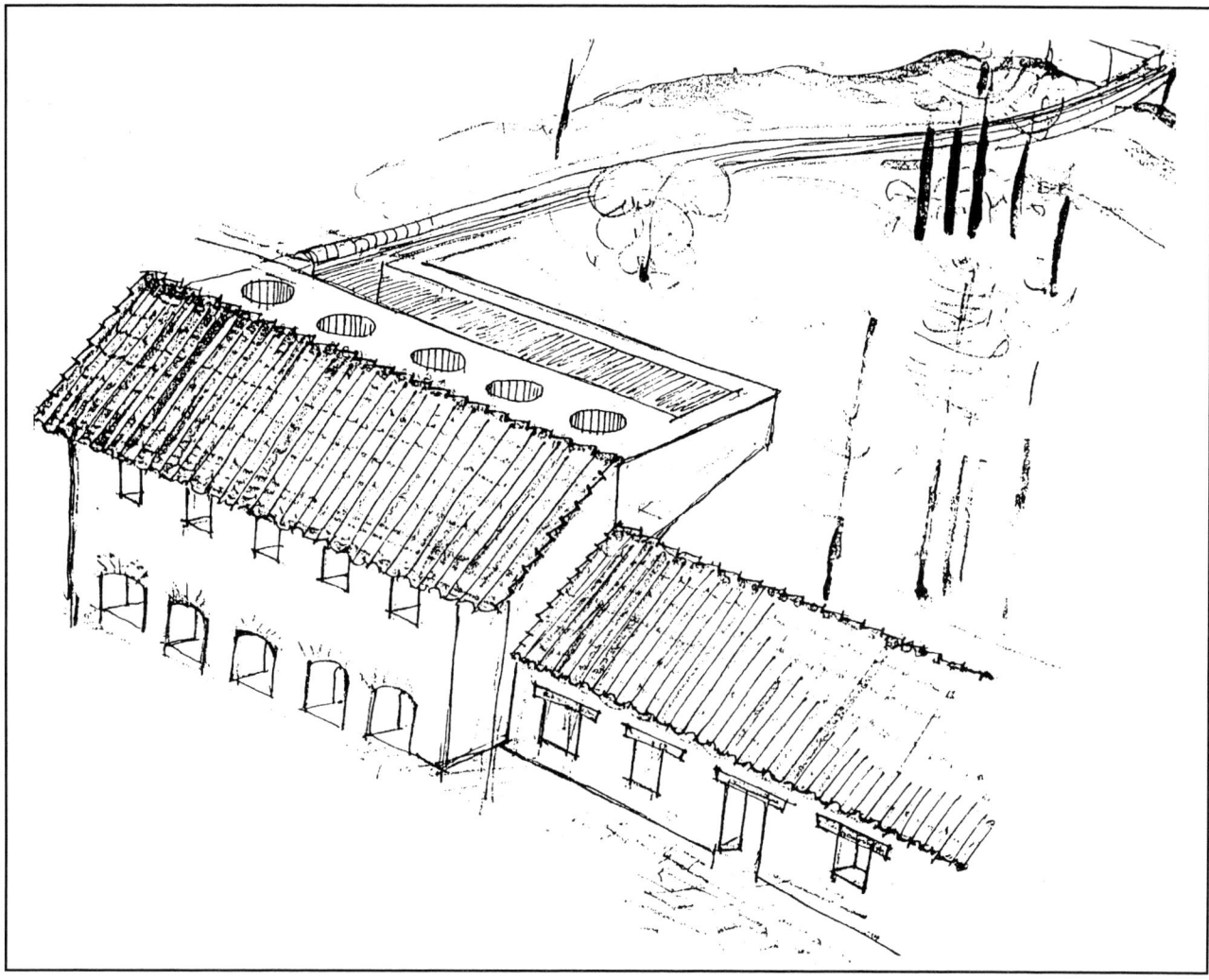

Figura 8.4 Perspectiva del molino Arrivillaga

cochinilla y otras industrias de la época Colonial (1989); el Lic. Jorge Luján Muñoz ha publicado trabajos acerca de actividades productivas Coloniales (1988), mientras que el Historiador Julio Pinto Soria ha llevado a cabo trabajos referentes a aspectos económicos (1988).

Resultados de esta Investigación, y Perspectivas a Futuro

Nuestra investigación pretende contribuir a conocer mejor las estructuras hasta ahora desatendidas. En las investigaciones de campo se han localizado nuevas evidencias relativas a la ubicación de asentamientos Coloniales y estructuras que no aparecen registrados en las fuentes históricas. En este proyecto se ha iniciado el estudio de las estructuras arquitectónicas, realizando un catálogo preliminar de al menos cincuenta complejos y edificios. Dicha catalogación se ha elaborado con base en la información existente en la literatura contemporánea, datos de historia oral y los propios reconocimientos de campo (véase el apéndice 8.1), al realizar el Catálogo de la Arquitectura y el Urbanismo de Sacatepéquez, Guatemala.

Se han ejecutado planos preliminares de su localización (figuras 8.1, 8.2, 8.7), esquemas gráficos (figuras 8.3–8.6, 8.8–8.10), descripciones y fotografías de algunas estructuras, además de realizar registros acerca de los sistemas constructivos utilizados. Paralelamente se han ejecutado propuestas de rescate, valorización, conservación, reutilización y/o revitalización de algunas de ellas. Se planea documentarlas sistemáticamente, buscando información histórica, y realizando documentación gráfica y fotográfica en forma sistemática.

A la fecha hemos podido localizar e identificar rutas históricas (figura 8.1 y apéndice 8.1) y algunos de sus respectivos componentes arquitectónicos, como paradores que servían para dar servicio a los viajeros que transitaban por ellas, localizándose bebederos para los viajeros y los animales que transportaban a éstos o jalaban carretas y carretones, y puentes utilizados para salvar accidentes geográficos como ríos y barrancas, construidos de mampostería con uno, dos o tres arcos (figura 8.1).

Además, se han ubicado camposantos o cementerios, los más primitivos a los costados de iglesias y ermitas, y

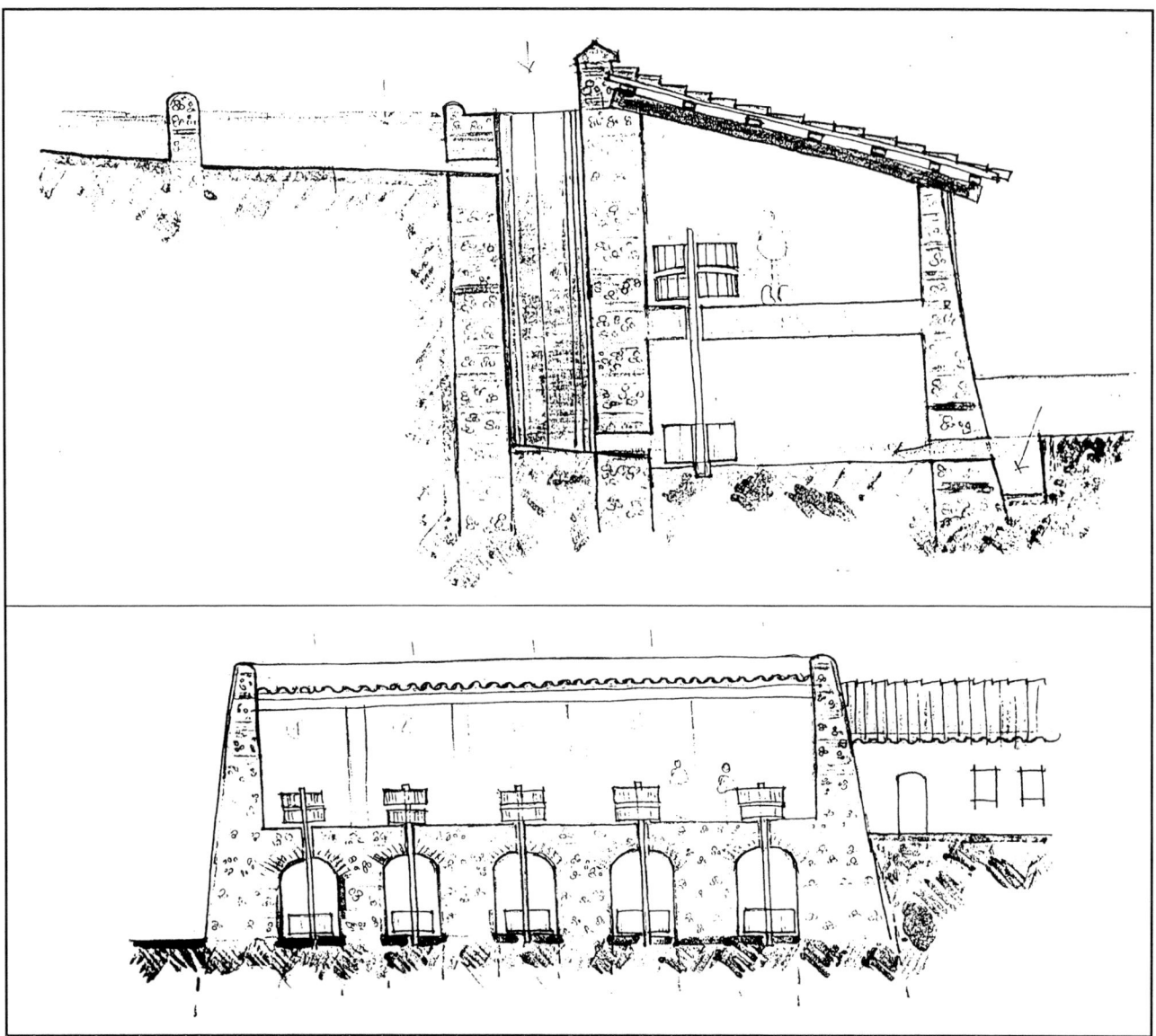

Figura 8.5 Secciones transversal (*superior*) y longitudinal (*inferior*) del molino de Arrivillaga

cementerios propiamente dichos, los cuales normalmente se localizan en lugares estratégicos cercanos o en montes o montañas vecinas a los poblados. También se encontraron fábricas de jabón y fábricas de cerámica conocidas en Antigua Guatemala como las locerías (figura 8.2), donde se producía cerámica vidriada, observándose aún hornos usados en la quema (figura 8.3).

Se ha realizado una amplia lista, la cual habrá que analizar en mayor detalle sobre las haciendas (figura 8.1) y sus componentes arquitectónicos como casas patronales, rancherías o casas del personal; puentes menores construidos en madera, así como sus respectivos abastecimientos de agua o acueductos menores; lecherías; complejos de la industria del azúcar como trapiches e ingenios (figura 8.1); instalaciones para extraer el añil y procesar la cochinilla (figura 8.1); imprentas (figura 8.2); rastros y tenerías (figura 8.7) y trojas; molinos de granos y de pólvora accionados éstos por agua que hacía mover ruedas ya fueran verticales u horizontales (figuras 8.4–8.7).

Cabe destacar en cuanto a los grandes sistemas de agua que abastecían la ciudad de Santiago con sus respectivos componentes arquitectónicos, que "era tan general la distribución de agua, que la mayor parte de las casas Coloniales ubicadas en la ciudad... poseían una fuente o un búcaro" (Annis 1968:28); el vital líquido era distribuido por gravedad (figura 8.1) hasta llegar a cajas de agua (figura 8.8), las cuales se ubicaban en cada manzana de la ciudad, y llegaba a su destino por medio de cañerías de barro cocido de dimensión variable. "Este sistema fue bastante adecuado para servir por más de cuatro siglos y todavía funcionaba bien en 1982 cuando fue sustituido por un sistema de presión con contadores" (Annis 1968:28–29). El sistema contaba además con una serie de estructuras y componentes adicionales como presas, cajas recolectoras, ataujía o acueducto propiamente

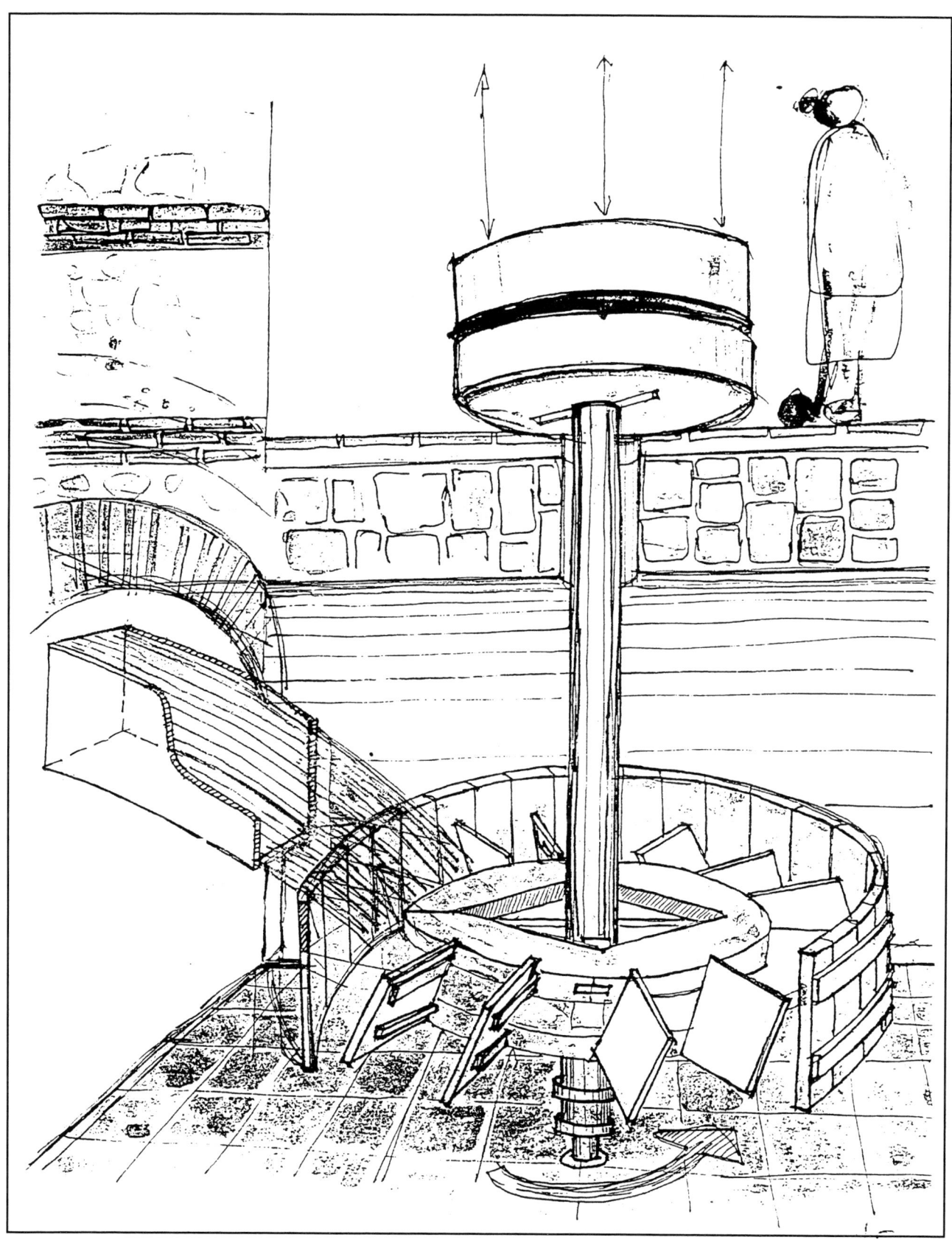

FIGURA 8.6 Perspectiva del mecanismo de molino de Arrivillaga

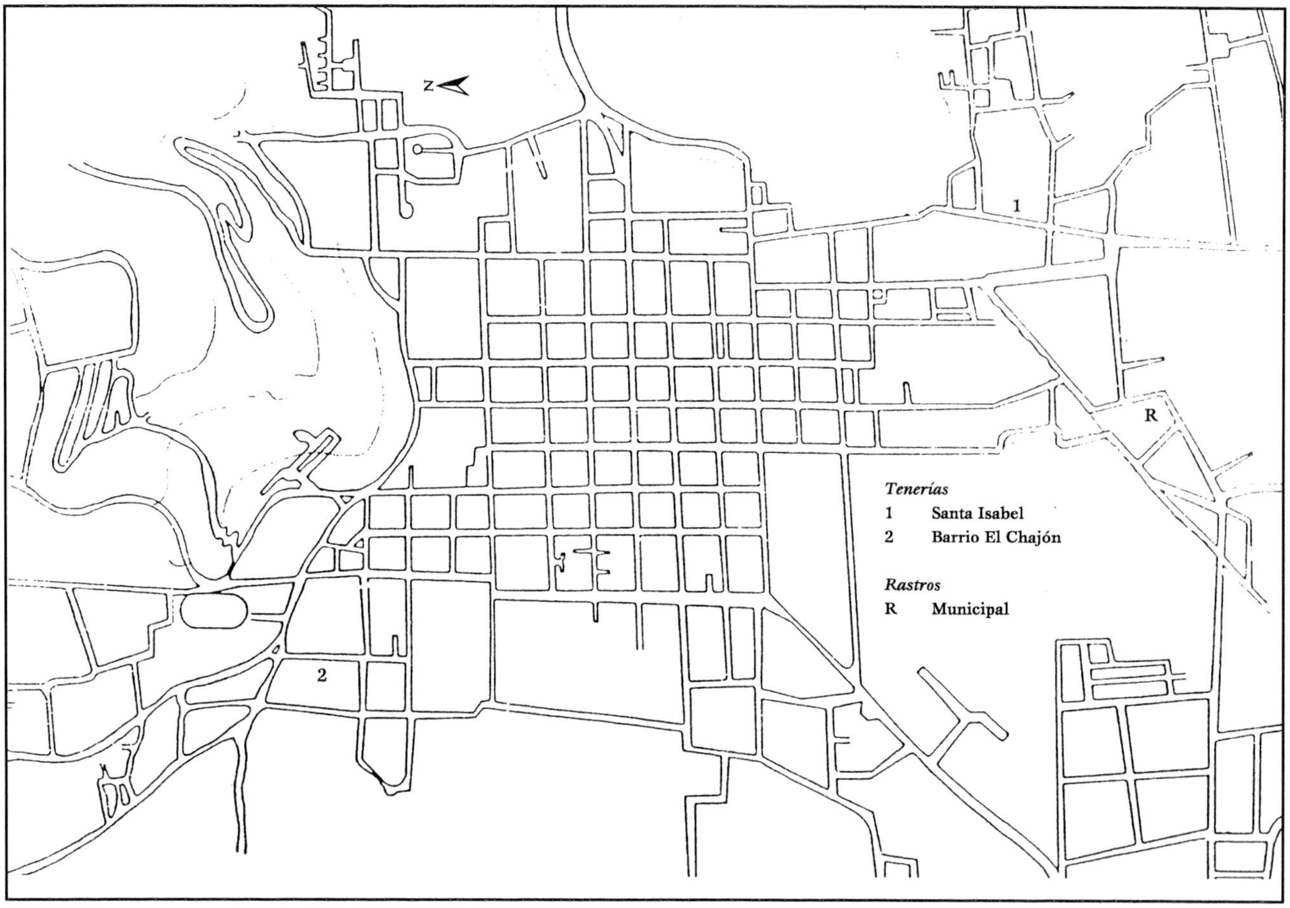

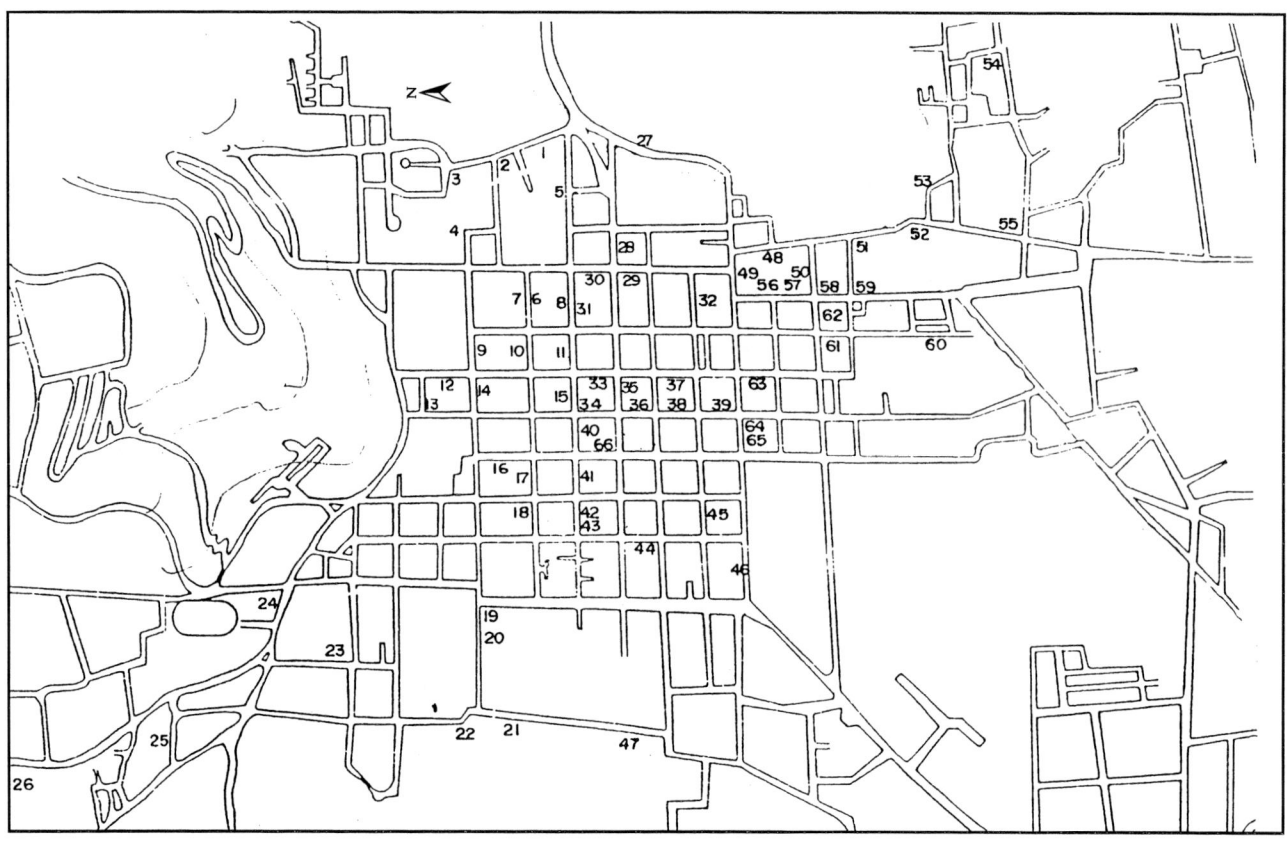

FIGURA 8.7 Ubicación de tenerías y rastros en Antigua Guatemala

FIGURA 8.8 Ubicación de cajas de agua en Antigua Guatemala

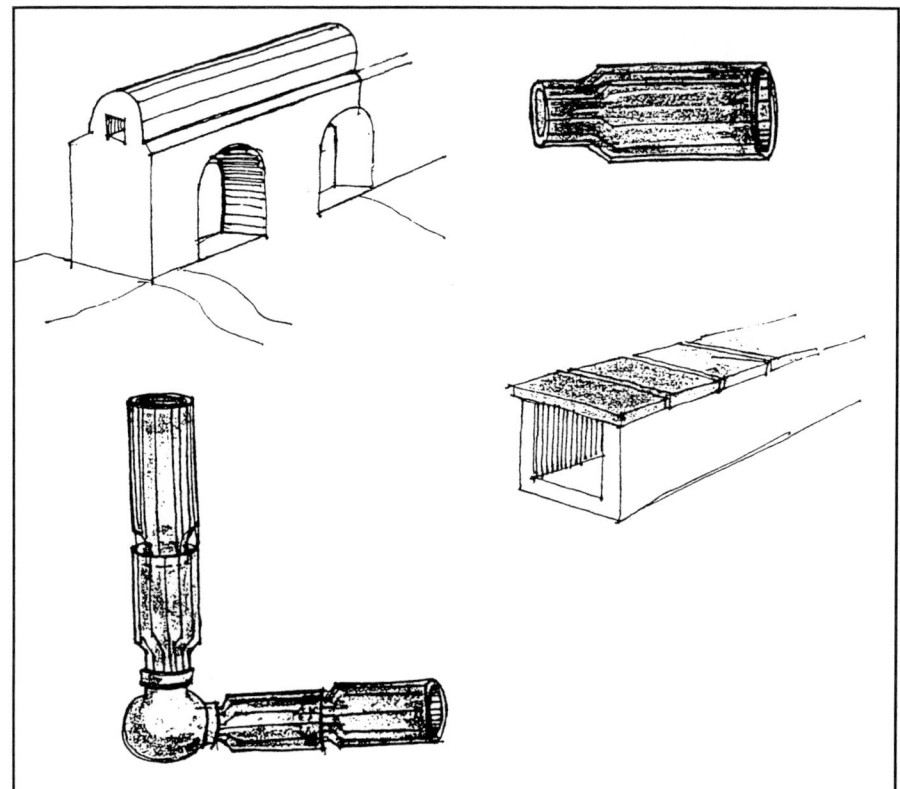

FIGURA 8.9 Detalles asociados con sistemas hidráulicos: *superior, izquierda,* acueducto; *inferior, izquierda,* conducción por tubería; *superior, derecha,* tubo de borro; *inferior, derecha,* ataujía

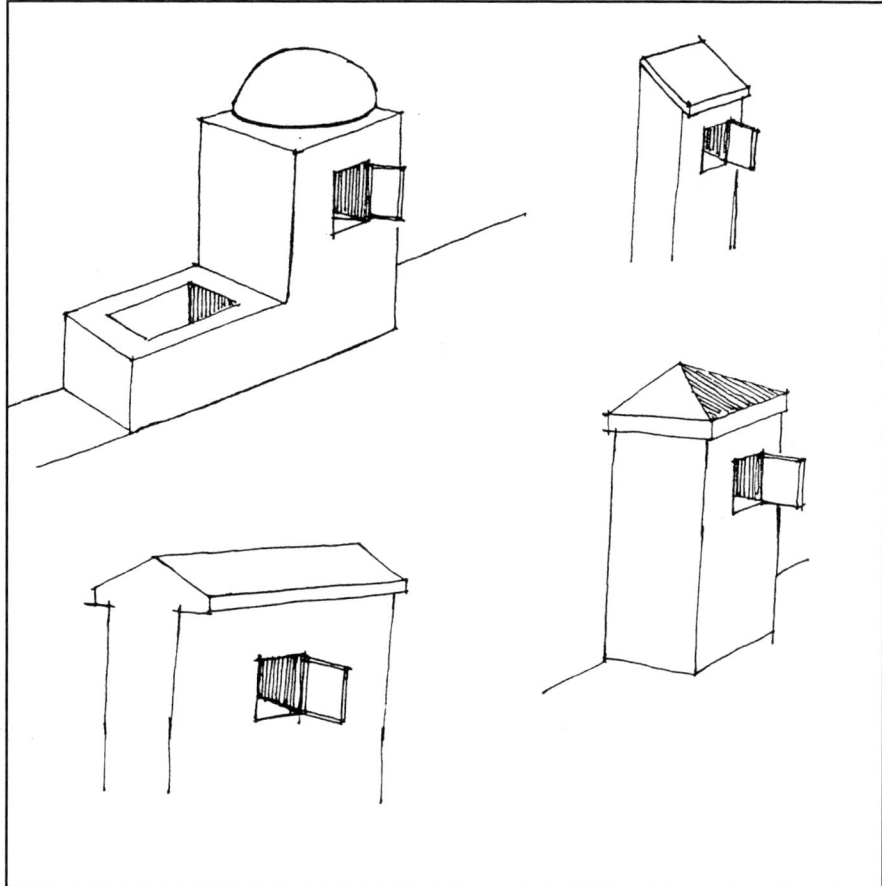

FIGURA 8.10 Tipos principales de cajas de agua: *superior, izquierda,* caja de agua y pila; *superior, derecha,* caja de agua; *inferior, izquierda,* caja adosada a un muro; *inferior, derecha,* caja

dicho, cajas de registro, desarenadoras, almacenadoras, de limpieza, sifones, rompe-presión, distribución o flautas, tapones, etcétera (figuras 8.9, 8.10). Asimismo, podemos encontrar otras estructuras auxiliares o complementarias para el servicio de la población, como los baños públicos y las pilas de lavar (figura 8.1); existen también estructuras que además de tener la función de contenedores de agua podrían usarse para embellecer y adornar la ciudad y sus edificios, como las fuentes y búcaros (figura 8.1).

La datación histórica de la arquitectura Colonial de Santiago ha sido determinada con base en un ciclo periódico de aproximadamente cincuenta años, determinado por la actividad sísmica: después de cada terremoto, los arquitectos experimentaron con nuevos materiales, nuevas técnicas constructivas y nuevos tipos de refuerzos, llegando a desarrollar y construir lo que los historiadores han denominado una arquitectura barroca asísmica (Kelemen 1967:13; Luján Muñoz 1972:1; Markman 1966:41).

Es común ver en los edificios de Santiago varias etapas constructivas en un solo elemento arquitectónico, únicamente adosando otra nueva etapa constructiva, muchas veces sin ni siquiera eliminar los antiguos revestimientos para lograr un buen anclaje entre la parte vieja y la nueva. La constante reconstrucción de las estructuras, así como la repetición a través del tiempo de los mismos sistemas constructivos, hace difícil determinar la edad de los edificios debido a la similitud de los materiales y métodos constructivos usados; es común ver en las estructuras de Santiago varias etapas constructivas en un mismo elemento arquitectónico, pues únicamente adosaban al antiguo elemento una nueva etapa del edificio, ya sea para repararlo y hacerlo más resistente si éste había sido dañado por un sismo, para ampliarlo si esto era necesario o para aplicar la decoración "de moda."

Con respecto a los métodos de construcción sabemos que al principio de la época Colonial los materiales fueron simples y pobres: se usó adobe y tapial para los muros, paja y artesonados de madera para las cubiertas. Algún tiempo después los muros se volvieron más gruesos y los arquitectos cubrieron sus edificios con bóvedas de cañón y bóvedas vaídas hechas de mampostería (Annis 1968:23; Luján Muñoz 1972:5; Markman 1966:42).

Las iglesias Coloniales de La Antigua Guatemala han sido fechadas con base en la decoración aplicada en sus fachadas, mayormente en los elementos verticales de soporte (columnas y pilastras), en el estuco o ataurique y en la capa de recubrimiento de piedra de sus fachadas. La adscripción cronológica de algunos edificios se ha hecho mediante la información encontrada en los documentos históricos Coloniales, básicamente en las solicitudes de materiales de construcción para la reparación de las mismas estructuras y en las solicitudes de pago a los trabajadores.

La diferencia en los tamaños de los ladrillos podría determinar diferentes épocas constructivas. Además, las construcciones que fueron realizadas de una sola vez, como los puentes de mampostería que no han sufrido mayores cambios ni modificaciones a través del tiempo, puedan dar alguna información al respecto.

El potencial histórico, arquitectónico y arqueológico y lo que podemos aprender de estos grandes complejos arquitectónicos o de las reminiscencias que aún existen de otros es inmenso. Muchas de estas estructuras han sobrevivido el paso del tiempo; algunas se conservan manteniendo su función original. Otras han desaparecido debido a su demolición, destrucción por los constantes terremotos y el subsecuente abandono; otras están ocultas bajo capas de remodelación y modernismo y muchas están sepultadas bajo los escombros de los mismos edificios, o de la arena de los desbordes y aluviones de los ríos y bajadas de agua de montañas y volcanes vecinos, quedando olvidadas después de su abandono.

Conclusiones

Esta investigación preliminar nos da a conocer el gran potencial que existe en el campo de la arqueología histórica en Guatemala, además de que demuestra la existencia de una gran cantidad de temas de estudio para profesionales en los campos de la historia, la arquitectura, la restauración, o en el del desarrollo mismo, que en gran medida hasta la fecha los han ignorado.

Las perspectivas a futuro incluyen no solamente posibilidades de investigación científica sino además un gran potencial en el sentido del aprovechamiento integral de estas evidencias para la educación cultural del guatemalteco y una gran fuente de explotación a través del turismo. Así, podría desarrollarse un programa planificando para el uso y aprovechamiento de los edificios y complejos arquitectónicos por medio de programas de rescate, valorización, restauración, conservación o reutilización de los mismos.

Estudios subsecuentes posibilitarán conocer aspectos adicionales de la vida económica Colonial en el Reino de Guatemala, además de que paralelamente será factible la preservación de monumentos históricos de La Antigua Guatemala.

Agradecimientos. Apreciamos la colaboración y la información que brindaran las siguientes personas: el Arq. Leonel Grajeda del Consejo Nacional para la Protección de La Antigua Guatemala, el Dr. William Swezey (QEPD), el Lic. Mario Álvarez, el Sr. Edgar Pérez, la Sra. Ana María Cofiño y la Profa. Elizabeth Bell, en Antigua Guatemala; el Sr. Adbel Guarán de San Antonio Aguas Calientes; el Sr. Antonio Núñez, administrador de la Finca Retana, San Bartolomé Becerra; el Dr. Christopher Lutz y la Plumsock Foundation.

Apéndice 8a
Conjuntos y estructuras arquitectónicas industriales y utilitarias en El Departmento de Sacatepéquez, Guatemala

Rutas históricas: Hemos tomado en consideración todos aquellos caminos que partiendo de Santiago, hoy La Antigua Guatemala, llevaban a otra población importante (véase la figura 8.1).

Fábricas de cerámica ("Locerías"): En un punto durante el período Colonial al menos seis fábricas producían cerámica vidriada hecha con torno en Antigua Guatemala (Sharer, Ashmore, y Hill 1970:2) y el mayor número de alfareros y talleres de alfarería registrados entre 1631–1773, registrados en fuentes documentales (Luján Muñoz 1982b:27; véase las figuras 8.2, 8.3). *Arriola* (sin uso actual; observaciones del autor): 4a Avenida Norte Pasaje Dolores o Calle del Obispo Marroquín Antigua Guatemala. La locería no se usa posiblemente desde los años 1920. Debido a su ubicación como parte del jardín de una casa en La Antigua, no se han destruido sus vestigios, los cuales son muchos; se conservan los dos hornos que la componían, el área para almacenar la leña y alimentar los hornos y otras estructuras asociadas con la misma. *Santo Domingo* (observaciones del autor): En terrenos del Complejo Santo Domingo Calle de la Nobleza y Calle de los Carros. *Montiel* (Luján Muñoz 1981; observaciones del autor): Ubicada en la Subidita a San Felipe 9 Barrio del Manchén, LaAntigua Guatemala. Es la única locería que aún se mantiene en uso en Antigua. Su forma de producción es la misma que se usaba en la época Colonial; desgraciadamente los actuales propietarios no están interesados en continuar la manufactura de cerámica, situación por la cual la locería funciona esporádicamente y está a punto de desaparecer.

Haciendas y sus componentes arquitectónicos ("Fincas"): En el caso de las fincas que pertenecen al municipio de Antigua Guatemala, se tienen registradas a la fecha 102, las cuales será necesario investigar para realizar un listado de estructuras de interés por su arquitectura (Markman 1966; véase la figura 8.1).

Imprentas: Los talleres de imprenta estuvieron ubicados dentro del tejido de la ciudad con excepción de los localizados en los conventos. La mayoría de estos talleres con toda seguridad no tuvieron grandes instalaciones arquitectónicas, exceptuando los mencionadas anteriormente, y en especial las ubicadas en San Francisco el Grande, en el cual hemos podido localizar el área donde se encontraban los diversos talleres que allí operaron; debido a esto es difícil ubicar con exactitud el lugar mediante reconocimientos de las casas existentes, sin embargo podrían ubicarse realizando investigaciones documentales (véase la figura 8.2).

Industria del azúcar ("Trapiches e ingenios"): En el valle central los trapiches "eran probablemenete medianos ingenios, y sólo dos o tres pueden catalogarse como tales" (Pinto Soria 1988) en el actual Departamento de Sacatepéquez (véase la figura 8.1).

Industria de la cochinilla (extinta): Véase la figura 8.1.

Molinos: Los molinos son accionados por agua y pueden ser de tipo horizontal o vertical (véase la figura 8.1). Según observaciones del autor, el molino de Arrivillaga (véanse las figuras 8.4–8.8) está ubicado en terrenos de la finca Chuito en una posición geográfica estratégica entre las poblaciones de San Lorenzo el Tejar, Chimaltenango y San Luis de las Carretas. El molino estaba conformado por cinco molinos y parece haber sido abandonado hace unos cien años; prácticamente ha sido devorado por la misma naturaleza, pues la vegetación ha ido creciendo y destruyendo lentamente todos sus vestigios, mas sin embargo no ha sido alterado por la mano del hombre. El molino está casi completo, existiendo los canales o tomas que se desvían del río para formar una caída, los canales, edificios, estanques, y los grandes silos que servían para darle presión al agua que hacía girar las piedras que molían el grano. Éstas se encuentran aún in situ, haciendo falta únicamente dos de las diez piedras que formaban los cinco molinos. En el cuarto de moler tan sólo hace falta la estructura del techo y su cubierta. También se encuentra en perfecto estado el sitio donde se ubicaban las ruedas, en este caso horizontales. El complejo sería fácilmente rescatable debido a que existen todos sus vestigios para restaurarlo.

Puentes de mampostería: Véase la figura 8.1.

Rastros: *Rastro Municipal de Antigua:* Localizado en el extremo sur de la ciudad, a inmediaciones del Río Pensativo; el rastro sigue en uso, siendo un complejo de grandes dimensiones donde se mata ganado mayor y menor, debido a su ubicación cercano al Río Pensativo y al final del Callejón del Rosito. El complejo seguramente ha sido asolvado por las constantes inundaciones del río y las bajadas de agua y arena que provienen de Santa Ana, Santa Isabel y San Cristóbal el Bajo, correntadas que bajan por el Callejón antes mencionado; debido a estos factores las posibilidades de realizar estudios arqueológicos en el complejo son muy grandes. Véase las figuras 8.1, 8.7.

Sistemas de agua: *Acueductos:* véanse las figuras 8.1, 8.8–8.10). *Baños públicos:* véase la figura 8.1. *Fuentes:* véase la figura 8.1 y Luján Muñoz 1977. *Pilas de lavar* ("lavaderos"): véase la figura 8.1. *Presas:* véase la figura 8.1.

Tenerías: Véanse las figuras 8.1, 8.7.

Chapter 9

The Mercedarians and the Missionization of the Lenca in Santa Bárbara de Tencoa, Honduras

Nancy Johnson Black

Abstract

The missionary operations and objectives of the Mercedarian Order influenced their encounter with the indigenous Lenca Indian population of western Honduras during the sixteenth through mid-eighteenth centuries. This chapter investigates factors and conditions in a frontier province in Mesoamerica during the Colonial period in order to provide an analysis of missionization processes at the local level. Such an examination may help to explain patterns of indigenous cultural continuity, change, and adaptive responses to Spanish colonialism, as well as infer the manner in which Indians and conditions in frontier areas shaped mission systems over time.

Resumen

Las operaciones misioneras y los objetivos de la orden mercedaria influyeron en su encuentro con la población indígena lenca del oeste de Honduras, desde el siglo XVI hasta mediados del XVIII. En este capítulo se estudian los factores y condiciones prevalecientes en una provincia fronteriza de Mesoamérica durante el periodo Colonial, con la finalidad de presentar un análisis de los procesos misioneros en el nivel local. Este examen puede ayudar a explicar de forma adecuada los patrones de continuidad cultural, cambio y respuestas adaptativas de los indígenas ante el colonialismo español, así como a inferir la manera en que los indios y las condiciones en áreas fronterizas le dieron forma a los mismos sistemas de misiones a través del tiempo.

THIS CHAPTER explores aspects of the interaction between members of the Mercedarian Order and the Lenca Indians during the Colonial period in Santa Bárbara de Tencoa, a frontier region of western Honduras. Previous research has examined pre-Hispanic Lenca social organization and the initial encounter between the Spaniards and the Lenca (Chapman 1978, 1985:39–86; Lara Pinto: 1985, 1991; Newson 1986; Stone 1948:195; Weeks, Black, and Speaker 1987; Weeks and Black 1991). Chapter 10 describes the archaeological investigation of the Lenca in the Santa Bárbara de Tencoa region, providing additional information about the historically defined mission stations organized by the Mercedarian Order.

An important avenue for research on Colonial Middle America is the role of the regular clergy during the initial encounter between Spaniards and native peoples and the subsequent colonization process. In its desire to expand its sphere of influence, the Spanish Crown sent more than fifteen thousand missionaries to the Americas from the time of Columbus' second voyage in 1493 to Spanish-American independence in the early nineteenth century (Van Oss 1986:181). Especially in frontier regions, the missions of the Catholic church were the dominant institution responsible for the maintenance of Colonial rule. In these regions, the initial task of Christianization of the indigenous population was entrusted to the regular clergy, such as the Dominicans, Augustinians, Franciscans, Mercedarians, and later the Jesuits. *Doctrinas* (Indian parishes) established by the mendicant orders have been singled out as having had a great impact on local indigenous populations (Chance 1986:173).

At the beginning of the evangelization process, regular orders tended to think that the Indians could best be nurtured and protected by limiting contact between Spaniards (other than themselves) and the natives. Members of the regular clergy tried to interpose themselves between Indian communities and Spanish settlers, and, by learning native languages themselves, hoped to keep "outside" contacts to a minimum. As a result, in frontier areas such as western Honduras, regular clergy served as intermediaries or "culture brokers" linking central authority to the local populations.

Tensions between missionaries and the indigenous peoples of Mexico and Central America were inherent in the evangelization process and in the establishment of Colonial society. An increasingly valuable area of research is the examination of these tensions at the level of local social processes. In the study area of western Honduras, a relatively small group of individuals from a single institution, the Order of Our Lady of Mercy for the Ransom of Captives (known officially as Ordo Beatae Maria

Virginis de Mercede Redemptionis Captivorum, but commonly referred to as the Mercedarian Order), played an important role in the cultural transformation of the indigenous Lenca population. Mission accounts may be used to better explain patterns of indigenous cultural continuity, change, and adaptive responses to Spanish colonialism as well as to infer ways in which native groups and conditions in frontier areas, in turn, shaped the mission system.

Documentary Sources

Ecclesiastical records, a rich source for reconstructing the social fabric of Colonial Latin America, have been utilized successfully by both anthropologists and historians (Borges Morán 1977; Clendinnen 1987; Farriss 1968; Marzal 1981, 1983; Schwaller 1985, 1987; Van Oss 1986). Little has been published concerning the Mercedarian Order in this region, however, compared to the Dominicans, whose activities in the Audiencia of Guatemala are well documented by that order's chroniclers, Remesal and Ximénez (Placer-López 1968–1983). More recently twentieth-century historians and a few anthropologists have examined Mercedarian activities in northern Central America. For example, Wasserstrom (1983) presents one view of early Mercedarian activities in Chiapas, Mexico; Collins' (1980:148–155) documentary ethnography on the Jacaltenango region discusses early Mercedarian activities in western Guatemala; and Van Oss (1986:31–35, 137–142) delimits Mercedarian territory through an investigation of parish history in Colonial Guatemala. In general, however, the activities and influence of the Mercedarian Order have been largely ignored in northern Central America.

Investigators have been relatively unsuccessful in finding historical information in local archives pertinent to Early Colonial activities of the Mercedarian Order in Honduras (Cruz Reyes et al. 1986). These archives include the Archivo Nacional de Honduras, Archivo del Poder Judicial, Archivo de la Catedral de Tegucigalpa, Archivo Eclesiástico de Comayagua, Biblioteca del Instituto de Antropología e Historia, Biblioteca Nacional, and Biblioteca de la Universidad Nacional Autónoma de Honduras. Finney has called attention to the absence of information on religious institutions in Honduras during Colonial times and has referred to extant material as "the somewhat nebulous influence of the Catholic church which has come down in bits and pieces" (1985:50).

In fact, historical material for the sixteenth and seventeenth centuries for the Tencoa region of western Honduras is generally scarce. Many factors have contributed to the lack of historical records in areas such as Tencoa. Considerable disruption in administration and record-keeping during the Colonial period resulted from natural disasters such as floods, fires, earthquakes, and epidemics and from lack of personnel. This lacuna has hampered research, and, until quite recently, many aspects of the Early Colonial period in Honduras have not been investigated and are terra incognita in comparison with other Central American regions such as Guatemala (MacLeod 1985:14).

Documentary evidence for missionary activities in the Tencoa region during the Colonial period would be quite meager were it not for the Archivo de los Padres Mercedarios de Guatemala (AMERGUA) and to a lesser extent the Archivo General de Centro America in Guatemala City. AMERGUA contains extensive documentation for the Mercedarian province in the Audiencia of Guatemala which was established in 1563. The Mercedarian province of Guatemala, *La Provincia de Nuestra Senora de la Merced Redención de Cautivos de la Presentación de Guatemala*, consisted of Guatemala, Chiapas (Mexico), El Salvador, Nicaragua, and Honduras.

In general, the archival material includes *probanzas* (investigations of an individual's conduct in office), *visitas* (inspections), censuses, and information concerning the reduction of indigenous peoples of the region. In addition, with a few quirks in the archival record, the complete records of the triennial reports of the *Capítulos Provinciales* exist for the period 1645 through 1757. Materials relating to Mercedarian personnel in the Audiencia include records of *Patentes* (1678–1712), *Hábitos* (1683–1791), and *Professiones* (1756–1828). Information regarding the visitas (1673–1808) refers to the objectives of the pastoral inspections, but also includes data concerning alms collected for redemptions, the actions of various religious personnel and their functions, the internal hierarchy of the order, and the construction of churches and convents. The broad focus is on the rules and regulation of behavior of the priests as opposed to information concerning the native groups, particularly the role of indigenous women.

Because the capital of Guatemala served as the dominant ecclesiastical and secular authority in northern Central America during the Colonial period, and because the regular orders had their principal seats in its capital, the emphasis of the materials is on the concerns and dominance of the administrative center of the Mercedarian Order located in the capital city, Santiago de Guatemala. More distant frontier areas, such as Tencoa, frequently were mentioned only in passing.

The Mercedarian Order

An account of the history of the so-called spiritual conquest of the Lenca people of western Honduras primarily involves the activities of the Mercedarian Order, a regular order that developed in Spain during the thirteenth century. Their involvement in the ransom or rescue of captive Christians from Muslim territory in Africa gave them a unique identity among the religious orders. An order that lives collectively by the rule of solemn vows of chastity, obedience, and poverty, the Mercedarian Order is distinguished by its fourth vow, *el voto de sangre* (vow of blood). This fourth vow of redemption or salvation was fulfilled either by paying ransom in monies they collected or by exchanging their lives for Christian captives within Muslim territory (Fortunato 1982:18). The number of Christians freed in exchange for Mercedarians in North Africa totaled approximately eighty thousand at the time of the last redemption in 1803 (Instituto Histórico de La Orden de La Merced 1986:351). Given the military association of the order, Mercedarian friars were appropriate chaplains to the conquistadores, and almost every expedition of importance to the Americas had a Mercedarian chaplain. A new interpretation of the specifics of the fourth vow of the order evolved at this time, so that those who came to the Americas did not come to redeem captives in the previous sense but to give form and focus to the new activities. In the countries colonized by the Spanish, the establishment of Mercedarian convents was guided by two objectives: to moderate the excesses of the conquistadores and to promote the Christian faith among the indigenous populations by imparting the principles of salvation and European culture (Vásquez Nuñez 1931).

Mercedarian expansion in Latin America was rapid. It was the first order to begin missionary work in western Honduras during the mid-sixteenth century, forming a human network that lasted into the eighteenth century. At the time of the formal establishment of its first missions in Honduras in 1552, the entire Mercedarian Order consisted of 106 convents with 934 religious members; of those, seven convents and fifty-four religious members were located in Central America (Vásquez Nuñez 1931). The distribution of the Mercedarian convents and their dependencies within the Audiencia of Guatemala in 1700 is illustrated in figure 9.1. Today, the total population is much reduced and estimated at 500 members, with only one house consisting of two members in Honduras (Actas del Capítulo General 1979:289).

Religious Administration in Colonial Honduras

The Spanish conquest of Honduras began in 1524, but it was not until 1539 that the Spaniards achieved military control. The region was administered under the Audiencia de los Confines, which was established in 1544, and later under the Audiencia de Guatemala (Chamberlain 1953:2).

During the Early Colonial period, the church in Honduras was not in a propitious position for a variety of reasons and had difficulty in complying with the government's wishes concerning resettlement of the indigenous population. The mountainous land held few economic attractions, human resources had been extremely diminished by the protracted conquest, and the remaining indigenous population was hostile. With relatively few Indians scattered throughout the region, communication, economic production, and evangelization were difficult. Without Indian labor, the mines and fields could not function, and the church could not become viable.

Ecclesiastical affairs initially were centered in Trujillo, but by the middle of the sixteenth century they had been shifted inland to Comayagua. The number of religious personnel in Honduras in 1550, as reported by Alonso López de Cerrato, president of the Audiencia of Guatemala, consisted of only three secular priests and one friar who did not administer to the indigenous population (Reina Valenzuela 1983:141). In general, members of the secular clergy did not readily engage in apostolic missionizing among the indigenous population; they preferred to meet the spiritual needs of the Spanish colonists in the cities and to satisfy their own material needs.

In Honduras, the bishop supervised all clergy, secular and regular, and it was necessary for the regular clergy to secure his permission to enter various regions to evangelize. Royal *cédulas* (decrees) of 1557 and 1558 instructed the Audiencia of Guatemala to keep the convents of different orders separated by a distance of at least six leagues outside the cities to minimize competition for territory and to reach more of the native population (Remesal 1966). The general pattern of the numbers of missionaries sent by the Crown reflects increased prosperity of the regular orders, favorable general economic activity during the Colonial period, and support of the Spanish monarchy. Therefore, the greatest number of missionaries were sent in the latter half of the sixteenth century, with an additional resurgence during the 1660s (Borges Morán 1977). Mercedarian and Franciscan missionaries laid the foundation for Christian conversion and carried out the major portion of evangelization in Honduras. In general, the Mercedarian missions were located in the western and central regions of Honduras, and the Franciscans concentrated their missionary efforts in eastern Honduras. Although the Mercedarians founded the earliest missions in Honduras and covered the most geographic territory, the Franciscans, who did not arrive until the 1570s, are generally credited with more conversions (Reina Valenzuela 1983:167).

Historical and philosophical differences governed the actions of the different religious orders, and the orders themselves changed through time. There is general agreement that a gradual deterioration in the quality and dedication of the European priests arriving in the Americas occurred over the Colonial period. Speaking broadly, early missionaries were not simple friars but were among the better educated Spaniards and noted for their zealous religious convictions. In addition, many Mercedarians had endured hard training as missionaries in the Muslim areas of Spain and Africa and were physically and mentally disciplined. After initial mass conversions of the indigenous population, evangelization activities gave way to more administrative concerns in the population centers, especially those of a financial nature. The very success of the mendicant orders led to a lessening of support by the Crown, which issued a series of decrees curbing their authority. The historical circumstances affecting the Catholic clergy directly influenced the number and role of missionaries in Latin America. This situation was exacerbated by the Mercedarian Order's neglect

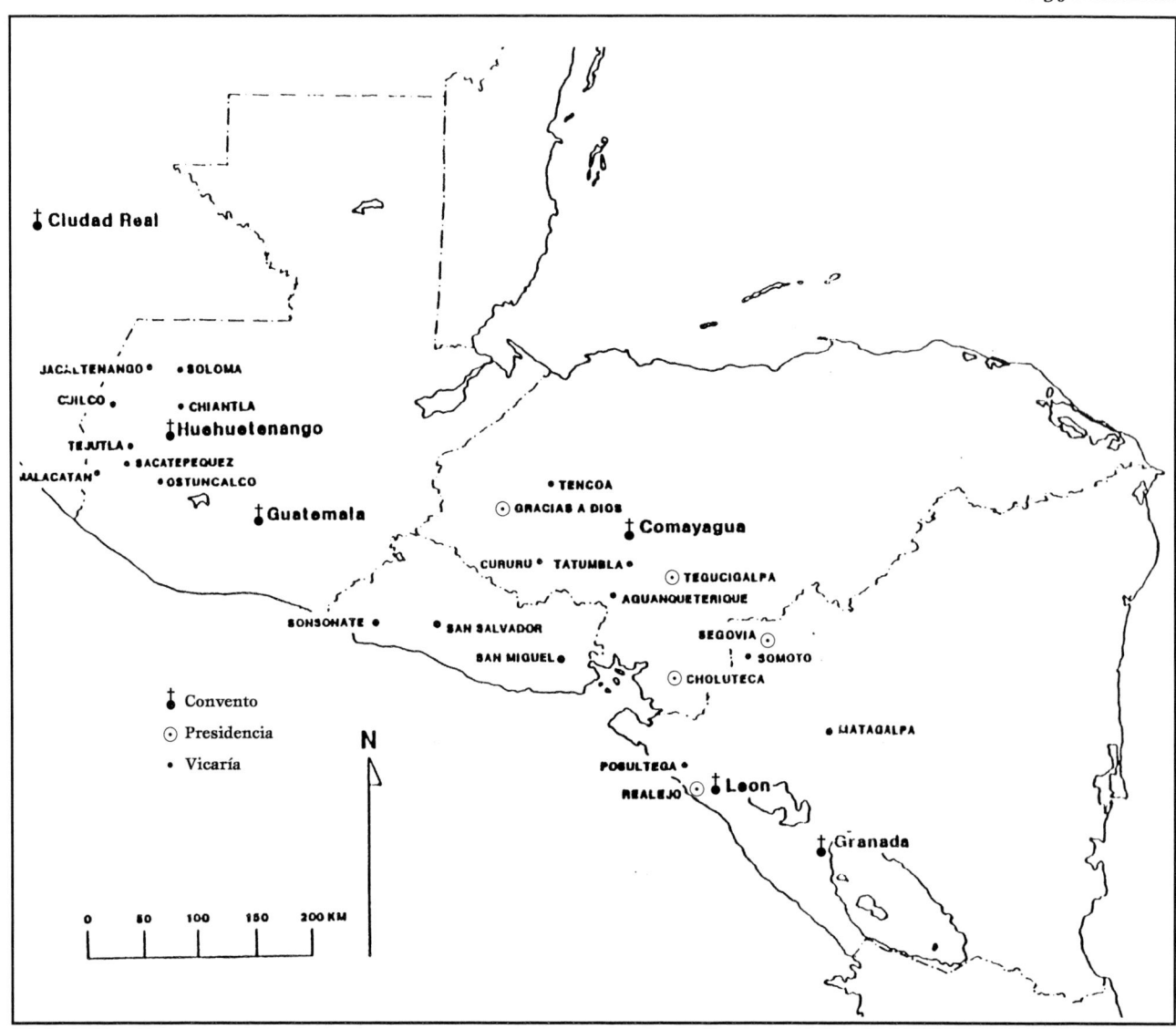

FIGURE 9.1 Colonial Central America and location of Mercedarian *presidencias* (a Mercedarian house having less than the required eight religious members to meet the daily obligations of mass, not located within encomienda territory, independent of the authority of a comendador and directly under the jurisdiction of the governing body in Guatemala), *conventos* (convent or monastery), and *vicarías* (a Mercedarian house having less than the required eight religious members to meet the daily obligations of mass, usually located within the encomienda territory and attached to a specific convent under the jurisdiction of the comendador), circa 1700. *Illustration by John M. Weeks*

of Indian vocations for the priesthood. As a result, the church did not have a broad base of support in northern Central America from which to draw much-needed personnel.

During the Early Colonial period, the secular clergy often were more reluctant than members of the regular orders to come to frontier areas. Secular clergy were not bound by vows of poverty and obedience and were accustomed to better material conditions of life than regular clergy; as a result, they were not as readily inclined to leave Spain (Borges Morán 1977:69-71). Not only were they insufficient in number but in many cases they also lacked competence to attempt the massive task of Christian conversion in the Americas (Ricard 1966:111). Further, during the early period, clergy in Spain had heard conflicting information concerning economic resources and conditions in Honduras, and it was known that the natives had not been pacified completely.

As an incentive for departure from Spain, as well as a means of controlling the activities of the regular orders in the Americas, the Crown paid the expenses for sending missionary personnel, and no member of the clergy could travel to the Indies or return from there without royal permission. To give consistency to the missions, royal decree prohibited clerics from returning to Spain for ten years. This same period of ten years was initially envisioned by the Spanish Crown as the necessary transition period for the regular clergy to missionize the indigenous population. By that time, it was surmised that the indigenous population would have been turned over to the secular clergy and would have become integrated into Colonial society with the obligations of paying tribute and providing labor services. Missionaries were then to move on to more remote areas and establish new missions.

The mission illustrates the intimate relationship between programs promoted by the Catholic church and the secular wishes of the Spanish Crown. Not only did missionaries receive annual salaries and substantial initial grants for supplies and construction of mission establishments from the royal treasury, but they were also frequently accompanied and assisted by Spanish military personnel. Because expenses for *presidios* (forts) and missions were charged to the same financial account, the *Ramo de Guerra* (war fund), there is little doubt as to the intentions of the Spanish government.

Spanish authorities sought to implement Christian instruction through the policy of *congregación* (forced resettlement) within Honduras. Royal decrees in 1538 and 1540 directed that towns, known as *pueblos de indios*, be formed and that Indians be gathered into them by persuasion or through force if necessary[1] (see chapter 10). Mission towns were designed to give converts not simply salvation through Christian conversion but also new identities and allegiances. Missionaries became political, economic, and social agents who helped extend, control, and Europeanize the Colonial periphery (Gibson 1966).

From the latter half of the seventeenth century onward, the triennial reports are replete with fears of impending secularization of Mercedarian doctrinas. In Tencoa, the last Mercedarian priest served in 1773. For Honduras, complete secularization did not occur until 3 November 1829 with a decree of the Legislative Assembly following independence from Spain.

Mercedarian Activities

One of the earliest references to a religious presence in Tencoa is a 1539 report concerning Cristóbal Pedraza's election as bishop of the diocese of Honduras (Remesal 1966:413). Fray Jerónimo de Corella, who followed Pedraza as bishop, visited Tencoa in 1556 and stayed in the convent of Nuestra Señora de la Merced where he was well received. Although they are not mentioned by name, two Mercedarian missionaries attended him. Other sources indicate that these individuals were almost certainly Fray Nicolas del Valle and Fray Alonso Dávila. In Corella's 1559 report to the Crown, he commented on the difficulties of managing the terrain and travel and of carrying provisions over the mountainous region, as well as "la plaga de mosquitos y otros animales..." (*Relacíon hecha al Rey año 1559*, Fray Jerónima de Corella, AGI, quoted in Reina Valenzuela 1983:149).

Honduras remained a religious frontier compared with Mexico, which reportedly had more than eight hundred regular clergy and 160 convents established by 1559, as well as a considerable number of secular clergy (Ricard 1966:22). Secular and religious interests sometimes clashed, however. In 1554, for example, the governor of Honduras complained to the king that the Mercedarians were instilling obedience among the Indians to their order and not to secular authorities and accused the Mercedarians of using corporal punishment to effect compliance (Tojeira 1986:45).

With increasing political stability in Honduras after 1550, the Mercedarian Order in Santiago de Guatemala was asked to send members to evangelize in Honduras because of the great scarcity of clergy. In response to a petition from President Cerrato of the Audiencia of Guatemala, Fray Marcos Pérez Dardán, vicar provincial of the Guatemalan convent of Mercedarians, was ordered to found three houses in Honduras, at Comayagua, Gracias a Dios, and Tencoa (Castro Seaone 1943:419). The Christian conversion of the Lenca began at Comayagua in 1552 with the founding of the first Mercedarian convent (Carias 1985:63; chapter 10). Missionization efforts continued with the establishment of the two additional convents at Gracias a Dios and Tencoa in 1554.

The basic structure of Mercedarian frontier missions consisted of the *partido* (mission district) with a single *cabecera de doctrina* (headquarters church) and a number of *visitas* (or outlying towns) that were cared for by the priests resident at the cabecera. Missions with resident priests were called doctrinas; villages in which no priest resided but which served as satellites of a doctrina were called pueblos de indios or visitas. The Mercedarian mission objective was to establish a relationship with the Lenca in pueblos de indios within frontier regions such as Tencoa.

Tencoa began as a cabecera de doctrina, as did the majority of Mercedarian centers. This administrative center was located among villages that had been created for the purpose of religious administration. The Colonial policy of congregation, so important in the reduction of other Indian groups such as the Maya, does not appear to have been easily implemented in the Tencoa region, however. Congregación had obvious advantages for missionaries because, if the indigenous population was grouped together, fewer priests would be needed for their spiritual and worldly administration. This practice facilitated the evangelization task of the missionaries, as well as their more secular duties involving the compilation of population, tribute, and labor lists (Lovell 1985:75–94; MacLeod 1973:120–142). Congregación is also credited with having the unforeseen consequence of contributing to Indian population loss through epidemic disease. Nevertheless, congregación was seen as necessary because of the dispersed settlement pattern of the Lenca population and the shortage of trained clergy in Honduras. Because of the poverty in Tencoa, many villages could not provide sufficient food and services to support visiting priests for any length of time.

The Mercedarian friars who were assigned to the partido of Tencoa appear to have been serving more as parish priests than as cloistered monks. The word *convento* in reference to describing the early mission center at Tencoa cannot be translated as monastery, friary, or convent because it appears to have been none of these. In 1700, it was mandated that all regular orders have at least eight members in residence to hold the status and privileges of a convent and receive significant financial support from the Crown (Black 1989:314). After that date, Tencoa was reduced to the status of *vicaria* (vicarage) while it remained under Mercedarian control.

Briefly, the evangelization duties of these missionaries included the Christian instruction of the Indians, administration of some of the sacraments, and suppression of such practices as idolatry, witchcraft, and concubinage. From their experiences among indigenous populations elsewhere in the Americas, the order devised a plan for missionizing that embraced organization, tools, and supplies adapted to the varying local conditions and groups. Friars introduced European plants and animals and modified methods of cultivation for indigenous subsistence crops such as corn. Indeed, accounts of priests' suffering from not having wheat bread to eat are frequent in the documents. Indians were to support mission efforts by building churches, providing goods and services for the friars, contributing alms for redemption, and making donations for services such as marriages and burials. Detailed information concerning the organization of Lenca labor in the Mercedarian missions is scant, however (Newson 1986:199).

By the end of the sixteenth century, the Mercedarian province of Guatemala had approximately two hundred friars residing in sixteen convents. At that time, the partido of Santa Bárbara de Tencoa consisted of eleven pueblos de indios serving a Christian population of 1,100 with three Mercedarian priests in residence (Samayoa Guevara 1957). As a frontier location distant from the Guatemala headquarters, friars in Honduras were frequently isolated for long periods of time. Undoubtedly, frontier conditions affected the health and life span of priests. Documentary evidence includes repeated requests for additional religious personnel and supplies. Despite an acute shortage of personnnel, a strict separation in terms of race and class was maintained between the religious specialists of the Mercedarian Order and the indigenous Lenca population. Requirements concerning legitimacy and non-Indian birth for admission to study for the priesthood continued to be strictly enforced in the province throughout much of the Colonial period. To be considered a candidate for study with the Mercedarian Order, legitimate birth, purity of blood, and proof of Catholic faith had to be ensured through written proof of the legal marriage between the mother and father—and the grandparents as well—as was done in Castile.[2]

The geographic distances between the Mercedarian operations in Spain and Santiago de Guatemala and its personnel in the frontier impeded communication, supervision, and delivery of supplies. Nonetheless, the order attempted to regulate minutely the behavior of its members and their interaction with the Lenca population. In 1650, reports indicate that Tencoa was among the convents most needing priests who spoke the indigenous Lenca language.[3] Records show that Mercedarian priests became certified by examination in Lenca, as well as Mam, Jacalteca, Mexicana, Lacandon, and Cuilqueña.[4] Until friars had successfully mastered the language of their convent, they were to be given only half their ration of chocolate.[5]

Regulations designed to enforce compliance with vows of poverty, obedience, chastity, and redemption—and with the Constitution of the Mercedarian Order—were abundant. These regulations were far-reaching. The vow of poverty, for instance, dealt with rules concerning individual inheritance, disposition of a priest's property (for example, clothing and jewelry), down to the number of mules an individual could have in his possession. *Doctrineros* (friars or priests) were allowed to have two mules because their occupation required extensive travel, while their superiors were permitted to have only one mule.

The relationship between *encomenderos* (holders of an encomienda) and doctrineros appears to have been a particularly fractious one. The governing body of the province sent down regulations and continuing financial demands to the encomenderos on the frontier. Some regulations were somewhat modified from Spain, but, in essence, the order was trying to use a set of European precepts to operate under different environments and conditions in the Americas. Friction between encomenderos and priests may have been caused by the inability of doctrineros to comply with the governing body's unrealistic demands, which were the superior's responsibility to impose. What is somewhat surprising is that the provincial offices, which changed every three years, were generally composed of individuals who had served throughout the distant province. These individuals should have been cognizant of the conditions and limitations imposed throughout much of the frontier province.

Conclusions

The centralized bureaucracy and dedication of the religious orders as well as the substantial support of the Spanish Crown enabled the Catholic church to undertake Indian missionization programs on a large scale in Central America. The distribution of Mercedarian missionaries in Honduras and the geographic dispersion of their convents show that they preferred to install themselves in areas that had been subjugated by the Spaniards and in which Spanish administration had been instituted. As has been confirmed from the archaeological research (see chapter 10), the convento in the case of the partido of Santa Bárbara de Tencoa was established in one of the more densely populated indigenous centers in Honduras at the time of contact. Undoubtedly, Lenca society was undermined by depopulation, disease, warfare, and perhaps factionalism shortly after Spanish contact. Because of this great devastation of the population and ensuing social disorganization during the Early Colonial period, it is difficult to reconstruct precisely the magnitude and nature of the processes of the Spanish encounter.

In the Early Colonial period, Mercedarian missionaries in Honduras appear to have undertaken a spiritual conquest of the indigenous people with dedication and determination under quite difficult physical conditions. Given their previous military and redemptive tradition, the Mercedarian Order would seem to be well suited to the vicissitudes of the conversion task in the Americas. In mapping the dynamics of the encounter between the Mercedarians and the Lenca in the frontier of western Honduras, we see both an attempted spiritual conquest and the role of religion in the formation and maintenance of Colonial rule. Clearly, Mercedarian missionaries viewed Christian life as a totality involving many facets of cultural life. Such policies in a frontier have implications for both the missionaries and the missionized. For example, it is frequently the case that the successful missionary is promoted within the order's hierarchy, and thus has less direct contact with the target population. Another dilemma is that, if a missionary is successful and the group is converted, there is no longer a need for the missionary's presence.

Mercedarian activities in Tencoa were governed by climate, terrain, personnel and financial resources, the state and nature of Lenca society, the rules and regulations of their order, and the bishop and the Crown. Conditions promoting early conversion efforts included similarities between pre-Hispanic and Spanish religious beliefs and practices, considerable financial and military support by the Crown, religious zeal as exemplified by the dedication of the sixteenth-century missionaries, and social disruption caused by the conquest.

Mitigating against conversion efforts were the brutal treatment of Indians by the Spanish colonists and the example their behavior set for expectations of Christian life, indifference or hostility by encomenderos to fulfill their obligation of Indian conversion, heavy financial demands on the local convents of religious orders after the initial conversion, internal conflict between Catholic regular and secular clergy concerning administration of the indigenous population, and perhaps an unwillingness on the part of the Lenca to be converted.

It is disappointing that few sources apart from church records exist regarding missionary and Indian interaction in frontier regions, but archival records contain revealing data in many areas. In particular, the mission monologue contrasts the rules and expectations of the Mercedarian Order with the actions of its members in remote areas. Rules are prescriptive and do not always resemble actual behavior, especially when operating under differing conditions and environments. Although many of the Mercedarian missions such as Tencoa were far from Santiago de Guatemala, and quite distant from Spain, they were connected to both by religious and civil controls. Mercedarian missions were expected to operate under highly restrictive sets of regulations and legal requirements emanating from within the order in Spain, as well as those prescribed by the Crown.

The inter group contact over time between the Guatemala province and the Mercedarian Order in Europe reveals that the province thought of itself as increasingly dissimilar in conditions and objectives. As their records so fully demonstrate, all daily activities were to be carefully regulated, and obligations, particularly financial ones, were abundant in the frontier. What we find in these records is more of an internal dialogue within the Mercedarian Order itself which governed its action in regions such as Santa Bárbara de Tencoa in western Honduras. These data are valuable as guides to processes that influenced culture change within the mission system and for making inferences concerning the indigenous groups.

Acknowledgments. I am grateful for the support provided by the following archives: Archivo de los Padres Mercedarios de Guatemala, Archivo General de Centro América in Guatemala City, Archivo Eclesiástico de Comayagua, and the Archivo Nacional de Honduras in Tegucigalpa. Initial funding was provided by the National Geographic Society to the Santa Bárbara Archaeological Project, co-directed by Wendy Ashmore, Edward Schortman, and Patricia Urban. Subsequent funding was made available by the National Endowment for the Humanities and a Benevolent Association Fellowship from the State University of New York at Albany. I thank John M. Weeks for providing figure 9.1. I appreciate the support of my colleagues Julie C. Benyo, Janine Gasco, and Beverly Hill in the preparation of this chapter.

Notes
1. Archivo General de Centroamérica, Guatemala City (AGCA). A1.23 4575, f. 38; A1.23 1511, f. 10.
2. Archivo de los Padres Mercedarios de Guatemala, Guatemala City (AMERGUA). Capítulos Provinciales, 1645–1757: 1659, f. 121.
3. AMERGUA. Capítulos Provinciales, 1645–1757: 1650, f. 33.
4. AMERGUA. Patentes de Guatemala, 1678–1828.
5. AMERGUA. Capítulos Provinciales, 1645–1757:1662, f. 140v.

Chapter 10

The Mercedarian Mission System in Santa Bárbara de Tencoa, Honduras

John M. Weeks

Abstract

Archaeological and historical research concerning the Postclassic and Colonial settlements of western Honduras offers new information regarding the development of Hispano-Indian society along the southeastern periphery of Mesoamerica. This chapter describes the Postclassic and Colonial settlement system of the Lenca within the historic partido of Tencoa, focusing on the transition from prehistoric to historic periods. The relationships between changes in location, size, and configuration of Lenca settlement systems is discussed, particularly as it was influenced by the imposition of the European mission system.

Resumen

La investigación arqueológica e histórica acerca de los asentamientos posclásicos y coloniales del oeste de Honduras aporta nueva información respecto al desarrollo de la sociedad hispano-indígena en la periferia del sureste de Mesoamérica. En este capítulo se describe el sistema de asentamiento posclásico y colonial de los lenca en el partido histórico de Tencoa, con énfasis en la transición entre los periodos prehistórico e histórico. Se analizan las relaciones entre los cambios en ubicación, tamaño, y configuración del sistema de asentamiento lenca, en particular en función de la influencia de la imposición del sistema de misiones europeos.

IN WESTERN HONDURAS, the spiritual conquest of the Lenca people is largely an account of the activities of the Order of Our Lady of Mercy for the Ransom of Captives (Black 1989:87; see also chapter 9). The Mercedarian friars were the first to begin mission work in western Honduras. While many of their missions were eventually taken over by the secular clergy, the Mercedarians were responsible for the initial conversion and baptism of the Lenca and for their education in the basic tenets of the Catholic faith. This chapter reviews recent archival and archaeological work that has examined the physical sites of Mercedarian-Lenca contact in the Tencoa region of western Honduras (figure 10.1).

Historical Background

The Spanish conquest of Honduras began in 1524, but it was not until 1539 that the Spaniards achieved effective military control of the region. Unlike Central Mexico and parts of the Maya region, pre-Hispanic Honduras had little political cohesiveness, and territory had to be subjugated piecemeal. Frequently, areas had to be reconquered from the indigenous Lenca (Weeks and Black 1991).

The Spaniards recognized the need to gather new Lenca converts into permanent Christian communities soon after the initial pacification of western Honduras. In 1549, the reformist administrator president of the Audiencia de los Confines at Gracias a Dios, Alonso López de Cerrato, petitioned Fray Marcos Pérez de Dardán, vicar provincial of the Guatemalan convent of Mercedarians, to establish a series of convents in western Honduras to begin Christian instruction (Castro Seaone 1943:419; Vázquez Núñez 1968). Dardán sent a mission of Mercedarians to found houses at locations deemed convenient, far from each other and where needed most. The principal *pueblos de españoles* (Spanish towns) at the time, Valladolid de Comayagua and Villa de Gracias a Dios (figure 10.1), were selected to serve as mission centers from which Mercedarians would instruct the Lenca throughout the region.

The first Mercedarian base mission was founded by Fray Jerónimo Clemente and Fray Juan Ramos at Comayagua in 1552. The first church construction consisted of coarse wooden walls, a tamped earth floor, and a palm or thatch roof (Carias 1985:63; Reina Valenzuela 1983:161). Thirty years later, the population of Comayagua consisted of fifty Spaniards and 1,800 indigenous tributaries distributed in fortyeight pueblos over a circuit of 250 leagues. These were eventually grouped into six *partidos* (religious districts) administered from Comayagua by the Mercedarians (Pérez Rodríquez 1966:99).

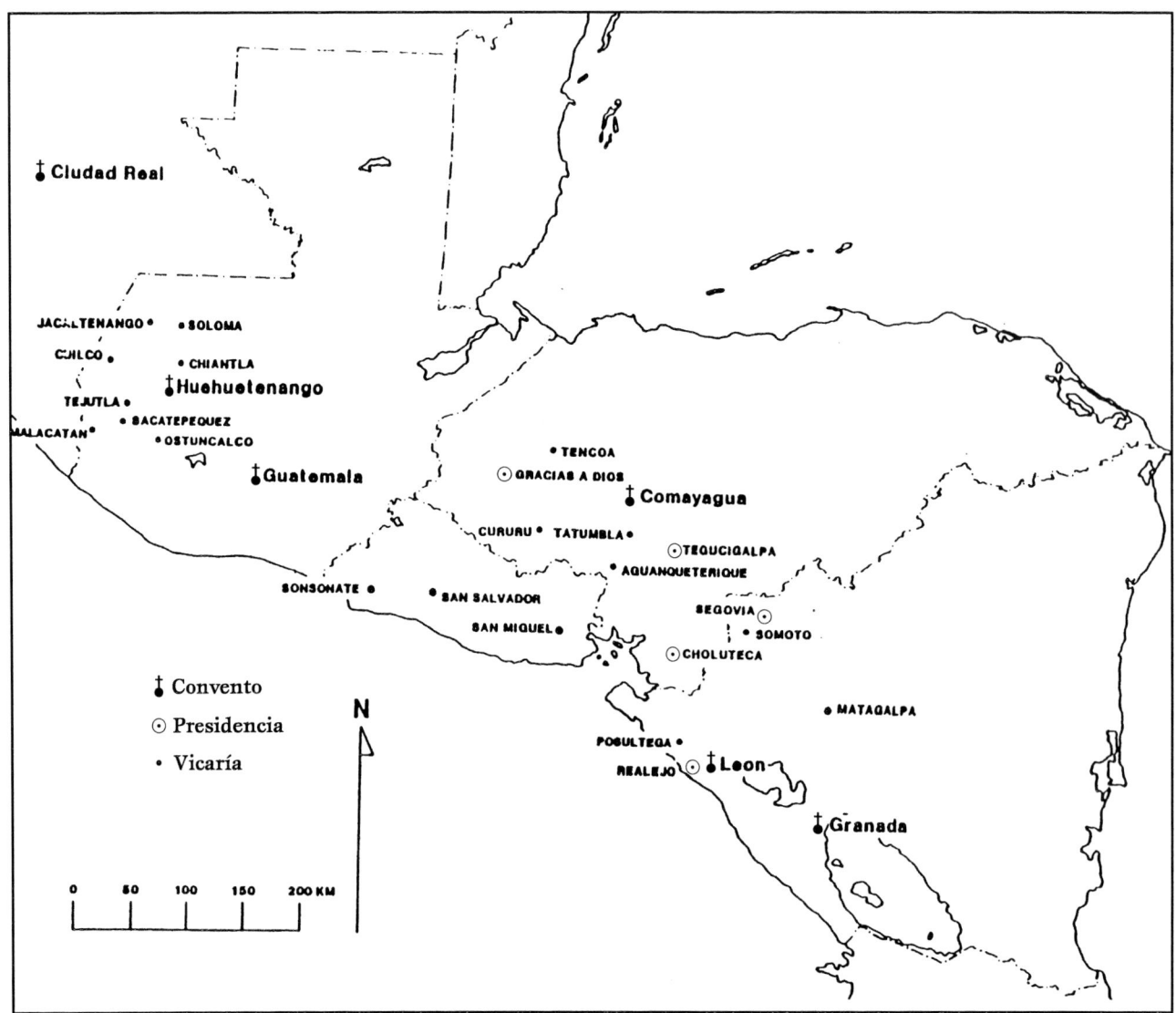

FIGURE 10.1 Colonial Central America and location of Mercedarian *presidencias* (a Mercedarian house having less than the required eight religious members to meet the daily obligations of mass, not located within encomienda territory, independent of the authority of a comendador and directly under the jurisdiction of the governing body in Guatemala), *conventos* (convent or monastery), and vicarías (a Mercedarian house having less than the required eight religious members to meet the daily obligations of mass, usually located within the encomienda territory and attached to a specific convent under the jurisdiction of the comendador), circa 1700. *Illustration by John M. Weeks*

A second base mission was established in 1552 at Gracias a Dios, a pueblo de españoles 30 leagues west of Comayagua, which had been founded in 1536. By 1582, Gracias a Dios had thirty Spaniards and 2,100 tributaries in fifty-six pueblos over a circuit of 1,280 leagues. These pueblos were eventually organized into six partidos.

A third base mission was founded at the end of 1554 at Santa Bárbara de Tencoa, 14 leagues northeast of Gracias a Dios. The number of Spaniards who lived in Tencoa is unknown, although by 1582 the mission comprised 900 tributaries in twenty-two pueblos. There does not appear to have been much initial resistance to the Mercedarian efforts (Pérez Rodríguez 1966:101).

Santa Bárbara de Tencoa Mission System

The Tencoa region was not especially attractive for Colonial settlement (figure 10.2). The rugged terrain offered few easily extractable resources, the indigenous population had been reduced by the military campaigns, and the remaining groups were antagonistic. Bernal Diaz del Castillo (1912) states that the Lenca in the vicinity of Tencoa offered little resistance during the expeditions into the area led by Cristóbal de Olid during the early 1520s. By 1536, several Spaniards received *encomiendas* (grants of Indians and their tribute to an individual Spaniard) in the region. Chuchepeque was given to Luis Diaz, Gualalá to Luis del Puerto, Ilama to Pedro de Alvarado, and Yamalá to Cristóbal Gallego (Alvarado 1871:5–

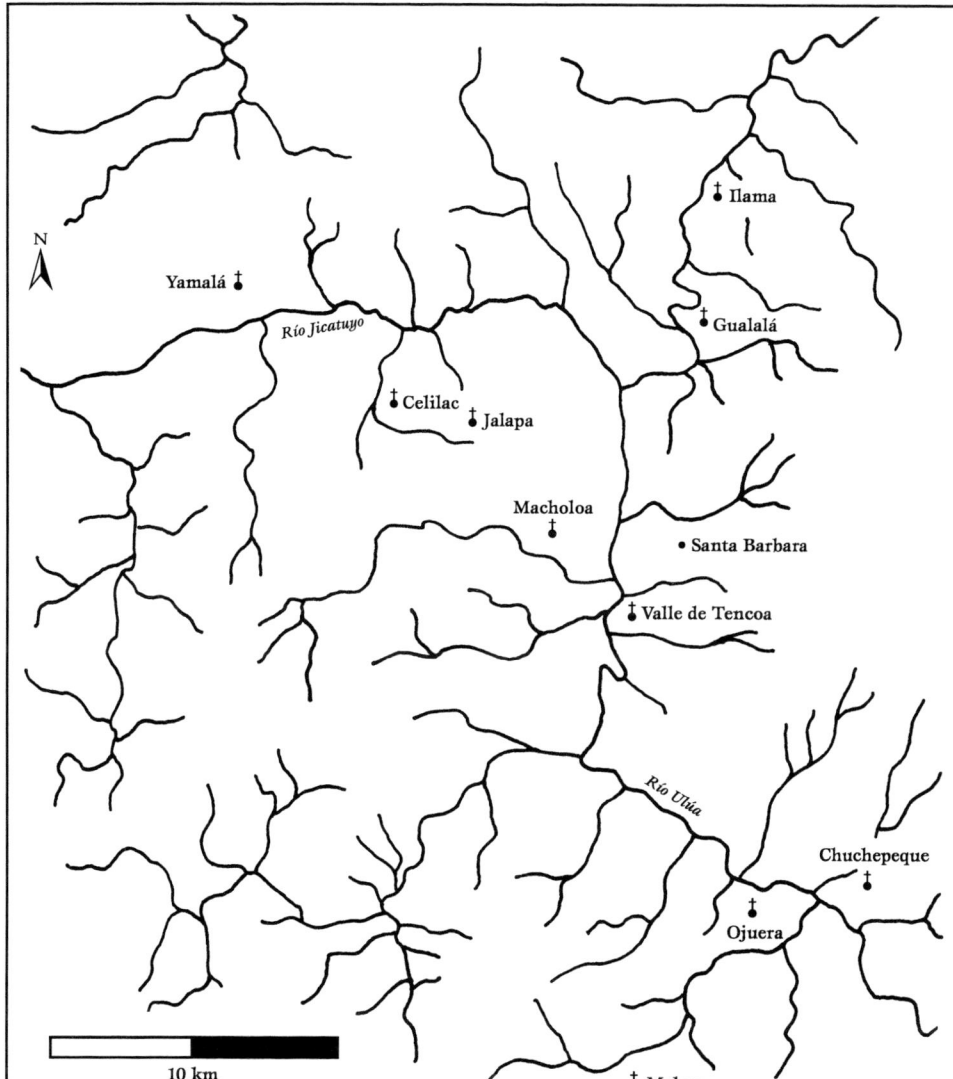

Figure 10.2 Ecclesiastical topography of the Mercedarian province of Tencoa

20). These settlements would become important *pueblos de indios* (Indian towns). Tencoa, itself, was assigned as an encomienda in 1544. The number of tributaries in each settlement is unknown, although Newson (1986:102) states that the largest number of tributaries assigned to a single *encomendero* (grant holder) was 380, and most had fewer than two hundred.

Very little substantive information is known about the first Mercedarians at Tencoa. A sum of 25 pesos was paid to an Indian named Luis Pérez for teaching the Christian doctrine in the vicinity of Tencoa from September 1553 through September 1554. During this time, there were no Mercedarians at Tencoa, and Pérez, presumably a Lenca, was probably a *fiscal* (an Indian official who was charged with the daily observation of Catholic ritual and a variety of other conversion and education activities; see Collins 1977:246). The following year, a little over 176 pesos in gold were paid to the Mercedarian Nicolás del Valle for evangelizing at Tencoa from November 1554 to December 1556. Del Valle served at Tencoa as superior and principal friar for some years and evidently gained considerable respect. He was fluent in the Lenca language, was a highly effective preacher, and was successful in destroying numerous places of traditional Lenca worship. By 1565, he was the most senior preacher in the province of Honduras. Similar to Bartolomé de las Casas in Guatemala, del Valle used flute music in his ministrations. The *oidor* (Audiencia judge), Dr. Anton Mejía, declared in 1565 that del Valle taught the Indians well and was a very good model for his followers. The Mercedarians emphasized the acquisition of vernacular languages, and there is abundant documentation to indicate that the friars at Tencoa had mastered Lenca.[1] Mastery of an indigenous language was expected within a year (Zúñiga Corres 1968), and until the friars learned the required native language they received only a half ration of chocolate (Black 1989:158; chapter 9).

By 1568, the doctrina included Tencoa, Quezaltepeque (Quesailica), Camala (Yamalá), Aracagua (probably Macholoa or Gualala), Calaca (Celilac), and Lamatepeque (Ilama; figure 10.2; Zúñiga Corres 1968).

The operation of the Mercedarian mission system in the Tencoa region was difficult for various reasons. The terrain is described as rugged and existing road conditions as generally poor, especially during the rainy season when travel was virtually impossible.[2] All of the Lenca pueblos de indios were dispersed, and a single priest was insufficient to provide adequate instruction or administration of the sacraments. In addition, the pueblos de indios were very small and were unable to support a visiting priest. The *limosna* (charity) received by the Mercedarians from the Crown was also meager, and the friars lacked basic necessities. A sum of 60 pesos was given to the Mercedarians in 1556 for one complete set of vestments and a silver chalice to be used to celebrate the Mass at Santa Bárbara de Tencoa and its dependencies within the doctrina. Several years later, in 1600, some fifty images were sent to Honduras to address the lack of *retablos* (altarpieces), images, and missals.[3] By 1740, the *vicaría* (vicarage) of Tencoa was sustained by three Mercedarians, a *vicario* (priest), a *cura doctrinero* (the priest in charge of the parish), and a *coadjutor* (assistant to the bishop).[4]

The organization of the Tencoa mission system was generally similar to the model developed in Mercedarian provinces in Chiapas, Guatemala, and Honduras (Zaportes Pallares 1983:170–171). Mission stations, governed from a centrally located mission at Santa Bárbara de Tencoa, were established throughout the region. The operation of the mission system was rapidly disrupted, however, by the decimation of the Lenca through disease, dislocation, and abuse by the encomenderos.

Eventually, a series of reforms was imposed to curb the abuses of the encomenderos and to give the religious orders new powers to protect and regulate the Lenca (Sherman 1971). The most significant of these measures was the Spanish policy of *congregación* in which the inhabitants of scattered indigenous settlements were forced to resettle into a single community. These settlements were organized into a network of mission towns under Mercedarian control (MacLeod 1973:122; Newson 1986:206). The new towns were located at existing Lenca centers, now greatly enlarged and reorganized according to Spanish urban patterns.

Each *cabecera* (base mission), such as Santa Bárbara de Tencoa, housed several friars who led instruction in Christian doctrine, attended various fiestas, offered Sunday services, and provided generally for the spiritual and corporal needs of the community. The territory assigned to the Mercedarians at Santa Bárbara de Tencoa was large and relatively unpopulated, and many Lenca fled to more remote and mountainous regions. Because it was not possible to position a friar permanently in each indigenous village, a system of *visitas* (inspections) was implemented in which missionaries visited the smaller outlying communities periodically, celebrated the Mass, and taught Christian doctrine. This pattern of religious service continues today in many rural or remote regions of Honduras and elsewhere in Latin America.

The initial conversion of the Lenca emphasized the indigenous nobility. Influential Lenca were instrumental in attracting their subjects to the new religion. Another method, used extensively during the early years of evangelization, consisted of removing Lenca children from their parents in pueblos de indios to the Mercedarian convents at Comayagua, Gracias a Dios, and Tencoa, where they received special instruction in reading and writing and learned Catholic doctrine and ritual. Eventually these children were returned to their own villages to promote the acceptance of Christianity and to assist the friars in teaching in the Lenca language.

The religious province of Honduras was constantly reorganizing throughout the seventeenth century. Crown support for the regular orders was diminishing. Visita districts were deteriorating because of indigenous population loss, and convents could no longer be sustained (Black 1989:123–124; chapter 9). In 1683, when the Bishop of Guatemala attempted to replace the Mercedarians with secular clergy, the convents were forced to rely upon donations. In October 1700, it was mandated that all regular orders had to have at least eight members in residence to hold the status and privileges of a convent and to receive support from the Crown.

Archaeological Reconnaissance of the Colonial Partido of Tencoa

Sixteenth-century Honduras occupied an ethnographically and linguistically complex transition zone that separated the elaborate state-level Maya civilization of southern Mesoamerica from the chiefdoms of lower Central America (Schortman et al. 1986:259). Despite the relative archaeological and historical importance of the region, however, systematic research has begun only recently (Black 1989; Chapman 1978; Lara Pinto 1980, 1982, 1985, 1991; Richter 1971; Weeks and Black 1987, 1991; Weeks, Black, and Speaker 1987). An adequate understanding of the region is complicated by a number of factors, including a lack of reliable ethnographic studies (Chapman 1985) and the rapid extinction of many indigenous groups following the arrival of the Spaniards (Healy 1984:115).

The late prehistoric and Early Colonial archaeology of the region is complicated by numerous factors, including the apparent lack of deeply stratified deposits, the small number of identified or excavated late pre-Hispanic components, and the general disinterest in the historical archaeology of settlements other than *pueblos de españoles* (Spanish towns). Because of these problems, the late prehistoric archaeology of western Honduras has been difficult to identify, define, and monitor through time and space. Despite these difficulties, recent research makes it possible to identify general characteristics of the Postclassic and Colonial periods.

Definition of the Study Area

The study area comprises most of the Colonial partido of Tencoa (figure 10.2). More specifically, it includes the territory drained by a 70-km–long segment of the north-south–trending Río Ulúa and 25 km of the east-west–flowing Río Jicatuyo. The area is bounded on the north by the Early Colonial town of Ilama, situated some 10 km north of the confluence of the Río Jicatuyo with the Río Ulúa; to the southeast by Chuchepeque, located at the confluence of the Río Gualcarque and the Río Ulúa; and to the south by the Colonial town of Malera. The community of Yamalá, situated on the banks of the Río Jicatuyo, defines the western limit of the study area.

The study area, which covers 2,300 km², has been divided for analytical purposes into ten survey zones defined on the basis of historical evidence. These zones are small *vegas* (intermontane depressions) known to have supported ten Mercedarian visita stations maintained during the late sixteenth and early seventeenth centuries. These vegas are Celilac, Chuchepeque, Gualalá, Ilama, Jalapa, Macholoa, Malera, Ojuera, Tencoa, and Yamalá (figure 10.2).

Historical documentation suggests that these vegas were preferred settlement locations during Protohistoric and Early Colonial periods because of the potentially fertile alluvial and savanna microenvironments (Chapman 1978; Herrera y Tordesillas 1726–1730:4:140–141). The surface surveys were limited spatially to floodplains and adjacent alluvial terraces, the most attractive areas for sustaining human habitation.

An archaeological reconnaissance of the ten vegas within the Mercedarian partido of Tencoa resulted in the identification of sixty-four archaeological sites. The settlement system represents continuous human occupation extending from the Late Preclassic (ca. 400 BC–AD 200) through the Historic period (after AD 1540) and thus provides an opportunity to examine settlement continuity and modification during these periods.

Sites of the Postclassic Period

In contrast to the great demographic growth and settlement expansion of the preceding periods, the Early Postclassic period (ca. AD 950–1200) is characterized by population reduction and site abandonment throughout western and central Honduras. External influences are evident from the appearance of copper bells, Plumbate and Fine Orange pottery, Naco Polychrome pottery, and an increase in the frequency of obsidian. Although some contacts with Mesoamerica are apparent, cultural assemblages exhibit close relationships with the south. Pottery and lithics, and some architectural features (such as paved walkways) are similar to those found in lower Central America, especially Atlantic coastal Nicaragua and Costa Rica (Healy 1984).

Recent archaeological research in the vicinity of Tencoa is variable in its coverage of the Postclassic period (Ashmore 1987; Ashmore et al. 1986, 1987; Benyo and Melchionne 1987; Schortman and Urban 1987; Schortman, Urban, and Ashmore 1984, 1986; Urban and Smith 1987). Surface survey and excavations at the site of Gualjoquito, a large regional center located at the confluence of the Río Ulúa and the Río Jicatuyo, suggest a cessation of all monumental architectural construction by the end of the Late Classic period (ca. AD 950). Population in the sustaining area continued without any significant decline well into the Early Postclassic (ca. AD 950–1200) when construction techniques changed to low earthen platforms roughly faced with a single course of unmodified stone. Structural form changed to emphasize long, proportionately narrower structures. There is no evidence that an administrative center had developed to replace Gualjoquito. Early Postclassic pottery in central Santa Bárbara is generally a simplified continuation of Late Classic–period types (Urban 1993:137–138).

Sites of the Historic Period

Nine sites of the Historic period were located during the survey. Seven were identified from the remains of churches at Celilac, Chuchepeque, Gualalá, Jalapa, Ojuera, Tencoa, and Yamalá. The churches at Chuchepeque, Jalapa, and Ojuera were deliberately constructed on or near large pre-Hispanic Lenca sites. Raised above former platforms, these structures were conspicuous symbols of the triumph of Christianity. Two Colonial churches at Ilama and Macholoa are still being used by parishioners. The Mercedarian mission station associated with the vega at Malera has not been identified.

The historical architecture associated with the mission stations included in the survey of the partido of Tencoa consisted of peripheral pueblo de indios (or visita) churches and one pueblo de españoles church at Tencoa. The church identified at Tencoa may not have been the main Mercedarian cabecera convent—excavation revealed a modest construction with little architectural or other elaboration.

Unlike the elaborate religious architecture preserved in the great Colonial centers at Comayagua, Antigua Guatemala, and San Cristóbal de Las Casas (Markman 1966, 1984; Palacios 1987), pueblo de indios churches in the partido of Tencoa exhibit a distinctive simplicity influenced by isolation, poverty, and regional conservatism, possibly a function of the Mercedarian ideal of austerity. The indigenous Lenca presence is also felt. Although construction was initiated by missionaries, it could not have been accomplished without the efforts of the Lenca.

From the beginning, the churches were the focus of an investment of labor and wealth into the construction and maintenance of buildings. Stone was the construc-

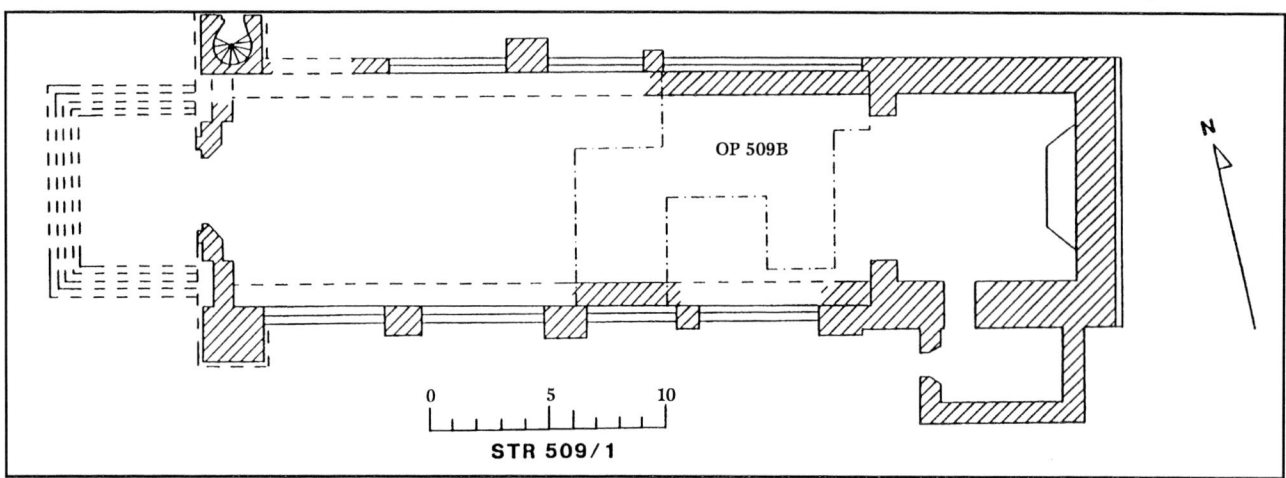

Figure 10.3 Plan drawing of colonial church at Yamalá (site 509)

tion material of choice, and piles of riverine cobbles were readily available from the Río Ulúa and Río Jicatuyo. Basic masonry techniques, familiar to both Spaniard and Lenca, involved laying up courses of rubble in a matrix of clay mud mortar. Dressed and cut stone, removed from pre-Hispanic ruins, was used to frame the windows, doorways, and corners of the buildings.

The first visita churches situated in the smaller pueblo de indios settlements that supported the main church at the cabecera of Tencoa in the task of evangelization were little more than primitive, simple structures made of perishable materials (Palacios 1987; Pérez Rodríguez 1966). As the partido was able to accumulate sufficient capital, these early buildings were replaced by more substantial masonry structures. Appendix 10.1 provides a late eighteenth-century summary of the condition and construction characteristics of churches throughout the partido of Tencoa at that time.[5]

The standard plan for pueblo de indios churches (figure 10.3) was more economical than the more elaborate churches in pueblos de españoles. Single nave in plan, wall construction was of adobe or wattle-and-daub. Interior and exterior wall surfaces were covered with stucco. Masonry buttresses used to reinforce adobe walls are evident at Celilac, Macholoa, and Yamalá. The main façade was treated as a freestanding wall on which the nave of the stabilized adobe abuts. When towers were added, they were placed to one or both sides of the façade from which they projected beyond the nave. Roofing materials were clay tile or thatch on a wooden roof frame.

An important innovation in eighteenth-century churches was the addition of an *atrio*, a walled open space that enclosed the front of the church where the Mercedarians baptized, catechized, and preached to the Lenca and staged religious processions and dance dramas.

It is difficult to describe the portable material culture associated with the interiors of visita churches because most has been lost through neglect or vandalism. Surviving examples at Chuchepeque, Gualalá, and Macholoa demonstrate that church art was less opulent than in richer provinces and can be divided into two primary categories: stonework and painted woodcarving. Mural painting is rarely visible today, although some polychrome painting still exists on the molding of the doorways at Celilac and Yamalá.

Because of its greater durability, stonework has survived better than the more perishable wooden artifacts. Stonework was almost exclusively a Lenca skill, and it ranged from simple to sophisticated. *Canteros* (itinerant masons) went from church to church executing the stone carving under the supervision of friars or professional architects. The bulk consisted of exterior detailing: door frames, columns, carved niches, and belfries. Ornamental stonework, such as the carving of religious symbols and Mercedarian *escudos* (insignia), was probably also the work of the Lenca and appears on many buildings. Interior stonework was largely confined to fonts and holy water stoups and seems to have been the work of local stoneworkers.

The craft of religious woodcarving and finishing sprang from entirely different sources. Production of the *retablo* (the painted or carved altarpiece attached to the back of the altar) was restricted to artisans trained in the European tradition. The finished retablo was the result of a complex series of steps involving a team of skilled and specialized craftsmen.

Scarce resources and lags in fashion in remote areas like western Honduras resulted in simpler, less elaborate altarpieces. In many pueblo de indios churches where there was little money for even the simplest altarpiece, cloth hangings or painted backdrops adorned the sanctuary.

Appendix 10.2 is an inventory of the possessions of a parish priest at Santa Bárbara de Tencoa in the late eighteenth century and provides an excellent idea of the range of material culture associated with the residential quarters of a church.[5]

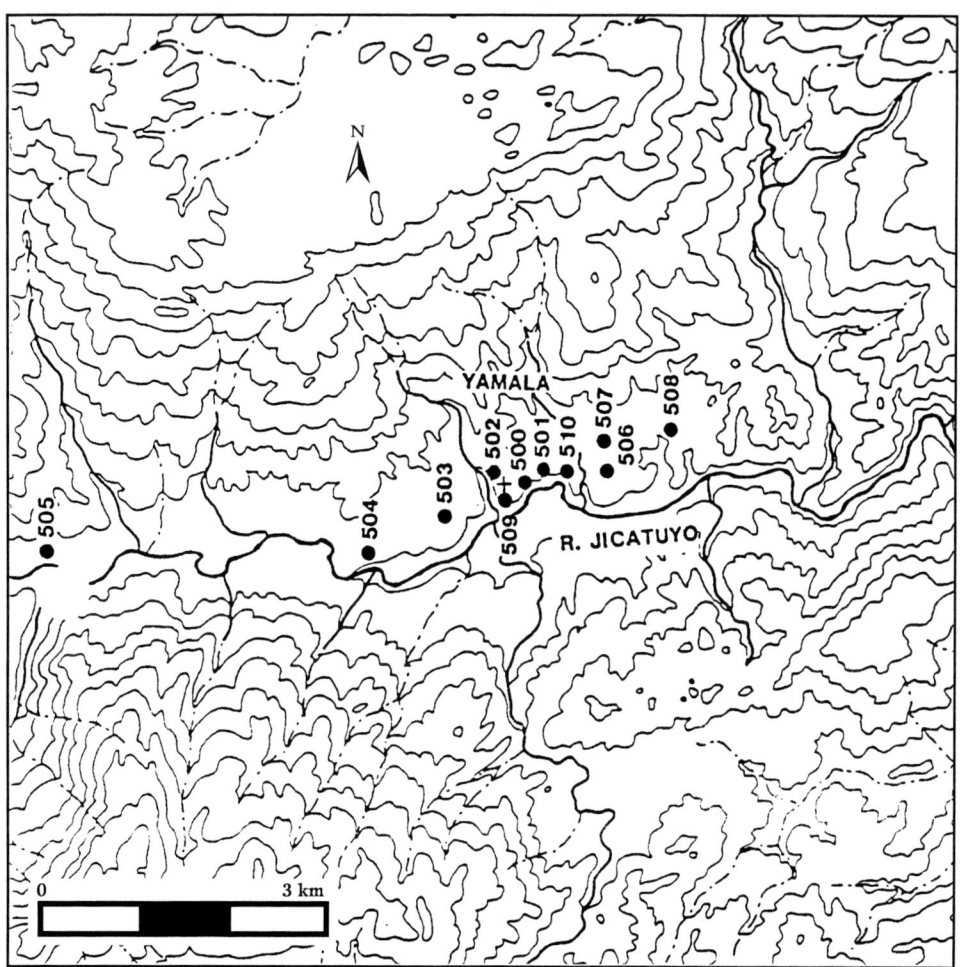

Figure 10.4 Sites in the Yamalá vega mentioned in the text

Settlement System in the Yamalá Vega

The most complete settlement system information available comes from Yamalá, a small vega measuring 4 km east-west and 0.5 km north-south, on the Río Jicatuyo (figure 10.2). This vega probably represents the eastern limit of Classic-period Maya sites in western Honduras (Pahl 1988). The survey at Yamalá identified eleven prehistoric and Historic period sites (figure 10.4), comprising thirty-nine individual structures, of which twenty-two were partially excavated. Extensive mapping, systematic surface collection, and selective excavation permit the reconstruction of a continuous settlement sequence from the Late Preclassic through the Historic periods, based on evidence from seven of these sites (table 10.1).

The vega appears to have been settled as early as the Late Preclassic period (ca. 400 BC–AD 200). A concentration of ceramic fragments, lithic debris, and shell fragments from this period can be found eroding out of an alluvial terrace (site 501) north of the Río Jicatuyo. Less significant Late Preclassic occupations have been identified at sites 500, 502, and 503. During the Early Classic period (AD 200–600), sites 502 and 503 were abandoned and light occupation continued at sites 500 and 501. A moderate occupation began at site 504, a group of at least ten platforms situated at the western limit of the vega at Yamalá.

Seven sites were occupied in the valley during the Late Classic period (AD 600–950), more than doubling the number of sites occupied in the Early Classic period. All earlier sites either continue to be occupied or are reoccupied. Particularly strong Late Classic occupations are noted at site 504, continuing an Early Classic occupation, and site 509, a deposit buried beneath the nave of the Colonial church on the east side of the town plaza. A modest Late Classic period occupation is found at site 506, consisting of two platforms located on a terrace overlooking the eastern edge of the Yamalá vega, and at site 500, a group of three large cobble platforms arranged in a plaza configuration located some 100 m east of the Colonial church (site 509).

During the Early Postclassic period (AD 950–1200), the number of Late Classic sites decreased. Occupations at sites 500, 502, 503, and 504 continued from the Late Classic period, although occupations were lighter; sites 506 and 509 were abandoned.

The number of sites occupied during the Late Postclassic period (AD 1200–1540) increased. Sites 500, 502, 503, and 504 continued from light Early Postclassic occupations. Site 506, which had not been occupied since the Late Classic period, exhibits a moderate occupation.

Table 10.1 Periods of occupation for Yamalá vega sites

SITE	LATE PRE-CLASSIC	EARLY CLASSIC	LATE CLASSIC	EARLY POSTCLASSIC	LATE POSTCLASSIC	COLONIAL
500	X	X	X	X	X	
501	X	X	X			
502	X		X	X	X	
503	X		X	X	X	
504		X	X	X	X	
506				X	X	
509				X		X

Historical documents indicate that the vega of Yamalá was a settlement zone of some importance in western Honduras by the early sixteenth century. It was cited in a *relación* (account) written in 1536 by the conquistador Pedro de Alvarado (1871). A letter to the Spanish Crown pertaining to the governance of Francisco de Montejo in 1539 provides an account of the military siege of the Lenca stronghold at Yamalá (site 504):

> Disturbing news reached Gracias a Dios where Montejo was traveling with eleven Spanish soldiers. The Indians were preparing stubbornly to resist him. At Yamalá, a nearby village, they were building many houses on a great, very strong peñol which they have, and providing them with provisions. The Spanish chieftains sent a Negro spy, who knew the language of the Indians, to enter the stronghold and bring back a report. The frightened Negro found there four houses built very large, and four more larger ones full of corn. He set fire to the houses and to the corn (Montejo 1864:216–217).

With the end of the siege of the Lenca *peñol* (fort), the pre-Hispanic settlement system in the Yamalá vega collapsed and the settlement around the church, represented by site 509, became the focal point, a pattern that continues unchanged to the present. The residential or sustaining zone associated with the church at Yamalá has yet to be fully identified.

In 1536, the vega was assigned to the encomendero Cristóbal Gallego. In 1580, support was extended from the Mercedarian convent at Gracias a Dios to the Mercedarian friar Leandro de Santa María to support a doctrina at Yamalá (Zúñiga Corres 1968:89), although it is possible that evangelizing had begun in the 1560s. The Historic period population of the vega was small, as evidenced by the first enumeration in 1582, when it was populated by thirty *tributarios* (Indian tributaries), through 1804 when it was comprised of 279 souls and sixty tributarios (Anguiano 1946:139; Contreras Guevara 1946:9). In 1778, a petition was filed for funds to reconstruct the church, then in ruins. Appendix 10.1 includes a description of the physical condition of the church and its contents in 1791. The vega was finally abandoned in the early nineteenth century, but it was repopulated in the 1970s when a group of families from Erandique in the Department of Lempira established a satellite settlement. In 1973, it was recognized as a *caserio* (small settlement) of the municipality of Nuevo Celilac.

Conclusions

The evangelical task awaiting the Mercedarians was a formidable one. They were faced with numerous problems, including difficult topography, encomenderos, disinterested government officials, numerous vernacular languages, and an antagonistic indigenous population. For the Mercedarians, the Lenca settlement pattern was not conducive to the process of Christianization. Some Lenca lived in modest or even large villages, but most lived in dispersed settlements scattered throughout the countryside. For example, there were at least five Late Postclassic settlements in the Yamalá vega. The Mercedarians, well aware of their lack of manpower, realized they had little hope of Christianizing without profound reorganization of the indigenous society. It was thought that the Indians could never be reduced to a so-called civilized life unless they were congregated into nucleated settlements. In the Yamalá vega, five settlements were reduced to one.

Throughout the middle of the sixteenth century, scattered Lenca populations were reduced to *congregaciones* (Spanish colonial institution of forcible removable of native peoples from dispersed settlements into a centralized community). In some cases, smaller villages were moved into a central one or one convenient to the missionaries.

It is difficult to evaluate the indigenous reaction to the policy of congregación, although evidence suggests generally that the operation was conducted with little disruption. Congregación greatly helped the evangelical effort, and missionaries and civil officials worked through the Indian *caciques* (village chiefs; Remesal 1932–1933:179–180; Vázquez 1937–1944:1:108; Ximénez 1929–1931:1:483–484). Whatever its popularity among the Indians, congregación was a temporary success for the Spaniards. For the friars, it made the spiritual conquest; for the colonists and Colonial officials, it facilitated tribute collection and control and distribution of labor. For the indigenous Lenca, it marked the end of a settlement pattern that had existed as early as the Late Preclassic period.

Notes

1. Archivo General de Centroamérica, Guatemala City (AGCA). A1.24 1582 10226, f. 222. R.P. Fr. Fernando Izaguirre, religioso de la Orden de Nuestra Señora de las Mercedes, es presentado para la doctrina en lengua lenca del pueblo de Tencoa en el

obispado de Honduras, 1717.
2. Archivo General de Indias, Seville, Spain (AGI). Guatemala 164, Relación de los beneficios del obispado de Honduras por fray Gaspar de Andrada, obispado de Honduras, 20 de abril de 1591 y 12 de octubre de 1598.
3. AGI. Contaduría 245A. Cédula de S.M. para que el Presidente de la Casa de la Contratación de Sevilla envie a ellas 50 imagines para las iglesias, 24 de mayo de 1600.
4. AGCA. A1.18.1 211 5025. Relación histórica de la Orden de Nuestra Señora Redención Cautivos, 1740.
5. Archivo de los Padres Mercedarios de Guatemala, Guatemala City (AMERGUA). Legajo 27a, Estado que manifiesta el numero de almas que se han confirmado en su ultima visita espiscopal, las capellanías, y cofradías que obtiene, curato de Tencoa, 11 de junio de 1791.

Appendix 10.1
Churches in the Partido of Tencoa, 1791

By 1791 the church at Malera had apparently been abandoned. These descriptions include the church at Tencoa, as well as a second, recently established church at nearby Santa Bárbara de Cataquiles. See Archivo de los Padres Mercedarios de Guatemala, Guatemala City (AMERGUA). Legajo 27a, Estado que manifiesta el numero de almas que se han confirmado en su ultima visita espiscopal, las capellanías, y cofradías que obtiene, curato de Tencoa, 11 de junio de 1791, and Weeks and Black 1991. Translation by author.

Tencoa: It is made of adobe and wood but is incomplete. The church has three complete vestments of white, pink, and black, with their choir-cope, altar hanging, linen tabernacle veil, with a pair of altar cloths, all for the altar, a silver monstrance, a ciborium and a chalice, a crown of the Pura y Limpia Concepción, a *resplandor* [resplendent image] of the Virgin Dolores, and a pair of wine vessels. Also a pair of silver candlesticks, a missal, and two bronze bells with three cruets for holy oils; with an incensory with spoon.

Chichitepeque [Chuchepeque]: It is made of wood and has walls of lath and mud. It has two complete vestments, a choir-cope, an altar hanging, linen tabernacle veil, two altar cloths, a corporal cloth, with purificators; all is well used; a missal and a manual; two silver complete chalices, a small cross, six candlesticks, three containers for the holy oils; an incensory with spoon; an aspergillum and wine vessels with small hoop; two small bronze bells.

Ojuera: It is made of wood, covered with roofing tile, and walls of lath and mud. It has a complete vestment and an altar hanging; there is a silver complete chalice, two wine vessels, two candlesticks, an incensory with spoon and three cruets for the holy oils; it has a missal and a manual; a pair of altar cloths and two small bronze bells.

Macholoa: It is made of adobe and roofed with thatch; it has a complete vestment and an altar hanging; it has a complete silver chalice, two cruets and its tray, two large candlesticks; an incensory with spoon; three cruets for holy oils; a missal and a manual; a pair of altar cloths; two bronze bells, one small and one medium.

Jalapa: It is adobe and covered with palm; and very deteriorated; has a complete vestment; a choir-cope, an altar hanging; of silver, a complete chalice, two wine vessels; an incensory with spoon; three cruets for holy oils; a missal and a manual; a pair of altar cloths; two small bronze bells; four metal candlesticks.

Celilaca: It is constructed of adobe with its ... intervening area made of stone because it is strong and measures two and a half persons in thickness and a good *arco toral* (arch), which divides the *capilla* (chapel); its roof and *coro* (choir) are made of wood; it is covered with roofing tile and has a large capacity; has complete vestments; a choir-cope and an inexpensive altar hanging; of silver, a complete chalice, two wine vessels; a crucifix; an incensory with spoon; and three cruets for holy oils; a missal and a manual; a pair of altar cloths; three bronze bells; two candlesticks of silver.

Yamalá: It is made of adobe; only the capilla is completed; roofing is of wood covered with roofing tile; and has an attractive façade with two plaster-surfaced towers; has two good vestments and one very used; a choir-cope very used; linen tabernacle veil; two corporal cloth holders; three altar cloths; two veils; three purificatories; two manos a Nuestra Señora; a towel; a Santo Cristo; two missals well used; a manual; a gold-plated monstrance; a complete chalice; two wine vessels and their tray; a cross; three chrismatories; the crown of the Virgin Mary; a diadem with two large candlesticks; an incensory with spoon; two bronze bells; an inexpensive altar hanging.

Ilamatepeque: It is constructed of adobe and covered with palm. It is very deteriorated. It has a complete vestment; a choir-cope; an inexpensive altar hanging; two altar cloths; a complete silver chalice; two wine vessels; an incensory with spoon; three chrismatories; it has two small bronze bells; a missal and a manual.

Gualalá: The construction work on this church has been suspended and only consists of a small chapel of walls of lath and mud with a roof covered with palm; it has two complete vestments; a choir-cope; an altar hanging; linen tabernacle veil and two cloths; two embroidered altar cloths; a missal and a manual; a silver monstrance; two complete gold-plated small crosses; an incensory and spoon; a baptismal font and a resplandor of the crucified Jesus Christ, gold-plated with some keepsake of little consideration; two small bronze bells.

Santa Bárbara: It is constructed of adobe with roofing of wood and roofing tile. It has four complete vestments of black, pink, white, and brown; a choir-cope; an altar hanging; two missals and a manual; a gold monstrance; a ciborium; a complete chalice; an incensory with spoon; a pair of cruets with tray; an altar cross; a pair of candlesticks; a resplandor; corporal cloths; two linen tabernacle veils and three altar cloths with three bronze bells, one large and two medium.

Appendix 10.2
Inventory of the possessions of Fray Joaquin Baquero, Tencoa, 1791

See Archivo de los Padres Mercedarios de Guatemala, Guatemala City (AMERGUA). Legajo 27a, Estado que manifiesta el numero de almas que se han confirmado en su ultima visita espiscopal, las capellanías, y cofradías que obtiene, curato de Tencoa, 11 de junio de 1791.

Currency and commodities: 50 pesos of currency; 44 pesos, donations found in a money box pertaining to the ransom of captives; and 8 *cargas* (load, approximately 50 pounds) of pepper stored at Ilama.

Religious objects: 2 plates, silver; 1 bowl, silver; 1 cup, silver; 1 tinplate platter without cover, and nine plates; 1 reliquary, large, with various relics; 1 bottle case, small, with eight bottles; 1 rosary; 2 altar cloths; and 1 *santo* (image) of Jesus Christ.

Books: 12 books, Christian year; 6 books, choral; 6 books, February; 6 books, small; 4 books, pertaining to donations for the ransom of captives expenses and receipts, and financial obligations; 3 books, breviaries; 2 books, small, nosegays; 2 books, saving of souls; 2 books, religious compendia; 1 book, Council of Trent; 1 book, deaths; 1 book, Fr. Corella; 1 book, Fr. Serrano [Fr. Juan Serrano, Mercedarian, served as comendador at Tencoa from 1696 to 1700, and as vicario at Tatumbla between 1724 and 1727]; 1 book, Mercedarian saints; 1 book, minutes of triennial chapter meetings; 1 book, new use service; 1 book, preaching subjects; 1 book, sermons; 1 book, sermons of Fr. Leal with declaration of possessions at the pueblo of Ojuera, the *paraje* (rural place) of Ceguaca, the paraje of Las Lagunas, and the pueblo of Santa Bárbara; 1 book, small, Holy Week; 1 book, small, Spanish eloquence; 1 book, explanatory grammar; 1 book, detailing the evangelical triumph at San Ysidro of San Juan.

Clothing: 6 linen stockings; 4 kerchiefs; 4 lapels; 3 shirts; 3 trousers; 2 napped cloth, 1 white; 3 underwear, cotton; 2 waistcoats; 2 aprons, black; 2 aprons, white wool; 2 cassocks, flannel; 1 buckle set, iron; 1 riding cloak, long, black wool; 1 hat, black oakum; 1 eye glasses; and 1 belt buckle, small, silver.

Other: 4 bed sheets; 4 jars, glass; 1 barber's cloth; 1 towel, used; 1 towel, hand; 1 bedspread, wool; 1 pavilion, with six curtains and striped gingham canopy; 1 pavilion, old; 1 carpet, cotton, with fringe; 1 curtain, cotton; 1 wine bag, leather, old; 1 mattress; 1 pack saddle; 1 camp bed, folding; 1 skeletal framework for a parasol; 1 traveling bag, canvas or leather, for mattress with case and mule chair; 1 whetstone, with five razors; 1 drinking horn for *aguardiente* (brandy); 1 chocolate vessel, porcelain; 1 writing desk; 1 inkstand made from cow horn; 1 baton, wood, with silver knob; and 1 cattle brand, iron.

Livestock: 2 mules; and 2 horses

† Chapter 11

Setting an English Table
Black Carib Archaeology on the Caribbean Coast of Honduras

Charles D. Cheek

Abstract

The Black Caribs were deported from their homeland, St. Vincent Island, to Honduras in 1799 by the British, who had recently defeated them in battle. The Black Caribs, or Garifuna, entered Honduras at Trujillo and quickly spread along the coast of Central America from Guatemala to Nicaragua, establishing settlements where they could participate in a money economy. In spite of their treatment at the hands of the British, the Black Caribs came to model themselves on the British rather than on the Spanish, with concomitant effects on their material culture, particularly their ceramics. This chapter compares two excavated assemblages from Trujillo: a Black Carib assemblage and probably a "French Republican Negro" assemblage from a site inhabited by refugees from Haiti. These assemblages are also compared with those noted during a survey of the Caribbean coast in Guatemala and Honduras.

Resumen

En 1779 los caribes negros de la isla de San Vicente fueron deportados a Honduras por los ingleses, que recientemente los habían vencido en el campo de batalla. Los caribes negros, o Garifuna, llegaron a Honduras por Trujillo y rápidamente se distribuyeron a lo largo de la costa de centroamérica, desde Guatemala hasta Nicaragua, fundando asentamientos donde podían participar en una economía monetaria. A pesar de este tratamiento a manos de los británicos, los caribes negros adoptaron los modelos ingleses en lugar de los españoles, con los efectos concomitantes en su cultura material, en particular la cerámica. En este capítulo se comparan dos conjuntos de excavación de Trujillo, en Honduras: uno corresponde a caribes negros y otro probablemente a "negros republicanos franceses", sitio habitado por refugiados de Haití. A su vez, se comparan estos conjuntos con los que se detectaron a partir de reconocimientos de superficie en la costa caribeña de Guatemala y Honduras.

THE BLACK CARIBS—or Garifuna as they call themselves today—have the appearance of African Americans, speak a South American Indian language, Carib, and have South American foodways (for example, they make a cassava bread, called *areba*). Their home in Central America is the Caribbean coast of Belize, Guatemala, and Honduras. This chapter, which relies on theories of ethnogenesis (the process of forming an ethnic group), examines how the Black Caribs used material culture to create a new identity for themselves in the nineteenth century.[1] They used behavior and material culture to aid in this process. Specifically, the focus is on English tablewares and the frequency of cups and saucers, and how such everyday items helped to both differentiate and affiliate the Black Caribs with respect to Europeans and European-affiliated groups as well as Native American groups on the Caribbean coast of Central America.

The Black Caribs could have affiliated with a number of groups when they reached Honduras. In addition to the dominant or co-dominant English and Spanish groups, there were Native Americans. Primary among these were the Miskito, a native client group of the British who helped the British in their conflict with the Spanish. The Miskito had close relations with the Black Caribs, and their ranges overlapped in eastern Honduras. Other Native American groups tended to stay in the interior, and, since the Black Caribs were a coastal people, they seem to have had little contact with these groups. Among other blacks on the coast were English blacks, slaves concentrated in British Honduras (now Belize) and possibly in Honduran logging camps. Free English and French blacks were refugees living in Trujillo when the Black Caribs arrived (González 1988:52–53).

Why the Black Caribs affiliated with English culture rather than with Hispanic or other cultures is a result of the particular historical forces at work in that part of the Caribbean. Their identity as an ethnic group was redefined in Honduras during the early 1800s as a result of interactions and unstated negotiations among the Black Caribs, other African Americans, native Indian groups, the Spanish, and the English. These negotiations involved Black Carib responses to

Spanish and English fears that the Caribs were French Republicans wedded to the Haitian ideology of liberty, equality, and fraternity. Such beliefs could translate into an overthrow of the existing slave-based economic system. Furthermore, because they affiliated with a European group rather than with Native Americans like the Miskito, the Black Caribs were perceived as part of the European sphere rather than the native or wild sphere. This perception was useful because of Spanish and British concerns that the Caribs were not reliable allies and might foment slave revolts (González 1988:55–56).

As Hodder and others have said, ideas are real resources in negotiations of power relations among groups, and material items are part of the ideological apparatus (Hodder 1984:351). In the Black Carib situation, the idea, which was the real resource, was their identity as an ethnic group, different from other groups in their environment. Because of their skin color, however, they were associated with another ideology, French republicanism, which could be dangerous for the European groups in power. This situation suggests that the Black Caribs took on English culture, even though they should not have been particularly friendly to the English, because it helped give them an identity separate from French Republican revolutionaries. The use of English tableware aided in this perceived transformation from a wild, uncivilized people who associated with the French Republicans to a group respected for their work habits and thought to be, by the English at least, the only civilized non-European group on the coast of Honduras.

History

The Black Caribs began, as far as we know, with a population of Africans from a Dutch slave trader wrecked off the coast of St. Vincent, an island in the Lesser Antilles. The Africans intermarried with the Caribs who inhabited the island, and, over the next 150 years, their descendants created a new society that interacted with the increasingly diverse Caribbean societies. The French and English were in conflict with each other and with the Black Caribs for control of the island. The last event in this contest was the Carib War, 1795–1796, between the Carib/French alliance and the British. The Black Caribs were also allied with a French mulatto revolutionary who was a serious enemy of the English. The Black Caribs lost and were deported by the English to the island of Roatan in the Bay Islands off the Caribbean coast of Honduras, opposite the Spanish town of Trujillo (González 1988:14–24).

It is not clear why the Black Caribs were sent to Roatan rather than elsewhere. The English and Spanish were contesting for control of the Honduran coast. Trujillo was a fortified Spanish outpost located in the center of the coast. To the east toward the Patuca River and Nicaragua, the English had client societies, the Miskitos and Sambos, whom they supplied with guns and encouraged to raid the Spanish and other inland groups (Floyd 1967; González 1988:52; Helms 1976:9–10). The English were also well established in what is today Belize. Perhaps the English wanted the Black Caribs to be another thorn in the side of the Spanish, although one would have thought that after their defeat and expulsion from St. Vincent by the English, they would not have been particularly amenable to being used in that fashion. Indeed, the Spanish from Trujillo sent an emissary to Roatan, and the Black Caribs moved immediately from the island to the mainland.

During the next thirty years, the Black Caribs spread along the Caribbean coast. The two criteria they used to select a site were nearness to wage labor and to land suitable for their tropical agriculture (Cheek and González 1986). Because virtually any location along the shore was suitable for tropical agriculture, the controlling variable in locating their settlements was the distance to wage labor opportunities. By the 1830s, the Black Caribs had spread along the entire Caribbean Coast from central Belize to Río Patuca, with the exception of a portion of the eastern shore of the Honduran coast which had no European settlements.

In the early 1800s, the primary opportunities for wage labor were around Trujillo, where the Black Caribs could also sell their produce to the Spanish, who were ineffective in establishing an agricultural economy. The second important source of wage labor was the English logging camps, which included areas east of Trujillo on the Aguan River and Sangreleya, or Black, River, as well as Belize.

Besides the three thousand or so Black Caribs, there were other African Americans in Trujillo in 1800 and possibly even on the ships that brought the Black Caribs to Roatan. Slightly fewer than three hundred French Republican blacks had been deported from Santo Domingo because they had been tainted by the revolution in Haiti. Various records place either forty or 300 English blacks (former slaves of the English colonists) and an unspecified number of free blacks, perhaps from Grenada, in Trujillo (González 1988:53).

According to their tradition, the Black Caribs never intermarried with other groups. Recent ethnohistoric research by Nancie González (González 1988) and physiological data gathered by her colleagues from Belize (Crawford 1984), however, strongly indicate that this tradition is a fiction developed to maintain the group's identity. All other African Americans in Trujillo in the early 1800s vanished from the historic records as individual populations. They could not be traced in the historic records partly because the Spanish applied such terms as *morenos, caribes morenos, morenos franceses,* and *caribes pardos,* more or less indiscriminately, to people who looked black (González 1988:62). They probably disappeared, however, because they were absorbed into

Setting an English Table

the numerically superior Black Carib ethnic group (González 1988:113–114)

Project History

The material for this study is derived from a larger ethnographic, ethnohistoric, and archaeological study, called Proyecto Garifuna, of historic and modern Black Carib settlement patterns. The goal of the 1982–1984 project was to identify the forces that controlled the initial settlement pattern of the Caribs after their landing at Trujillo in 1797. Several authors (Beaucage 1982; Bolland and Shoman 1977; Davidson 1984) had suggested or assumed that the Black Caribs were primarily interested in finding agricultural lands and that their economy was based largely on fishing and agriculture. Thus, they would locate in sites suitable for these pursuits. Cheek and González (1986), based on their study of the economic activity of the Black Caribs in St. Vincent, felt that they established settlements near locations where they could obtain wage labor and participate in the market economy. A survey of the coasts of Guatemala and Honduras supported this interpretation.

In addition to the survey, the excavation of Black Carib sites in and around Trujillo was undertaken to provide a sample that would allow definition of the material culture the Black Caribs utilized to establish and maintain their identify within the multicultural environment of the Caribbean coast.

Three of the sites are used for analysis in this chapter: Campamento, west of Trujillo, was occupied by Black Caribs as early as 1799 (González 1988:54,62); site 8, located southeast of Trujillo proper on uplands overlooking the city, seems, on the basis of archaeological evidence, to have been occupied from 1800 to 1820 or 1830; and site 1 in Cristales, on the west edge of Trujillo, also based on archaeological evidence, was occupied from the 1830s to the 1880s.

Campamento was a military camp occupied by at least some Black Caribs in 1799 (González 1988:62), just two years after their arrival, when they helped defeat an attack by the English whom they said they hated (González 1988:54). All ceramics from this site are majolica or fragments of olive jars.

The site at Campamento could be a predominantly Spanish site, as there is only documentary evidence that Black Caribs occupied it for a short time, but it is very unlikely that sites 1 and 8 could be Spanish. First, no document or informant has ever suggested that Spaniards had lived in these places; second, both contained white clay pipes, generally not found in Spanish sites—a circumstance true in Colonial Florida for the earlier periods as well as for Colombia (Deagan 1983:246). Recently, a lack of clay pipes has been noted at a late nineteenth-century Puerto Rican site (Cheek et al. 1987:63) indicating that Spanish populations in the Caribbean may never have developed the habit of smoking tobacco in clay pipes.

The second site, site 8, located in the hills above Trujillo, may be the area given in 1803 to French Republican blacks as a reward for their service in the militia (González 1988:109). Several lines of evidence support this assumption:

- The ceramics belong to a very limited time period. There is some creamware, a majority of pearlware, and very little whiteware, which suggests a date of 1800 to 1825. There are also Bristol Glazed "ginger beer bottles," which can be dated no earlier than the 1840s when this glaze was developed. Thus, the site may have been occupied somewhat later, and the ceramics represent out-of-style wares still favored by the local consumers. The ceramics from site 8, partially benefiting from the relaxed Spanish trade laws, were primarily English with other components which will be reviewed later.

- There are no grater stones.

- Several pieces of military hardware—such as a bayonet, a piece of a gun mechanism, and gun flints—were found (figure 11.1).

The third site, site 1, is from Cristales, an area on the beach and lower slopes below and to the west of Trujillo proper. This site does not have a ceramic assemblage as chronologically restricted as that at site 8. The major occupation was probably from the 1830s to the 1880s. There are a few ceramic markers from the early 1800s, including majolica, and a few from the late 1800s, including red, white, and blue annular ware and decal-decorated porcelain.

This site did produce grater stones. A grater stone is a piece of quartz placed in a *egei* (wooden board) and used to grate manioc root. Manioc bread is a South American tropical forest product made on the Caribbean coast of Central America only by the Black Caribs. These grater stones can be differentiated from nonutilized pieces of quartz found in the soil. Their use in the *egei* creates a polish on one end that is identifiable under a microscope. Items relating to the sea orientation of the Black Caribs, such as fish-hooks and copper boat nails, were also found here.

Ceramics and Ethnicity

The title of this chapter comes from an observation by an English trader named Young that the Black Caribs set an English table . In 1847, he listed plates, dishes, cups, mugs, jugs, saucers, and basins as goods wanted by the Black Caribs (Young 1847:126–127). The question is why the Black Caribs were perceived as the most English of the non-European groups along the Honduran shore. The Miskitos had closer

FIGURE 11.1 Military-related artifacts from site 8, Trujillo, Honduras. Gunflints (*left*), rifle or musket side plate (*top right*), three unidentified metal artifacts, round shot, and projectiles. *All photos by Sheree Lane and Nancy Chabot*

ties to the English, had been their clients for years, and had even been crowned as kings in Jamaica. They had the same access, through traders like Young, to these goods. It was the Black Caribs, however, who had been deported by the English from their homeland, who emulated the English ways.

With the loosening of trade restrictions by the Spanish Crown during the years 1785 to 1815, the inhabitants of the Spanish possessions in the Americas became part of the market for the industrialized ceramic products of England. Some of these products had been smuggled into Spanish ports during the preceding years, but there was a major increase in their purchase and use beginning at the turn of the nineteenth century. For example, non-Hispanic ceramics constituted between 25 and 55 percent of the ceramic sherds from the Ballajá area of San Juan, Puerto Rico (Joseph and Bryne 1992:54) dating from the first decades of the nineteenth century. English ceramics have been excavated from this period at the fort of Omoa on the west end of the Honduran coast.[2]

How Spanish and non-Spanish groups on the Honduran coast took advantage of this access was controlled by their decisions concerning not only what they wanted to buy but also whether they had the means to buy it. It is clear from Young's report and from the results of the survey (Cheek and González 1986) that the Black Caribs bought and used many more items and classes of European goods than did the Miskito or non-European groups. Archaeological assemblages in other Spanish possessions (Felton and Schulz 1983; Joseph and Bryne 1992) demonstrate that Hispanic groups were a major market for English ceramics. No one has yet explored the differences that might exist, however, in the kinds or frequencies of decorative types and forms purchased by the Spanish as opposed to, for example, North Americans.

Another factor that may have affected the ability to acquire English ceramics relates to work. Because the Caribs worked in Belize, they had access to British goods from stores as well as from traders like Young who cruised the coastline. Well known and respected workers (González 1988:125–143), the Black Caribs were able to obtain jobs in the cash economy which might have given them an advantage in purchasing items from such traders. Young, however, does not talk about differences in the ability to pay but about differences in desires for different kinds of items. One would not expect that the Spanish were less able to acquire goods than the Black Caribs, although this has not been explored either from the historic record or archaeologically. The Proyecto

Garifuna was originally intended to collect a sample from a nineteenth-century Spanish site at Trujillo, but that part of the project remains to be completed.

Ceramic Assemblage

The Black Carib ceramic assemblage is similar in its composition to other nineteenth-century assemblages from other Spanish Republican areas (see, for example, Joseph and Bryne 1992) and must be examined as a whole to be understood. The Black Carib assemblage is composed of three separate ceramic traditions: a non-Hispanic European component, an Hispanic component, and an indigenous component. The non-Hispanic European component was composed exclusively of British wares until the later nineteenth century when other European whitewares and porcelains appeared.

In site 8, English wares were composed of hand-painted and blue transfer-printed pearlware, as well as some annular ware (figures 11.2, 11.3). In site 1, hand-painted, sponged, and transfer-printed whitewares and annular whitewares were recovered (figure 11.4). There was no evidence in the material collected of an African American component nor of North American ceramics.

The indigenous ceramic tradition was represented by handmade, red-painted, buff water jars that informants said were still being brought to Trujillo for sale in the twentieth century. Other coarse wares, some unglazed and unslipped, were present but are much rarer.

The Hispanic component was represented by chronologically distinct wares: the fine-paste majolicas and olive jars typical of the late eighteenth century and a wheel-thrown redware cooking pot. The early majolicas and olive jars were very rare in nineteenth-century collections and may have been relict wares. The Hispanic redware is a wheel-thrown, restricted-neck cooking bowl, 8 to 11 inches in diameter, with red-orange paste and greenish lead glaze, primarily on the interior but sometimes spilling over onto the exterior (figures 11.5, 11.6). Rolled vertical handles are found occasionally. These vessels are common from the early 1800s (site 8 at Trujillo) to at least the late 1800s (at various sites on the Honduran coast) when they seem to drop out of the assemblage. Sherds from several similar vessels were found in a trash pit of a wealthy family in Ponce, Puerto Rico, dating to the beginning of the twentieth century (Cheek et al. 1987:63).

It is not known how common these redware vessels were in Puerto Rico or other areas of the Caribbean. Deagan (1987:247–253) neither discusses nor illustrates such a type or form in her review of the lead-glazed, coarse earthenwares from the Spanish colonies of Florida and the Caribbean from 1500 to 1800 (Deagan 1987:247–53). This redware could be one of the many kinds of locally made miscellaneous redwares that have not yet been defined, or this ware could have been produced after 1800. It is interesting, however, that none of the redwares Deagan discusses were said to have been used for cooking. Such a function recalls the use of ceramics for cooking in Jamaica (Armstrong 1990:146–158) and other areas inhabited by African Americans such as the southeastern United States (Ferguson 1978; Wheaton and Garrow 1985). Although it has been suggested that similar redware vessels (El Morro ware) in Puerto Rico may have been part of the Afro-Caribbean ceramic tradition, this idea has not been pursued (Joseph and Bryne 1992:53).

A similar class of lead-glazed, coarse redware vessels may be found in Jamaica. Armstrong (1990:146) calls these wares imported coarse earthenwares because they exhibit European technology and were composed of clays and tempers not found in Jamaica. They are described as "thick, fine-grained, and often massive sherds that were fully fired (no core) and wheel made" (Armstrong 1990:146). The rim profiles in Armstrong's Figure 41 are similar to the rims from Trujillo. He notes, however, that this ware was used primarily for storage. Another group of coarse redwares was used for cooking: open bowls or simple restricted-orifice vessels that were handmade of a clay that fired generally brown/red and was often incompletely oxidized (Armstrong 1990:147). The rim forms are direct and not rolled as are those from Trujillo. One vessel with a red-brown paste was found in site 8 at Trujillo, the probable settlement of the Afro-Caribbean, French Republican blacks; however, the rim of this vessel was also rolled.

Older Black Caribs were interviewed to ascertain if there was a tradition of ceramic manufacture among them. Only one of those interviewed suggested this was a possibility, although even she was uncertain. One contemporary household in the Río Negro barrio (located on the east side of Trujillo) had curated a similar vessel that had a slightly larger diameter than the archaeological examples. The recollection of the vessel's function was that it was not used for cooking but for preparing some liquid, possibly beer, for use in ceremonies.

Ceramic Analysis

Following classification, the minimum number of vessels were calculated for all wares. Minimum vessel analysis is necessary to examine the functional characteristics of a ceramic assemblage, and it provides a better basis on which to count and calculate percentages. Sherd counts are affected by vessel size and friability and distort the real frequencies of particular wares, types, and forms. Vessel forms are used in the current analysis because they are an important source of information about the foodways of different groups. Minimum vessel counts have been used to understand ethnicity (Otto 1977), class (for example, Garrow 1987; Shephard 1987), and regional differences (Yentsch 1991) in North American cultures.

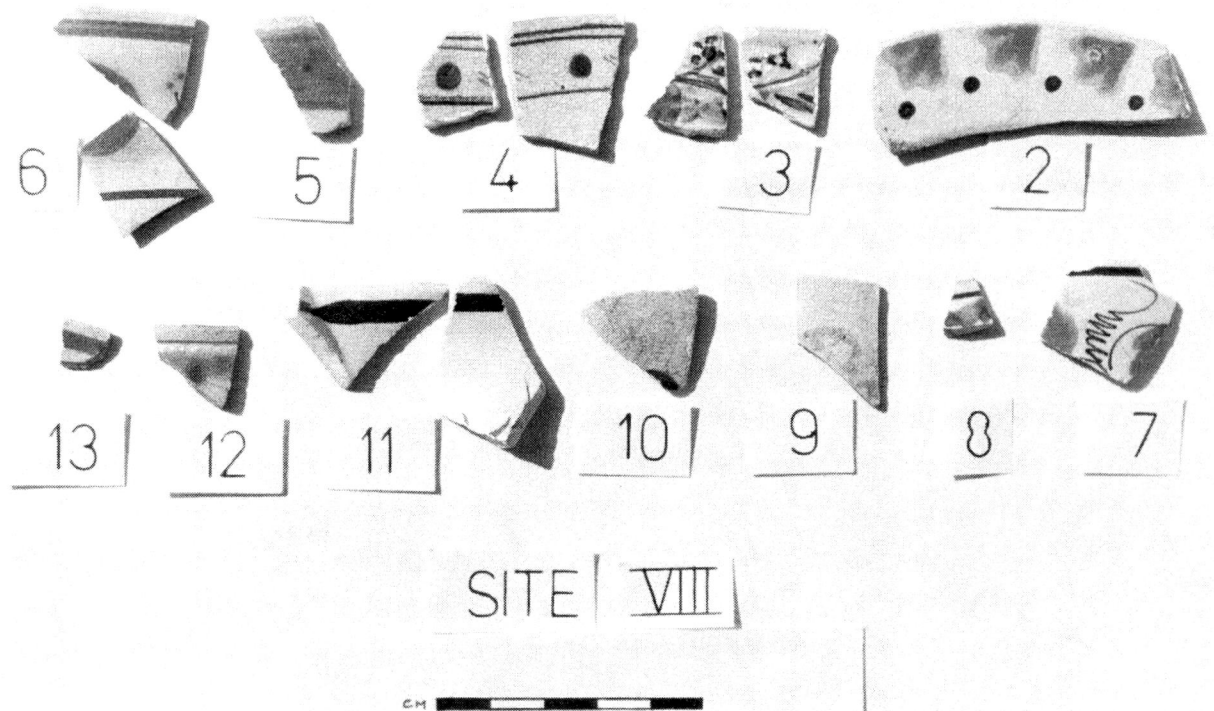

FIGURE 11.2 Staffordshire ceramics from site 8, Trujillo, Honduras. Hand-painted pearlware: plates (vessels 2 through 4); bowls (vessels 5, 6); cups (vessels 7, 8); teapot (vessel 10); unidentified (vessels 12, 13). Hand-painted creamware: cup (vessel 9); pitcher (vessel 11)

FIGURE 11.3 Transfer-printed pearlware cups and saucers from site 8, Trujillo, Honduras. Interior and exterior of blue cup (vessel 63); blue saucer (vessel 64); interior and exterior of blue cup (vessel 78); and interior and exterior of blue cup (vessel 79)

FIGURE 11.4 Staffordshire ceramics from site 1, Trujillo, Honduras. Pearlware: edged plates (vessels 89, 90); hand-painted bowls (vessels 91, 92, 102); hand-painted cups (vessels 101, 103); hand-painted lid (vessel 93). Whiteware: spattered chamber pot (vessel 94); sponge-stamped cup (vessel 95); sponge-stamped plate (vessel 96); sponge-stamped bowls (vessels 97, 98); hand-painted cup (vessels 99, 104); hand-painted saucer (vessel 100); and hand-painted plates (vessels 105, 106)

Gaining an understanding of actual behavior through mass-produced wares with standardized forms is more difficult than studying assemblages from cultures that produced local forms for local foodways. One set of mass-produced English forms, associated with tea and coffee, reflects specific foodways. These forms include cups, saucers, tea and coffee pots, and creamers and sugars.

Most historic archaeologists are aware that the tea ceremony which penetrated English society in the seventeenth century was an important component of social interaction among the elite, and later among the general populace. Both tea and coffee penetrated the foodways of European societies and their colonies. In the nineteenth century, teaware was provided for the masses in a variety of differentially priced decorative ceramic types. Although teawares may have been of varying quality, they are ubiquitous on North American sites. It is difficult, if not impossible, to identify the beverages and in what circumstances cups and saucers were used; yet, it is possible to identify the forms and to be aware that they were different from previous forms. It is suggested that an increased use of cups and saucers is a signal of an attempt to emulate the English food and drinking habits, whether or not tea or coffee were drunk regularly.

The transformation to an English orientation can be seen in the ratio of plates to cups in the everyday material culture of the three Trujillo sites: Campamento, site 8, and site 1. Ratios of plates to cups, rather than percentages, are used. Thus, a site assemblage characterized as having sixty plates per cup would mean that teawares were not as important as in an assemblage that had a ratio of two plates per cup.

As discussed above, the occupants of site 1 and Campamento are Black Carib. The occupants of site 8 are probably French Republican blacks possibly mixed with Black Caribs. While it would be better to have a collection from an early Black Carib site, site 8 is used because its occupants were in the process of being absorbed into the Black Carib community and may have wanted to distance themselves from a revolutionary label.

A number of sites in the Mid Atlantic area of North America from the mid-1800s were used as a familiar com-

FIGURE 11.5 Lead-glazed, coarse redware from site 8, Trujillo, Honduras

FIGURE 11.6 Lead-glazed, coarse redware from site 1, Trujillo, Honduras

parative standard. All deposits were from white, middle-class households. The ratios generally ranged from 0.8 to 1.5 plates per cup (see Garrow 1987; LeeDecker et al. 1987; Shephard 1987). This fairly large number of cups reflected the importance of this class of ceramics in middle-class homes in North America.

In Trujillo, the cup ratio indicated an increase in the relative number of cups over time. At Campamento, only Hispanic wares from the late eighteenth century were found, indicating no participation in English foodways. In site 8, the cup ratio was 4.9 plates per cup. In site 1, there were 3.8 plates per cup. The number of cups was increasing with respect to the number of plates but did not reach the levels of the Mid-Atlantic ratios.

It is also instructive to compare these ratios to those of the slave and free Afro-Jamaicans at Drax Hall in Jamaica (Armstrong 1990). The plate-to-cup ratio at Drax Hall underlines Armstrong's observations about the lack of tea wares. The ratio varies from almost thirteen plates per cup to sixty plates per cup. It seems clear that, for whatever reasons, the Afro-Jamaicans did not take up the use of cups and saucers, and possibly tea or coffee drinking, to the same extent as the Black Caribs.

The plate-to-cup ratio among the Black Caribs clearly indicates a distinct appreciation of tea and coffee wares and possibly of the use of these beverages. Tea and coffee wares were less integrated into their foodways than in middle-class households in North America, but such ceramics were more important to the Black Caribs than to the Afro-Jamaicans.

This appreciation may have developed as the Black Caribs freely came to emulate the English in their consumption patterns. The Afro-Jamaican slave populations did not have the same latitude of choice and may have had less incentive to imitate the former masters when given their freedom. As part of developing an ethnic identity which affiliated them with the British rather than the French or Spanish, the Black Caribs increased the use of tea and coffee wares over time.

Conclusions

These observations should be considered preliminary because analysis of the collection is not complete. Furthermore, there is no excavated collection from a Spanish site in Trujillo that can be compared to the Black Carib sites. Such a comparison is crucial in understanding the Black Carib material culture, especially the range and selection of material items available to this group during the nineteenth century.

Three observations can be made with some certainty, however. First, the Black Caribs are an example of the groups created as a result of the intersection of cultures from disparate areas of the world. Second, like other groups during this period, Black Caribs helped to create themselves and their identity. They drew upon their historically based behavior patterns and combined them with new elements from their increasingly complex social and cultural environment. They used these elements as the raw material from which they formed their new culture. Finally, as demonstrated by comparison with the material culture of other non-European groups in the Caribbean and Honduras, part of the tools they used to create their culture were material items like mass-produced English ceramics, which had symbolic value to them and to the societies with whom they intersected.

Acknowledgments. The first field survey, in the winter of 1982–1983, was funded by the Graduate School, the Division of Behavioral and Social Sciences, and the Department of Anthropology at the University of Maryland. In the following year, further research was made possible through a Fulbright-Hayes Group Projects Abroad, the Fulbright Council for the International Exchange of Scholars, and the Wenner-Gren Foundation for Anthropological Research. John Milner Associates, Inc., West Chester, Pennsylvania, provided a leave of absence for the author. The Honduran national host institution was the Instituto Hondureño de Antropología e Historia. Sheree Lane, the archaeological project assistant, also supervised the archaeological work in my absence. Archaeological students Nancy Chabot and Martin Dudeck supervised excavations, cataloged the artifacts, conducted the minimum vessel count, and photographed the artifacts. Thanks are also due to the many Garifuna who assisted us.

Notes

1. The Black Caribs have created or redefined themselves at least three times while maintaining their basic identity as a group: in the late seventeenth century, in the nineteenth century, and in modern times (González 1988:32, 70, 186).
2. This material was excavated by George Hasemann, an archaeologist with the Instituto de Antropología e Historia and examined by the author in 1984.

✝ Chapter 12

Monumentos y Fragmentos
Arqueología Histórica en el Ecuador

Jozef Buys

Resumen

En el marco del Proyecto de Cooperación Técnica Ecuatoriano-Belga "La Preservación y Promoción del Patrimonio Cultural del Ecuador," se está llevando a cabo la investigación arqueológica del Convento de Santo Domingo de Quito, sede del mencionado proyecto, como paso previo a la restauración y la adecuación del museo. Las excavaciones van dirigidas a conocer la historia constructiva del convento, desde su inicio hasta la fecha, pero tratan de resolver, a la vez, preguntas arquitectónico-estructurales con miras a la posterior restauración del monumento. Los resultados hasta ahora obtenidos permiten establecer una secuencia cronológica que comienza en el período de Integración (500–1500 dC) con los restos de un cementerio aborigen, sobre el cual se construyó el primer convento en la segunda mitad del siglo XVI. El claustro principal y la iglesia del monumento actual se sobreponen a la construcción primitiva y datan de principios del siglo XVII, luego de lo cual se añadieron numerosas dependencias hasta la fecha.

Abstract

The Ecuadorian-Belgian Technical Assistance Project "La Preservación y Promoción del Patrimonio Cultural del Ecuador" is conducting the archaeological investigation of the Convento de Santo Domingo in Quito as a prelude to its restoration and the installation of a museum in part of the monument. The excavations are designed to unravel the construction history of the monastery from its beginnings until today. In addition, they also will resolve architectural and structural questions regarding its future restoration. The results to date have established a chronological sequence starting during the Integration period (AD 500–1500) with the remains of an aboriginal cemetery, on top of which the first convent was built in the second half of the sixteenth century. The main cloister and church of the present monument overlay the earliest building and date to the beginning of the seventeenth century. Since then other constructions have been added.

D**URANTE VARIAS TEMPORADAS** entre 1988 y 1992, el Área de Arqueología del Proyecto de Cooperación Técnica Ecuatoriana-Belga "La Preservación y Promoción del Patrimonio Cultural del Ecuador" se encargó de la investigación arqueológica del Convento de Santo Domingo en Quito, Ecuador, como estudio previo a la restauración del edificio y su futura adecuación como museo (Buys 1989; Buys y Camino 1991; Buys y Domínguez 1988; Buys, Domínguez, y Andrade 1988). Simultáneamente y como consecuencia directa de las excavaciones, se inició el estudio comparativo de la cerámica colonial en el Ecuador, un campo que sólo ahora empieza a ser explorado de una manera sistemática (Buys 1990, 1992; Holm 1971). En este capítulo se pretende resumir y relacionar los resultados de ambas investigaciones, con el fin de proporcionar una visión general de la arqueología histórica en el Ecuador, en particular en la región de Quito (véase capítulo 13).

El Convento de Santo Domingo

La evolución de un monumento con la importancia del Convento de Santo Domingo representa un proceso continuo de construcciones, modificaciones, reparaciones y restauraciones que reflejan las necesidades y usos cambiantes de la comunidad que siempre lo habitó. A la vez puede explicar la razón de su emplazamiento: topografía adecuada, ubicación ventajosa dentro de la incipiente planificación urbana de la colonia, así como ocupación intencional de elementos prehispánicos importantes.

Antes de la llegada de los españoles, el sector de la "Loma Grande," en donde actualmente se ubica el Convento de Santo Domingo, formaba parte del asentamiento aborigen que se organizaba alrededor del *tianguez* (mercado) precolombino, un lugar de intenso intercambio con alcance extrarregional (Salomon 1980). El hallazgo de varias tumbas secundarias in situ con el ajuar típico de la zona, permite inferir la existencia de un cementerio perteneciente al período de Integración (500–1480 dC).

La dominación inka del sector se evidencia por la presencia de cerámica dispersa, pero en un solo sector se encontró una

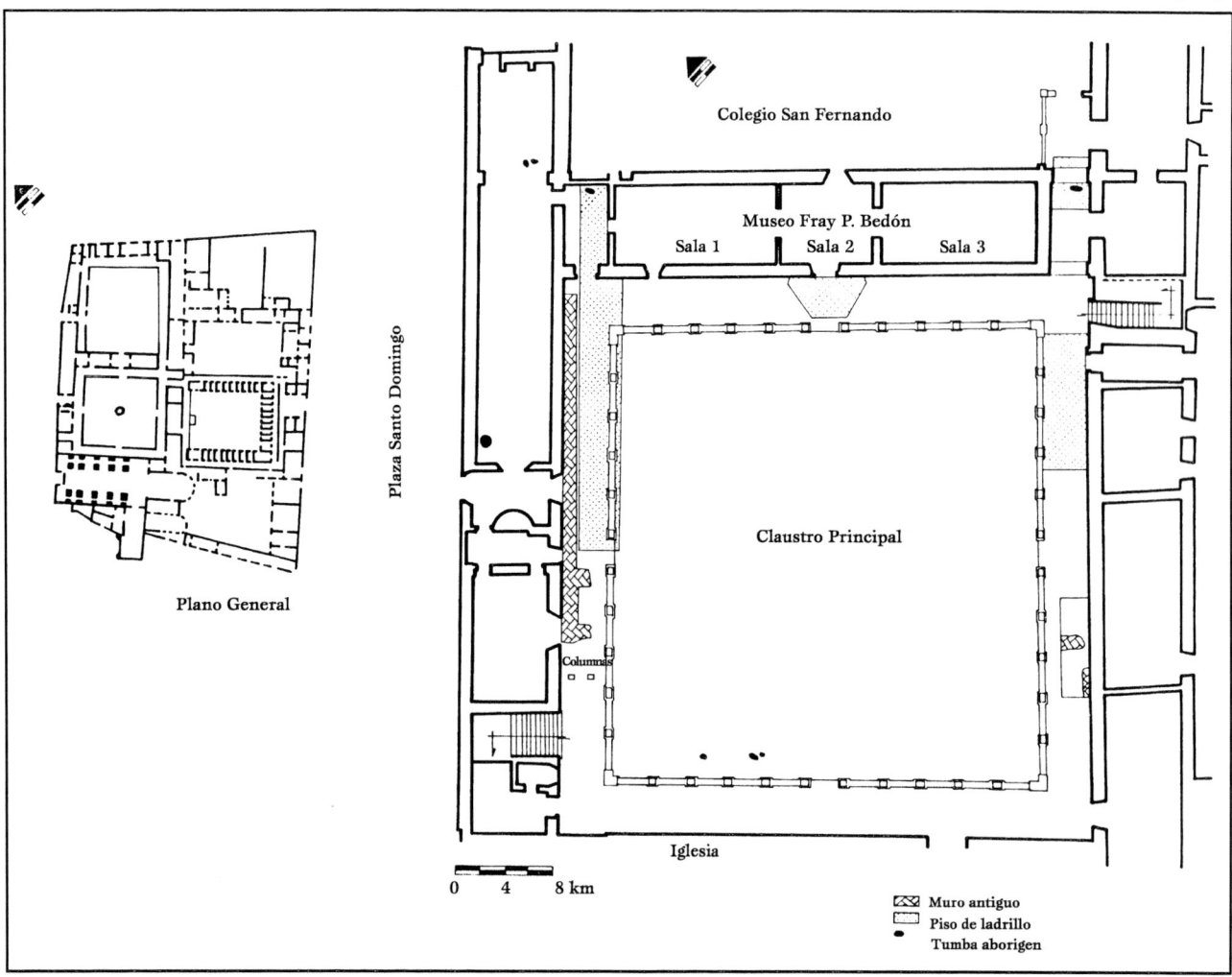

FIGURA 12.1 **Planta del Convento de Santo Domingo en Quito.** *Todas las ilustraciónes son por el Proyecto de Cooperación Técnica Ecuatoriano-Belga "La Preservación y Promoción del Patrimonio Cultural del Ecuador." Ilustraciónes y fotografías del autor*

concentración de esta alfarería junto a un fragmento de muro muy alterado posteriormente. Resulta aventurado inferir la existencia de alguna construcción inka con los pocos datos ahora conocidos, pero la presencia de un muro inka grande bajo la iglesia de San Francisco (Terán de Rodríguez 1991) indica que no se debe descartar esta posibilidad.

En 1541 el cabildo de Quito entregó algunos solares del sector "Loma Grande" para la ubicación del convento (Vargas 1986:30). No existe información histórica sobre lo que se edificó inmediatamente después de esta asignación, pero entre 1561 y 1565, bajo el impulso del Fray Jerónimo de Cervantes, se cercó la propiedad y se inició la construcción del claustro principal (Vargas 1967:49). Deben haber sido estructuras poco imponentes para que Pedro de Aguayo, en 1573, hablara de "edificios humildes" (citado en Vargas 1967:55).

En las excavaciones del claustro principal se han descubierto varios elementos de este primer convento fechado en la segunda mitad del siglo XVI (figura 12.1): varios tramos de un piso de ladrillo con el diseño "espina pez" y un muro de adobe sobre base de piedra (figura 12.2); conforman por lo menos tres alas de un claustro primitivo desplazado hacia el norte con respecto al monumento actual. En el centro de esta configuración se han encontrado los restos de un piso hexagonal con un canal abierto alrededor y tubería debajo, la base de la pileta original (figura 12.3). El ala sur funcionaba como iglesia, a juzgar por la cantidad de entierros cristianos y los datos históricos que aseveran que el templo antiguo coexistió con el actual (Terán Najas 1991). Parece que la iglesia estaba un poco retirada para dejar espacio a un atrio en el cual se deben haber ubicado las dos columnas, cuyas bases se excavaron hacia la esquina suroeste del claustro principal actual. De esta información resumida se puede visualizar un convento de 42 m de lado en su interior y alas entre 6 y 8 m de ancho, con iglesia en el ala sur. Esta configuración postulada se asentaría perfectamente centrada sobre la loma natural original y no habría necesitado de movimientos de tierra. Como fue edificado en adobe y de un solo piso, este convento debe haber originado la descripción de "edificios humildes" en la pluma de Pedro de Aguayo.

La falta de recursos para edificar un monumento grande

Monumentos y Fragmentos: Arqueología Histórica en el Ecuador

FIGURA 12.2 Corredor occidental del Convento de Santo Domingo en Quito. Se nota el muro de adobe enlucido de blanco y piso de ladrillo (diseño de "espina de pez" con orla alrededor). La zanja diagonal que destruyó parcialmente el piso obedece a un canal posterior; la tubería es muy reciente. El piso de piedras cuadradas indica el nivel actual de los corredores. *Todas las fotografías son por Jozef Buys*

FIGURA 12.3 Corredor norte del Convento de Santo Domingo en Quito (frente al museo). Se aprecian restos del piso de la pileta central del primer convento, de ladrillos y con un pequeño canal abierto alrededor de forma hexagonal, que está cortado por un canal posterior.

desde el inicio, se debía a que los dominicos no recibieron el respaldo del sector más rico de la sociedad, por su posición en defensa de los indígenas. Sólo tiempo después llegaron las donaciones importantes de comerciantes pudientes que fundaron y financiaron las capillas menores o altares laterales de la iglesia, con el fin de que en ellos se dispusiera su sepultura y la de sus descendientes (Terán Najas 1991:2).

En 1581 había llegado a Quito el español Francisco de Becerra. Este arquitecto de buena reputación elaboró los planos de la iglesia y convento, pero al parecer sólo construyó los cimientos del templo. Más bien fue el Padre Rodrigo de Lara Manrique quien, a partir de 1595, llevó adelante la verdadera edificación (Vargas 1967:56). La necesidad de un convento nuevo y definitivo se había hecho impostergable con la creación, en 1584, de la provincia dominicana de Santa Catalina Virgen y Mártir, por lo cual el monasterio de Quito adquirió la categoría de Convento Máximo; el subsiguiente crecimiento del número de religiosos exigía una infraestructura extensa (Terán Najas 1991:3).

A principios del siglo XVII se inició, entonces, la edificación grande con la colocación de los cimientos profundos. El único testigo de los trabajos de construcción queda en el Museo Fray Pedro Bedón, bajo la forma de una superficie de uso en la cual se observan hoyos de poste grandes y pequeños, seguramente para andamios, además de restos de los materiales de construcción. Aquí también se localizó el refectorio original, un solo espacio en el cual se podían ubicar los setenta religiosos que se estima habitaban en el convento (Vargas 1986:176). Atestigua este evento un piso de ladrillo con banco alrededor, en las salas 2 y 3 (figura 12.4), y el umbral en la puerta de entrada. La sala 1 actual debe haber tenido el carácter de sala "de profundis." Cabe señalar que

FIGURA 12.4 Museo Fray Pedro Bedón, esquina sureste de la sala 2. El piso de ladrillos muestra diseño de "espina de pez" y orla, banco de ladrillos y adobe adosado al muro. Se nota bien cómo este piso pasa debajo el muro que separa las salas 2 y 3. El muro en primer plano pertenece a modificaciones posteriores.

en los siglos XVI y XVII la costumbre era de ubicar el refectorio en el ala opuesta de la iglesia (Sebastian, J. de Mesa, y T. Gisbert de Mesa 1985:156).

A partir de mediados del siglo XVII el segundo claustro, hoy Colegio de San Fernando, estaba en plena construcción. En 1688 el refectorio actual, en el ala oriental de este claustro, fue terminado. Alrededor de la misma fecha el refectorio antiguo debe haber cambiado de función y se postula que fue a finales del siglo XVII o principios del siglo XVIII cuando se edificó el segundo piso de ladrillo en el Museo Fray Pedro Bedón. Creemos que simultáneamente se construyó también el sistema de las bóvedas en la parte occidental del museo y, posiblemente, en el resto del convento. Este sistema podía funcionar como ventilación del edificio, para contrarrestar la humedad capilar, a la vez que era una manera de elevar el nivel de los pisos.

En la transición entre los siglos XVII y XVIII se consolidaron los rasgos básicos de la fisonomía del convento y se amplió con el noviciado o coristado (1730), para terminar el conjunto hacia fines del siglo XVIII con la gran muralla que hoy rodea el convento (Terán Najas 1991:4–7). El análisis de los datos de archivo permite aseverar que el resto del siglo XVIII fue un período más bien de reparaciones y adecuaciones, no de grandes construcciones (Kennedy T. 1989:25).

Las edificaciones posteriores se refieren principalmente a otras partes del monumento y no vienen al caso aquí. En realidad, la actividad arquitectónica continúa hasta la actualidad. En lo que respecta al claustro principal, las modificaciones posteriores deben haber sido de poco alcance, lo que hace difícil detectarlas e interpretarlas. Se limitarían a subdivisiones cambiantes dentro de la configuración grande existente y obedecerían a los múltiples cambios de funciones de las diferentes partes del monumento. Lamentablemente, con la información histórica disponible no es posible inferir la ubicación de ambientes específicos.

La Cerámica Colonial

La cerámica encontrada en las excavaciones del Convento de Santo Domingo refleja bastante bien la variabilidad de la alfarería Colonial del Ecuador en general: terracota Colonial ordinaria y fina, mayólica de diferentes calidades y porcelana. La cerámica vidriada es casi inexistente. En el resumen que se presenta a continuación, se trata de tomar en cuenta todos los vestigios de cerámica Colonial procedentes tanto de la Sierra (Bolaños y Manosalvas 1989; Rousseau 1989, 1990; Terán de Rodríguez 1989), como de la costa (Bushnell 1951; Lanning 1967) y Amazonia (Porras 1974).

Terracota Ordinaria

Esta cerámica sólo puede ser fehacientemente definida como Colonial cuando acusa formas o decoraciones no aborígenes, ya que la continuidad de la tradición alfarera mantenía los mismos procedimientos tecnológicos que durante la época Prehispánica. Normalmente esta cerámica es de una pasta bastante gruesa, desgrasante mediano a grande y una variedad de acabados de superficie, desde un simple alisado hasta un pulido ligero.

Los jarrones grandes o botijas en las cuales se transportaba el aceite de oliva, vino, brea, etcétera, se encuentran tanto en las colecciones existentes como en las excavaciones. Casi todos los ejemplos conocidos pertenecen al estilo Medio de la clasificación de Goggin (1960), es decir que cronológicamente se ubican entre 1570 y 1770. Tal es el caso de los hallazgos en las excavaciones del Convento de Santo Domingo (Buys 1990:68, Lám. 6) (figura 12.5f), en el Hospital de San Juan de Dios (Rousseau 1990) y en el Convento de San Agustín, todos en Quito. En este último sitio se encontró una buena cantidad de botijas en el relleno de la bóveda entre la planta baja y el piso alto, visible en la escalera de la esquina sureste.

La colección más grande de botijas se halla indudablemente en el Museo del Banco Central de Cuenca, y muestra una amplia variedad de las formas características de los períodos Medio y Tardío de Goggin. Aunque no se debe excluir la posibilidad de unos pocos casos del estilo Temprano, hasta la fecha no existen fragmentos que indicarían botijas anteriores a 1570.

Los cántaros grandes constituyen los mejores ejemplos de sincretismo cerámico. En sus formas despliegan claras reminiscencias inkaicas, pero en la decoración muestran una gran influencia española. En efecto, muchos ejemplos acusan las características del *arίbalo* inka, con asas verticales e incluso la clavija en la base del cuello, pero normalmente con una base plana en vez de puntiaguda. Usualmente se caracterizan por un engobe rojo oscuro y frecuentes decoraciones al pastillaje.

En los diseños se observan elementos foráneos como rostros alados y motivos florales no andinos. Cronológicamente estos cántaros parecen cubrir un tiempo largo, desde los primeros todavía muy prehispánicos fechables en el siglo XVI, hasta los ejemplos completamente Coloniales de los siglos XVII–XVIII (figura 12.5a–b). Así, también las ollas muestran una cronología prolongada y una asignación Colonial sólo con base en la decoración, ya que las formas cambian muy poco hasta nuestros días.

Por definición, los jarros (figura 12.5c–f) son claramente definibles como Coloniales. El cuerpo de estas vasijas puede adquirir diversas formas, de simplemente esférico hasta alargado o de contornos complejos, pero siempre tienen una sola asa vertical y a veces una vertedera. La vertedera normalmente es abierta y no muy grande, pero en unos pocos casos existe un pico vertedero cerrado. La mejor colección de jarros se halla en el Museo del Banco Central de Cuenca: son de tamaño mediano y acusan una decoración bastante compleja mediante la aplicación de medallones, la incisión de motivos, elementos sellados, etcétera (Idrovo Uriguen 1990:33–34). Algunos ejemplos, con caras modeladas en el cuello, al lado opuesto de la asa, indican el elemento aborigen. El acabado de la superficie de los jarros puede ser muy sencillo, simplemente alisado o con engobe. En la Plaza de Santo Domingo de Quito se encontraron en excavaciones dos jarros con engobe rojo ligeramente pulido en el exterior (Rousseau 1991). La pasta y el acabado son idénticos a las técnicas aborígenes y constituyen buenos ejemplos de la continuidad técnica en formas nuevas. Es posible que varios fragmentos de este tipo de terracota, relativamente comunes en todas las excavaciones, representen el mismo tipo de jarro.

Las otras categorías de terracota están representadas por muy pocos ejemplos: cuencos medianos para uso doméstico, fuentes grandes de tipo "lavacara," *comales*

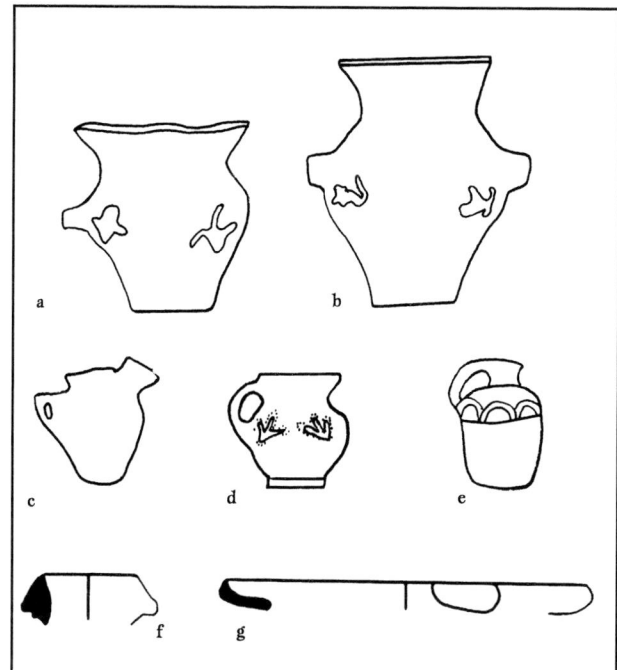

FIGURA 12.5 Principales tipos de terracota encontrados en el Convento de Santo Domingo

(figura 12.5g), y crisoles.

Terracota Fina

A esta categoría pertenecen los fragmentos de cerámica sin vidriar no esmaltada correspondientes a recipientes de forma no siempre definida pero que, con seguridad, no son aborígenes. En las colecciones del Hospital de San Juan de Dios de Quito se puede reconstruir parcialmente un jarro pequeño. Este ejemplo al igual que un buen número de fragmentos en varios lugares excavados dentro de la ciudad de Quito, tienen el cuerpo lobulado que, muchas veces, representa la imitación del repujado en metal. Un hallazgo procedente de la Plaza de Santo Domingo muestra, incluso, una cara humana elaborada en uno de los lóbulos mediante repujado e incisión. Las asas siempre son verticales y de corte tubular, aplicadas sencillamente hacia un costado del jarro, pero es otra vez en la Plaza de Santo Domingo donde se halló el ejemplo único de una asa pequeña, delicadamente enrollada en forma de una oreja. Esta terracota se caracteriza por una pasta fina, bien cocida, y un engobe rojo altamente pulido. Su presencia es mínima pero recurrente a través de todos los monumentos Coloniales hasta ahora investigados. A diferencia de la terracota ordinaria, hecha a mano, pensamos que la categoría fina, por lo complicado de los contornos lobulados, debe estar hecha en moldes verticales.

Mayólica

La mayólica constituye el elemento Colonial más diagnóstico porque está omnipresente. Existe en varias calidades pero la gran mayoría pertenece a un segundo grado del tipo verde

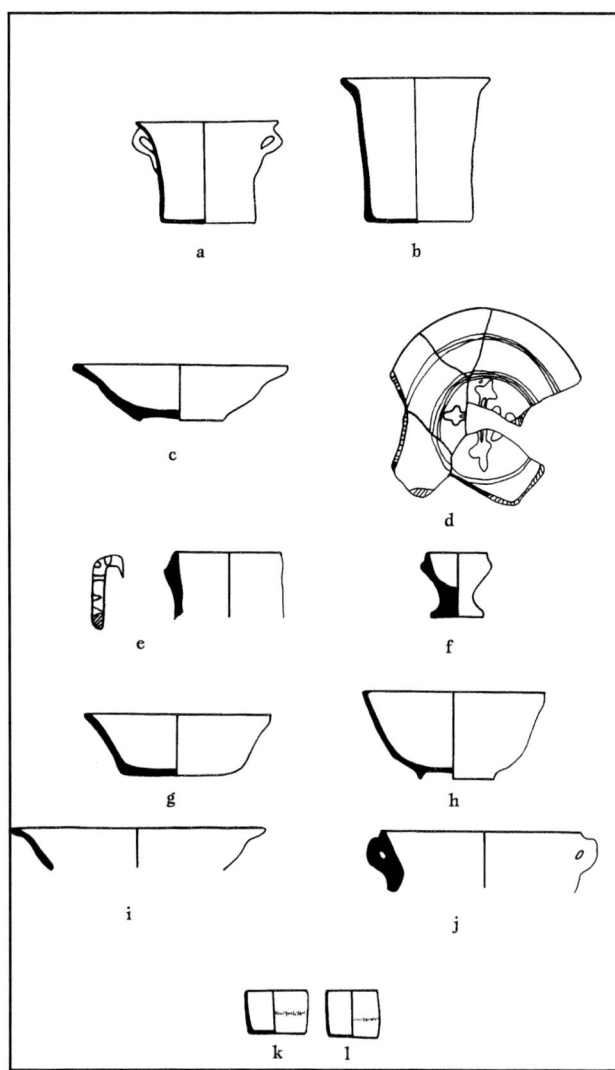

FIGURA 12.6 **Principales tipos de mayólica:** *a–h*, **verde-crema**, *i–l*, **azul-blanco**

sobre blanco (figura 12.6a-h). Pocos ejemplos pueden ser definidos como entrefino y algunas excepciones se clasifican como de primer grado. Estos últimos son normalmente de una mayólica azul sobre blanco (figura 12.6i-l), aparentemente importada.

Mayólica verde sobre blanco cremoso. La casi totalidad de la mayólica se caracteriza por un esmalte delgado con diseños de color verde sobre un fondo blanco (véanse capítulos 13, 18). Se halla en todos los sitios Coloniales hasta ahora investigados de la Sierra, la Costa y Amazonia. Muestra una pasta bien cocida y de grano fino, sin desgrasante observable a simple vista y de color anaranjado. El espesor de las paredes varía entre 2 y 15 mm. La baja calidad del esmalte se evidencia a través de su poco espesor (menos de 0.5 mm), el craquelado de la superficie, la presencia de pequeños huecos y la variación del color que va de blanco, crema, grisáceo, hasta verdoso.

La decoración pintada se aplica directamente sobre el esmalte y consta de varios diseños, principalmente en color verde esmeralda de diferentes tonos, a veces combinados con elementos decorativos en color marrón, amarillo y muy raramente en azul.

En cuanto a formas se han podido establecer varias categorías morfo-funcionales: platos hondos, lebrillos, bacines (figura 12.6a,b), cuencos, copas, jarros, y fuentes.

Los platos hondos (figura 12.6c) presentan un borde evertido y el cuerpo convexo, con base convexa y anular. Tanto el interior como el exterior de los platos están cubiertos por el esmalte, pero sólo el interior muestra decoración (figura 12.6d). La decoración es pintada a mano y en el caso del Convento de Santo Domingo representa una estilización del emblema de la Orden Dominicana, las cuatro espadas cruzadas. En el Convento de San Francisco son pocos los diseños que pueden ser reconstruidos, pero todos parecen ser de tipo floral. En la Plaza de Santo Domingo, en cambio, los platos hondos muestran una decoración más variada y alegre. Son frecuentes las representaciones de caras humanas rodeadas de diferentes motivos como semicírculos, líneas onduladas y combinaciones de varios elementos. También hay ejemplos zoomorfos, todos pájaros ubicados en medio de motivos florales. Uno de estos platos, mejor conservado que la mayoría, ilustra que en los casos zoomorfos los bordes presentaban una decoración compleja de tipo floral y geométrica. Un ejemplar interesante muestra una figura humana de una mujer indígena con vestido y poncho, un collar en los hombros, frente a una planta.

Los cuencos tienen cuerpo convexo, borde directo o ligeramente evertido, base convexa y soporte anular (figura 12.6h). En el Convento de Santo Domingo, los pocos fragmentos pertenecientes a esta clase de forma, y un solo ejemplar completo, parecen indicar que la decoración se ubicaba sólo en el interior y que era sobre todo del tipo floral. Una variante más ordinaria, procedente de la Plaza de Santo Domingo, tiene únicamente esmalte verde uniforme en el interior. El exterior parece intencionalmente ahumado porque el color negro penetró hasta la mitad de la pasta. Un tercer tipo tiene el esmalte verde uniforme tanto en el interior como en el exterior y una asa horizontal.

Las copas (figura 12.6f) tienen el cuerpo convexo y el borde directo, con un reborde exterior muy pronunciado, de 7 a 8 mm bajo el labio. La base es un pedestal sólido campaniforme. El esmalte que cubre todo el artefacto se acerca al gris verdoso y no tiene decoración.

Pocos son los restos de lebrillos, cuencos de bases planas, cuerpo recto divergente y borde directo o corto y horizontal (figura 12.6g). En el Convento de Santo Domingo se halló un ejemplar pequeño con decoración floral en el interior. Es mucho más complejo el tratamiento que recibió el fragmento encontrado en la Plaza de Santo Domingo. Los lados interiores están divididos en un sinnúmero de pequeños cuadros, alternando blanco (a veces con punteado), verde, amarillo y café. El fondo acusa parte de un escudo con un diseño floral alrededor del centro.

Las jarras se caracterizan por un borde directo, paredes rectas y el cuerpo posiblemente cilíndrico, sin que puedan determinarse las características de la base (figura 12.6e). La asa aplicada en forma de oreja tiene pequeñas líneas verdes horizontales. El resto del recipiente está totalmente cubierto por esmalte, pero muestra como única decoración una línea verde en el labio. En la Plaza de Santo Domingo se encontró una variante con la misma decoración en la asa, pero con el cuerpo del jarro de forma esférica y cuello recto.

De la Plaza de Santo Domingo y del Hospital de San Juan de Dios se conoce una forma llamada *bacín*, recipientes de base plana, lados rectos y un borde ancho evertido u horizontal (figura 12.6a,b). Normalmente tienen dos asas verticales junto al borde (figura 12.6a). El esmalte puede variar desde un verde bastante oscuro hasta casi blanco verdoso y se ubica principalmente en el interior, aunque puede aparecer en zonas de la parte superior de la pieza en el exterior. Se nota claramente que fueron manufacturados mediante la técnica de enrollado.

Mayólica azul sobre blanco. Pocos son los ejemplos de una mayólica de excelente calidad, tipificada en general como azul sobre blanco. La pasta es muy parecida a la de la verde sobre blanco aunque de color más oscuro. El esmalte es de una calidad netamente superior y consta de una capa gruesa, aproximadamente de 1 mm de espesor, de un blanco opaco brillante, sobre la cual se ubica la decoración azul.

En el Convento de Santo Domingo las pocas formas reconocibles incluyen un tipo de cuenco, diferente al de la mayólica verde sobre blanco. Se caracteriza por el borde evertido casi horizontal y el cuerpo convexo, aunque no pudo identificarse la base (figura 12.6i). La decoración se compone de un complicado diseño que combina elementos geométricos y florales. La decoración de tipo floral parece la más común en este tipo de mayólica, a juzgar por los fragmentos de platos hondos y otras formas (figura 12.6j) que se han encontrado.

Al lado de esta mayólica fina existe una de segundo grado, caracterizada por un esmalte menos espeso, con múltiples fallas pequeñas, sobre todo un fuerte craquelado, y de color más bien crema. En las excavaciones del Convento de Santo Domingo se recuperó un fragmento de plato hondo con una estilización del emblema de la Orden Dominicana. Otros dos fragmentos de plato hondo muestran parte de la inscripción "IHS" (en latín, Jesús Salvador de los Hombres), con otros elementos rodeándolo. En estos últimos casos el fondo blanco acusa un color y una consistencia de tiza, o sea un acabado mucho menos brillante que de costumbre pero más claro.

En el Convento de San Francisco también es escasa esta mayólica, pues sólo hay unos cuantos fragmentos de bordes de plato y posibles tazas y un fragmento de asa. En estos casos resulta imposible de reconstruir la decoración, pero un fragmento definido como perteneciente a una jarra muestra las llagas de San Francisco en el exterior (Terán de Rodríguez 1989, Anexo 22). La calidad es de segundo orden.

De la misma categoría de mayólica se encontraron, en la Plaza de Santo Domingo de Quito, dos pequeños recipientes a manera de tazas. Tienen la base plana y los lados casi rectos (figura 12.6k,l). La pasta es idéntica a la de la mayólica verde sobre blanco cremoso, pero aquí el esmalte, aunque delgado, es de un color bastante blanco. La decoración, de color celeste, se conforma de una línea en el labio y una banda central en el exterior.

Azulejos. Aunque no son muy comunes en las excavaciones, todos los monumentos Coloniales tienen una gran variedad de azulejos. En el Convento de Santo Domingo se encontraron varios fragmentos de azulejos cuadrados, de 180 mm de lado y de dos tipos de espesor, 15 y 22 mm, esmaltados de blanco y con una decoración floral, combinando verde esmeralda, azul, marrón y amarillo. A esto se deben añadir varios centenares de azulejos ubicados en las cúpulas de la iglesia y que fueron trasladados ahí en una fecha no determinada. Originalmente se hallaron en los zócalos de los corredores del claustro principal, donde fueron colocados en la década de 1760 (Terán Najas 1991:33). Muestran una gran variedad de motivos y acabados: representaciones zoomorfas, antropomorfas, florales y geométricas en muchos colores diferentes. Sus dimensiones varían entre 180 y 190 mm de lado y su espesor es de 17 mm. Casi todos tienen en el centro, debajo del esmalte, la impresión de una flor redonda, formada por seis u ocho pétalos. Otro tipo está constituido por azulejos de un solo color, normalmente verde pero a veces blanco. Tienen las mismas dimensiones que los azulejos figurativos y muchos acusan la idéntica impresión de flor en su centro; otros tienen como marca un motivo geométrico. Son los elementos más comunes para cubrir las azoteas y cúpulas de los edificios Coloniales, por ser impermeables.

En el Convento de San Francisco de Quito se hallan azulejos para pisos de 187 mm de lado y 26 mm de espesor, con los lados biselados y decoración floral o geométrica en verde, azul y marrón sobre un fondo blanco cremoso. Acusan el mismo tipo de sello: una flor de ocho pétalos (Terán de Rodríguez 1989:15). El segundo tipo de azulejo, para recubrimiento de exteriores, mide 170 mm de lado y 19 mm de espesor y tiene los bordes biselados pero es de un solo color verde oscuro. Muestra una impresión de diseño más complicado: un círculo de 42 mm de diámetro impreso con una flor de tres hojas y una mariposa sentada sobre ella. Finalmente hay azulejos más grandes, de 270 mm de lado y

19 mm de espesor, sin biselado, decorados en verde y marrón sobre blanco cremoso, con motivos florales y un caso con el cordón y las cinco llagas de San Francisco de Asís (Terán de Rodríguez 1989:15).

Los azulejos de mejor calidad se encuentran en la Capilla de Villacis, al lado norte del altar mayor de la iglesia de San Francisco. Son cuadrados, de 128 mm de lado, entre 17 y 20 mm de espesor, y conforman un zócalo compuesto de varios paneles sencillamente cuadrados con diferentes diseños, pero que siempre combinan elementos geométricos con motivos florales abstractos. Uno de estos paneles es idéntico al de la Iglesia de Santa Ana en Triana, el barrio alfarero de Sevilla. La mencionada iglesia constituyó, además, la iglesia parroquial de los ceramistas y data de 1575 (Lister y Lister 1987:140). Desconocemos los colores empleados en España, en los cuales se observa una mejor ejecución en el trazado de las líneas y motivos florales, pero no cabe duda que los azulejos ecuatorianos constituyen una copia muy exacta del estilo Morisco Andaluz. Un aspecto sumamente extraño es que estos azulejos tienen en el reverso el mismo tipo de decoración, pero de pésima calidad. Sólo se puede interpretar este hecho como un fracaso del esmaltado durante la cocción y la subsiguiente reutilización de los mismos azulejos.

Porcelana

La ocurrencia de porcelana es mínima en todos los sitios hasta ahora investigados. En el Convento de Santo Domingo su presencia se limita a pocos fragmentos con decoración azul sobre blanco, aparentemente del tipo floral. Las formas no siempre son definibles pero por lo menos existe evidencia de platos. El fragmento mejor conservado de un plato no muy grande, muestra una flor separada mediante una línea vertical de un campo con líneas horizontales. Este diseño resulta típico de la porcelana Ming de Carraca de 1580–1610 (Deagan 1987:97–99).

En algunos museos como por ejemplo de Jijón y Caamaño, se pueden observar bellas piezas de porcelana importadas directamente desde China. La porcelana siempre debe haber sido muy limitada en cantidad aunque posiblemente estuvo presente desde el siglo XVII y durante todo el período Colonial y Republicano. Entre las formas características se pueden señalar tazas, botellas, platos y jarrones. Las decoraciones normalmente son realistas pero varían entre diseños sencillos y motivos muy complejos. No hay que excluir la existencia de porcelana japonesa a partir de la segunda mitad del siglo XVII, ya que formaba parte del comercio con Manila, Filipinas.

Presencia y Función de los Diferentes Tipos de Cerámica

Para evaluar la importancia de cada tipo de cerámica Colonial sólo podemos remitirnos a las excavaciones realizadas en el Convento de Santo Domingo de Quito. A partir de la figura 12.7 se puede concluir que la gran mayoría de

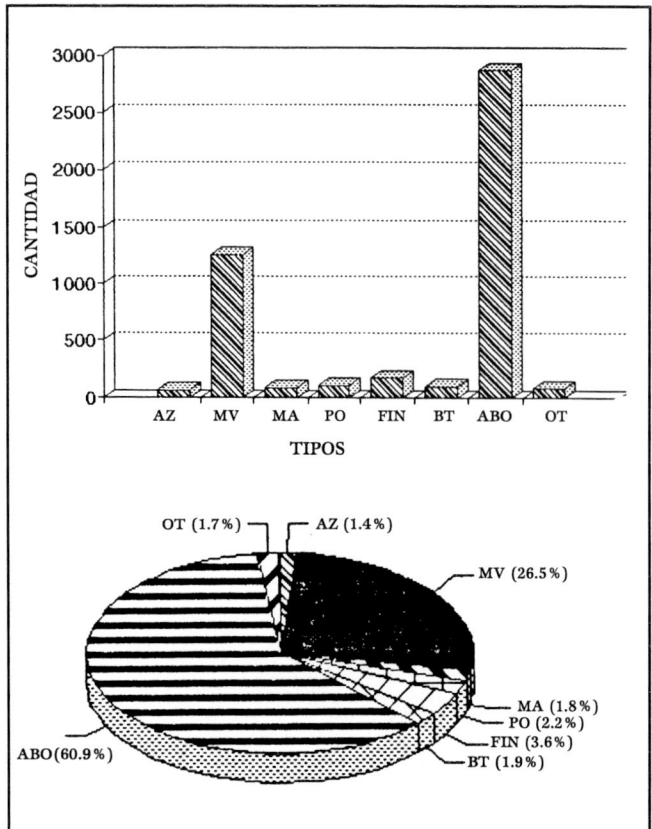

FIGURA 12.7 Gráficas con frecuencias comparativas de diferentes tipos cerámicos, colecciones del Convento de Santo Domingo. *superior*, Totales de tipos de cerámica; *inferior*, porcentajes de tipos de cerámica. AZ = azulejos; MV = mayólica verde sobre crema; MA = mayólica azul sobre blanco; PO = porcelana; FIN = terracota fina; BT = botijas; ABO = terracota aborigen; OT = otros

fragmentos cerámicos corresponde a terracota aborigen (ABO = 60.9%). Cabe hacer énfasis en el hecho de que, no obstante el nombre de "aborigen," una buena parte de esta categoría debe ser Colonial, pero no se le puede distinguir como tal debido a la falta de rasgos diagnósticos. Se han cuantificado las botijas (BT) aparte y constituyen 1.9 por ciento de la colección. Otros elementos Coloniales como tejas, fragmentos de tubos, etcétera (OT), conforman tan sólo 1.7 por ciento, y la terracota fina (FIN) sólo ocupa el 3.6 por ciento.

La mayólica constituye aproximadamente la tercera parte de toda la cerámica (29.7%), pero con una gran preponderancia del tipo verde sobre crema (MV = 26.5%), en relación con la mayólica azul sobre blanco (MA = 1.8%) y los azulejos (AZ = 1.4%). Finalmente, la porcelana está presente en una cantidad mínima (PO = 2.2%).

Esta simple cuantificación de los hallazgos en el Convento de Santo Domingo indica la importancia de la continuidad de la alfarería tradicional, con el énfasis en la producción de terracota ordinaria para los usos diarios de preparación y almacenamiento de alimentos y líquidos. La terracota fina se volvió el principal portador de las nuevas influencias, pero la baja cantidad, así como la calidad decorativa, refleja adecuadamente una utilización restringida; debe haber desempeñado un papel parecido al de la mayólica de buena calidad, es decir para objetos decorativos exclusivamente o para un uso poco intensivo, relacionado con actividades poco frecuentes. Si consideramos que la terracota con engobe pulido conformaba la vajilla de lujo en el período Aborigen y constatamos una baja frecuencia de ella durante la Colonia, podemos inferir que, posiblemente, fue intencionalmente sustituida por la mayólica. En la mayólica se repite el fenómeno de la superioridad numérica de la calidad más baja. La relación entre la mayólica verde sobre crema y azul sobre blanco resulta muy parecida a la de la terracota ordinaria/fina. En este caso, también se puede postular la misma diferenciación funcional. La porcelana, por su alto costo y difícil acceso, siempre fue escasa y sirvió para aspectos muy excepcionales de la vida.

Una breve evaluación cuantitativa y funcional de los diferentes tipos de cerámica Colonial, según su presencia en el Convento de Santo Domingo de Quito, no necesariamente reflejaría la situación general del Ecuador Colonial. No podemos olvidar el contexto conventual en teoría de pobreza por voto que se usó para este análisis. Sin embargo, basándonos en nuestras observaciones hechas sobre las diferentes colecciones arqueológicas del país, las proporciones de las diferentes categorías parecen mantenerse a grandes rasgos ya sea que se trate de la Plaza de Santo Domingo, otros conventos en Quito u otros sitios en el resto de la nación. Más bien se observa una variación en las formas y las decoraciones de la cerámica, y esto es sobre todo obvio en la mayólica.

Como mejor ejemplo podemos citar el contraste entre el Convento y la Plaza de Santo Domingo, por tratarse de elementos contiguos en el espacio pero con funciones completamente distintas. En ambos casos existe una gran cantidad de terracota ordinaria de características iguales, porque básicamente obedecía a un mismo fin: la organización doméstica del convento y la logística de un espacio público que prestaba servicios generales a la ciudadanía. La mayólica, empero, se distingue claramente en la cantidad de formas y en la calidad de la decoración. La calidad técnica general no difiere mucho porque se trata de una mayólica de segundo grado con bastantes imperfecciones. Sin embargo, las formas son más variadas y la decoración refleja aspectos alegres y paganos de la gente común, en contraste con la estilización severa de los pocos elementos decorativos de la vajilla conventual.

Conclusiones

A partir de este breve panorama de la cerámica Colonial en el Ecuador se ha podido establecer, no obstante las dificultades inherentes a su estudio, las principales variaciones de un aspecto de la cultura material en la cual se expresaba una sociedad a la vez tradicional e innovadora. La terracota ordinaria y fina siguieron mayormente los cánones milenarios del período Aborigen, pero se adaptaron ocasionalmente a las nuevas condiciones. La producción alfarera se diversificó incorporando a la mayólica, pero la moldeó discretamente con motivos de la vida diaria, elementos autóctonos de tiempos inmemorables.

Esta dualidad de lo nuevo en lo viejo y de lo tradicional en la innovación, es el fiel reflejo del sincretismo cultural que originó el encuentro de dos mundos profundamente diferentes. Por consiguiente, esta dualidad se expresa en todos los niveles de la sociedad Colonial, sean éstos el pensamiento intelectual, la organización social, el sistema económico o las distintas expresiones artísticas. Desde la colonia y hasta nuestros días el curso de la historia ha transformado y continúa modificando este sincretismo inicial en lo que constituye hoy la identidad propia de la sociedad ecuatoriana, diferente de los demás pueblos andinos por su singular proceso histórico.

Futuras investigaciones de arqueología histórica en el Ecuador permitirán abundar en interpretaciones y reforzar las que hemos presentado, acerca de la variabilidad cerámica en sitios Coloniales destinados a diversas funciones.

✝ Chapter 13

Settlements and Ceramics of the Tambo River, Ecuador, from the Early Nineteenth Century

Karen E. Stothert, Kevin Gross, Anne Fox, and Amelia Sánchez Mosquera

Abstract

This chapter describes sites and ceramics of the late eighteenth and early nineteenth centuries in southwestern Ecuador. Surface collections and excavated assemblages from farmsteads along the Tambo River of the Santa Elena Peninsula allow us to begin to reconstruct the settlement strategy and economy of the rural population of this region. The ceramic evidence from house sites along the Tambo River indicates that residents were linked to regional and international commercial networks, using locally produced pottery as well as imported glazed wares. Yet people also continued to rely heavily on a pre-Columbian diet and to produce goods for household consumption.

Resumen

En este capítulo se describen los sitios y cerámica de fines del siglo XVIII y principios del XIX en el suroeste de Ecuador. Las colecciones de superficie y de excavación procedentes de ranchos ubicados a lo largo del Río Tambo, en la Península de Santa Elena, son la base para iniciar la reconstrucción de la estrategia de asentamientos y de la economía de la población rural en esta región. La evidencia cerámica de sitios habitacionales localizados a lo largo del Río Tambo indica que los residentes estaban integrados a las redes comerciales e internacionales de comercio, consumiendo alfarería de factura regional así como lozas vidriadas importadas. No obstante, los individuos continuaron dependiendo en gran medida en la dieta precolumbian y en la producción de bienes para el consumo doméstico.

THIS DESCRIPTION of some of the sites and ceramics of the Historic period characteristic of the Santa Elena Peninsula of southwestern Ecuador (figure 13.1) is significant because little is known about the material culture of the Colonial and Republican periods in coastal Ecuador (Goggin 1968:47-48; Lister and Lister 1974). Bushnell (1951) mentioned some sites of the Historic period, and Lanning (1967) named a Santa Elena phase, but it was never defined. Smith and Westbury (1985) and Westbury (1984) have described some of the Santa Elena ceramics very briefly. At this time, there is insufficient evidence upon which to base any comparison between sites from the Historic period found in the coastal zone and those known from the highlands of Ecuador (Buys 1990; Holm 1971; Idrovo 1990; Kennedy 1990; chapter 12).

The ceramics found at rural sites along the Tambo River (figure 13.2) are described here as a first step toward creating a framework for reconstructing the history of the region. In addition, an interpretation is offered based on excavations at one house site belonging to the Santa Elena phase. It is remarkable that the rural people, described as poor "Indians" in early-nineteenth-century sources, maintained a traditional lifestyle while gaining access to a variety of imported goods.

Santa Elena Peninsula

Historical descriptions from the eighteenth and nineteenth centuries provide few details abut rural life on the coast. What is known comes primarily from the work of Hamerly (1973). In order to add to these information sources, continued archaeological research in Santa Elena is important.

The semiarid Santa Elena Peninsula figured prominently in early Colonial history because Spanish ships stopped there to take on supplies and to pitch their hulls and rigging with refined petroleum from the local tar seeps (Stothert 1994). Despite this strategic resource, there is little description of local life, in part because the population was mainly Indian.

The native people of the Santa Elena Peninsula, classified as *indios* until at least the middle of the nineteenth century, maintained a low-energy agricultural system not unlike that of their prehistoric ancestors. They combined agricultural activities with the exploitation of natural resources, particularly marine fish, and they manufactured craft items in house-

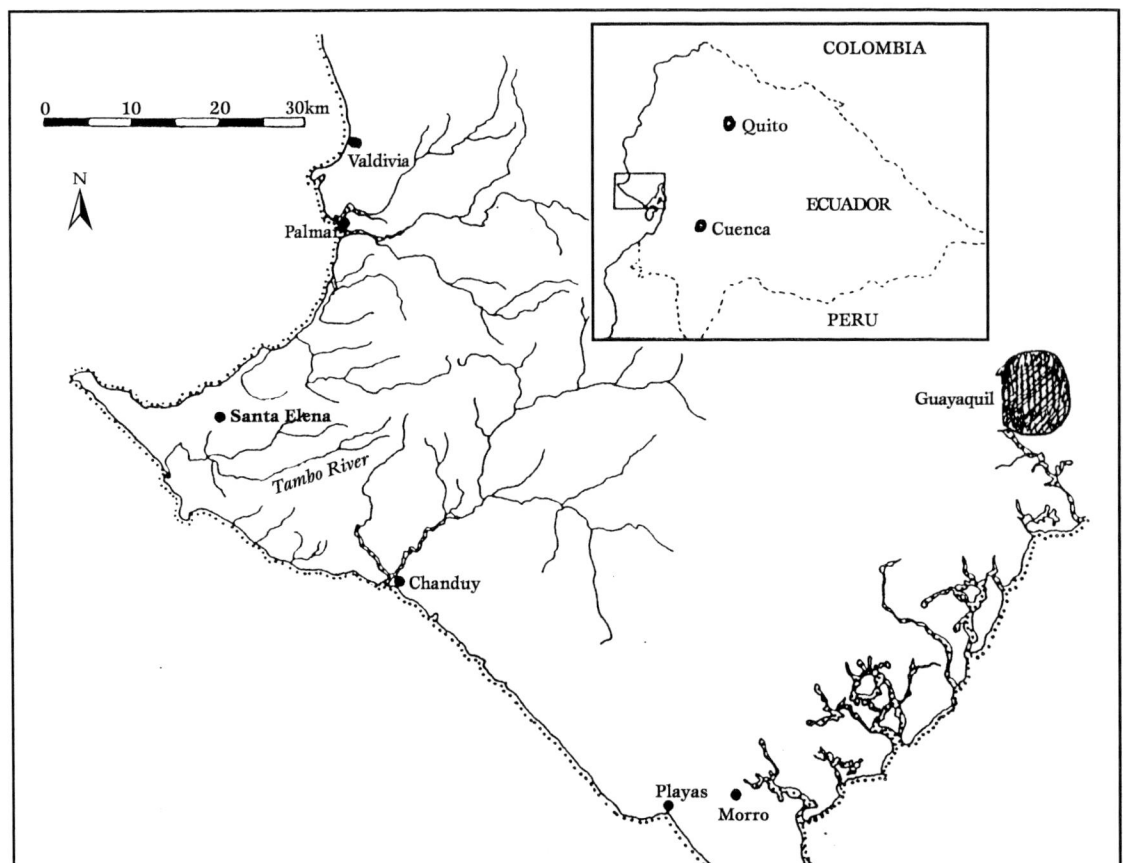

FIGURE 13.1 Southwestern Ecuador, showing the Tambo River drainage on the Santa Elena Peninsula. *All drawings by Kevin Gross*

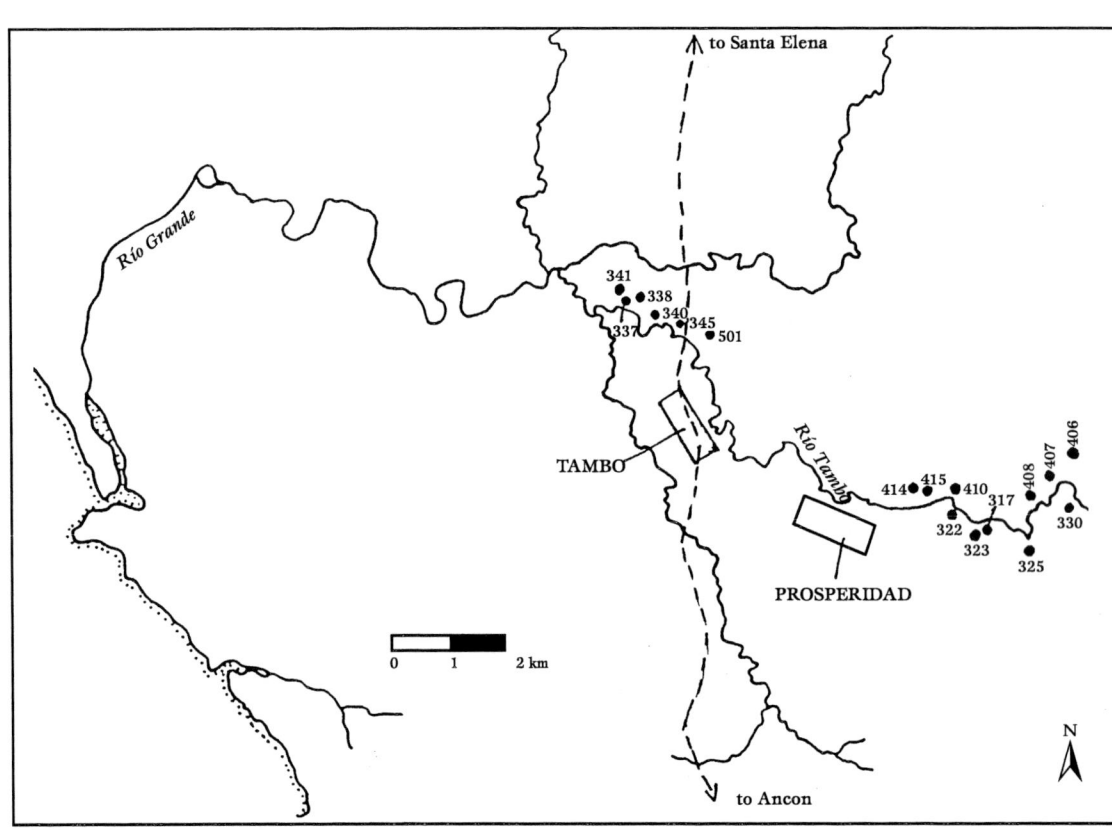

FIGURE 13.2 Plan of the Tambo River showing the locations of sites identified during the survey

hold contexts. Hamerly (1973:102) noted that, at the beginning of the nineteenth century, the people of Santa Elena produced fish, salt, Panama hats, and hand-spun cotton thread dyed purple using local shellfish—all of which was sold for money used to pay tribute (Hamerly 1973:104). Non-Indians controlled the tar-boiling industry (refining tar from petroleum) in the eighteenth and early nineteenth centuries, and a few wealthy people owned land and cattle, but few Europeans lived in Santa Elena in the early nineteenth century (Hamerly 1973:102). Throughout the Historic period, animal husbandry was an important element of the local economic system.

Ecuador gained its independence from Spain in the 1820s, but it is not known how rural life may have changed at that time. Many of the same economic activities persisted with little change. In 1858, Villavicencio (1984:256–257) noted that the important regional products were cattle, mules and burros, dried fish, salt, wax, purple-dyed yarn, black lacquer, gypsum, and tar.

What is interesting about the natives of Santa Elena is that they have maintained a unique ethnic identity through modern times. Perhaps because sparse rainfall limited the agricultural productivity of the region, European colonizers did not take control of the land, and it remained in the hands of indigenous people (Hamerly 1973:103–104; Alvarez 1987a).

Hamerly (1973) reported demographic expansion in the early nineteenth century, possibly related to the cacao boom in the region north of Guayaquil (figure 13.1). In Santa Elena, the activities most important to the economic elite were the production of tar for export and cattle ranching. The indigenous people included independent farmers who were partially integrated into the national economy, wage-earning *jornaleros* or *peones* (day laborers) employed by cattle owners, and those employed in the tar works.

Santa Elena was not a major trade center, but in the nineteenth century it was (as it is today) connected to the nearby city of Guayaquil, a busy port (Hamerly 1973:124, 132). The Partido de Santa Elena grew rapidly between 1763 and 1840. Even though Santa Elena was characterized by a predominantly Indian or *cholo* (mixed ancestry) population that was mostly rural and very poor (Hamerly 1973:79, 91, Tables 11, 22), the town in the early Republican period boasted the largest of the very few schools within the ancient Province of Guayaquil. Hamerly (1973:140–143) attributes this to the political independence of the people, who maintained their ethnic lands (Alvarez 1987a, b) and were not subordinated as laborers on large haciendas.

Tambo River Survey and Settlements

The Tambo River is the principal seasonal river of the western peninsula (figure 13.2). Today, after serious deforestation in the Historic period, it carries surface water only in years when there is good rainfall. The traditional *chacras* (agricultural plots) of the people of Prosperidad and El Tambo are located in the river bottom. In the rainy years, families cultivate maize, manioc (*yuca*), sweet potato (*camote*), squashes, beans, chili peppers, and various fruits. A generation ago, they cultivated various species of useful trees and native tree cotton (Lindao and Stothert 1994). This system has changed little since the prehistoric period.

During a foot survey in 1981, 115 sites were located along the drainage of the Tambo River between its confluence (at Tambo) and a point about 18 km upstream. Seventeen sites with lead-glazed earthenware sherds on their surfaces were selected for the study of Historic settlement (figure 13.2). In many of these sites no midden was preserved underground; as a result, the ceramic samples are small.

The sites chosen form two clusters near the modern towns of Tambo and Prosperidad, located on low hills just outside the flood plain of the Tambo River where the agricultural potential is particularly high. Contemporary people use both zones for chacras and modern, pump-irrigated fields.

The Historic sites that form the two clusters are known only from archaeological survey. There is no written historical information, but, according to an oral tradition, the original inhabitants of Prosperidad (formerly called Tambo de Arriba) came from Santa Elena in the 1820s. Because many of the archaeological sites reported here were occupied in the 1830s and 1840s, it appears they were the residential sites of these early settlers.

Although the ceramic collections from some of these sites are heterogeneous, they do not appear to be mixed. The excavations at site 406 (table 13.1) demonstrate the deposition of a variety of ceramics in a shallow, intact midden that accumulated during a short period of occupation. Surface collections from other sites show similar associations (table 13.2); this is taken as evidence of heterogeneity and not as evidence of lengthy occupations or conflated contexts.

The seventeen sites in the sample contain wares that date to the first half of the nineteenth century, and their respective periods of occupation probably overlap. The sites in table 13.2 are ordered from left to right in a hypothetical chronological order based on the datable ceramics found at each site, but the sites should be considered roughly contemporaneous.

A wide variety of vessels and artifacts was found at sites 406 and 410, both of which produced large sherd samples. Site 338 also produced a large sample, but the assemblage differed dramatically from that of all other sites. While site 338 may have been occupied later than other sites, it is distinctive because of its original function. Since it was located near the modern main road and showed heavy concentrations of bottle glass and "china" ware, it may have been a store, saloon, or house of wealthier persons located along the old roadway that led to the town of Santa Elena.

The settlement strategy of the nineteenth-century people resembles that of both the prehistoric period and the present. In all cases, small houses were dispersed along the low hills just outside the floodplain of the

Table 13.1 Distribution of ceramics recovered from the surface and from excavated contexts at site 406

	UNIT A	UNIT B	UNIT C	UNIT 21	UNIT 20	UNIT 34	UNIT 22	UNIT 7	TOTAL
SOFT-PASTE GLAZED EARTHENWARE									
Lead glazed: Local Folk ware									
Rims	62	14	11	2	4	4	3	10	
Painted decoration	59	13	18	1	8	5	3	8	
Plain glazed body	106	40	15	1	5	5	2	11	
SUBTOTAL	227	67	44	4	17	14	8	29	410
Brown glazed									
Rims	6	0	2	1	0	2	1	1	
Body sherds	7	0	0	0	0	4	0	0	
Decorated	2	0	0	0	0	1	0	0	
SUBTOTAL	15	0	2	1	0	7	1	1	27
Tin glazed: Local imitation majolicas									
Rims	2	0	2	0	0	0	0	0	
Body sherds	16	2	0	1	0	0	0	0	
SUBTOTAL	18	2	2	1	0	0	0	0	23
Imported Puebla ware	1	0	1	0	0	0	0	0	
SUBTOTAL	1	0	1	0	0	0	0	0	2
HARD-PASTE/REFINED EARTHENWARE									
Undecorated whiteware	10	3	0	1	2	1	1	2	
Transfer printed	23	1	2	0	1	0	0	1	
Flow blue	0	0	0	0	0	0	0	0	
Hand painted	0	0	1	1	0	0	1	0	
Edgeware	2	0	(1)	(1)	0	0	0	0	
Spongeware	0	0	0	0	0	0	0	0	
Banded slipware		0	0	0	0	0	0	0	0
SUBTOTAL	35	4	3	2	3	1	2	3	53
Porcelain	1	0	0	0	0	1	1	0	3
Stoneware gin jugs	0	0	0	0	0	0	0	0	
UNGLAZED EARTHENWARE									
Redware	8	3	0	10	24	35	2	19	101
Spanish-style storage jars	1	1	0	0	0	0	0	0	2
TOTAL	306	77	52	18	44	58	14	52	621

Note: ( ) = sherds counted in two categories

Tambo River. Even today, during rainy years, some families temporarily leave their houses in town to reoccupy the rural hilltops where they build houses, plant crops, and raise animals in the manner of their ancestors.

Excavations at Site 406

Site 406 was selected for excavation because the surface collection was not mixed with twentieth-century pottery. The excavations yielded ceramics from intact midden deposits, faunal remains, and other artifacts and features. The ceramics recovered have led to the conclusion that the site was occupied around 1840. This is the first time that remains from the Historic period from Santa Elena have been reported in detail.

The site is located on a low hill just above the river bottom where Silvino Balón Limone, a native of Prosperidad, cultivates maize, beans, manioc, camotes, and various fruits when it rains. His hand-dug well taps the underground water resources of the dry river bed. Even several years after the last significant rainfall Mr. Balón continues to find water only a few meters below the surface.

Sections A and B of the archaeological site (table 13.1) yielded a large surface collection of material from the Historic period. The test excavations made along the top of the

Settlements and Ceramics of the Tambo River, Ecuador

Table 13.2 Distribution of sherds in Tambo River sites

Site #	310	317	323	345	341	406	407	408	410	414	415	322	330	325	337	338	340	TOTAL
SOFT-PASTE GLAZED EARTHENWARE																		
Lead glazed																		
Local Folk ware	16	10	5	31	14	227	18	11	71	16	19	41	11	5	9	1	4	509
Brown glazed					15			4	5	1	4	1			1			31
Tin glazed																		
Local imitation	1	4	2	23			18	11	6	6		7	2	8	1			89
Puebla ware	1	3						1			1							6
Monterey ware	2						3											5
HARD-PASTE/REFINED EARTHENWARE																		
Undecorated whiteware				6		10	4		2		1	2	2			35	39	101
Transfer printed						23	1	2	20	*	1	11	8			91	3	160
Flow blue													1	20		21		
Hand painted															52	3		55
Edgeware				2				1								1		4
Spongeware																37		37
Banded slipware																5		5
Porcelain						1			1									2
Unidentified decorated whiteware											4							4
Stoneware gin jugs									12						4	1		17
UNGLAZED EARTHENWARE																		
Redware				6		8		3	2	22		1	8	1				51
Spanish-style storage jars						2			6			2				1		11
TOTAL	20	17	7	66	14	306	37	23	125	43	26	69	32	14	15	245	49	1108

Note: * = present but not counted

hill showed scattered remains from the Historic period in sandy soil, with some prehistoric material at deeper levels. A few features were uncovered which suggest this portion of the hilltop was a work zone where kitchen/patio activities took place.

One feature consisted of the base of a circular clay wall, resting on a large circle of fire-reddened earth (about 44 cm in diameter) and showing compacted ash in the center. This ash has been interpreted as the remains of a small mud oven (*horno* or *hornilla*). Today, in rural areas, a woman will construct a similar oven in the form of a volcano which, is used to toast tortillas, an important food in the local diet.

Unit 34 revealed a group of features including a refuse pit and a single deep posthole. The post, apparently removed and replaced by sand and refuse, would have been adequate to support a house. Traditionally, houses were made of wood and cane. Informants say they used to be raised about 80 cm from the ground on a series of posts. In the old days, people removed good posts for reuse at a new house site. The empty posthole may be evidence of the relocation of the house following several years of occupation.

In addition to ceramics, artifacts found in the excavated refuse include glass fragments (early-nineteenth-century medicine bottles and imported wine bottles), an iron knife with brass fittings, spent bullets and lead shot, and a few stone artifacts, including hand stones (natural cobbles used for grinding) and flakes of stone that may have been used for cutting. Two sherds, one a local majolica (tin-glazed) and the other a piece of refined earthenware plate, had been worked into disks. Today on the peninsula, perforated ceramic disks are used as spindle whorls for spinning cotton thread.

Faunal remains in the midden included several edible mollusks: turbans (primarily *Astrea buschii* and two species of *Turbo*), *Tegula* sp., chiton, and urchin. All are found today along the rocky coast 7 or 8 km from the sites. At a nearby nineteenth-century site, a handmade mother-of-pearl button was found, indicating that local people used shellfish as both food and raw material.

The portion of the vertebrate faunal assemblage studied by Sánchez Mosquera (1991) consisted of 1967 bones from 103 individuals. Of these, 89 were fish, 11 were mammals, 2 were reptiles, and 1 was a frog or toad. Compared to prehistoric samples from Santa Elena, this assemblage was unusual because it lacked bird bones. Sánchez noted a very high proportion of marine fish (55% of the assemblage). Forty-two species of fish were identified, most of which occupy estuaries and inshore waters of the continental shelf. The wild mammal species included deer and peccary, which are hunted today in the seasonally dry forest at the northern edge of the peninsula.

Because spent lead shot and bullets were found in the

midden, it seems likely that the people of this site hunted deer with some sort of firearm, although animals might also have been trapped in the garden plots. In any case, the prey was apparently butchered where it was killed and brought to the site in parts. These parts were then broken apart with a hatchet or machete, leaving a pattern of cut marks and blows on the long bones.

Two domestic animals not native to America were identified at site 406: cow, identified from several teeth and a single metapodial bone, and pig, identified from a tooth. Both species were important commercially in nineteenth-century Santa Elena, and so their underrepresentation in the midden at site 406 is surprising. The presence of only teeth and a single foot bone of a cow indicates that cows and pigs were not butchered at the site, and it is not clear whether or not they were eaten. The householders may have had no domestic animals at all, acquiring only hooves (and teeth?).

Alternatively, occupants of the house may have raised domesticated animals for sale. They may not have eaten beef and pork regularly, or they may have eaten meat that was butchered elsewhere. Family members may have labored as peons or jornaleros who tended animals for the owner, and they may have consumed little meat themselves, a pattern known from the early twentieth century.

With respect to fishing, several methods might have been employed to catch the species represented at site 406: net fishing in the estuary or at the edge of the sea, the use of seines or fish poison (in the estuaries), or fishing with line and hook. These methods are suggested because the species represented come from habitats near the beach and in estuaries. Because few head elements were found, it seems likely that fish were partly cleaned before they came to the site. It is not possible to infer whether they arrived salted, smoked, or fresh. Only two fish vertebrae were found burned, suggesting that the majority of the fish were not cooked directly over a fire. Today, fish are commonly steamed with rice or boiled in soup.

Little has been written about hunting patterns and subsistence in the Historic period in coastal Ecuador, but the late eighteenth-century watercolor drawings made in a similar ecological zone by the Bishop of Trujillo, Martínez-Compañón (1985), show many scenes of northern Peruvian Indians fishing, setting traps for wild animals, and hunting with clubs and blowguns. It is surprising that the faunal remains from site 406, presumably deposited around the year 1840, consisted largely of fish and wild animals such as deer and peccary. That part of the diet based on meat reflects a pattern of fish and deer utilization that is similar to prehistoric faunal samples from the Santa Elena region (Reitz 1989; Stothert 1993).

In summary, the remains at site 406 indicate a rural house site, probably occupied by a family that cultivated the adjacent river bottom. Wild foods may have been acquired directly by family members, although fish also may have been obtained from villages along the shore or from itinerant fishmongers of the sort that walked from village to village on the peninsula in the early twentieth century (Lindao and Stothert 1995). If this family kept pigs and cattle, it is likely that they did not consume the flesh regularly—at least the bones were not discarded in the household refuse sampled.

Evidence indicates that the diet of the people who lived at site 406 consisted of fish, shellfish, peccary, deer, and other wild animals. Surely plant foods were important, but evidence is not preserved. It is likely that people consumed plantains, maize, peanuts, sweet potatoes, squash, and manioc. Traditional farmers today value tropical fruits grown in their river bottom gardens. Judging from early twentieth-century patterns, earlier people might also have acquired food from part-time traders who brought plantains, rice, and cane sugar to the peninsula on donkeys and mules along the dry-weather dirt roads (Lindao and Stothert 1994, 1995).

Domestic pursuits along the Tambo may have included cotton spinning and weaving, both of which continued to be important activities undertaken by women in the twentieth century (Parker and Stothert 1983; Stothert and Parker 1985). With enough labor (daughters and daughters-in-law, for example), the production of textiles might have been a substantial source of income, and the family might have marketed dyed yarn.

There is no evidence that the people at this site wove hats, although such weaving was commonly practiced by men and women all along the coast in the nineteenth and early twentieth centuries. Sources of cash income for men may have included wage labor (in tar boiling or cattle ranching); raising and selling cattle and pigs; collecting honey, wax, and salt; and salting fish or shellfish.

This evidence offers a unique view of the poor but politically independent natives of Santa Elena. The following analysis of the pottery from site 406 and others shows that the rural people from Santa Elena accumulated a varied inventory of local and imported vessels.

Ceramics from the Historic Period

The ceramics collected from sites along the Tambo River (table 13.2) fall into three general ware categories: soft-paste glazed earthenwares, hard-paste/refined earthenwares, and unglazed earthenwares.

Soft-paste glazed earthenware. These earthenwares are handmade or wheel-thrown vessels fired at low temperatures. They include lead- and tin-glazed wares produced in ceramic centers and smaller workshops from Mexico to Peru.

Lead glazed: Local Folk ware. Lead-glazed earthenwares, presumably produced in Ecuador for popular consumption, were acquired and used by rural people in large quantities. One known center of ceramic production in the nineteenth century was Cuenca in the highlands of Ecuador, but it is likely that lead-glazed wares were produced elsewhere as well. These are denominated "folk" pottery because they are poor imitations of the finer lead-glazed wares produced in Europe or at principal centers in New Spain. This tradition of the local production of lead-glazed wares continues today in the folk pottery produced in many areas of Mexico, Colombia, Ecuador, and Peru. These wares were used to define the group of sites from the Historic period in the Tambo River sample.

The Local Folk wares vary little in paste, which is soft, terracotta in color, with sandy temper. Sherds break roughly. The vessels may have been handshaped or wheelmade, and many are covered with an almost clear glaze over terracotta-colored paste. Glaze colors range from white through yellow to green. Some glazes are thick and opaque, showing a tendency to flake off, but they do not show crazing. Other glazes are thin, almost transparent, and often sloppily applied to the interior of the vessel. The glaze usually covers the rim, stopping about 0.5 to 1 cm below the exterior of the rim. Vessel exteriors, however, are generally unglazed. A "chalky, crackly and pale" appearance on many vessels may be the result of insufficient heat during firing (Schuetz 1969:53).

Vessel forms are mostly open (figure 13.3), with painted decoration on their interior surfaces and pronounced angles between the sidewalls and flat interior bottoms. Other forms have restricted necks (probably jars and cooking ollas, figure 13.4). Several handles and ring-shaped bases are present (figure 13.5).

The vessels in the sample included several with painted decorations made with copper oxides. The predominant designs are green fern motifs executed on either terracotta, white, or yellow grounds (figure 13.3a). The leaves vary in thickness: some designs were executed using thin lines to create a sharp image, whereas others feature fat, bulbous leaves. The bottom of the interior of unrestricted vessels frequently bears a floral motif. It is interesting that no modeling or impressed decorations are found on the Tambo River glazed vessels, in contrast to styles common in the highlands during the Historic period (Idrovo 1990).

Comparisons of ceramic data from published reports and collections from the highlands and coastal regions of Ecuador (Holm 1971; Idrovo 1990; Kennedy 1990) suggest that the Historic assemblages in Ecuador are heterogeneous, reflecting both many loci of production and the well-documented social and geographical divisions within Ecuador.

Stothert examined materials from La Merced, a probable habitation site located near Quito which, according to the excavator, dates to the end of the eighteenth century (Kimball Smith 1991). In general, the green (and yellow) lead-glazed earthenwares from La Merced were like wares from the Tambo River. There were similarities in the glazes, design motifs, and colors, but the vessel forms differed from those found in Santa Elena. Also, the impressed decorations frequently found under the glazes (apparently on the shoulders of restricted vessels) of vessels from the highlands did not appear in the coastal material.

Brown glazed. The brown lead-glazed pottery found in the sites on the Tambo River and at the Alamo in Texas has a fine, homogeneous tan to red or brick-orange paste and a dark brown, vitreous glaze. It corresponds to what Schuetz defined as Guadalajara Red ware which was produced in Mexico in the early nineteenth century: "The clay is red, and hematite has probably been added to the lead glaze. The deeper red-brown tone, instead of orange, separates it from the Jalisco ware" (Schuetz 1969:51). Black linear decorations are present on some sherds. The forms apparently include plates or shallow bowls, with rounded direct rims.

Tin glazed: Local imitation majolica. The common term "majolica" refers to a category of "glazed, wheel-thrown ceramics, distinguished by its soft earthenware paste covered by an opaque vitreous enamel or glaze" (Deagan 1987:53; chapters 12, 18). The glaze is usually whitish because of tin oxides in the lead glaze. There are several famous centers for the manufacture of these wares in Italy, Spain, Mexico, and Panama. But tin-glazed earthenwares also were produced in less well-known centers. The ability to recognize and date these wares is very limited.

In the Tambo River collections, eighty-nine sherds (table 13.2) were from a high-quality ware, probably an imitation of imported majolica, which was finished with an opaque, glassy glaze applied to both the interior and exterior of the vessel (fig. 13.6). These local sherds varied in color from chartreuse to white to green and were decorated with brown, yellow, and green painted motifs, sometimes with a floral design (figure 13.6c). The colors were more vibrant than those of the lead-glazed Local Folk ware. The ware was very hard, and the sherds were thicker than the more common lead-glazed Folk ware. The paste was homogeneous and completely oxidized, often fired to a bright color, with no visible temper. Sherds of this type consistently occurred in the same contexts with lead-glazed sherds, but they were easily differentiated because the sherds of local majolica were glazed on both sides, while the Folk ware sherds showed glaze on just the interior of the vessel. Samples are inadequate to define differences in decoration between the two types.

Westbury, who found a single majolica sherd during a survey on the peninsula, noted that Andean majolicas produced in Cuenca, Ecuador, and Arequipa, Peru, in the later eighteenth century were fired to a brick red. He argued that the majolica in the Santa Elena site "may very well be a piece from an Ecuadorian majolica industry yet to be defined" (Westbury 1984:33).

Tin glazed: Imported wares. Several sherds from the

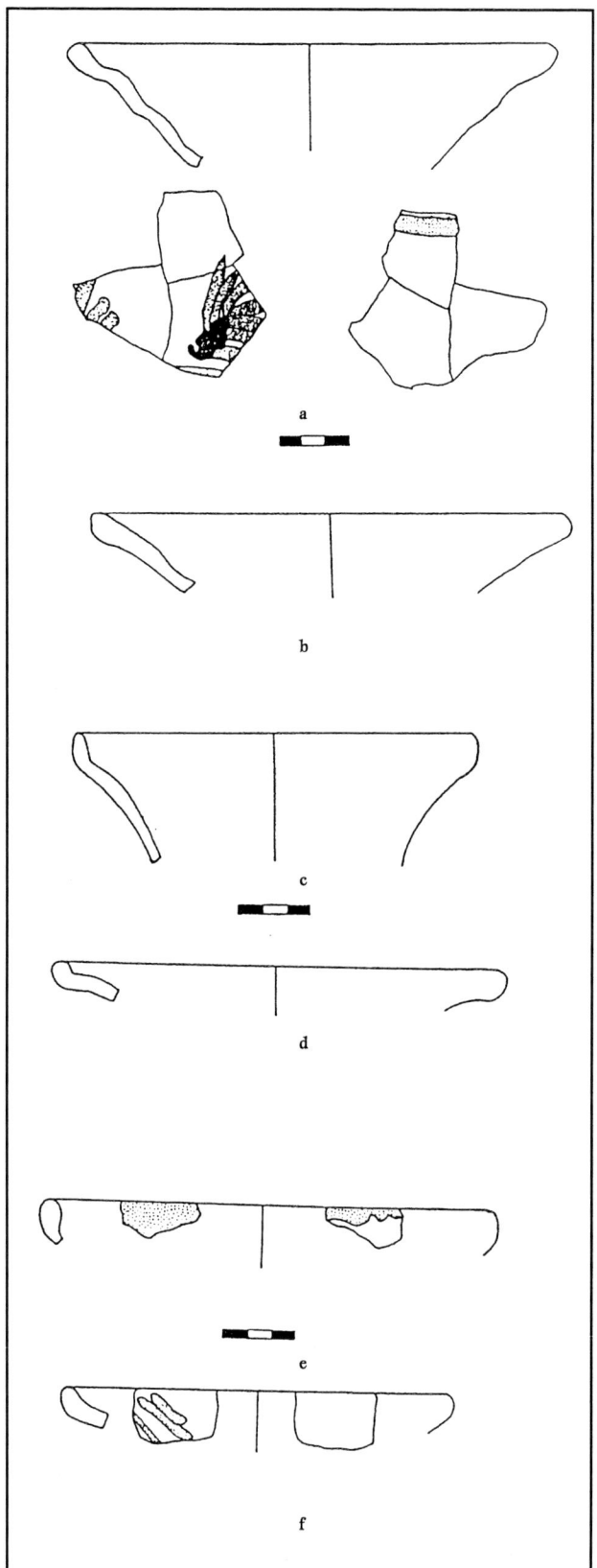

FIGURE 13.3 Forms of open vessels, Local Folk ware characterized by yellow glazed interiors with green floral decoration, and an irregular rim band of glaze on the exterior. *a*, site 410A; *b*, site 410B; *c*, site 406, unit 21; *d*, site 322, unit D1; *e*, site 330, unit A2; *f*, site 406A.

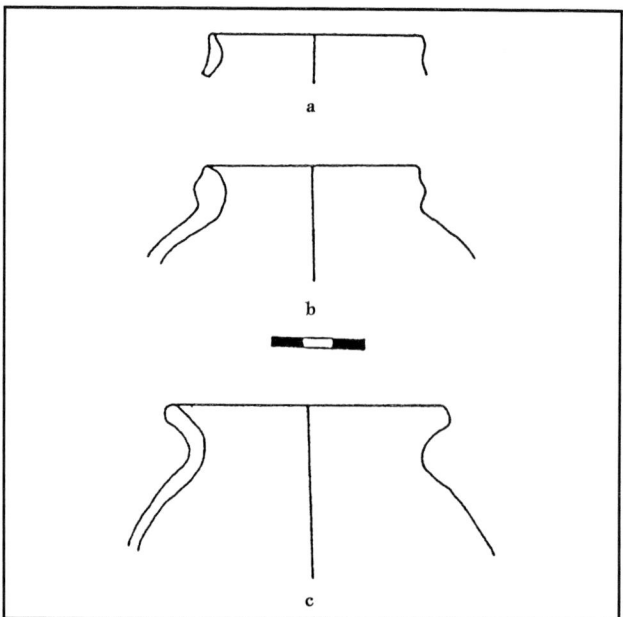

FIGURE 13.4 Forms of restricted vessels, Local Folk ware with glazed rims. *a*, site 406; *b*, site 325C; *c*, site 406C.

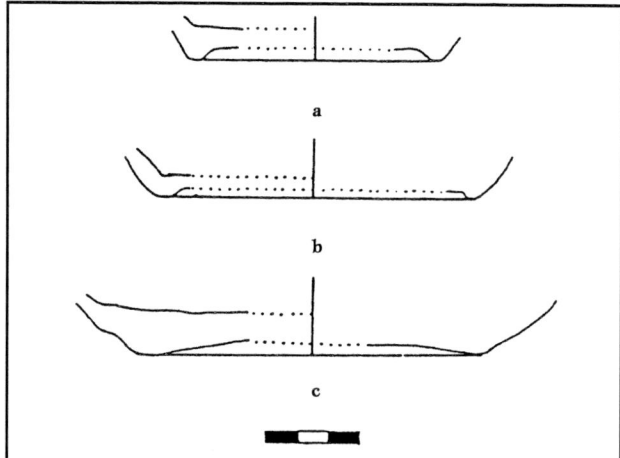

FIGURE 13.5 Base forms of Local Folk ware with glazed interiors and floral designs. *a*, site 406; *b*, site 301, with glazed exterior; *c*, site 407B.

Tambo River collections have been identified as belonging to the "Puebla Tradition." Deagan (1987:78-79) described this as a series of blue-and-white wares produced from the seventeenth to the early nineteenth centuries in Puebla, Mexico. While the Tambo sherds do not have the diagnostic decorations of Puebla majolica, they do have the characteristic creamy white background enamel and some blue decoration. We cannot be sure that this finely made ware was produced in Puebla because there are no rim sherds and no basis for reconstructing vessel form. They might be imitations produced elsewhere, but they are consistent with wares made in Puebla between 1780 and 1810.

Other sherds have been identified by Fox as Monterey Polychrome, a tin-glazed ware produced in Mexico (Barnes and May 1972:36). This ware, popular during the early nine-

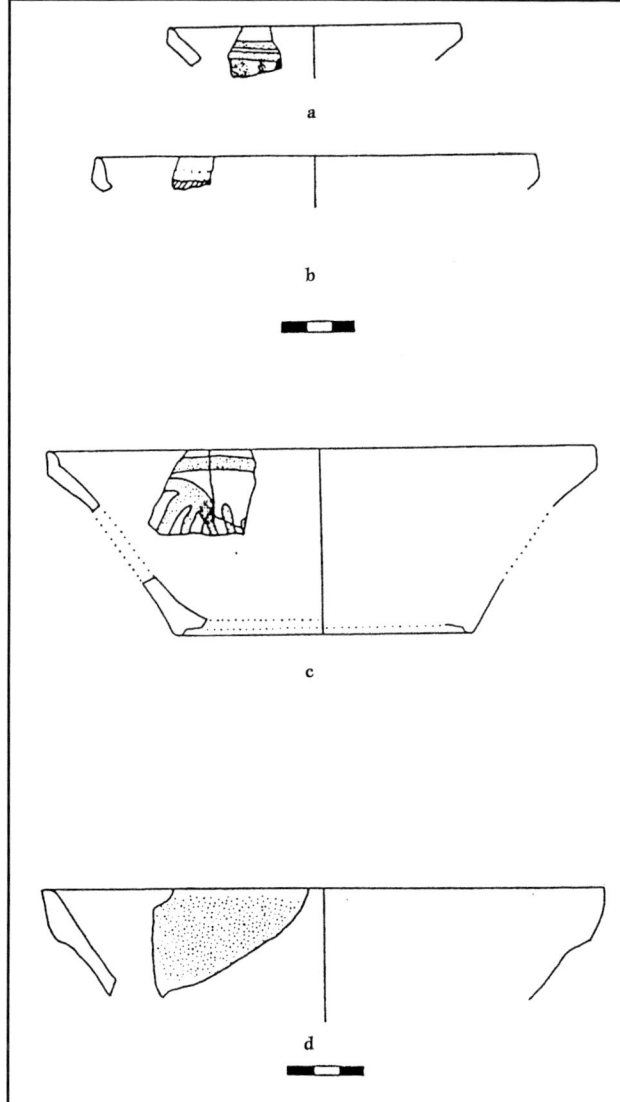

FIGURE 13.6 Local imitation majolica characterized by opaque glazes on both interior and exterior surfaces with interior decorations. *a*, site 406A; *b*, site 406A; *c*, site 345C; *d*, site 410G, pea-green glaze on interior and on exterior rim only.

teenth century, was widely traded.

Analysis. James Burton of the Laboratory for Archaeological Chemistry, University of Wisconsin, Madison, has analyzed the paste of twenty-three sherds from the Tambo River collections, classified as lead-glazed earthenwares, Brown lead-glazed wares, and tin-glazed local wares (imitation majolicas), as well as two brown-glazed sherds from the site of Alamo Plaza in Texas. The data from the analysis of constituent elements in the paste of these sherds resulted in the identification of six robust clusters. In terms of many constituent elements, nine of the lead-glazed sherds (cluster 1) were generally similar to one another, with probable variation within the cluster, but the sample was too small to assess that variation. Distinct from this group were four local tin-glazed (imitation majolica) sherds (cluster 2) from sites 406A and 345C. Two sherds from site 406 formed another small group (cluster 3), and one lead-glazed sherd was unique (cluster 4). Two lead-glazed sherds from sites 406A and 345C were alike (cluster 5) and different from the rest. Cluster 6 included three very similar brown-glazed sherds, one from site 406A and two from Alamo Plaza, and a green lead-glazed sherd from site 345C. It seems likely that the brown-glazed ware common at the Alamo was made in Mexico and also exported to Ecuador, perhaps with other lead-glazed vessels from the same workshop.

Although Burton cautions that the functions of vessels have effects on the chemical constituents of the paste which should not be ignored, it may be tentatively concluded that the observed variation in the paste composition indicates many different centers of manufacture for the ceramics in the sample.

Hard-paste/Refined Earthenwares. Hard-paste/refined earthenwares were manufactured in the late eighteenth and nineteenth centuries in Europe, principally England, and in the Americas. They were all produced with refined clays and fired at high temperatures. They have vitreous glazes and exhibit a range of decorative motifs.

Historical documents tell us these imported wares were fairly common in Ecuador (Kennedy 1990:55-56), and that while some people used these wares for decoration, most families of the middle to upper classes owned and used imported "china" dinnerware. A factory in Quito produced refined earthenware at the end of the eighteenth century, and some production occurred in Cuenca (Kennedy 1990). Except for figurines produced in Quito, these products have not been identified.

These imported wares were found in excavated contexts at site 406 in association with soft-paste earthenware, suggesting that their association on the surface is not owing to the mixing of several occupations but is rather the result of the disposal of those wares at the same time in the first half of the nineteenth century. Site 338, interpreted above as a store or saloon, was unique among all the sites. It had not only the largest quantity but also the greatest variety of decorated refined earthenware.

Undecorated whiteware. White sherds that lacked decoration or other distinctive features were classified as miscellaneous whiteware. This category includes fragments of ironstone and pearlware (Boger 1971:163, 258) as well as the undecorated portions of vessels classified as transfer printed, stamped, hand painted, edgeware, and so forth. Some may be early nineteenth century in date, but surface collections could include unidentified twentieth-century plates and cups.

Transfer-printed ware. Transfer printing became a standard technique for decorating inexpensive chinaware beginning in the mid-eighteenth century in England, France, and elsewhere (Boger 1971:347). The Tambo River collections contain a variety of transfer-printed sherds, but only sixteen patterns were identified with certainty at seven sites. Twelve of the sixteen patterns have been useful in dating (table 13.3).

Based on identified patterns on transfer-printed wares in the large sample from site 338, that site can be assigned occupation dates ranging from pre-1835 through 1897, but the likely time of occupation was after 1850. Sites 322, 408, and 330, with small sherd counts, contained wares produced between 1833 and 1847. Sites 406 and 410, based on blue transfer-printed sherds (Pollan 1992), may date before 1835.

The computer software program called CERAMDATE (Carlson 1985) estimated a median date of occupation for a group of eleven Tambo sites with transfer-printed wares. CERAMDATE is based on an earlier Mean Ceramic Date formula (Carlson 1983; Salwen and Bridges 1977; South 1972). The program calculates the midpoint of production for fifty-one types of European refined earthenwares and five types of Asian porcelain.

The sample of 229 sherds, consisting of ten refined earthenware types, was used for analysis of the eleven Tambo River sites. Using CERAMDATE, an occupation date of 1836.6 was estimated. Because 76 percent of the refined earthenwares in the Tambo River sample were recovered at site 338, that site was tested separately. The 175 sherds from site 338 produced a median occupation date of 1841.4, which supports our perception that this site may have been occupied slightly later than some of the others. These median dates of occupation are consistent with our interpretations of the entire ceramic assemblage.

Flow blue ware. This transfer-printed ware is characterized by a white background bearing a transfer-printed blue design that appears blurred. A "considerable international trade was developed in this cheaply produced and attractive ware" in the second and third decades of the nineteenth century (Boger 1971:117–118).

Hand-painted ware. Hand-painted floral motifs were common throughout the nineteenth century. The Tambo River collection includes sherds from vessels with hand-painted polychromatic floral designs under the glaze.

Edgeware. These vessels have special edge treatment consisting of molded and/or hand-painted interior rim bands. The decoration may include "cockled" edges, also called "shell" edges a sculptured or scalloped edge, and the surface just inside the rim may be impressed. The interior rim may bear distinctive brush strokes that create a feather design called feather edge (Brown 1990:19). Recent research by Randy Moir (1991) has suggested that the cockled edge is an early feature, produced between 1775 and 1825. Plates in our collections exhibit impressed edges in combination with a freehand painted floral decoration, which may have been

Table 13.3 Distribution of identified transfer-printed patterns by sites

	406	408	410	414	322	330	338
Palestine/ Damascus 1819–1864							X
Mare & Foal 1825–1848			X				
"Deep cobalt" ?–1835	X						
Florentine Fountain 1830–1835	X						
Beverley 1832–present							X
Camilla 1833–1847		X	X	X	X		
Italian 1833–1847		X	X		X	X	
Byron Views/Grecian Border 1833–1847							X
Medina 1845–1870							X
Roselle 1848–1897							X
Columbia ca. 1850							X
Toro ca. 1859							X

Note: Some identified patterns, whose chronological distributions are very broad, have been omitted from this table.

added after the original manufacture.

Spongeware. The technique of decorating whitewares by hand application of floral designs using carved sponge stems was popular from 1845 until the early 1880s (Robacker and Robacker 1978:97). Hand-painted and sponged sherds from our collections are similar to each other in color and design and can be dated to the second half of the nineteenth century. The techniques of hand painting and applying sponged designs may be combined in the decoration of single vessels. Both techniques have been identified on individual sherds in the Tambo River collections. The vessel forms represented include plates and shallow bowls.

Three sherds in the collections represent a variant which is called Spatterware, characterized by daubed-on color that does not make recognizable shapes.

Banded slipware. Banded slipwares are whitewares decorated with painted bands presumably applied while the vessel was spun on a lathe. Tambo River sherds feature blue bands on white ground. Similar wares were popular in North America from the 1790s until the 1850s.

Porcelain. The two decorated porcelain sherds from the Tambo River are probably soft paste or semiporcelain. They come from small plates presumably produced in Asia (Deagan 1987:96). By the end of the eighteenth century, ships from Manila passed through Callao (Peru's chief port) bringing Asian goods to the Andes. Artisans in Cuenca also claimed to have made porcelain in 1781 (Kennedy 1990:54), but there are no descriptions of those wares.

Stoneware gin jugs. These handmade stoneware bottles are shaped like cylinders. Gin jugs, found at three sites on the Tambo River, exhibit a clear glaze on the exteriors. In the mid-nineteenth century, these containers were imported in quantities into the United States from Germany and Holland.

Unglazed Earthenware. ***Redware.*** A small portion of each assemblage consisted of rim and body sherds from plain, low-fired earthenware vessels with red-slipped surfaces (Munsel 10R 4/6). Figure 13.7 shows the rim forms, which include both open bowls and collared vessels, possibly cook pots or storage jars. This ware has fine-sand temper, with some larger grit, and may be completely oxidized or show gray cores. The paste is coarse and breaks roughly. The surfaces are often streaky polished, as if with a narrow, hard polishing tool. The slip paint is frequently thick and finely crazed. This is probably the Crackled Red ware that Lanning (1967:26) described as diagnostic of the Santa Elena phase, which has never been defined. These vessels were probably made locally and acquired directly from the potters. Early in the twentieth century, the local ceramic production center was the community of Río Verde, where several elderly potters still work (Alvarez 1987b; Holm 1968). If sherd samples were larger, it might be possible to address the question of continuity between the ceramic technology of the middle nineteenth century and contemporary Río Verde.

Spanish-style storage jars. Spanish-style storage jars, or "Iberian Storage Jars," including olive jars, were imported into the Americas throughout the Colonial period (Deagan 1987:37–39; Goggin 1960). Many examples of *botijas españolas* (earthenware vessels) are known from the highlands of Ecuador (Holm 1971; Kennedy 1990). Although Stothert found Goggin's "Middle" style olive jar necks on the surfaces of sites in the study area, none are present in this collection. There are rims and body sherds of several kinds of Spanish-style storage jars.

An important variant is the large wide-mouthed jar with thickened rim and pronounced external ridge located below the rim (figure 13.8c, e). Terracotta in color, the jars have thick walls and coarse paste heavily tempered with sand and other grit particles. These vessels belong to a tradition of tar-boiling kettles used in northern Peru and on the Santa Elena Peninsula in the late eighteenth and nineteenth centuries (Stothert 1994). The tar-boiling vessels used in Amotape, Peru, were manufactured in Catacaos in northern Peru, but we do not know the site of manufacture of those used in Santa Elena. These vessels are found in abundance at industrial sites on the peninsula, and a few sherds, not impregnated with tar, have been found in habitation sites along the Tambo River.

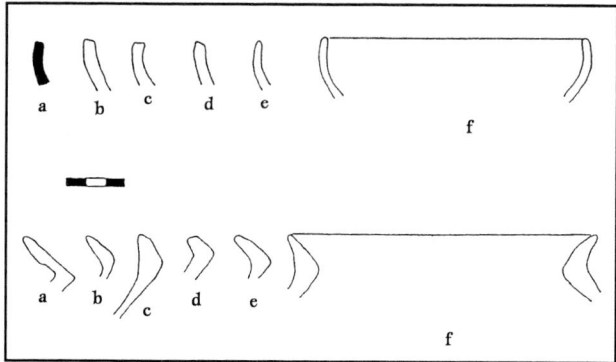

FIGURE 13.7 Redware: First row: *a*, site 406, unit 11, 0-10cm; *b-c*, site 414G; *d*, site 325C. Second row: *a*, site 415A; *b*, site 408C; *c*, site 406, unit 9; *d-e*, site 345C; *f*, site 406, unit 28.

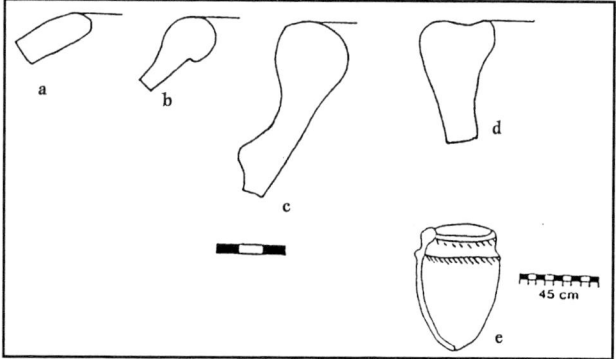

FIGURE 13.8 Earthenware storage jars: *a*, site 406B; *b*, site 406A; *c*, site 406, unit 11, 0-10cm; *d*, site 322, unit 5, 0-5cm; *e*, form reconstructed from sherd found at site OGSE-84

Antique *pipas* (water-storage vessels) are still in use on the peninsula (figure 13.8a, b). They are reported to have been made in the nineteenth century at Sanborondón, just north of Guayaquil, in the nineteenth century (Treacy 1982:4). In the Colonial period, large earthenware jars were used for storing and transporting honey, milk, clothing, cereals, beans, gunpowder, and oil (Holm 1971:272-273). These vessels derive their shapes from olive jars, but they do not have the diagnostic necks and rims.

The origin of these vessels is unknown; there is little information about pottery production in coastal Ecuador, in part because it was a lower-class activity (Holm, 1971:274). No craft guilds were reported for the entire province in the late eighteenth and early nineteenth centuries (Hamerly 1973:145; Treacy 1982:5). In 1840 the only tax-paying potters in all of the Province of Guayas were at Sanborondón (Hamerly 1973:113-116). Treacy (1982:6) states that pots were inexpensive even in the twentieth century and that potters traveled from Sanborondón to exchange wares for goods or money. Some storage jars and other wares might have been brought to Santa Elena by these traders or carried by families back to their homes. There was significant seasonal movement of people with cattle between the Sanborondón region and the peninsula at the beginning of the nineteenth century (Hamerly 1973:68).

Interpretation

The archaeological remains from house sites along the Tambo River are evidence that the rural people of the Santa Elena Peninsula were connected to the national and international commercial network in the early days of the Republic. They used not only cooking pots and bowls made locally (Redware) but they also acquired storage vessels perhaps from specialized communities near Guayaquil (such as Sanborondón); Lead-glazed platters and bowls similar to vessels made in the highlands today; finer Tin-glazed vessels (imitation majolica) probably produced in Ecuador; imported brown-glazed, Puebla, and Monterey wares from Mexico; refined earthenwares from England, France and Belgium; porcelain from Asia; wine bottles from abroad; and gin jugs from Germany or Holland. Because these arrived by sea and would have been relatively cheap and abundant in coastal towns, it is not surprising that in the expanding economy of the first half of the nineteenth century the local people acquired imported wares.

The archaeological evidence from the Tambo River, taken in combination with historical data, shows us the way of life of rural people, classified as *indios* (indigenous people), who were engaged in subsistence agriculture and who carried on a variety of other economic activities including spinning (from which we infer weaving), fishing, shell fishing, deer hunting, and perhaps animal husbandry. The presence of stone tools, handmade buttons, homemade spindle whorls, and the dietary emphasis on fish and wild game all suggest that people used local materials to produce goods and food for domestic consumption.

Nineteenth-century written sources indicate that households in Santa Elena produced items for trade or sale, including salt, wax, woven hats, purple-dyed thread, and textiles. Craft and commercial activity apparently permitted indigenous families to buy such imported goods as metal knives, guns and ammunition, wine and other alcoholic beverages, Mexican ceramics, imitation majolicas, and British and Asian refined earthenwares.

The material culture analyzed here supports the idea that the Indian communities of the Santa Elena Peninsula had a cultural strategy which was to acculturate while maintaining their ethnic identity and distinct life-ways. In the Colonial and early Republican periods these communities participated in the national economy (by engaging in exchange and paying tribute and taxes), accepted national language and dress, took advantage of the national legal and educational systems, and adopted some new technologies, but they also conserved other aspects of their traditional productive, social, and ideological systems.

Acknowledgments. We acknowledge with gratitude institutional support from the Museo Antropológico, Banco Central del Ecuador, Instituto Nacional de Patrimonio Cultural (Guayaquil), Petro-Ecuador and Petro-Península (formerly CEPE). The project received support and encouragement from Olaf Holm, Sandra Pollan of the Brazosport Archaeological Society, Kimball Smith, Bill Westbury, James Burton, and Jozef Buys. In the field in the early 1980s, Stothert counted on the collaboration of Helaine Silverman, Leon Doyon, Karl Taube, Rita Molina and Neil Maurer. We also thank Richard G. Cooke for his guidance in doing the faunal analysis, and for permission to use the type collections of the Smithsonian Tropical Research Institute in the Republic of Panama.

✟ Chapter 14

Buenos Aires del Siglo XVI al XIX
Avances en Arqueología Histórica

Daniel Schávelzon

Resumen

En los últimos años se ha establecido un programa continuo de excavaciones arqueológicas en el área del asentamiento colonial de Buenos Aires. La zona sur, conocida como San Telmo, se seleccionó debido a su antigüedad y estabilidad constructiva; esta parte de la ciudad está parcialmente protegida por leyes para la conservación del patrimonio cultural. Con anterioridad jamás se habían realizado excavaciones arqueológicas en Buenos Aires, y gracias a nuestras investigaciones se han descubierto contextos que datan del siglo XVI al XIX, incluyendo cimientos de casas, pisos, muros y túneles subterráneos. Como consecuencia, ha sido posible identificar tipos cerámicos y ubicarlos cronológicamente, con lo cual es posible proponer nuevas ideas sobre la vida cotidiana en el ámbito urbano, en particular de los sectores populares.

Abstract

In the past few years a program of continuous archaeological excavations has been established in the area of the colonial settlement of Buenos Aires. The southern zone of the city, known as San Telmo, was chosen because of its age and structural stability; this part of the city is partially protected by law as part of the cultural heritage. Before this program was begun, archaeological excavations had not been conducted in Buenos Aires. These investigations have led to the discovery of deposits dating to the sixteenth to nineteenth centuries, including house foundations, floors, walls, and underground tunnels. As a result, it has been possible to identify and date artifact types that suggest new ideas about daily life and urban space, focusing particularly on the lives of common people.

EN BUENOS AIRES, hoy una ciudad de 10 millones de habitantes y con una historia que se remonta a su primera fundación en 1536, nunca se habían realizado excavaciones arqueológicas. El establecimiento de un proyecto continuo desde 1985 ha logrado iniciar su conocimiento desde una visión alternativa a la histórico-documental tradicional. En especial debido a la casi absoluta falta de legislación preservacionista en la ciudad, el desarrollo urbano ha destruido la mayor parte de los sitios con potencial arqueológico o lo hará en los próximos años en forma casi irremediable; incluso la ley que protege el área histórica—generalmente llamada San Telmo por su iglesia jesuítica—ha sido modificada en 1992 posibilitando la demolición de la zona. Esto obliga a que las intervenciones arqueológicas sean necesariamente tareas de rescate urgente y, paralelamente, a que se realice una labor de concientización sobre su importancia.

En Argentina la arqueología indígena o prehispánica tiene una larga historia y logros que no necesitan ser destacados, pero la arqueología histórica y en especial la urbana ha permanecido a la sombra de ésta (Fernández 1982).

Son un tema difícil de explicar aquí los motivos por los cuales los proyectos iniciados a principios de siglo y que en las décadas de 1940 y 1950 llegaron a ser grandes excavaciones—como las ruinas de Cayastá, Concepción del Bermejo y las misiones jesuíticas—que incluían la restauración y preservación de conjuntos de envergadura, fueron siendo dejadas de lado y olvidadas por las autoridades y por los especialistas (Schávelzon 1992a). Incluso en 1905 se hizo un descubrimiento casual de objetos indígenas en el patio central de la Casa de Gobierno, y que pese a ser controlado por arqueólogos no sirvió para despertar interés u otras inquietudes.

Pero la realidad es que la década de 1980 significó un reencuentro con la arqueología histórica en el país. Si bien en Buenos Aires hubo desde principios de siglo algunos estudios pioneros, entre 1928 y 1940 se hicieron algunos intentos de realizar investigaciones más amplias, pero nunca llegó a cristalizarse un proyecto continuo de investigación.

La Ciudad de Buenos Aires

Buenos Aires fue fundada en 1536 por Pedro de Mendoza como un puerto con un real o pequeña aldea cercana. Es muy poco lo que se sabe sobre la ubicación exacta y la estructura física de ese asentamiento inicial, el que fue abandonado y quemado en 1541 para que sus sobrevivientes viajaran a Asunción. La flota de Mendoza estaba compuesta de casi mil quinientos hombres y gran parte de ellos murieron en el sitio por hambre, asedio de indígenas, y en viajes al interior.

Existe una amplísima bibliografía sobre el tema, en especial compilaciones monumentales de documentos (Comisión Oficial del IVo. Centenario 1941), e incluso existe un sitio que ha sido institucionalizado por la historia como el lugar de fundación, pero nunca había sido excavado, hasta 1988 en que pudimos plantear, tras una temporada de trabajo de campo, que no había restos atribuibles a esa época.

Al parecer la ciudad fue fundada en esa primera oportunidad en algún sitio cercano a la barranca que limita las planicies de la zona con el gran Río de la Plata, que en algunos lugares alcanzaba hasta 15 m de alto, y cerca del Riachuelo, única entrada de naves de calado medio a zonas protegidas de los vientos y crecidas. El terreno era plano, sólo cruzado por arroyos producidos por las lluvias y los desniveles que son poco marcados hasta hoy; esa falta de accidentes topográficos es precisamente lo que hizo que no hubiera referencias geográficas precisas en las primeras descripciones. Pero la segunda fundación de la ciudad, en 1580 por Juan de Garay, sí prosperó; la zona es la misma según las crónicas, ya que sobrevivientes del primer viaje acompañaron al segundo, aunque posiblemente se ubicó un poco más al norte, en una meseta sobre la barranca, limitada por dos arroyos al norte y sur, con posibilidades de crecimiento ilimitado hacia el oeste. Ésta fue la estructura física que se mantuvo hasta el siglo XVIII.

Desde el siglo XVI hasta la mitad del siglo XVII fue poco más que una aldea grande dependiente de la muy lejana Lima. Teniendo prohibido comerciar a través del puerto, sus posibilidades económicas se limitaban al contrabando, tanto en la entrada ilegal de productos de consumo básico como en la salida de plata desde Potosí. La gran producción de cueros y sebo vacuno, y más tarde carne seca y luego salada, fue haciendo surgir una burguesía local que utilizó todos los medios para hacer crecer sus fortunas. Así el siglo XVIII tardío vio, a la par de la apertura del comercio en 1774, y con la creación del Virreinato del Río de la Plata en 1776, cómo la ciudad aumentaba en forma acelerada su densidad, la ocupación de nuevos terrenos y la mejora de la calidad de la arquitectura: nuevos edificios públicos, empedrados, casas de dos pisos, mercados construidos, consolidación de la manzana urbana, construcción de medianeras entre lote y lote, y obligaciones de hacer fachadas a la calle. Incluso las técnicas constructivas, los materiales usados y la presencia de arquitectos profesionales trajeron cambios rápidos y evidentes.

En 1750 la ciudad sólo contaba con 14,000 habitantes, pero en 1790 alcanzaba ya los 32,000. La población era variada étnicamente aunque con una notable mayoría de blancos: para 1778 había 16,000 blancos, 6,800 negros y sólo 1,150 indios, aunque es posible que en el número de estos últimos sólo se incluyeran los residentes permanentes y censables (Besio Moreno 1934).

Para inicios del siglo XIX Buenos Aires era una ciudad importante en la región pero que mantuvo su identidad física colonial hasta medio siglo más tarde. Hacia 1850 empezó un proceso de europeización acelerado que permitió que en medio siglo prácticamente toda la ciudad colonial desapareciera. A diferencia de otros centros históricos de Latinoamérica, la ciudad no posee en su casco urbano ejemplos residenciales de la época de la dominación española, salvo algunas pocas iglesias, todas remodeladas o modificadas en el siglo pasado. Esto hace que la arqueología tenga un papel particularmente interesante en cuanto al rescate de un pasado que no está físicamente visible, que ha sido borrado de la memoria y de la identidad de la población con la ideología de la Gran Inmigración entre 1880 y 1920.

Ya para la década de 1870 se establecieron polémicas acerca del valor de los ejemplos de arquitectura colonial o anteriores a 1852, y el consenso de la intelectualidad era que, salvo algunos casos paradigmáticos, todo debía ser destruido y construido de nuevo en aras de progreso. Para el año 1889 llegaron al país más de 225,000 inmigrantes europeos, los que seguirían aumentando hasta 1914. Es así que llegó el momento en que el 50 por ciento de la población total no había nacido en el país. La ciudad tenía en 1855 unos 96,000 habitantes, es decir que triplicaban los existentes antes de la independencia, pero para 1890 había 527,000 personas viviendo en la ciudad y sus alrededores, que en 1914 llegaron a ser casi dos millones. De más está decir lo que esto significó no sólo para la arquitectura sino para toda la vida cotidiana y los objetos materiales que la acompañan.

Paralelamente a este proceso rápido de europeización se iniciaron las campañas de genocidio de la población indígena, la cual fue exterminada en las grandes guerras de la década de 1880, o reducida a reservas con la destrucción total de su cultura material (Martínez Sarasola 1992). De todas formas en Buenos Aires su presencia, importante hasta las guerras de la independencia, fue decayendo hasta desaparecer hacia 1840.

Lo que sí es un tema abierto para la arqueología es que la supuesta aculturación total de esos pobladores indígenas no lo fue tanto, por lo menos en cuanto a lo que su cerámica expresa hasta el momento; mayores estudios nos informarán al respecto. Por ejemplo, la excavación de una herrería ubicada debajo de la Capilla de Nuestra Señora de Belén, en la zona de San Telmo, y asociada a las obras de su construcción hechas a partir de 1740, dio varios fragmentos de tinajas de cerámica rústica, pero ningún fragmento de mayólica española. Pero una vivienda contemporánea, ubicada asimismo en un sector marginal de la ciudad, aunque atribuida a una familia de ciertos recursos, mostró un alto porcentaje de objetos importados (51%) en relación con los regionales (49%). Para finales del siglo XVIII se incrementa el porcentaje en las colecciones arqueológicas de loza crema (creamware) a la par de la lenta desaparición de la población indígena; hacia 1820 se encuentra tanta cantidad de esa cerámica como de las mayólicas españolas anteriormente. Para pocos años más adelante la totalidad de lo usado en la ciudad era importado, o manufacturado a partir de materias primas europeas.

Intervenciones Arqueológicas en Buenos Aires

Las excavaciones hechas se han centrado en diversos problemas que se consideraron prioritarios: el primero fue obtener un conjunto significativo de materiales culturales que permitieran construir una tipología cerámica, de vidrios, metales y otros objetos de la vida cotidiana, mostrando la presencia o ausencia más significativas; en segundo lugar establecer una secuencia cronológica de dichos materiales conjuntamente con su correlación con los sistemas y técnicas constructivas conexas (Schávelzon 1987, 1988, 1991, 1994, 1995). Una vez organizado esto y ya con una visión de conjunto, se comenzó con proyectos más específicos con el objeto de comprender mejor las formas de la vida cotidiana de las clases medias y bajas, excavando viviendas y edificios industriales o comerciales diversos. Más tarde se estableció el proyecto Primera Fundación con el objeto de excavar el área supuesta donde se hallaba ubicada la aldea inicial del siglo XVI. Por último se ha publicado el proyecto de estudio de la red de túneles hechos por los jesuitas en el siglo XVIII—aunque con precedentes desde el siglo XVII y obras posteriores hasta el XIX—y otras construcciones subterráneas conexas (Schávelzon 1992b). Actualmente se han iniciado en otros sitios del país proyectos similares y ya se ha excavado el cabildo de la ciudad de Mendoza (Bárcena y Schávelzon 1990), y se han completado dos temporadas en el cabildo de Buenos Aires (Schávelzon 1995).

El subsuelo urbano del área central de la ciudad ha tenido un proceso de acumulación y relleno importante; primero porque la ciudad fue renivelada en varias oportunidades dada la necesidad de crear desniveles artificiales para el desagüe pluvial, más tarde para instalar los primeros tranvías y luego por las obras de infraestructura de servicios urbanos, en especial cloacas y agua potable. Más tarde fueron rellenados los arroyos estacionales y las barrancas al río rebajadas.

En el siglo XVIII también se inició la costumbre de ganar terrenos al ancho río al que enfrenta la ciudad, por rellenado con basura y escombros de demolición de edificios, lo que ha permitido que la zona urbanizada avanzara en ciertos sitios un par de kilómetros. Estos enormes rellenos son una fuente inagotable para la arqueología histórica con grandes potencialidades para el futuro. En ciertos sectores del centro hemos excavado hasta 3 m de rellenos que llegan hasta el siglo XVI.

Un ejemplo interesante de las posibilidades que dan los trabajos hechos a partir de la hipótesis de la preexistencia arqueológica incluso debajo de grandes obras arquitectónicas (véanse capítulos 6, 15, donde se mencionan situaciones semejantes en México y el Uruguay, respectivamente), lo da lo hecho bajo Galerías Pacífico, un conjunto de grandes dimensiones construido en 1895 y actualmente reciclado, donde se logró el rescate de una buena colección de objetos fechados entre approximadamente 1780 y la época de construcción.

La cultura material está representada por cuatro grandes grupos de materiales: los de tradición indígena, los mestizos, los africanos y los europeos, sean españoles primero o de Europa Occidental más tarde. La correlación entre cada una de estas categorías está en estricta relación con la disponibilidad de bienes en cada época y para cada grupo social estudiado, y para los usos a que estaban destinados dentro de la vida hogareña.

Por ejemplo, la cerámica que llamamos indígena en realidad es una continuidad o tradición de los pueblos prehispánicos; existen dos grandes corrientes cerámicas que confluyeron en Buenos Aires, por una parte la de la cultura guaraní y por la otra la querandí. La primera de ellas es la que ocupó un considerable espacio geográfico de carácter selvático y fluvial desde Paraguay hacia el sur y que conforma más del 90 por ciento de la cerámica indígena. La otra tradición cultural es característica de la región que circundaba la ciudad pero cuya expresión cerámica es reducida, desapareciendo en el siglo XVII (Conlazo 1990).

La presencia guaraní era fuerte, ya que fueron usados como mano de obra de los constructores jesuíticos en sus grandes emprendimientos, por los virreyes para las obras públicas y por los artesanos en sus trabajos diarios por la alta calidad de su artesanía. Las cerámicas por ellos producidas o utilizadas eran en su mayoría hechas sin torno, por enrollado y alisado a mano, que a medida que pasa el tiempo van transformando su forma globular por bases planas y bocas más amplias, abandonando la decoración superficial en relieve por paredes lisas o sólo pintadas de rojo. No es una cerámica rica en ornamentación sino más bien sencilla, modesta, utilitaria tanto antes como después de la conquista.

Los tipos que denominamos mestizos son en cambio cerámicas que si bien tienen un origen indígena o que continuaron siendo fabricadas por ellos, están íntimamente ligadas a los gustos y a la tecnología española. Básicamente están compuestos por cerámicas hechas en torno pero con formas o decoración indígena, o la inversa pero con funciones

FIGURA 14.1 Cerámica Monocroma Roja de Cayastá, siglo XVII, uniendo la tradición prehispánica con las formas y técnicas españolas. *Del Museo Etnográfico, Sante Fe*

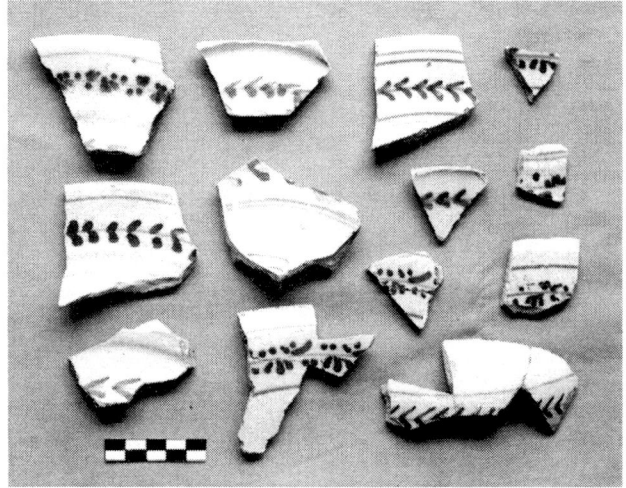

FIGURA 14.2 Mayólica española tipo Triana con decoración de la variedad Monocromo Azul de Ramazón, segunda mitad del siglo XVIII. *Colección C.A.U.*

europeas. Este tipo de cerámica es la que está menos estudiada en el país, pese a su constante presencia en la región litoraleña, e incluso muchas veces ha sido confundida con sus predecesoras inmediatas. La variedad es mucha y se ha logrado identificar varios tipos: la Monocroma Roja (figura 14.1) tanto pintada como pulida, la Policroma similar a la anterior pero con varios colores e incluso letras o guardas ornamentales españolizadas, aun inscripciones; las grandes pipas y tinajas de uso diario en la ciudad hechas siempre por enrollado, desde las grandes para el vino y agua hasta las de uso doméstico, y los candeleros para las velas, tanto en torno como a mano. Las afriicanas son modeladas y muy modestas.

Es evidente que existen otros tipos confusos o mal representados, e incluso situaciones intermedias que esperamos se irán clarificando con nuevas excavaciones. La falta de colecciones de comparación en el país hace difícil la situación, ya que cuando las hay no están clasificadas, como sucede en lo descubierto en Cayastá, donde pese a que hubo más de veinte años de excavaciones nunca se hicieron estudios sistemáticos de lo descubierto salvo una contada excepción (Ceruti 1983). La gran mayoría de estas cerámicas aumentan a medida que avanza el siglo XVII, son mayoría en el XVIII y desaparecen muy rápidamente hacia fines de ese siglo.

Las cerámicas españolas son en su mayor parte las habituales para Latinoamérica: las cubiertas con vidriados de estaño y las de plomo (véase capítulo 18). En las primeras la tradición Morisca es la más común (aproximadamente 90%) aunque hay de los tipos Sevilla y Triana en especial para el siglo XVIII, e incluso XIX temprano (figura 14.2). Las Moriscas son del tipo Columbia Liso, Santo Domingo Azul sobre Blanco, y Yayal Azul sobre Blanco, aunque hay algunas aún no bien identificadas. Entre las de cubierta de plomo hay los tipos Lebrillo Verde y Criollo tanto en los recipientes de gran tamaño—cerca de 1 m de diámetro (figura 14.3)—como en vasijas menores, y la cerámica tipo El Morro está bien representada (figura 14.4).

Para finales del siglo XVIII comenzó a difundirse lentamente por el territorio la loza inglesa tipo crema (creamware); no hay fechas muy exactas pero la apertura del comercio en 1774 aceleró el proceso de introducción de importaciones (véanse capítulos 17, 18). Esto se vio acompañado por botellas de vidrio negro sopladas provenientes de Inglaterra, cuchillos y otros instrumentos metálicos del mismo origen y diversos productos de consumo que se hicieron habituales para fines de ese siglo, como las pipas de caolín.

Con las dos invasiones que Inglaterra intentó realizar a Buenos Aires en 1806 y 1807, y su posterior instalación en la cercana ciudad de Montevideo, incrementó notablemente el mercado de esos productos y más tarde, hacia 1820–1830, los provenientes de Estados Unidos acompañando la gran importación de harina de trigo de ese país. Así, la ciudad vivió una transformación de su cultura material, acompañada de un cambio político—la libertad en 1810—y una reorganización de todo el territorio que significó desde un primer momento el abandono de lo español por las nuevas modas europeas. Desde inicios del siglo XIX el gres cerámico fue introducido con las botellas para cerveza y ginebra, las que venían con la marca del fabricante pero la etiqueta impresa en relieve era del comerciante nacional.

SUPERIOR: FIGURA 14.3 **Vasija de gran tamaño de tipo Criollo, siglo XVIII, producto regional para depositar agua.** *Museo Histórico del Cabildo, Buenos Aires*

FIGURA 14.4 **Fragmentos de El Morro, la más común de las cerámicas utilitarias en Buenos Aires durante 1750–1820.** *Colección C.A.U.*

INFERIOR: FIGURA 14.5 **Loza pearlware policroma importada de Inglaterra en los inicios del siglo XIX, símbolo de los cambios en la cultura material burguesa de la época.** *Colección C.A.U.*

Los años siguientes y casi hasta 1850 la cerámica tradicional fue la loza perla (pearlware, figura 14.5), y los platos españoles reemplazaron definitivamente las ollas indígenas de uso culinario, en especial al dejar de usarse el lebrillo de las comidas guisadas para pasar al plato con un nuevo tipo de forma de comer y de servir la mesa. Esto en realidad expresa un profundo cambio en las maneras de comer, cocinar y recibir invitados en la vivienda.

Para mediados de ese siglo comenzó a crecer la industria nacional, aunque la sustitución de las importaciones sólo comenzó hacia 1880 y se completó en 1914 con la Primera Guerra Mundial. En el ínterin la loza blanca (whiteware) inglesa reemplazó a la anterior loza perla (pearlware), llegando hasta los más alejados rincones del territorio (véase capítulo 13). De este tipo hay infinidad de marcas impresas provenientes de Checoslovaquia, Alemania, Francia, Italia y España.

Pero la estructura física de la ciudad fue cambiando rápidamente durante el final del siglo XVIII y al inicio del XIX: Buenos Aires pasó de una ciudad pequeña provincial, al centro del poder del virrey; el crecimiento de las exportaciones por el puerto, la producción ganadera y el contrabando consolidaron fortunas que permitieron la construcción de grandes iglesias y conventos, casas de dos pisos, edificios de gobierno y asentamientos rurales y suburbanos de importancia. La presencia desde finales del siglo XVII de constructores profesionales, ingenieros militares y arquitectos jesuíticos impulsó en mucho el desarrollo urbano y el mejoramiento de las técnicas constructivas.

Para una etapa tardía en la historia de la ciudad tenemos una excavación interesante por lo significativa y porque el edificio excavado, el Caserón de Rosas, aportó buena información sobre el cambio de función arquitectónica y su correlato en los objetos materiales. Este edificio de enormes dimensiones rodeado de parques y jardines fue iniciado entre 1837 y 1838 para residencia, luego pasó a ser sede del gobierno provincial y nacional, más tarde fue abandonado, olvidado, luego fue cuartel militar, escuela de artes y oficios, colegio militar y liceo naval, para ser demolido en 1899. Esta continua transformación del edificio y de sus pobladores pudo ser detectada en los restos de ocupación (Ramos y Schávelzon 1992; Schávelzon y Ramos 1991).

Conclusiones

Si se resumen los logros de los diversos proyectos arqueológicos realizados en Buenos Aires, podemos citar en primer lugar la comprobación de la presencia de materiales culturales en el subsuelo de la ciudad, pese a los grandes cambios sufridos en el siglo XIX, en que casi toda la ciudad fue renivelada. Algunas zonas donde hay hasta 3 m de rellenos muestran el potencial para futuros trabajos. En segundo lugar se ha logrado apreciar que la cultura material sufrió profundos cambios a finales del siglo XVIII.

Prácticamente la cultura material desde el siglo XVI se expresa como una continuidad en que si bien los tipos cerámicos cambiaban, incluso eso era lento. Hay presencia de materiales regionales, como las cerámicas indígenas y de tradición indígena, o los tipos mestizos, pero la vida cotidiana tuvo siempre una marcada presencia de objetos españoles. A partir del siglo XVIII tardío el reemplazo fue abrupto, siendo las botellas inglesas y la loza crema quienes ocuparon los rangos de mayor porcentaje. Es decir que la arqueología puede confirmar la interpretación histórica de que los cambios sufridos en la sociedad en esa época fueron fuertes, e implicaron no sólo la desaparición del indígena de la ciudad hacia 1830, sino también el surgimiento de la clase burguesa urbana de formación cultural europeizante.

✝ Chapter 15

La Arqueología Histórica en el Uruguay
Historia, Análisis, y Perspectivas

Nelsys Fusco Zambetogliris

Resumen

La arqueología histórica en el marco de nuestro continente se ocupa de los episodios cronológicamente ubicados a partir del impacto de contacto entre las sociedades americanas y los europeos, evento que en el territorio del Uruguay se remonta a los inicios del siglo XVI. Es objetivo de este estudio explicar el camino recorrido por la arqueología histórica en el Uruguay. En este sentido se darán a conocer diferentes momentos del proceso de su desarrollo, los procedimientos seguidos y los resultados obtenidos, estableciendo los enfoques teóricos que enmarcan las acciones a través del tiempo.

Abstract

The field of historical archaeology in South America pertains to the period following the initial contact between indigenous societies and Europeans. In Uruguay this period begins in the early sixteenth century. The objective of this study is to explain the history of historical archaeology in Uruguay by describing the historical development of the field, the methods and procedures followed, and research results, establishing theoretical outlooks that have influenced the field through time.

Para abordar la temática del desarrollo de la arqueología histórica en el Uruguay, hay que considerar que durante el convulsionado siglo XIX se da la búsqueda de la identidad nacional, misma que se refleja en la investigación histórica, la literatura, y las artes plásticas y en la preocupación por la educación popular. Hacia fines del siglo, al cobrar importancia los vestigios culturales prehistóricos, se esbozó la arqueología, sumando más tarde a sus intereses los restos monumentales pertenecientes al período Colonial, mismo que se extiendió hasta 1810 cuando se inició el proceso independentista del Uruguay.

Numerosos vestigios testimonian el pasado histórico de la nación. En la actualidad es posible observar algunos monumentos auténticos y también otros que han sido reconstruidos; estos últimos son fruto de acciones emprendidas en las primeras décadas de este siglo y muestran los inicios de la arqueología histórica en el país.

Primer Período

Los estudios precursores vinculados con la arqueología histórica ocurrieron en las primeras décadas de este siglo. El tema atrajo la atención de estudiosos de distintas disciplinas, quienes para abordar ese patrimonio pusieron en práctica formas de trabajo que permanecerían vigentes hasta la década de los años cincuenta.

La óptica predominante de este período abarcaba los estudios de las fuentes históricas y los monumentos arquitectónicos, con el propósito principal de reconstruir el bien patrimonial. En ese sentido se emprendieron numerosas acciones en edificios vinculados con la presencia española y portuguesa, cuyas ruinas eran visibles en distintos puntos del territorio (figura 15.1). Algunos testimoniaban la demarcación de fronteras, como los fuertes de Santa Teresa y San Miguel; otros la ocupación española, como el Cabildo de Montevideo, y los fuertes de Maldonado e Isla Gorriti; o la presencia portuguesa representada por la ciudad de Colonia del Sacramento.

La Fortaleza de Santa Teresa

Este baluarte se ubica al este del Uruguay, en el Departamento de Rocha a escasos kilómetros del Océano Atlántico. Se erigió en el límite de la frontera hispano-portuguesa a fines del siglo XVIII y fue el escenario de una constante pugna territorial mantenida por ambas potencias ibéricas; este litigio se inició en el siglo XVI y se dilucidaría definitivamente con la independencia consumada en 1830. Ilustrativa de estos acontecimientos es la propia historia de la fortaleza, construida por los españoles de acuerdo con un plan ideado por el ingeniero Bartolomé Howel en 1780, el que se llevó a cabo en el lugar geográfico elegido por los portugueses para

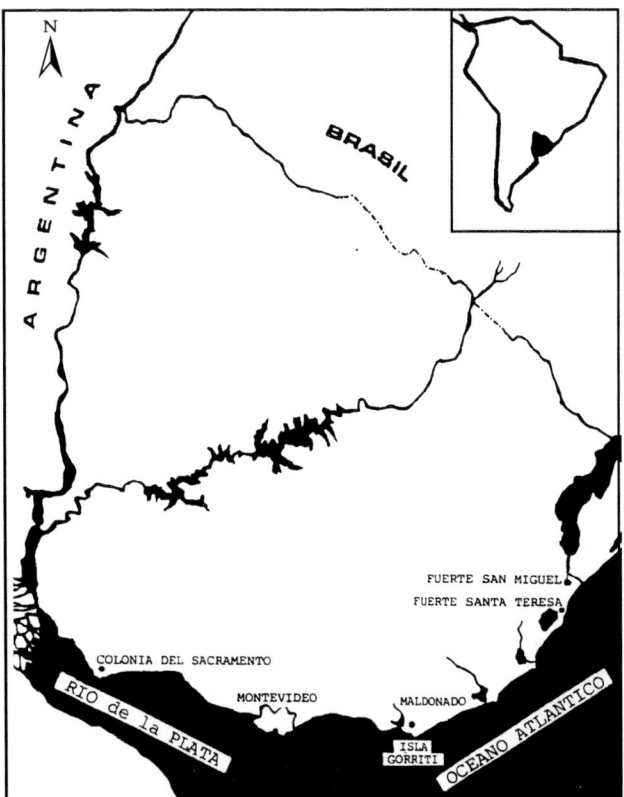

FIGURA 15.1 República Oriental del Uruguay

el emplazamiento del modesto Fuerte de Santa Teresa, cuya piedra fundamental fue colocada por el Coronel Osorio el 4 de diciembre de 1762.

Los restos monumentales de este bastión no habían pasado desapercibidos, pues existen varias referencias de fines del siglo XIX que evidencian el interés que ellos despertaban. Durante la dictadura de Latorre (1876–1880), éste propuso inspeccionar las ruinas con el fin de conservar lo que pudiera tener valor material e histórico (Arredondo 1955:41).

En 1881 Luis Melián Lafinur escribe:

> Pronto va a desaparecer el Fuerte de Santa Teresa dejando en las páginas de la historia la estela de sus desgracias y las glorias de que ha sido teatro. Viento de ruina sopla en sus almenas; el salitre de las aguas del Océano alcanza a dos cañones sin cureña que yace allí fuera de su sitio; la herrumbre descascara la antes tersa y bruñida superficie del metal y arranca en costra rojiza, las armas de Castilla en él grabadas.... Las dunas que lo asechan desde el pie de sus murallas, concluirán por tragarlo, sepultándolo en honda tumba de arena. (citado en Arredondo 1955:39–40)

Más adelante los jefes políticos del Departamento de Rocha, Pedro Lapeyre (1892) y Manuel González Rodríguez (1895), impulsaron ante los respectivos gobiernos constitucionales decretos presidenciales, con el fin de propiciar la reparación de las ruinas y su utilización. Es la segunda iniciativa la que se llevó a la práctica y por ella se procedió a limpiar el fuerte y el parque circundante, así como a restaurar parte de las ruinas.

Respecto a la reconstrucción del monumento, a raíz de la visita de Arredondo en 1917 en el área, éste aprovechó la oportunidad para proponer que se escribiera su historia, se realizara su restauración y se contuvieran las dunas con plantaciones (Arredondo 1955:50).

Paralelamente se procuró sensibilizar a las autoridades políticas de estos propósitos, y como consecuencia en 1923 se formó una comisión para preparar las obras; cuatro años más tarde se declaró monumento nacional la Fortaleza de Santa Teresa, siendo el primer bien patrimonial que recibió esta denominación. Se establecieron en la misma resolución los trabajos de reparación y reconstrucción del monumento que se efectuarían, así como también se estableció un parque público en los terrenos circundantes.

Previo a la ejecución de las obras se reunió información histórica, arquitectónica, de historia del arte, derivada de tradiciones orales y de artículos periodísticos. Con base en esta reunión, Arredondo propuso la reconstrucción del monumento:

> expresé que sostenía con pleno convencimiento de razón la tesis de la reconstrucción total en forma de retrotraerla a fines del S. XVIII, por cuanto estimaba bastantes los planos disponibles—en su mayoría inéditos—más que suficientes para hacer una restauración fidelísima. (1955:90)

En oposición a esta teoría surgió la de conservar como ruina el monumento, posición sostenida por el Coronel Arquitecto Alfredo Campos, con base en las entonces recientes resoluciones de los Congresos de Arquitectos (Arredondo 1955:90).

Marco Jurídico y Académico del Período

Hacia la década de los años cincuenta y utilizando las mismas pautas puestas en práctica para Santa Teresa, se reconstruyeron el Fuerte de San Miguel en Rocha y la Fortaleza del Cerro en Montevideo. Paralelamente se amplió el marco jurídico relacionado con los vestigios monumentales, y por la Ley de Homenajes a Artigas promulgada el 10 de agosto de 1950, se creó la Comisión Nacional de Monumentos Históricos; entre los cometidos de dicha comisión se encontraba realizar un inventario de los monumentos históricos nacionales. Como consecuencia del minucioso relevamiento llevado a cabo por este organismo, se propuso declarar como monumentos históricos los vestigios relacionados con la evolución nacional y los personajes destacados, así como también aquéllos que son considerados representativos de la cultura de la época.

Así, se recabó una extensa lista de los inmuebles y monumentos que se decidió ameritaban ser conservados—

en su mayoría de los siglos XVIII y XIX—su estado de preservación, sugerencias para reconstruir algunos, datos acerca de su origen y construcción, y eventos históricos que ahí se dieran, además de la función original a que estaban destinados. Las categorías empleadas en la clasificación y catalogación de los monumentos incluían la arquitectura militar, la religiosa y la civil, marcos delimitadores, esculturas religiosas, cementerios rurales, y arquitectura del medio rural (Arredondo 1955:297–305). La iniciativa permitió proteger valiosos testimonios del período histórico.

Esta preocupación por los vestigios monumentales encontró su expresión en los ambientes universitarios. Así, en 1938 se creó el Instituto de Arqueología Americana en la Facultad de Arquitectura de Montevideo, orientado hacia la investigación arqueológica en la arquitectura; su prédica creó las bases doctrinarias y metodológicas que posteriormente permitirían su transformación en Instituto de Historia de la Arquitectura, en 1948.

Segundo Período, las Décadas de los Años Sesenta y Setenta

Este fue un período de cambios en lo relacionado con los enfoques para abordar los monumentos históricos, durante el cual surgieron iniciativas que abarcaban la teoría de la restauración y las orientaciones jurídicas y académicas.

Respecto a la teoría de la restauración, los sostenedores de esta postura pusieron en práctica la reconstrucción de diversos monumentos. En ese sentido, el Cuartel de Dragones de Maldonado es un ejemplo de su vigencia, mientras que los estudios relacionados con la Puerta de la Ciudadela y el Cabildo de Montevideo aportan conceptos nuevos, que pretenden dejar atrás la teoría de la restauración. Un singular ejemplo lo constituyen las obras encaradas en la ciudad portuguesa de Colonia del Sacramento.

El Cuartel de Dragones

Según Alfredo Castellanos, este monumento originalmente

> ocupaba toda una manzana ("una cuadra en quadro") de la ciudad de Maldonado; fue construido entre los años 1793 (fecha de los planos existentes en el Museo Histórico Municipal), y 1806, en que fue parcialmente destruido cuando la toma de aquella ciudad por las fuerzas invasoras inglesas. Por dichos planos se sabe que contaba con numerosas y amplias crujías para la tropa, alojamientos para la oficialidad y gentes a su servicio, cuarto de guardia, comandancia, almacenes de armas y víveres, capilla, cocinas, etc.; en el centro había una amplia plaza de armas con pozo de agua potable. (1974:33)

Al iniciarse este segundo período que analizamos, el Cuartel de Dragones se hallaba en ruinas, conservando sólo su portada y una pared perimetral. En conocimiento de esta situación algunos estudiosos propusieron su restauración, mientras que otros se opusieron tenazmente:

> Querer arrancar de esos "restos insignificantes" para restituir el panorama urbano de Maldonado el cuartel desaparecido es vana y desacertada labor, meritoria y útil como trabajo de taller o academia para la reconstrucción en vía de hipótesis sobre papel o en la maqueta, pero absolutamente inaceptable como testimonio histórico. La reconstrucción del cuartel, si se realizase, no sería en verdad más que un infeliz remedo—por más que ella se realizase basándose en dibujos y planos auténticos—del edificio ya desaparecido y no podría cumplir ni con su función de cuartel ni con su función de documento auténtico. (Bausero 1959)

De cualquier manera, en el caso de este monumento se emprendió su reconstrucción y aún en la actualidad se llevan a cabo obras con ese propósito (figura 15.2).

La Puerta de la Ciudadela de Montevideo

En 1957 se iniciaron estudios con el propósito de emplazar la Puerta de la Ciudadela de Montevideo en su ubicación original, ya que en 1877 había sido desmontada y posteriormente armada en la entrada sur de la Escuela de Artes y Oficios, lejos de su contexto original.

Éste es el único elemento que se conserva de la más notable construcción militar española del Montevideo Colonial; su construcción se inició en 1742 y se concluyó más de cuarenta años después, ocupando aproximadamente la mitad de la actual Plaza de Independencia de la capital del Uruguay (Castellanos 1974:27).

El proyecto de emplazamiento dio lugar a una investigación enmarcada en un campo que en su momento se denominara "arqueológico-histórico" (Bausero y Bonino 1957). Esta investigación abordaba el relevamiento arquitectónico y el estudio de los planos Coloniales con el propósito de ubicarla en el lugar donde originalmente se encontraba, contemplando los aspectos planimétricos y altimétricos, así como también la historia del propio monumento.

En este estudio se realizaron aportes novedosos para el tratamiento de los vestigios monumentales, ya que se apartó del purismo estilístico predominante hasta ese momento, e incorporó aspectos relacionados con la arqueología y la arquitectura clásica al proponer trasladar el monumento sin desmontarlo y además sugerir excavaciones para ubicar los cimientos originales, de manera que fuera factible emplazar la Puerta de la Ciudadela en su primitiva ubicación.

En la actualidad este monumento no se encuentra en su lugar original, sino que está desplazado en dirección sur para armonizar con la urbanización de la Plaza de Independencia.

El Cabildo de Montevideo

Esta construcción es considerada uno de los más valiosos

FIGURA 15.2 Cuartel de Dragones (Maldonado). Reconstrucción iniciada en el segundo período. Actualmente continúa en obras. *Todas las fotografías son de la autora*

monumentos coloniales de la ciudad, el cual se estableció en el mismo lugar que ocupara el primer edificio de Ayuntamiento y Reales Cárceles entre 1737 y 1758, mismo que se demolió en 1804. Bajo la dominación española se iniciaron las obras de la planta baja del Cabildo, culminándose ocho años después, y la ampliación de la misma planta correspondió al período de la dominación brasileña; instalada la República en 1830 se culminó la planta alta. La construcción había sido realizada con piedra granítica y, hacia la segunda mitad del siglo XIX, se complementó el coronamiento de las fachadas utilizando ladrillo revocado.

En el momento en que se inició la restauración del inmueble, era sede del Museo Histórico Municipal, habiendo albergado con anterioridad a los poderes legislativo y judicial, al gobierno de Montevideo, la Jefatura de Policía y el Ministerio de Relaciones Exteriores.

Las acciones emprendidas con motivo de su restauración levantaron voces de adhesión y de divergencia. Al plan para restaurar el Cabildo se opuso la propuesta para su consolidación, cuyo objetivo principal era conservar la historia del edificio abarcando no sólo su período constructivo, sino también los testimonios de las distintas funciones que tuviera a lo largo de un siglo. En un artículo periodístico de la época se señaló que

> Durante mucho tiempo hemos luchado en la medida de nuestras limitadas fuerzas, porque el edificio civil con más carga histórica que tiene nuestro país, fuese respetado, conservado y consolidado, y no se borrase de él aquello precisamente que lo hacía venerable y augusto ....

> Lamentablemente este fervor por volver a la época colonial ha hecho perder a los restauradores la visión de conjunto de nuestra historia—viva y palpitante en el monumento a restaurar. (Bausero 1958)

Desde la década de los años sesenta al paisaje urbano de Montevideo se sumó el edificio reconstruido del Cabildo (figura 15.3).

Alfredo Castellanos señala que

> Las obras de restauración procuraron devolver al viejo edificio colonial su primitiva estructura interior, para lo cual fue necesario reabrir galerías que habían sido tapiadas para acondicionar oficinas; demoler entrepisos modernos, y cielos rasos de yeso y molduras que ocultaban las bóvedas; quitar las inapropiadas ventanas de vitrales que cerraban los pórticos del clásico claustro, cuyos arcos fueron reconstruidos retirándose los muros que los cubrían; restaurar en piedra la escalera central, retirando los modernos escalones de marmol blanco, así como el plafón y claraboya de su caja, cubriéndola con una bóveda; reacondicionar el primitivo piso de piedra del vestíbulo de acceso, oculto bajo uno de marmol; colocación de baldosas coloradas semejantes a las originales encontradas en algunos pisos interiores del edificio; obras de carpintería y herrajes, manteniendo el estilo de los pocos elementos que había subsistido. (1974:55–56)

Colonia del Sacramento

La Colonia del Sacramento, fundada por los portugueses en 1680, fue uno de los primeros centros poblados del Uruguay. Su posición estratégica la vincula simultáneamente con el

FIGURA 15.3
El Cabildo (Montevideo), reconstruido durante el segundo período

interior de América del Sur y con el Océano Atlántico. Emplazada en los territorios disputados durante siglos por España y Portugal, se convirtió desde su nacimiento en un símbolo de esa contienda. En la década de los años veinte el asentamiento evidenciaba fuerte deterioro aunque parte de su arquitectura se observaba:

> El aspecto general de la Ciudad Vieja, al recorrer sus calles, es sugestivo; todavía quedan algunas notas interesantes que permiten y estimulan a la imaginación reconstruir el ambiente, si no propiamente del Fuerte Portugués, sí...postcolonial; el primitivo ambiente patricio, derivado del primero colonial; la planimetría general, el pavimento de algunas callejas, uno que otro ejemplar de arquitectura portuguesa y española, viviendas modestas o ejecutadas con restos de ambas, las ruinas de la Comandancia, los restos de la casa del virrey, los muros negruzcos del convento de San Francisco, complementado todo ello por las masas informes de las baterías de San Pedro y de Santa Rita y por los trozos despedezados de murallas, presentan en conjunto un cuadro evocador y emotivo, que se hace sentir más aún por la tranquilidad, quietud y silencio que imperan en la histórica ciudad. (Capurro 1928:106)

Durante el período que aquí nos ocupa se iniciaron las obras para conservar esta ciudad colonial; a diferencia de los otros ejemplos ya señalados donde se abordó el monumento como una unidad, en el caso de Colonia del Sacramento el objetivo principal lo constituía el conjunto del casco histórico (figuras 15.4, 15.5). Así, se emprendieron bajo la dirección del Arquitecto Miguel Angel Odriozola la consolidación de la Iglesia del Santísimo Sacramento, iniciada en 1957, y la reconstrucción del tramo este de la muralla con su puerta de ingreso (figura 15.6); esta última quedó al descubierto a través de excavaciones asistemáticas que se iniciaron en 1960, concretándose la obra a principios de la década de los años setenta (Odriozola 1970).

Los criterios que se siguieron en las intervenciones son:

- Consolidación integral de la iglesia, en lo posible sin elementos extraños a su estructura original.
- Respeto al máximo de los valores históricos y artísticos existentes, dejando a la vista las partes ocultas de sus distintos períodos, totalmente desconocidos hasta nuestros días.
- Aumento de la capacidad locativa.
- Adecuación a las nuevas normas de la liturgia.
- Integración del edificio al medio en que está enclavado y de acuerdo con las obras que allí se realicen. (Odriozola 1970:49)

Paralelamente numerosas viviendas del lugar fueron consolidadas y destinadas para usos públicos y privados. Desde 1968 el Consejo Ejecutivo Honorario de las Obras de Preservación y Reconstrucción de la Antigua Ciudad de Colonia del Sacramento, es el que vela por esta importante área histórica.

Marco Jurídico y Académico

A partir de 1971 una nueva ley (14.040) regula los aspectos vinculados con el patrimonio cultural, integrándose la Comisión del Patrimonio Histórico, Artístico y Cultural de la Nación, dependiente del Poder Ejecutivo, en la órbita del

FIGURA 15.4
Paisaje actual de la Colonia del Sacramento (Sacramento)

FIGURA 15.5
Una de las casas de la Colonia del Sacramento (Sacramento)

Ministerio de Educación y Cultura. Dicha comisión está facultada, entre otras funciones, para promover que bienes se declaren monumentos históricos velando por su conservación así como por la de los sitios arqueológicos, además de proponer la adquisición de fuentes y obras relacionadas con la historia del país, sean éstas de índole artística, arqueológica e histórica. Asimismo, emite permisos para la exploración de sitios arqueológicos y yacimientos paleontológicos por parte de personal especializado; una vez que se autoriza la afectación de un sitio, se establecen los principios técnicos mínimos que deberán seguirse (levantamientos topográficos, excavaciones estratigráficas,

FIGURA 15.6
Puerta de la Ciudadela de Colonia del Sacramento (Sacramento). Reconstrucción del segundo periódo.

toma de registros fotográficos y de dibujos, conservación de muestras de la estratigrafía, cernido de la tierra removida, entrega de informe en el que se incluya diario de campo e inventario de piezas a la comisión).

Por otra parte, en la ley citada se especifica la prohibición de que salgan del Uruguay objetos arqueológicos, paleontológicos, y artísticos, manuscritos históricos y literarios, o piezas de numismática nacional, a menos que la comisión autorice la salida temporaria de los bienes referidos. Cabe destacar que las piezas de carácter arqueológico o paleontológico que se obtengan al realizarse trabajos por particulares, instituciones privadas u oficiales, son propiedad del Estado.

En el ámbito académico, la creación de la licenciatura de ciencias antropológicas con especialización en arqueología dentro del Instituto de Historia de la Arquitectura preexistente, constituye el hecho más destacado del período, así como la feliz culminación de dos décadas de perseverantes esfuerzos llevados a cabo por los estudiosos de la prehistoria.

Tercer Período: La Arqueología Histórica en la Actualidad

Este período se inició en la década de los años ochenta, y se ve marcado por el nuevo impulso que cobra la arqueología histórica en el Uruguay, siendo el hecho más novedoso el estudio por parte de arqueólogos de sitios históricos. La madurez de la arquitectura, la arqueología, la antropología y la historia contribuyen a calificar este período, en el marco interdisciplinario que permite una mejor comprensión de la evolución de la historia Colonial del país.

La Restauración

Las acciones de restauración o reconstrucción van perdiendo vigencia; aunque en la actualidad felizmente no se persiguen esos objetivos, a inicios del período perduraban algunos ejemplos de intervenciones de esa clase. Testimonio de ello son los trabajos emprendidos en la batería del sureste de la Isla Gorriti, la cual se reconstruyó en su totalidad, así como la continuidad de las acciones ya iniciadas con anterioridad en el área del Cuartel de Dragones.

Las Investigaciones de Arqueología Histórica

Los estudios arqueológicos en sitios históricos se centran en los Departamentos de Maldonado, Colonia y Montevideo.

Departamento de Maldonado. Isla Gorriti. Esta isla está ubicada al este del Uruguay, en el área de ingreso al Río de la Plata. Junto con Punta del Este en la actualidad forma el área turística más prestigiosa del territorio, mientras que en la época Colonial sus baterías complementaban a las del puerto de Maldonado en lo relacionado con la defensa en la zona de acceso del Río de la Plata.

En 1977 se establecieron las pautas para construir un lujoso y amplio complejo turístico en la isla, mismas que en relación con los vestigios coloniales estipulan que "Los lugares de interés histórico no podrán ser modificados ni alterados por edificación o instalaciones de ninguna especie y por el contrario serán realzados o restaurados según corresponda" (Diario El País 1977:44).

En 1984, junto a otros bienes culturales del Departamento de Maldonado, se declaró monumento histórico la Isla Gorriti, y un año después se solicitó a la Comisión del Patrimonio Histórico, Artístico y Cultural de la Nación que autorizara la construcción del complejo turístico citado en el lugar. En consecuencia, las autoridades de dicha comisión a su vez solicitaron a su Departamento de Arqueología la realización de reconocimientos sistemáticos en el área, con el fin de determinar las características de los vestigios arqueológicos y conocer los riesgos a los que éstos se expondrían a raíz del proyecto propuesto.

Durante la prospección arqueológica de la isla, se relevaron las baterías coloniales, obras de arquitectura militar cuya importancia había sido destacada desde 1950. A través de pequeñas excavaciones se identificaron también construcciones totalmente desconocidas hasta ese momento. Los hallazgos se integraron en dos conjuntos: uno formado por las unidades de carácter militar construidas para la defensa del área a mediados del siglo XVIII, y el otro constituido por las unidades de carácter civil pertenecientes a la Real Compañía Marítima de España, fundada en 1789 y dedicada a la caza e industrialización de la ballena (Fusco Zambetogliris et al. 1987:108–109).

En 1991 y en el marco del "Proyecto de Recuperación y Puesta en Valor de los Bienes Histórico-Culturales de la Bahía de Maldonado," propuesto por la Comisión del Patrimonio, se inició la excavación del "conjunto funcional militar" ubicado al noreste de la isla, e integrado por la Batería de Santa Ana, el polvorín correspondiente y una represa de agua (Curbelo y Cabrera 1993:27). Respecto al carácter de las intervenciones cabe citar que

> Las técnicas de excavación...comprenden el destape dentro de las áreas de desmoronamiento (estructura) o en relación con los distintos "pisos" de ocupación, utilizándose pala recta y niveles artificiales en las áreas de relleno eólico (arena clara medanosa).... Las operaciones metodológicas tendieron a invertir el proceso natural de formación del sitio abordando cada uno de los eventos por separado. Primero se eliminó la disposición reciente de arena que cubrió las ruinas tanto de la construcción militar como de las instalaciones que luego la reutilizaron. Luego se abordó la estructura interna de la batería correspondiente a un momento posterior al abandono de la misma con fines militares, perteneciendo por lo tanto, a algún período del siglo XIX. Por último, la construcción militar y su uso como tal (fines del siglo XVIII y primeras décadas del XIX). De esta forma, se pretendió aislar los restos y vestigios correspondientes a los distintos eventos ocupacionales y las diferentes actividades desarrolladas en dicho espacio. (Curbelo y Cabrera 1993:28–29)

Departamento de Colonia. Colonia del Sacramento. La planificación de la remodelación de la Plaza Manuel de Lobos, una de las principales áreas verdes del Barrio

FIGURA 15.7 **Enterramiento completo puesto al descubierto en el cementerio Colonial (siglo XVIII) de Colonia del Sacramento (Sacramento). Norte de la Plaza "Manuel de Lobos."**

Histórico, da lugar a la intervención de los arqueólogos en esta ciudad Colonial.

Al iniciarse las obras en 1987 quedaron al descubierto cimientos de muros, ubicados en el sector sur y en el norte de la plaza; en este último que limita con la Iglesia del Santísimo Sacramento se produce además el hallazgo de varios esqueletos humanos. La importancia de estos vestigios trae como consecuencia la intervención de la Comisión del Patrimonio Histórico que, a través de su Departamento de Arqueología, lleva adelante dos proyectos de investigación.

El primero de estos estudios se realizó en 1988, en el Cementerio Colonial ubicado en el sector norte de la plaza, y abordó su problemática temporal y espacial; el área no alterada era muy reducida y ahí se procedió a través de pequeñas excavaciones.

Pese a haber sido una respuesta de salvamento, la investigación permitió identificar los usos del espacio a través del tiempo: (a) la ocupación prehistórica, representada por el hallazgo de cerámica indígena en los niveles de la base; (b) los episodios de principios del siglo XVIII, a través de los muros de las primitivas iglesias construidas en el área; (c) la

FIGURA 15.8
Planta de la Casa de los Gobernadores Portugueses del siglo XVIII. Puesta al descubierto al sur de la Plaza "Manuel de Lobos." Colonia del Sacramento (Sacramento).

identificación del área del cementerio y su utilización por un prolongado período de tiempo (figura 15.7); (d) los episodios de combustión correspondientes a los incendios registrados a nivel histórico (1799 y 1823). Concordante a esta cronología, se presentaron hallazgos de loza, vidrio y metal, destacándose entre ellos el de una moneda portuguesa de 10 reis de 1719 (Fusco Zambetogliris 1990).

El segundo proyecto de investigación se inició en 1990, previo a la transformación para uso peatonal de la vía de tránsito vehicular ubicada al sur de la plaza.

El estudio de los documentos históricos, bibliográficos, iconográficos, y cartográficos nos permitió conocer peculiaridades de este sector del Barrio Histórico, en particular el hecho de que allí, en el siglo XVIII, estuvo emplazada la Casa de los Gobernadores Portugueses (figura 15.8).

Los objetivos de la investigación eran bien precisos: ubicación de testimonios de la Casa del Gobernador del siglo XVIII, reconocimiento de su estructura (muros exteriores e interiores), diagnóstico de su estado de conservación e interpretación cultural de los diferentes espacios a través de la identificación de áreas de actividad que surgieran del análisis de los materiales arqueológicos recuperados. Fueron objetivos también del proyecto las operaciones de conservación y consolidación, así como también el asesoramiento al proyecto urbanístico y la difusión a la comunidad (Fusco Zambetogliris y López Mazz 1992:10).

En 1992 quedó al descubierto la totalidad de la planta de la Casa de los Gobernadores Portugueses. Con base en la comparación de esta estructura con evidencias de planos de viviendas del siglo XVIII, así como con el análisis de los vestigios hallados durante las excavaciones, se pudieron identificar el área de las habitaciones, el de la cocina, los brocales de agua y varias estructuras subterráneas, entre las que destaca una circular interpretada como la base de la torre de vigilancia (figura 15.9).

Los hechos arqueológicos que presentan relevancia para una investigación sobre el llamado proceso de conquista en el área de la "Casa del Gobernador" son los siguientes:

- Material lítico y cerámico en posición estratigráfica inferior (más antigua).

- Estructuras pertenecientes a los cimientos y parte de los muros de las ex-casas de los gobernadores portugueses, las correspondientes a los planos de 1731 y 1762, así como aquellas posiblemente anteriores.

- Al interior de la estructura de la casa, los bélicos, como la piedra lenticular de honda, típica de los indios de la región, así como piezas de balística europeas de diferente calibre.

- Una gran variedad de recipientes cerámicos en diferente grado de fragmentación, de modalidad técnica y materia prima también diversa. Los tiestos que señalan desde el objeto suntuario o decorativo, a las tinajas culinarias y domésticas en general, presentan características propias a los patrones clásicos de las culturas del contacto. Así encontramos desde las diferentes cerámicas europeas a la típica indígena con características del área del río Uruguay, pero pasando también por la cerámica criolla o mestiza, donde coexisten aspectos técnicos de la cultura autóctona y se recrean formas influenciadas por los

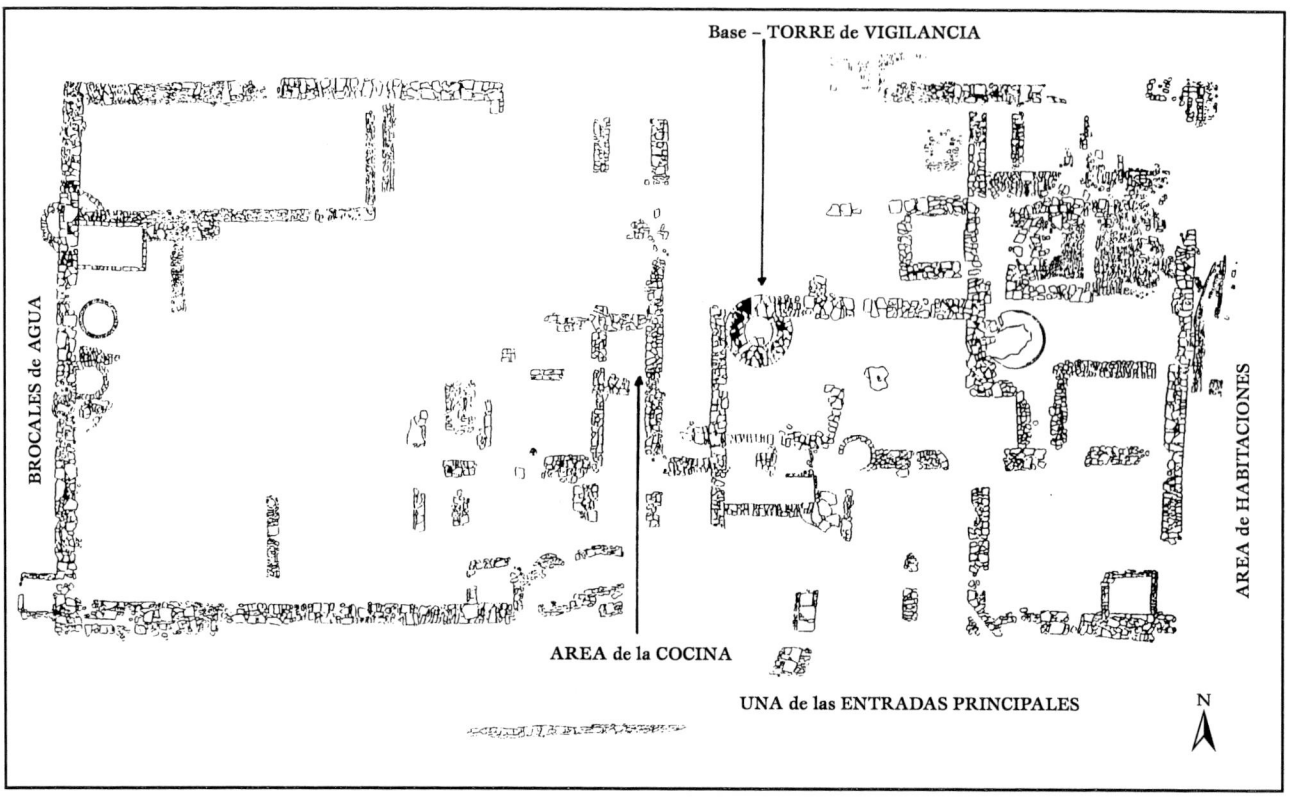

FIGURA 15.9 **Planta de la Casa de los Gobernadores Portugueses del siglo XVIII. Identificación de las distintas áreas de la vivienda (dibujo de Norma Calgaro). Colonia del Sacramento (Sacramento).**

patrones de funcionalidad europeos, particularmente tapas y asas. Si bien los análisis de laboratorio están en curso, un reciente trabajo del Arq. Daniel Schávelzon, da una referencia para Colonia del Sacramento de los tipos de loza europea.... Cream ware 15 por ciento—Pearl ware 20 por ciento—White ware 65 por ciento.

‡ Los hallazgos de pipas se reparten en dos grandes grupos: uno representado por las típicas de los guaraníes históricos y otro característico de las pipas europeas de caolín.

‡ Herrajes, restos de recipientes de vidrio, así como abundancia de vestigios de combustión; de particular interés resulta el hallazgo al interior de la casa de una moneda española de 1772, confeccionada en plata, que luce la silueta de Carlos III y en el anverso el escudo de la Corona.

‡ Las zonas de la casa presentan un importante grado de perturbación, debido a lo que los arqueólogos llaman procesos post-deposicionales. Esto se refleja en la disposición del material exhumado al interior y que conforma rellenos, y el deterioro de parte de los cimientos. Como parte de estos procesos vemos la reutilización del espacio por construcciones posteriores de los siglos XIX y XX, y una limitación importante al reconocimiento de áreas de actividad en la estructura del siglo XVIII.

‡ Una paleosuperficie correspondiente a una calle de tierra del siglo XIX, estratigráficamente ubicada encima de los cimientos de las casas de los siglos XVII y XVIII, y por debajo de la arena sobre la que asientan los adoquines de la calle actual. Sólo técnicas de excavación arqueológicas hubieran permitido recuperar esa paleosuperficie en buenas condiciones, donde se aprecian huellas de carros y caballos planteando actualmente un serio problema de conservación (adaptado de Fusco Zambetogliris y López Mazz 1992:11).

Respecto a la importancia del sitio en el desarrollo de la arqueología histórica en el país, paralelamente se realizaron los primeros análisis de materiales históricos en el Uruguay, iniciándose las investigaciones de laboratorio conjuntamente a las de campo (Onega, Caporale, y Mata 1991).

Asimismo, las numerosas obras que aún se emprenden en la antigua Colonia del Sacramento motivan la intervención constante de los arqueólogos en el lugar, que se enlistan a continuación.

La adaptación de una construcción del siglo XIX, para instalar el Hotel Plaza Mayor, permitió luego de la participación de los arqueólogos que quedara al descubierto debajo de uno de los deteriorados pisos de madera, el interior de una casa portuguesa del siglo XVIII.

En 1993 el Banco de Seguros del Estado planificó la

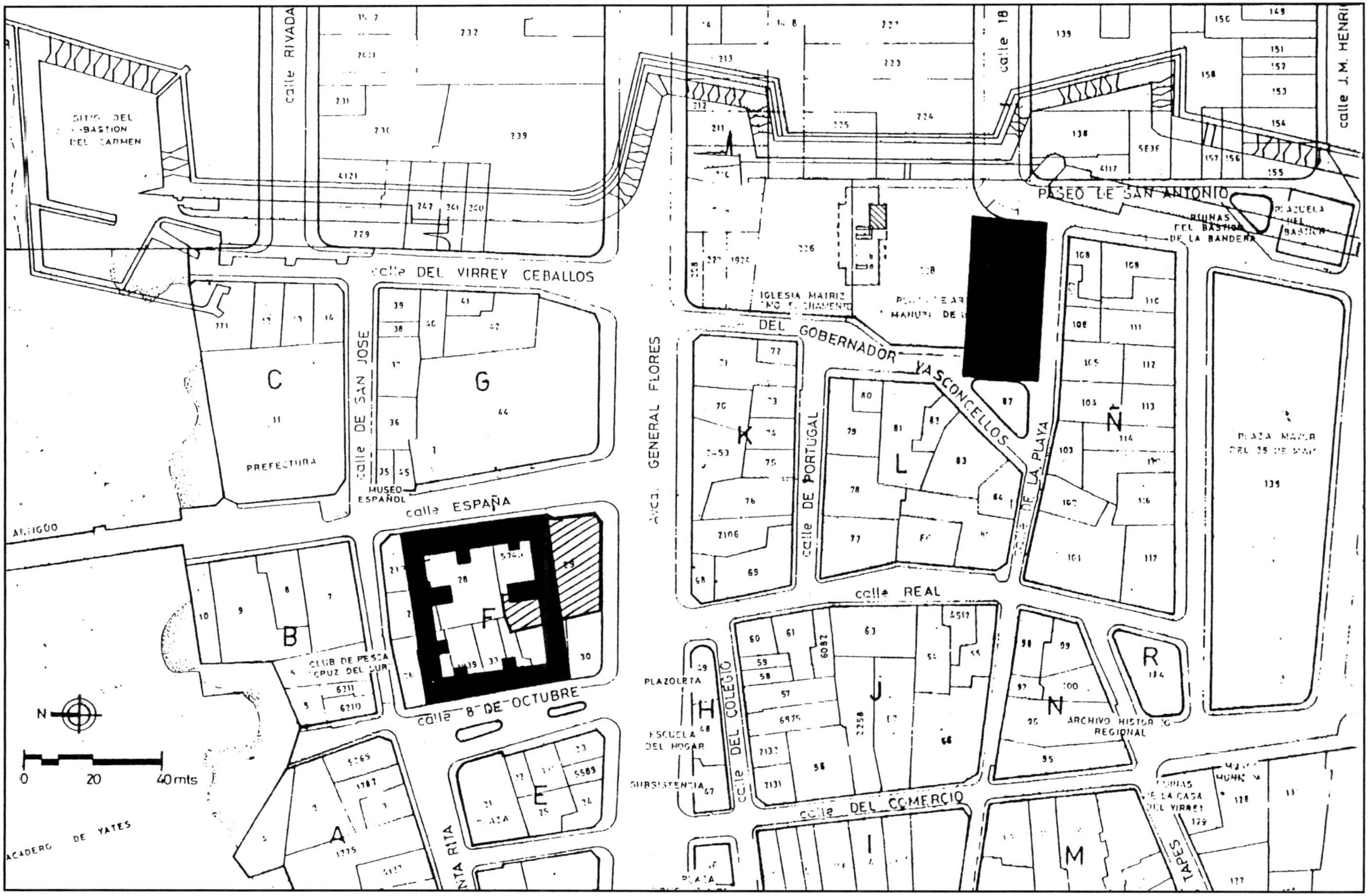

Figura 15.10 Barrio Histórico. Antigua ciudad de Colonia del Sacramento, mayo de 1977. Manzana moderna "F" con el padrón 29, donde se planifica el Banco de Seguros del Estado y el montaje de la construcción del siglo XVIII, que aparece arriba de éste. La zona sombreada al este señala el área de ubicación de la Casa de los Gobernadores Portugueses, puesta al descubierto durante la investigación arqueológica (1991–1992).

construcción de su sucursal en un lote baldío, de manera que arqueólogos y arquitectos realizaron paralelamente reconocimientos del terreno. Así, la tradición oral, las observaciones efectuadas en el predio, los registros fotográficos y las fuentes documentales fueron utilizados para llevar a cabo estas acciones. A ellas se sumaron los datos arqueológicos provenientes de la Casa de los Gobernadores Portugueses, fundamentalmente la ubicación exacta de esa planta y el perfil estratigráfico relativo a ella (figura 15.10).

El concurso de estas líneas de evidencia permitió conocer que el predio estuvo ocupado durante el siglo XVIII por un conjunto de casas particulares, mientras que en las primeras décadas de este siglo la zona estaba ocupada por una casa de reciente construcción. La investigación arqueológica permitió identificar los cimientos de las construcciones dieciochescas, así como también dos canaletas de desagüe, una relacionada con la calzada y la otra directamente vinculada con la construcción colonial (figura 15.11). Paralelamente se demostró que en la estructura de principios del siglo XX se habían reutilizado parte de los cimientos coloniales (Fusco Zambetogliris 1993).

Departamento de Montevideo. Montevideo, la capital del Uruguay, fue fundada por los españoles en las primeras décadas del siglo XVIII. La ciudad se desarrolla a orillas del Río de la Plata, y ese antiguo emplazamiento es conocido en la actualidad con el nombre de "Ciudad Vieja."

Al principio del período de la arqueología histórica antes expuesto y en la órbita del gobierno del Departamento de Montevideo, se creó la Comisión Especial Permanente de Ciudad Vieja, cuyo objetivo principal es velar por el patrimonio de esa área. En el marco de dicha comisión se han llevado a cabo numerosas obras de reciclaje, generalmente emprendidas desde la arquitectura, en las cuales la intervención de arqueólogos se ha limitado a actividades de rescate e interpretación de hallazgos.

Una excepción a esta realidad la constituye la obra de reciclaje emprendida en 1991 por la Comisión del Patrimonio, junto con el Ministerio de Transporte y Obras Públicas. Estas instituciones llevaron adelante una investigación interdisciplinaria donde la historia, la arquitectura y la arqueología actuaron en conjunto con el fin de habilitar la Casa del General Manuel Oribe, uno de los personajes más relevantes en la historia del país (Abdala 1992) (figura 15.12).

Un amplio consenso a escala americana y mundial, admite hoy que dislocar los ámbitos físicos sin una visión razonable de conjunto, conlleva disminuir al habitante en sus potencialidades individuales, grupales, comunitarias. Borrar las trazas visibles, eliminar masivamente los monumentos, desdibujar los lugares y los sitios con los que el usuario se identifica y en los cuales se reconoce, implica desconocer sus derechos y menospreciar el respeto que ese usuario merece.

Estamos convencidos que nuestro pasado forma parte de nuestro futuro, y convencidos asimismo, que no es posible eliminar sustentos básicos de nuestra memoria colectiva, sin mengua de nuestra gente y de nuestro ser nacional. La ciudad nos pertence a todos. Por eso todos debemos actuar (Arana 1983:6).

Cabe señalar que numerosos vestigios escultóricos y arquitectónicos pueblan la totalidad del área urbana y rural del Departamento de Montevideo, testimoniando así su historia de tres siglos; su recuperación y salvaguarda ha sido abordada mediante diversas estrategias y, al mismo tiempo, ha sido tema de debates.

Nuestras ciudades tienen su paisaje individual, histórico, propio sobre el cual progresó la vida de las mismas, creció la familia, se desenvolvió el comercio, maduraron las luchas políticas, se amplió el mundo cultural. Es el paisaje que es fondo irrenunciable de la acción ciudadana, mucho más marcado en nuestro ser, en nuestra memoria, que la sospecha de ello. Este paisaje merece especial consideración, y tanto, que el mismo monumento histórico, desgajado de él, cae, se reduce, se aminora y no es más que sombra de aquello que tiene que ser y, a veces, puede perder significado como una palabra arrancada de su texto (Bausero 1981).

Marco Jurídico. La Comisión del Patrimonio Histórico, Artístico y Cultural de la Nación debió adecuar la ley 14.040 en 1991, después de casi veinticinco años de su vigencia, de acuerdo con las exigencias contemporáneas. En ese sentido se elaboraron normas relacionadas con las investigaciones arqueológicas que promulgan un mayor rigor técnico y metodológico de éstas; resalta el hecho de que para la consecución de trabajos arqueológicos se estipule que, en cuanto a aval, la responsabilidad técnica del proyecto deba recaer en un egresado de la licenciatura de ciencias antropológicas, con especialización en arqueología de nivel universitario. Además, debe asegurarse la disponibilidad de recursos económicos para llevar a cabo las intervenciones y, así, garantizar que no se perjudique al sitio dejando inconclusas las operaciones.

Conclusiones

La arqueología histórica es impulsada en el Uruguay por los estudios del pasado, quedando vinculada estrechamente desde que surgiera con la arquitectura y la historia, y en el caso de esta última a través del tradicional análisis documental además de los testimonios orales. El papel protagónico de la arquitectura surge de la importancia del vestigio monumental, el cual siempre estuvo presente en los sitios históricos abordados y constituyó el objetivo primordial de las acciones emprendidas. La meta de estos pioneros era la reconstrucción

FIGURA 15.11 Canaleta de la calle Colonial, puesta al descubierto durante la investigación en el predio del Banco de Seguros del Estado. Colonia del Sacramento (Sacramento).

FIGURA 15.12 La Casa del General Manuel Oribe. Proyecto de puesta en valor en "Ciudad Vieja," Montevideo.

del monumento, acorde con los conceptos vigentes en ese momento, aunque dicho objetivo perdurara por varias décadas durante las cuales se alejó de las propuestas modernas surgidas principalmente desde la arqueología clásica y la arquitectura misma. Testimonio de esta situación son las referencias que hemos citado en el caso de la Puerta de la Ciudadela de Montevideo y el Cabildo.

La necesidad de un marco legal que protegiera estas

evidencias del pasado pronto propició la integración del derecho jurídico. En este sentido el concepto de "monumento histórico" como bien material, protegido legalmente por el Estado, es una aspiración que está presente desde los primeros momentos, como en el caso de la Fortaleza de Santa Teresa que en 1927 se declarará monumento histórico.

Aunque durante el primer período que hemos analizado la arqueología participa, de ninguna manera desempeña su rol específico como disciplina social, ya que meramente propicia la elaboración de una síntesis integradora de todos los estudios del pasado, en la búsqueda nostálgica de la identidad del pueblo uruguayo. Un ejemplo claro de este papel secundario es el de la Sociedad Amigos de la Arqueología, fundada en 1926 como organización civil:

> Nuestra Sociedad nació con el propósito y el humano interés de unificar aspiraciones y esfuerzos en torno a problemas de arqueología como una faz inquieta de nuestro desarrollo cultural...su afán de universalismo la muestra abierta a todas las disciplinas de la arqueología y a sus infinitas inquietudes. (Bausero 1974:3)

Los cambios sustanciales que permiten recuperar el retroceso comparativo que la arqueología histórica poseía desde la década de los años setenta, están formulados por la arquitectura, la historia y la arqueología misma. Así, la arquitectura reformula su lenguaje, con términos como *consolidar*, *recuperar*, *reciclar*, y *poner en valor*, además del concepto de reconstruir, y paralelamente innova a nivel de las técnicas utilizadas para conservar bienes materiales.

Por su parte, la arqueología interviene directamente en los sitios históricos a través de la puesta en práctica de métodos, técnicas y lecturas específicas. Asimismo, alcanza los objetivos propios de la disciplina al diferenciar las áreas de las actividades humanas, estudiar los procesos de formación de sitios, y develar los aspectos no conscientes de las sociedades históricas.

La arquitectura y la arqueología verán beneficiadas sus acciones por un abordaje moderno de la historia, que nos parece más antropológico y más vinculado con lo social respecto a desarrollos anteriores, al alejarse de fechas y héroes, además de vincularse con lo cotidiano de una sociedad; el más notable ejemplo de esta tendencia es la obra del profesor Pedro Barrán (1990), *Historia de la sensibilidad en el Uruguay*.

De esta forma, las tres disciplinas se transforman en protagonistas principales en un accionar interdisciplinario, y reciben en conjunto los aportes provenientes de otros estudios acerca del pasado. Desde la década de los años ochenta un producto de este cambio es la estrecha asociación de la arquitectura, la arqueología y la historia en la conformación de la esencia de la arqueología histórica en el país.

Desde nuestro punto de vista nos parece significativo realizar algunas precisiones ilustrativas de la pérdida del papel minimalista de la arqueología:

- Respecto a la arqueología sistemática, la primera referencia acerca del tema data de 1981 (Austral y Rocchietti 1981), paso inicial para el abordaje de los sitios históricos, que difiere radicalmente de tendencias previas en las cuales sólo se consideraba de competencia del arqueólogo el tratamiento de la prehistoria.

- Desde 1986 los trabajos sobre arqueología histórica realizados en el país han sido presentados en varios eventos sobre patrimonio, arquitectura y arqueología, tanto en el Uruguay como en Argentina, Brasil, Chile y los Estados Unidos de América; esto ha permitido no sólo la difusión de los avances logrados, sino también la comparación de su calidad a nivel internacional. Culminaron estas acciones en la celebración de la primera Conferencia de Arqueología Histórica en Colonia del Sacramento, Uruguay, en noviembre de 1993, evento que por iniciativa de los investigadores participantes de Argentina, Brasil, Estados Unidos, México y Uruguay será bianual; así existirá un foro de difusión y discusión de los logros de la disciplina en Iberoamérica y el norte del continente.

- La arqueología histórica en el Uruguay actualizó su rol en lo relacionado con el patrimonio natural, como lo testimonia el acercamiento con la "Sociedad Ecológica de San Gabriel," cuyos miembros requieren la óptica de los arqueólogos para ofrecer una respuesta a los vestigios culturales de la isla San Gabriel, reserva ecológica única en el país situada frente a la ciudad de Colonia del Sacramento. La intervención de los arqueólogos dio lugar a la elaboración de un proyecto para poner al descubierto las numerosas evidencias materiales que guarda la isla, correspondientes al siglo XVI y épocas posteriores; sin embargo, por iniciativa de la Sociedad Ecológica, el proyecto quedó en suspenso hasta que se generen propuestas que posibiliten que las intervenciones en el lugar den unidad tanto al patrimonio natural como al cultural.

- El abordaje de los sitios exige acciones de conservación y de almacenamiento, para las cuales debemos con urgencia prepararnos. Los estudios de conservación y exhibición museográfica no acompañan el ritmo de desarrollo de la arqueología histórica.

Es con base en la arqueología que surgen las respuestas para comprender el significado de los elementos de cultura material, desde fragmentos de vidrio, metal, loza, etcétera, hasta los vestigios monumentales. La conservación necesita una respuesta institucional, que acompañe la dinámica académica señalada; es una urgencia que reclamamos desde la arqueología histórica y a la cual no es ajena la arqueología subacuática. El reclamo requiere una respuesta política que globalice todos los aspectos derivados de las investigaciones. En el Uruguay el logro nos permitirá socializar los resultados obtenidos durante los estudios, difundir el conocimiento, en la certeza de que el patrimonio es el único bien que posee la singularidad de ser individual, de cada uno de los ciudadanos, y colectivo, es decir de la sociedad en su conjunto.

Agradecimientos. Agradecemos a los siguientes investigadores, colegas y organismos su apoyo para la realización de este estudio: Prof. Luis Bausero, Prof. José de Torres Wilson, Dr. José López Mazz, Lic. Roberto Bracco Boksar, Dr. Stanley South, Dra. Patricia Fournier, Dib. Norma Calgaro, Arq. Miguel Ángel Odriozola, Arq. Sara Abdala, Sociedad Ecológica de San Gabriel, Sacerdotes Pedro Wolcan y Edgardo Rodríguez, Periodista Artigas Mariño.

Chapter 16

Continuity or Change?
Vertical Archipelagos in Southern Peru During the Early Colonial Period

Mary Van Buren

Abstract

This chapter reexamines Murra's vertical archipelago model of Andean socioeconomic organization. Archaeological investigations at the transitional Late Horizon/Early Colonial site of Torata Alta provide confirmation of many aspects of Murra's original model. A review of the historical record, however, suggests that the existence of a highland settlement in the Moquegua Valley during the Early Colonial period can be attributed as much to the strategic decisions of Andean actors as to the persistence of ancient traditions. Because of the problems of equifinality in the archaeological record, the choice of interpretation is influenced as much by contemporary political discourse regarding the nature of Andean societies as by the data available in archaeological and historical sources.

Resumen

En este capítulo se reexamina el modelo de archipiélago vertical de Murra para la organización socioeconómica andina. Las investigaciones arqueológicas en el sitio de Torata, transicional entre le Horizonte Tardío y el Colonial Temprano, sirven para confirmar muchos aspectos del modelo original de Murra. Sin embargo, a partir de la revisión del registro histórico, se sugiere que la existencia de un asentamiento en las tierras altas en el valle de Moquegua durante el periodo Colonial Temprano, puede atribuirse tanto a las decisiones estratégicas de los actores andinos como a la persistencia de tradiciones ancestrales. Debido a los problemas de la equifinalidad en el registro arqueológico, la selección de la interpretación se ve influenciada tanto por el discurso político contemporáneo respecto a la naturaleza de las sociedades andinas como por los datos disponibles en las fuentes arqueológicas e históricas.

IN 1972, JOHN MURRA PROPOSED a model of Andean socioeconomic organization that influenced much of the anthropological research conducted in the Andes during the following decades. On the basis of information contained in early Spanish censuses, Murra demonstrated that direct colonization of altitudinally determined ecological zones was practiced by several ethnic groups during the Early Colonial period. One of his most important cases was the colonization of coastal valleys in southern Peru by the Lupaqa, a polity located in the Titicaca basin. Both Murra (1972) and another historian, Franklin Pease (1982), view the continued existence of these colonies after the Spanish conquest as evidence of an enduring Andean adaptation based on an ancient ideal of community self-sufficiency.

This chapter examines Murra's model and its implications for our understanding of indigenous culture from two perspectives: first, in light of archaeological evidence from the site of Torata Alta and second, in terms of changing conceptions of indigenous Andean history. Although the archaeological data tend to confirm the existence of a highland colony in the Moquegua Valley during the Early Colonial period, the contention that such a situation resulted from the simple persistence of traditional Andean organization can be challenged on both theoretical and historical grounds.

Dating Torata Alta

Torata Alta is a planned settlement located on a tributary of the Osmore drainage at an elevation of about 2700 m (figure 16.1). The preserved section of the site consists of twenty-four rectangular compounds that contain the stone foundations of domestic structures and storage bins (figure 16.2). These compounds are enclosed by low walls and separated from one another by relatively straight streets. A small plaza is located in the north-central part of the site adjacent to a complex of nondomestic architecture that includes a sixteenth-century church.

Unfortunately, the period during which Torata Alta was actually founded has not been established with certainty (see Van Buren, Bürgi, and Rice 1993 for a full discussion of this issue). Volcanic ash from the explosion of Huaynaputina in

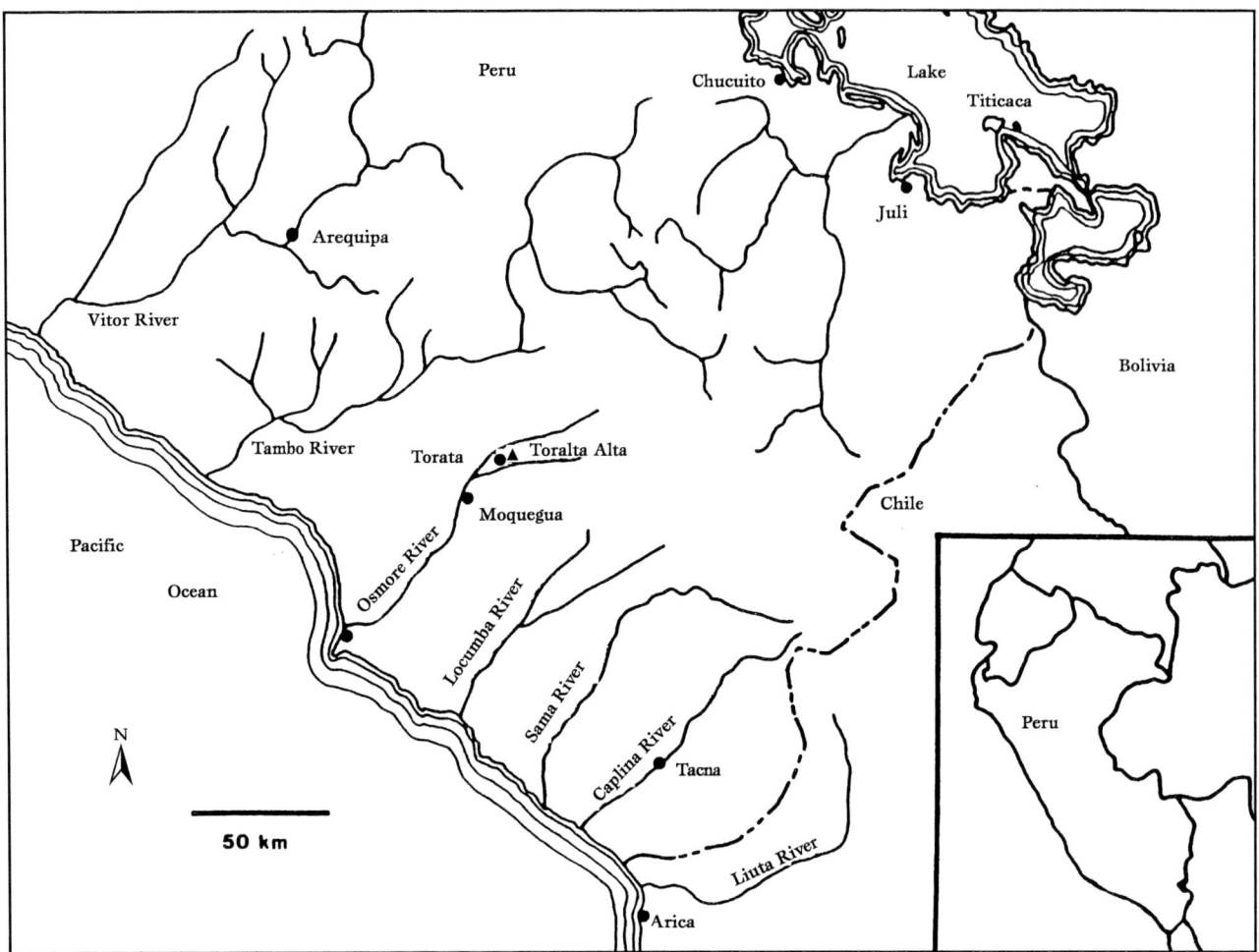

FIGURE 16.1 Southern Peru showing Osmore River and Torata Alta. *Map by Mary Van Buren*

1600 (Barriga 1951), both within and abutting most buildings, indicates that the settlement was constructed before the seventeenth century. Small quantities of European artifacts were encountered below and, in greater frequency, above the ash. The majority of artifacts recovered from the site, however, are of indigenous manufacture and are stylistically tied to the Late Horizon, the period of Inka expansion dating from approximately AD 1476 to 1534.

The architectural plan of the settlement is also difficult to use as the basis for making temporal inferences about the construction date. Although orthogonal planning is rarely found at indigenous sites in the Andes, Inka planners may have used this type of layout to construct a number of settlements in southern Peru (Hyslop 1990: Chap. 7). The plan of Torata Alta also bears a striking resemblance to Colonial *reducciones* (centralized communities established by Spanish authorities to resettle indigenous people; Gade and Escobar 1982; Núñez 1984).

The stratigraphy, artifact content, and plan of the site do not provide unambiguous evidence for the date of construction, which could have occurred during the Late Horizon or early in the Colonial period. What is clear is that the site was inhabited during the late sixteenth and early seventeenth centuries. The Colonial occupation is the temporal component addressed here.

Highland Colonization at Torata Alta

Torata Alta is located in a warm, arid environment dominated by xerophilic vegetation. The region is well suited for the production of maize, the primary exchange good sought by populations living on the higher, and much colder, altiplano. Ethnographic records indicate that people living at higher elevations regularly exchanged live llamas and such animal products as dried meat and wool for maize grown in the Moquegua Valley (see Brush 1977:114; Custred 1974; Fonseca 1972; Inamura 1981; Webster 1973). Murra's model, however, does not focus on exchange between different populations but on the establishment of maize-producing colonies by highland groups.

Murra's (1972) definition of a colony includes a number of elements that can be assessed on the basis of archaeological evidence (Mujica, Rivera, and Lynch 1983). According to Murra, colonies consisted of intrusive populations that permanently resided in an area outside the core territory of the parent group and maintained an ongoing relationship with that group. Although the exact identity of the inhabitants of

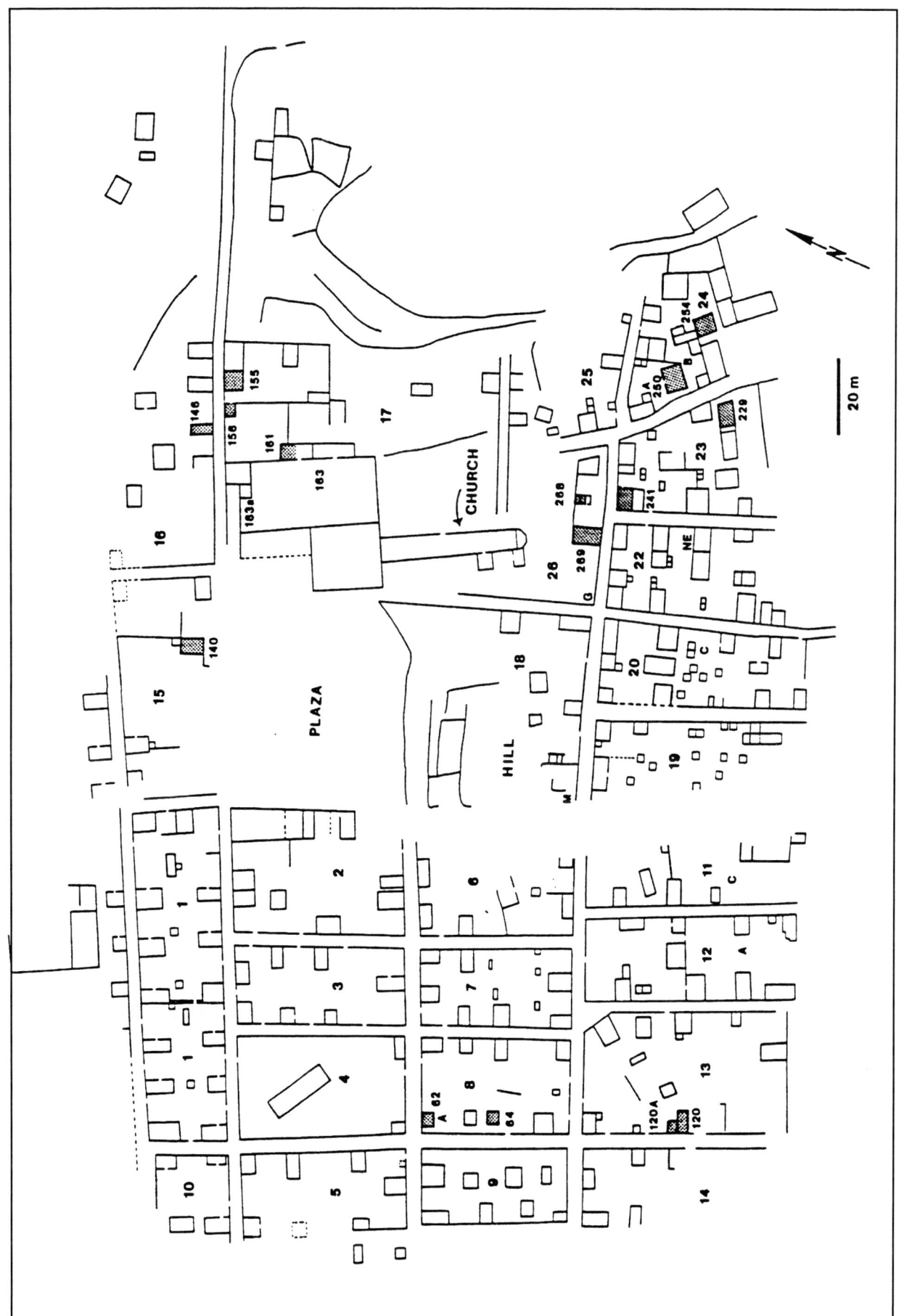

FIGURE 16.2 Excavated and analyzed contexts at Torata Alta. Ceramics from structure 250 were not completely analyzed. *After Stanish and Pritzker 1983*

Table 16.1. Nonceramic artifacts recovered from excavations in residential structures at Torata Alta (by structure)

	62	64	120	140	146	155	229	241	250	254	269
Whorl	0	1	7	0	2	0	8	0	4	8	3
Wichuña*	0	0	1	1	0	0	0	0	2	2	0
Needle	0	0	0	1	0	0	0	0	0	0	0
Thimble	0	0	0	0	0	1	1	0	0	0	0
Straight pin	0	0	0	0	0	0	8	0	2	8	0
Glass bead	0	0	1	0	0	1	2	10	6	4	0
Shell pendant	0	0	1	1	0	0	0	0	1	0	0
Metal ornament	0	0	0	0	0	0	5	4	2	1	4
Pestle	0	1	2	0	2	0	1	0	0	0	0
Mano	0	0	4	1	1	1	1	1	1	0	0
Mortar	0	0	1	0	0	0	0	0	0	0	1
Ground stone (misc.)**	1	0	6	3	2	0	3	0	2	4	1
Palette	0	0	0	0	1	0	0	0	0	0	0
Pigment	0	0	1	0	0	0	0	0	0	1	1
Stone/lime plug	0	0	0	1	0	0	0	0	1	1	0
Gass shard	0	0	1	0	0	0	35	1	1	5	0
Shell abrader	0	0	1	0	0	0	0	0	0	0	0
Sherd (worn/worked)	0	1	1	2	0	1	13	13	9	15	9
Stone flake	2	5	7	21	4	5	6	7	13	11	5
Stone core	0	0	2	1	1	0	0	0	0	1	1
Iron knife	0	0	1	0	0	0	0	0	0	0	0
Iron nail	1	0	0	0	1	1	6	1	3	2	1
Horse shoe fragment	0	0	1	0	1	0	3	1	0	0	1
Copper chisel	0	0	0	0	0	0	1	0	0	0	0
Copper hook	0	0	0	0	0	0	0	0	0	0	1
Copper tweezers	0	0	0	0	0	0	0	1	0	0	0
Brass bell	0	0	0	0	0	0	0	0	0	0	1
Bone tool?	0	0	0	0	0	0	0	0	0	1	0
Plumb bob***	0	0	0	0	0	0	0	0	0	1	0
Bola weight****	0	0	2	0	0	0	0	1	0	4	0
Lead slug	0	0	0	0	0	0	0	0	0	0	1
Coin	0	0	0	0	0	0	1	0	0	0	1
Figurine fragment	0	0	0	1	0	0	2	0	4	1	0
Stone dice	0	0	1	0	0	0	0	0	0	0	0
Bone flute	0	0	1	0	0	0	0	0	0	0	0
Iron fragments	0	0	3.0 g	10.7 g	0	0	55 g	11.8 g	11.5 g	196 g	28.2 g
Copper fragments	0	0	7.6 g	0	0	0	0	9.2 g	16.7 g	1.8 g	2.8 g

Notes: This table does not include material from structures 156, 161, or 168 because they were not residential in nature. Artifacts from structure 120A are included in the figures for structure 120. Frequencies are for artifacts found below surface deposits consisting of aeolian dust, wall fall, and in some cases volcanic ash; they include items from floor assemblages as well as secondary trash deposited in abandoned structures. Structures 62 to 155 were abandoned prior to 1600, and structures 229 to 269 were abandoned after that date. * A bone tool used in weaving. ** Includes unidentified fragments as well as unidentified complete specimens, many of which appear to have been used for polishing. *** Plumb bob was manufactured from soft stone. **** Includes both stone and copper bola weights.

Torata Alta cannot be determined with certainty, the archaeological data support the proposition that the settlement was occupied by a permanent intrusive population that maintained ties with the highlands.

Permanent Occupation at Torata Alta

The facilities and artifacts at Torata Alta reflect an investment of labor and range of activities indicative of permanent occupation (see Mujica, Rivera, and Lynch 1983). Storage bins, large slab grinding stones, and areas for raising guinea pigs are associated with most excavated domestic structures. Although tombs are absent from residential compounds, human burials were encountered beneath the church floor. The ceremonial architecture and a small complex that appears to have served an administrative function also suggest a permanent occupation.

While no evidence of specialized manufacture has been encountered at the site, individual households engaged in a wide range of productive activities. Tools used in the manufacture of cloth are particularly abundant, but flake tools, abraders, various types of grinding stones, bola weights, and palettes for crushing pigments are among the objects found in domestic structures (table 16.1).

In short, the material culture at Torata Alta is consonant with the activities of a permanent agrarian community and is comparable to the assemblage from Kjula Marca (Rydén 1947), the only other contact period site in the south-central Andes for which data are available.

Intrusive Nature of Torata Alta

One way to determine whether Torata Alta was an ethnic enclave of the type Murra described is to ascertain whether the inhabitants continued the stylistic traditions indigenous to the valley. Stanish argues convincingly that domestic contexts yield the best evidence of ethnicity because they reflect the every day activities of the resident population and are less likely than burial or ceremonial contexts to contain items produced by or in imitation of other groups (1985, 1989a, 1989b, 1992).

Three classes of material remains associated with domestic activities at Torata Alta were selected for analysis on the basis of their ubiquity and potential for yielding stylistic information relevant to the expression of ethnicity: residential architecture, ceramics, and spindle whorls. To assess the possibility of stylistic continuity, these materials were compared to slightly earlier remains in the upper Osmore drainage They were also compared with the limited amount of published information on artifactual remains from contemporaneous sites in the western Titicaca basin.

The fact that Torata Alta was part of a large empire complicates the assessment of ethnic identity on the basis of material culture. Even household items are sometimes acquired from sources outside the ethnic group in complex societies, and states often intervene in the expression of group identity. For example, both the Inkas and Spaniards regulated their subjects' use of clothing and other ethnic markers. As a result of these and other mechanisms, different classes of material culture provide more or less precise information regarding group identity.

Architecture. Torata Alta is clearly a planned settlement constructed over a short period of time. While blocks 19 through 24 display some features indicative of modifications made to accommodate household growth or other internal demographic shifts, the village did not develop in an organic manner according to the evolving needs of the inhabitants. The planned nature of the site, its orthogonal layout, and the configuration of the residential structures bear little resemblance to local architectural traditions. Although rectilinear architecture was the norm in the Osmore drainage during the Late Intermediate period (AD 1000–1476), single-room dwellings and grid layouts have no indigenous antecedents.

A brief comparison of Torata Alta and the nearby Late Intermediate site of San Antonio should make these differences clear. San Antonio, like most other Late Intermediate sites in the area, is a fortified settlement situated in a defensible location. The ridge on which it was constructed was terraced to provide level surfaces for housing and outdoor activities. Unlike Torata Alta, the architecture at San Antonio is agglutinated (figure 16.3). Patterns of wall abutment and bonding suggest that domestic units were constructed at different times (Borstel, Conrad, and Jacobi 1989), perhaps to house related families (Conrad and Webster 1989).

Household units always contain a large living area and a small kitchen, though additional rooms are often present. Differences in floor elevation and low partitions were used to demarcate space in the kitchen areas. Circular tombs are commonly found within living spaces, and drains are occasionally found as well (Conrad and Webster 1989: Fig. 3).

Neither the overall plan nor the details of the domestic structures at San Antonio are similar to the architecture at Torata Alta. The majority of the buildings at Torata Alta consist of a single room, are free standing or abut only the compound wall, and are surrounded by open space. Floors do not display elevational differences, interior partitions are rare, and stone platforms are relatively common. The only known instance of a separate kitchen is a simple addition of stones attached to the exterior wall of structure 120. No burials were found within domestic structures.

In terms of overall conception and specific structural details, the domestic architecture at Torata Alta is clearly distinguishable from that of San Antonio. Such a disjunction in architectural styles suggests that Torata Alta is an intrusive settlement with no cultural ties to the indigenous population. The distinctive layout of the site is most likely linked to the resettlement programs instituted by either the Inkas or Spaniards, the only societies known to have used orthogonal planning in the Andes.

Ceramics. The ceramic assemblage from Torata Alta also indicates a lack of continuity between the residents of Torata Alta and the local population. The decorated pottery found at the site bears little resemblance to the ceramics from San Antonio or other Late Intermediate sites in the area. Vessel forms, surface treatment, and paste characteristics are all different. Late Intermediate Estuquiña wares include shapes such as incurved bowls and boot pots that are entirely absent at Torata Alta. The most distinctive vessel forms found at Torata Alta, such as deep dishes with horizontal handles and long necked jars, do not occur in local Late Intermediate assemblages.

Even when utilitarian vessels are considered, the differences between the two assemblages are considerable. For instance, cooking pots at Torata Alta typically have dark brown paste with relatively fine temper, and the rims and necks are often slipped with a purplish-red pigment. These characteristics are not found in the San Antonio assemblage in which light brown paste, coarse temper, and orange slip are common features. The only point of overlap is in the paste characteristics: some large jars at Torata Alta are similar to those of the paste most commonly used at San Antonio. This similarity may reflect use of the same local source of raw material.

The majority of the decorated ceramics at Torata Alta are very similar to the Chucuito-Inka wares found in the Lupaqa

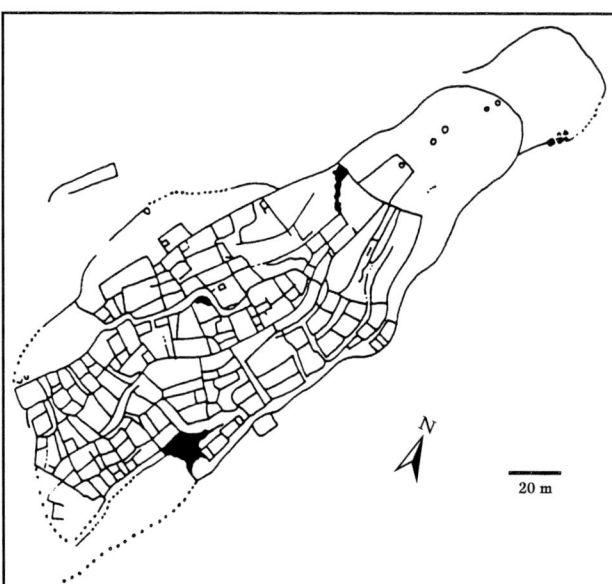

FIGURE 16.3 Site of San Antonio. *After Conrad and Webster 1989:405*

region southwest of Lake Titicaca (see Van Buren 1993 for a detailed description of the ceramic assemblage at Torata Alta). The vessel forms, motifs, design structure, colors, and paste characteristics of the Chucuito-Inka ceramics illustrated by Tschopik (1946) and found by Stanish in the vicinity of Juli (figure 16.1) are almost identical to the pottery recovered from Torata Alta. Black-on-Orange and polychrome bowls, for example, are common in both places and display the same rim forms, designs, and technological features.

The similarities between the Torata Alta ceramics and the Late Horizon pottery found in the Lupaqa area are strong enough to suggest that vessels at the former site were either imported from the Titicaca basin or manufactured locally by Lupaqa potters. Unfortunately, the absence of information regarding the organization of ceramic production in the Titicaca area during the Late Horizon makes it difficult to use this pottery as the basis for inferring ethnic affiliation. While these vessels may have been manufactured by Lupaqa households or specialists who worked independently of the state and exported their wares to Torata Alta, the possibility that the Inka supervised pottery manufacture and distributed it to state installations irrespective of their ethnic composition must also be considered (see D'Altroy and Bishop 1990).

Spindle whorls. While both the Inka and the Spaniards required subject populations to produce cloth and often provided the fiber with which to make it, there is no evidence that spindle whorls were manufactured or distributed under state auspices. The large amount of variability within the assemblage of whorls from Torata Alta also suggests household manufacture.

Spindle whorls are highly variable across cultures (Raymond 1984) and thus, like pottery, can be used to make inferences about ethnic identity. In the Andes, however, this potential is somewhat limited by the infrequency with which researchers publish illustrations of excavated whorls.

The fifty-four whorls recovered from Torata Alta were made from a variety of materials, including clay, sherds, stone, and bone. Approximately half (25) the assemblage is comprised of fired-clay whorls; the most common type has flat upper and lower surfaces and either straight or convex sides. Ceramic whorls were often slipped red (12) and sometimes decorated with red, white, or black designs (9), usually a series of lines radiating from the central hole.

Comparing the Torata Alta whorls with those from San Antonio revealed little overlap between the two assemblages. Whorls from San Antonio are made almost exclusively from clay, are primarily dome shaped, and are rarely, if ever, decorated (Conrad 1990). As is the case with ceramics, the whorls from Torata Alta do not seem to have been derived from a local Late Intermediate tradition.

Few illustrations of spindle whorls from the Titicaca basin have been published. The available information indicates, however, that while the assemblage from Torata Alta shares much in common with whorls found at Late Horizon sites on the southwestern side of Lake Titicaca, it is not identical to collections from the Lupaqa region. Tschopik (1946: Figs. 30, 31) illustrated seven whorls found on the surface of Lupaqa sites in the Titicaca basin which she describes as "typical." Of these seven, four are similar in form to specimens commonly found at Torata Alta, but the remaining three are large, flat, and tiered, a type absent at that site.

The whorls from Torata Alta are also similar to specimens found at Sillustani (Tschopik 1946: Fig. 30) and Hatunqolla (Julien 1983: Fig. 98), both of which are Qolla sites to the north of the Lupaqa region, and at Palli Marca and Cchaucha del Kjula Marca, two Late Horizon/Early Colonial sites in the Pacajes region on the southern side of Lake Titicaca (Rydén 1947). Rydén published all the material recovered from his excavations, and so the full range of artifacts, including whorls, can be compared to those from Torata Alta.

The collection of spindle whorls Rydén illustrated is not identical to the assemblage from Torata Alta, but there is a substantial amount of overlap between the two. All three sites yielded whorls made of fired clay and stone, though the percentage of stone whorls at Torata Alta is much higher (35 percent at Torata Alta compared to 13 percent in the Bolivian collection). Most of the ceramic whorl types found at Palli Marca and Cochaucha del Kjula Marca are also present at Torata Alta but in different frequencies. The six whorls that lack ceramic counterparts at Torata Alta are instead similar in shape to stone whorls found at that site. The motifs on decorated ceramic whorls also overlap; in both areas, radial patterns painted on the upper surface of the whorls are most common, but in only one case are the designs identical.

The spindle whorls thus suggest a slightly different picture than do the ceramics from Torata Alta. While they do not appear to have been derived from local tradition, neither do they seem Lupaqa in origin. The resemblances to the whorls excavated by Rydén reinforce the impression that the Torata Alta residents were descended from an altiplano population.

Interestingly, the artifact collections illustrated by Rydén are strikingly similar to the Torata Alta assemblage. The shapes of both decorated and utilitarian vessels, ground stone, and metal objects are nearly identical at these three sites. The most notable difference between them is that, at the Bolivian sites, bowls are decorated in what some researchers have called the Saxamar style: stylized llamas painted in black on a well-burnished orange background.

One point of similarity that deserves special note is the presence of camelid mandible tools at both Torata Alta (deFrance 1993) and Palli Marca. The function of these objects has not been determined, but they appear to be characteristic of assemblages associated with the southern Titicaca basin. Bermann (1993:128–129) found a possible workshop for the manufacture of such tools at Lukurmata, a site on the southeast side of the lake, and states that they are characteristic of Tiwanaku IV sites. Goldstein (1993:31) found the same tool type at Omo, a Tiwanaku colony located in the middle Osmore drainage. The recovery of such tools from domestic deposits at Torata Alta thus constitutes another line of evidence suggesting that the settlement's inhabitants originated in the Titicaca basin.

Isotopic Evidence for Agro-Pastoral Exchange at Torata Alta

For Murra (1972, 1985), an ongoing relationship between an ethnic enclave and the population from which it was derived is a defining characteristic of an Andean colony. One important aspect of this relationship mentioned frequently in the Chucuito census is the exchange of highland animals and animal products for lowland goods such as maize. Detecting this type of exchange in the material record poses a difficult challenge for archaeologists because there is evidence that camelids were raised in prehistoric times in lowland, as well as highland, habitats. Distinguishing between locally bred and imported animals has been extremely difficult until recently (Shimada and Shimada 1985). Isotopic assessments of camelid diet provide a potential means for identifying the altitudinal zone in which such animals were bred.

In archaeology, stable carbon isotope analysis has been most frequently applied to human bone to acquire information about dietary patterns (DeNiro 1987). The same principles can be used to infer the diets of herbivorous mammals such as llamas and alpacas (Ambrose and DeNiro 1986, 1989; DeNiro 1988; Tieszen et al. 1979a). Because the plant species and thus the isotopic composition of forage vary in different habitats, the stable isotope content of camelid bone should indicate the environment in which the animal was raised.

Studies in temperate, subtropical, and tropical environments on different continents have demonstrated that the distribution of C_3 and C_4 plants varies with altitude (Boutton, Harrison, and Smith 1980; Livingston and Clayton 1980; Rundel 1980; Tieszen et al. 1979b; Wentworth 1985). Both the proportion of C_4 species and the amount of biomass they contribute to the total increase with decreasing elevation (Boutton, Harrison, and Smith 1980: Fig. 3). The relationship between altitude and the distribution of plants with these different metabolic pathways is most apparent in the grasses. A number of investigators have found that C_3 grasses practically disappear at low elevations, while C_4 grasses are often absent at high altitudes.

The microdistribution of such plants is controlled by a complex set of factors, but, in general, temperature and moisture underlie the relationship between altitude and the distribution of C_3 and C_4 species. Colder, wetter habitats at high elevations tend to be dominated by C_3 species, while C_4 plants are most commonly found in hot, arid environments (Teeri 1979; Teeri and Stowe 1976).

No studies of the distribution of plants with different metabolic pathways have been conducted in Peru, but a number of factors indicate that the relationship between altitude and the occurrence of C_3 and C_4 species documented in other parts of the world should obtain in the Osmore drainage as well. First, temperature and precipitation are directly associated with changes in elevation on the western slopes of the Andes. Second, an investigation of plant distributions in the mountains of northwestern Argentina revealed the same altitudinal trends in C_3 and C_4 species that occur elsewhere (Ruthsatz and Hoffmann 1984). Finally, species lists compiled by Weberbauer (1945) at different elevations in the Osmore drainage and in the wet *puna* (high plateau) surrounding Lake Titicaca show a clear relation between altitude and the proportion of C_3 and C_4 species. The only exception might be the coastal fog oases, or *lomas*, that may contain a higher than expected percentage of C_3 plants because they are winter phenomena associated with relatively cool, damp, and cloudy weather.

The isotopic composition of the two most important types of high-altitude pasture are well known. In the grassy wet puna surrounding Lake Titicaca 6 to 14 percent of the diet is composed of C_4 plants. In the *bofedales* (spring-fed marshes), which are the primary source of pasture in the higher dry puna, C_4 plant consumption is close to zero (Reiner and Bryant 1986: Table 2; San Martin 1987: Tables A.4, A.5).

Camelids are no longer raised at low elevations in Peru,

Table 16.2 Camelid specimens selected for stable carbon isotope analysis

SPECIMEN	ELEMENT	PROVENIENCE	RELATIVE DATE	$\partial^{13}C$ VALUE (PPM)
5	1st phalange	Str. 140	Pre-1600	−19.7
6	1st phalange	Str. 146	Pre-1600	−19.4
10	metacarpal	Str. 62	Pre-1600	−20.5
11	1st phalange	Str. 64	Pre-1600	−20.0
12	1st phalange	Str. 120	Pre-1600	−21.7
13	1st phalange	Tr.E, Bl.20	Pre-1600	−19.5
16	2nd phalange	Tr.E, Bl.20	Post-1600	−19.3
17	1st phalange	Tr.NE, Bl.22	Post-1600	−20.7
18	1st phalange	Tr.NE, Bl.22	Post-1600	−18.8
19	1st phalange	Tr.G, Bl.26	Post-1600	−19.2
20	1st phalange	Tr.G, Bl.26	Post-1600	−18.9
21	1st phalange	Tr.G, Bl.26	Post-1600	−21.2
22	1st phalange	Tr.G, Bl.26	Pre-1600	−19.7
23	1st phalange	Tr.G, Bl.26	Pre-1600	−19.4
26	1st phalange	Tr.G, Bl.26	Pre-1600	−20.5
27	2nd phalange	Tr.M, Bl.18	Pre-1600	−20.1
28	1st phalange	Tr.M, Bl.18	Post-1600	−19.2
29	1st phalange	Tr.M, Bl.18	Pre-1600	−20.9
30	1st phalange	Tr.M, Bl.18	Post-1600	−18.4
37(=23)	1st phalange	Tr.G, Bl.26	Pre-1600	−19.4
38(=30)	1st phalange	Tr.M, Bl.18	Post-1600	−18.2

Notes: Trenches are designated by both a letter and the number of the room block in which they were located. Relative date refers to stratigraphic position of the element relative to the 1600 volcanic ash deposit.

and so little is known about the precise composition of camelid forage in the coastal valleys. The composition of camelid diets, however, particularly those of llamas, tends to reflect species availability (San Martin 1987: Table 2.5). Because the percentage of C_4 plants, especially annual grasses, is relatively high at lower elevations and maize stubble was also available as forage, the proportion of C_4 plants in camelid diets is expected to be relatively high. This assumption is supported in the analysis of camelid feces from the site of El Yaral, located downstream from the city of Moquegua at an elevation of 1,000 m. Two prehistoric specimens from El Yaral yielded $\delta^{13}C$ values of −21.0 and −21.2 ppm, figures that reflect a diet consisting of approximately 30 percent C_4 plants.

Nineteen camelid bones from excavated domestic contexts at Torata Alta were submitted to Geochron Laboratories for analysis. The tightly clustered results show no patterned differences by provenience or temporal context. The $\delta^{13}C$ values of these specimens range from −18.2 to −21.7 ppm and average −19.85 pm (table 16.2).

The majority of these values fall within the range predicted for camelids grazing in the wet puna, suggesting that camelids recovered from Torata Alta came from the Titicaca basin. Although the ethnicity of the group that supplied the animals obviously cannot be determined in this manner, the isotopic data are in agreement with the historical record. Because so little is known about the distribution and isotopic composition of potential camelid forage in the Osmore drainage, this interpretation is highly tentative.

Continuity or Change?

The archaeological evidence from Torata Alta, while open to some degree of interpretation, tends to confirm statements made in the historical documents regarding the existence of highland colonies in the Osmore drainage during the Early Colonial period. These data by themselves cannot be construed, however, as confirmation of the model as a whole, which includes an implicit explanation for the persistence of vertical archipelagos after the Spanish conquest.

Murra (1972) defines verticality as the control of a maximum number of ecological zones by a community or ethnic group in accordance with an ancient Andean ideal of self-sufficiency. He is careful to note that the size and function of such colonies varied with the scale of the societies that established them. Despite his sensitivity to these different organizational contexts in which colonies occurred, however, Murra emphasizes the enduring and pan-Andean nature of the cultural principles underlying their use. In addition, vertical archipelagos are characterized as ecological adaptations that benefited the ethnic group as a whole (Murra 1972:465). From this perspective, colonies existed in the Colonial period because they constituted a successful adaptation that survived the initial disruption caused by the Spanish conquest. The continuity, resilience, and inherent value of traditional culture are emphasized, but the result is a static conception of Andean social organization.

The problems associated with the verticality model are perhaps best understood in terms of what Starn (1991) has called "Andeanism." He defines this concept, which is derived from Edward Said's notion of Orientalism, as "representation that portrays the contemporary highland peasants as outside the flow of modern history" (Starn 1991:64). As is the case with Orientalism, Andeanism is structured by the creation of a dichotomy between "Western" and "non-Western" cultures and the attribution of certain essential characteristics to the latter (Starn 1991:66). In terms of the concept of verticality, disparate cultures are depicted as sharing a cultural preference for economic self-sufficiency and direct control of distant resources. This quality distinguishes Andean culture from Western civilization in which market exchange is the way in which most resources are acquired.

Murra's ideas inspired much interesting and informative research in all branches of Andean studies. The negative consequences of such a perspective are apparent, however, in the explanation attached to the presence of Lupaqa colonies in the coastal valleys during the Colonial period. Their existence is seen as a result of the persistence of a stable ecological adaptation rooted in an ancient cultural tradition. The indigenous population simply continued to do what it seemingly always had done until forcibly stopped by outsiders.

All societies do, of course, build new structures from available materials, and these usually include previous forms of organization. Identifying the reasons why some traditional practices continue while others disappear must be part of any explanation of change. An alternative understanding of the Lupaqa case can be posited by examining the colonies in terms of their contemporary socioeconomic context and by recognizing that Lupaqa society was not a unitary whole; rather, it was comprised of people with differing levels of access to economic, social, and political resources. Three indigenous groups played important roles in the maintenance of Lupaqa colonies: Lupaqa leaders residing on the altiplano, the elites representing individual colonies, and the commoners who inhabited them.

The dissolution of Inka control created a temporary power vacuum in the Andes during which both individuals and communities had the opportunity to renegotiate their access to resources. Julien (1985:213) has noted that, during the Late Horizon, Lupaqa elites appear to have emulated the Inkas. She suggests that Inka control of coastal colonies was usurped by altiplano leaders in the years following the Spanish conquest. A Lupaqa leader named Cari did, in fact, declare himself "son of the Sun" just after the Inka empire collapsed (Rowe 1982:111), a title that would have legitimated his usurpation of imperial privileges. A more common strategy for asserting rights over resources was to claim that such rights had been held during or prior to Inka domination. Because Spanish law recognized traditional rights, claims made on the basis of customary usage were often honored.

The documentary record indicates that maize produced by Lupaqa colonists flowed through the hands of elites, but there is little evidence to suggest that they redistributed it for the benefit of the population as a whole. Instead, maize was used for private domestic purposes, to maintain political dependents, and to pay tribute to the Dominican friars (Diez de San Miguel 1964: 20, 21, 55, 94, 197). Lupaqa leaders thus had an interest in maintaining colonies in the coastal valleys, but the documents suggest that they could not have done so without the active consent of the colonists themselves. By 1567, the Lupaqa leadership had already lost control over the services that residents of nearby towns had performed for them (Murra 1964). Why, then, did distant colonists continue to labor on their behalf?

One possibility is that coastal settlements benefited from being Lupaqa colonies. The Lupaqa were one of the few groups held in *encomienda* (grant of Indians and their tribute to an individual Spaniard) by the Spanish Crown, a legal status that many seem to have preferred over private control (Davies 1984:25; Murra 1964:421). Although no systematic comparison of conditions associated with royal and private holdings has been made, there is evidence that both demographic decline and the rate of taxation were less severe among groups held by the Crown (Cook 1981:131, 144). In addition, because of their distance from the Titicaca basin, the Lupaqa population in the Osmore drainage may have been able to avoid labor service in the Potosí mines, a form of tribute altiplano populations considered particularly odious. Though information about the tribute obligations imposed on the residents of Torata Alta is lacking, testimony in the Chucuito census does indicate that two other Lupaqa colonies, Sama and Chicanoma, were exempt from labor service in the mines (Diez de San Miguel 1964:69–70,197).

Finally, leaders of Lupaqa settlements residing in the coastal valleys may also have found their position advantageous (see Spalding [1970, 1973] and Stern [1982] for the position of native elites during the Colonial period). Notarial records from Moquegua indicate that the leaders of Torata Alta arranged for community members to transport wine to the altiplano for local producers (Guíbovich 1984:337–338). These services provided revenue that was either pocketed or used to defray community expenses such as the annual tribute payments. Local elites were thus geographically and socially well placed to take advantage of the new economic conditions.

Conclusion

The archaeological evidence from Torata Alta supports statements made in Colonial documents regarding the presence of Lupaqa colonists in coastal valleys during the Early Colonial period. The explanation for their existence must be sought, however, as much in the contemporary socioeconomic context as in historical precedent. Both the archaeological and historical records indicate a continuity in organizational form, but this form was not the result of adherence to an ancient ideal or an enduring ecological adaptation. Instead, the residents of communities such as Torata Alta used their status as Lupaqa colonists to negotiate new and difficult circumstances.

Acknowledgments. A number of individuals and institutions made important contributions to this research. Work at Torata Alta was conducted as part of the Moquegua Bodegas Project directed by Prudence Rice; funding for excavations was provided, in part, by grants awarded to her by the National Endowment for the Humanities and the National Geographic Society. Peter Bürgi co-directed fieldwork at the site with the author during the 1988 and 1989 seasons. Special thanks go to Geoff Conrad, Susan deFrance, Greg Charles Smith, and Chip Stanish for providing advice and information and to Dimitris Stevis for commenting on an earlier version of this paper. Geoff Conrad and Don Rice also provided samples of camelid dung from El Yaral for isotopic analysis. Additional financial support for this research was provided by the Tinker Foundation, Sigma-Xi Grants-in-Aid of Research, and the Department of Anthropology at the University of Arizona. A Geochron Dietary Studies Award funded analysis of the site's camelid bones.

Chapter 17

Andean and European Contributions to Spanish Colonial Culture and Viticulture in Moquegua, Peru

Greg Charles Smith

Abstract

Viticulture was introduced in several Peruvian valleys during the sixteenth century to supply wine for both religious and everyday use. The wine industry provided an opportunity for interaction and acculturation between the indigenous and intrusive cultures. Historical and archaeological data concerning Colonial cultural formation in Peru, which form the basis for this research, have been largely unstudied to date. Spanish Colonial wineries in the Moquegua Valley were excavated and the recovered data were interpreted using Early (1541–1600), Middle (1600–1775), and Late (1775–1900) temporal distinctions. Results indicate that trait admixture characterized domestic and industrially related material culture and that European artifacts were rare prior to 1778 (when free trade was allowed.) This pattern suggests that a great deal of miscegenation and/or transculturation was taking place between Spanish and Andean inhabitants of the valley and is interpreted as an adaptive response to relative isolation, restrictive trade laws, and lack of access to imported goods. Acculturative influences appear to have been strong for both groups, due in part to the highly developed economic and technological elements of Andean culture over which the Spanish took control.

Resumen

Durante el siglo XVI se introdujo la vinicultura en varios valles peruanos, con la finalidad de proporcionar el vino requerido tanto en actividades religiosas como en la vida cotidiana. La industria del vino constituyó una oportunidad para la interacción y aculturación entre la cultura indígena y la intrusiva. Hasta la fecha rara vez se han analizando los datos históricos y arqueológicos de la formación cultural colonial en Perú, que forman la base para este estudio. Se excavaron vinaterías coloniales hispanas en el valle de Moquegua y los datos que se recuperaron fueron interpretados con base en las siguientes diferencias temporales: Temprano (1541–1600), Medio (1600–1775), y Tardío (1775–1900). Los resultados indican que la mezcla de rasgos caracterizó a la cultura material tanto doméstica como la relacionada con la industria, y que los artefactos europeos eran excasos antes de 1778 (cuando se autorizó el libre comercio.) Este patrón sugiere que se dio un fuerte grado de mestizaje y/o transculturación entre los habitantes españoles y andinos del valle, lo que se interpreta como una respuesta adaptativa al aislamiento relativo, las leyes comerciales restrictivas, y la falta de acceso a bienes importados. Al parecer las influencias de la aculturación fueron fuertes para ambos grupos, debido en parte a los elementos económicos y tecnológicos altamente desarrollados de la cultura andina que quedaron bajo el control de los españoles.

RESEARCH FOR THIS STUDY was conducted in the Moquegua Valley of far southern Peru (figure 17.1), where the Spanish introduced grapes and viticulture during the latter part of the sixteenth century. The valley is a 28 x 1.5 km strip of fertile land situated along the northern edge of the Atacama Desert. The Atacama is the driest coastal desert in the world, receiving an average of 1.7 mm of moisture each year. Significant rains occur only in association with strong El Niño climatic events; coastal fog, which contributes the bulk of the yearly moisture, supports scattered *lomas* vegetation on hillsides. Because of the lack of moisture, cultivation depends almost entirely on irrigation, using highland runoff and spring-fed river drainage that crosscuts the coastal strip. The Moquegua Valley represents the only extensive arable lands in the Osmore River drainage, lying near the confluence of the river's three tributaries at 1,000 to 1,700 m above mean sea level.

Moquegua, founded in 1541, is the principal town in the drainage, the department, and the valley and is situated 1,366 m above sea level. The adobe ruins of the *bodegas* (wineries) are scattered throughout the valley (figures 17.2, 17.3).

Historical Background

Isolated from the Iberian Peninsula in terms of distance, Peru was indispensable to Spain because of its riches in silver bullion. The mine at Potosí (in present day Bolivia), estab-

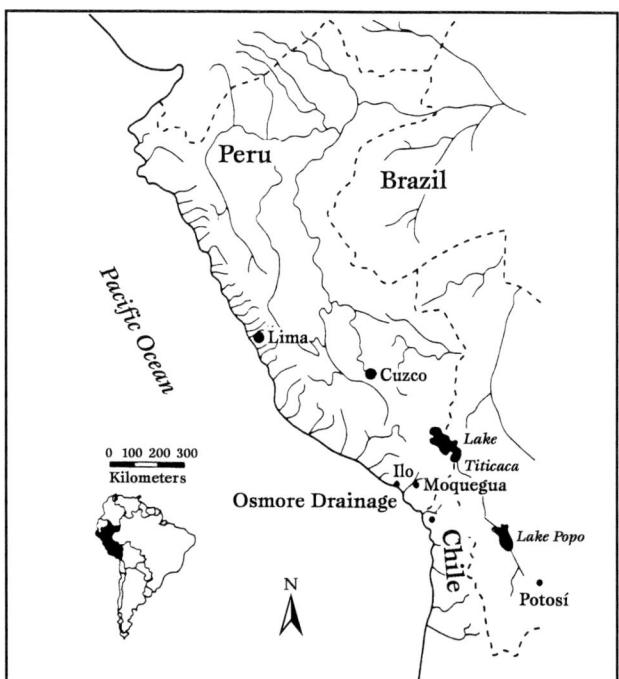

FIGURE 17.1 Location map showing Moquegua and Potosí. Drawing by Greg Charles Smith. Reprinted by permission of the Society for Historical Archaeology

lished in 1545, financed much of Spain's expansion in the Americas. Under Spanish direction, the Andean economy was shifted from a pre-Colonial emphasis on internal surplus production to a two-tiered Colonial export economy centered on silver. During the sixteenth and seventeenth centuries, bullion extraction and export were of primary importance. A necessary component in making that effort possible was basic subsistence, which for the Spanish included wine.

To accomplish their goals in Peru, the Spanish introduced controlling mechanisms very early and retained a modified form of the Andean *mita* system of labor extraction. The mita was one of a number of institutions that arose within pre-Inkan states and polities; most notable was service to the state in varied forms of obligatory labor. This system provided a structure for economy and society which the Spanish were able to tap. Between 1539 and 1600, administrative towns were set up and land was apportioned among Spanish settlers in the towns. Small holdings in grapes, sugar, and foodcrops were worked using labor provided by mita Indians and, in some areas, Africans.

Moquegua was one of several towns established along the coast which focused on growing grapes and making wine. The arrival of Indian laborers and subsistence goods to the Moquegua Valley is documented (Pease 1985), but no archaeological data exist from contact period sites within the town of Moquegua that reflect pre- and postcontact continuities (see chapter 16 for a discussion of nearby Torata Alta).

In addition to land and labor, Spaniards took over the rights of access to strategic resources such as water, trade routes, and irrigation systems. Their efficient use of these Andean infrastructural elements was made possible through arrangements with *kurakas* (local lords) who had served as managers of labor activities for the Inka. Kurakas were indispensable agents used by the Spanish in the early years of Andean settlement; they represent another economic resource of which the Spanish availed themselves (Spalding 1984).

Beginning in the late sixteenth century, significant modifications occurred in the labor system in Peru which would have lasting effects. Large encomiendas were taken over by the Crown, and indigenous laborers were largely absorbed into settler towns. A decline in the labor population was hastened to a great extent by the miscegenation of Spaniard and Indian. Anyone who could claim biological mixture was released from tribute payment and mita labor draft service (Faron 1985:22). These ex-tributary indios became part of a large rootless population referred to as *yanaconas* (sharecroppers), who worked for Spanish settlers in and around towns. When the intensity of mining activities dwindled in the seventeenth century, the Colonial economy shifted to agriculture, haciendas proliferated, and the number of yanacona families, and presumably mestizos, increased. Under these conditions, the stage was set for associated social, political, and economic developments in Colonial Peru which would lead the way to the Independence movement during the first quarter of the nineteenth century and the development of a Latin American culture that endures today.

Methodology

The goal of this study was to assess the degree to which elements from Andean and Spanish cultures influenced life and work in the Moquegua Valley and to interpret changes in material culture patterns through time. As part of the larger Moquegua Bodegas Project, this research owes much to the preliminary bodega surveys (Rice and Ruhl 1989) and related studies of the wineries (López and Huertas 1990). The fieldwork built upon these results and was composed of two distinct subsurface phases: shovel testing and excavation. Shovel testing, which was conducted on a 21.5 percent sample of the 130 bodega locations in the valley (figure 17.4), provided a general idea of site size and structure, occupational history and intensity, and the general distribution and nature of material remains at the wineries.

Results from shovel testing were used to establish a baseline view of the archaeological remains associated with the wineries and to select sites for excavation that held the potential for yielding primarily sixteenth and early seventeenth-century data. Data from the latter part of the Colonial period, which lasted until about 1826, were also recovered, as well as more recent remains from the nineteenth and twentieth centuries. Excavations were conducted at four wineries: Locumbilla, Chincha, Yahuay, and Estopacaje (figure

FIGURE 17.2 Locumbilla bodega. *Photo reprinted by permission of the* Society for Historical Archaeology

FIGURE 17.3 Chincha bodega. *Photo reprinted by permission of the* Society for Historical Archaeology

17.4). Field and laboratory research in Peru took place during fourteen months between 1987 and 1990.

Identification of early Colonial remains was facilitated by a layer of ash from the eruption of Huaynaputina volcano in February of 1600 (Cook 1981:172). This volcano, located approximately 53 km northeast of Moquegua, deposited a thin (1–10 cm) layer of white ash that remains undisturbed in the region and at some bodegas. The ash provided a stratigraphic marker for the separation of sixteenth-century deposits from later contexts and allowed for a less-than-ideal, but workable, means of drawing temporal inferences.

Three temporal periods were used to date proveniences and to interpret excavation results:

‡ Early contexts (pre-1600), situated below undisturbed volcanic ash deposits from the eruption of Huaynaputina, which provided a terminus ante quem (date before which)

‡ Middle contexts (ca. 1600–1775), which postdate the volcanic ash or lack eighteenth-century time markers such as pearlware and whiteware pottery

‡ Late contexts (1775–1900), which contain a wide variety of imported European goods, including pearlware

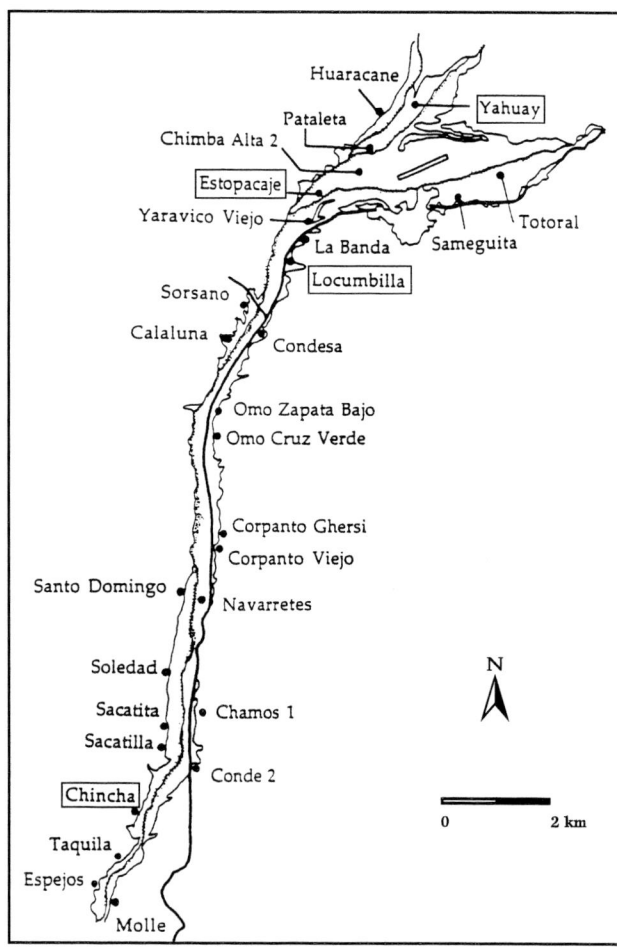

FIGURE 17.4 Map of shovel-tested bodegas. *Drawing by Greg Charles Smith*

and whiteware pottery, that have a terminus post quem (date after which) of 1775 (Miller 1987).

Excavations were designed to investigate artifact concentrations, methods of construction, and the range of Early, Middle, and Late contexts. Soils were excavated following natural deposition levels, which were distinguished by soil color, consistency, and nature of inclusions. Nonsoil lenses composed of concentrated organic material such as thatch, cane, or thick deposits of grape seeds and stems were frequently encountered. Arbitrary levels were excavated on occasion, particularly when removing upper soil zones that contained a large amount of animal guano and material from the late nineteenth and twentieth century.

During analysis, artifacts were grouped into twenty-six categories that described the range of materials recovered from the wineries. These groupings are similar to those used by South (1977) and others but were modified to account specifically for the Moquegua assemblage. The groups used to quantify and compare the excavated data are: adornment, activity-related artifacts, coarse earthenware, glass, horse hardware, industrial artifacts, lead-glazed coarse earthenware, other European pottery (post 1775), personal items, pre-Colonial artifacts, stoneware/porcelain, table/cooking utensils, tin-enameled pottery, unidentified metal fragments, weaponry, and wood construction material. To assess Andean, European, or other (such as Panamanian or Mexican) manufacture, the data were interpreted as they reflected the origin of certain artifacts. The artifact categories and their origins allow us to begin to understand how, when, and through which channels the inhabitants of Moquegua supplied themselves with domestic and industrially related goods. Regarding coarse earthenwares, a robust manufacturing and supply center is known to have existed in the Puno region near Lake Titicaca (Tschopik 1950).

In analyzing the material culture from the excavations, the following questions were asked. What are the patterns of artifact use during Early, Middle, and Late periods? Are the artifacts of Andean manufacture or were they imported? Do the artifacts show evidence of trait admixture in the combination of European and Andean elements? How and why do artifact patterns change over time, both within and between sites?

Results

Archaeological investigation of the bodegas has revealed that imported materials comprised a very small percentage of the material inventory of the earliest (pre-1600) Colonial residents. During the Middle period (1600–1775), we see trait admixture in material culture which reflects the combination of European and Andean elements in the formation of a new, mestizo-like assemblage. By the end of the Colonial period and during the early years of independence, a dramatic change is evident in material culture, with additions and replacements in the assemblage associated with the Industrial Revolution and the lifting of trade restrictions in 1778 as one aspect of the Bourbon reforms (Brading 1987:136).

A seriation of the sites is possible based on analysis of material from Colonial contexts representing Early, Middle, and Late periods at the four excavated wineries. Locumbilla is certainly the easiest to interpret because it is the only site that revealed sixteenth-century occupation. It is useful to assess the relationship between artifacts recovered and temporal occupation of all the sites, as seen in tables 17.1 and 17.2.

Artifacts recovered from excavations at all four bodegas indicate that Colonial residents of the bodegas were using products largely of Andean manufacture. This is especially true during the Early and Middle periods, although some imported products were reaching the valley despite trade restrictions.

Within the domestic sphere, almost all the tin-enameled pottery, lead-glazed pottery, and unglazed coarse earthenwares were local products that reflected a blending of Euro-

Table 17.1 Artifacts recovered by occupation period

	EARLY	MIDDLE	LATE
Locumbilla	54.%	50.3%	44.2%
Yahuay		51.0%	49.0%
Chincha		28.3%	71.7%
Estopacaje		16.3%	83.7%

Table 17.2 Artifacts recovered by place of manufacture

	ANDES	EUROPE	PANAMA	CUBA	MEXICO
Locumbilla	88.5%	10.7%	0.7%	0	0.03%
Yahuay	88.6%	9.7%	1.6%	0	0
Chincha	61.0%	37.8%	1.0%	0.08%	0.1%
Estopacaje	56.9%	41.1%	2.0%	0	0

pean formal and decorative attributes with Andean ceramic technology. Kitchen-related artifacts were the dominant feature of assemblages at all four sites, accounting for 78.8 to 90.4 percent of the site totals. Within this group, Andean-made Mas Allá and Estopacaje tin-enameled wares were produced (see chapter 18), probably beginning in the early seventeenth century, and were used increasingly in place of imported European tablewares. Hispanic tin-enameled pottery accounted for a very small percentage of each site assemblage; Panamanian pottery was the most common of the non-Andean wares. The high percentage of pottery in the bodega assemblages reflects the importance of pottery in daily life and parallels the predominance of ceramics at other Spanish Colonial settlements in the Americas (Deagan 1987). The fact that European ceramic types played such a minor role in Moquegua, however, illustrates a dramatic difference in the character of the archaeological assemblages.

Manufacturing of products other than pottery and textiles did not develop in Peru until the late nineteenth and twentieth centuries (Rippy 1946), which meant that other goods including glass, stoneware, porcelain, glass beads, and items such as sewing-related pins and thimbles, were present in Colonial contexts only through trade. These items were extremely few in number during the Early period, as seen at Locumbilla, and present in only slightly higher frequency in Middle-period contexts at all four sites. At all the sites, artifact categories including glass, stoneware/porcelain, construction materials, and personal artifacts, follow this pattern and show a steady increase in use through time.

It is during the Late period, after the declaration of *comercio libre* (free trade) in 1778 by Spain, that we see the influx of a variety of non-kitchen artifacts in the assemblages, especially activity-related artifacts, weaponry, and horse hardware. At the latest-dating sites of Chincha and Estopacaje, a much broader range of material culture items was identified. The nineteenth century was clearly a golden era for international commerce in Peru (Borah 1954; Brading 1987), as shown in the flood of products from Germany, Sweden, France, and England that found their way to Moquegua.

A few rare artifacts were found that were probably made locally, but, as at other Spanish Colonial sites, they cannot be clearly attributed to any one point of manufacture. These items include bone buttons, drilled stone beads, and earthenware pipes that specialists must analyze if more is to be known about their production. Other artifacts include gaming discs made of pottery, a spindle whorl made from a *tinaja* (large earthen jar) fragment, and a button made from gourd. These artifacts were clearly of Andean manufacture and indicate the recombination of a basic idea with a new raw material.

Although Middle and Late contexts were encountered at all four sites, only Locumbilla contained evidence for sixteenth-century Spanish Colonial occupation below a layer of volcanic ash. Both Locumbilla and Yahuay were sites of intensive domestic and industrial activity during the Middle period, while deposits at Chincha and Estopacaje reflect primarily Late-period occupation.

Results from Locumbilla indicate construction and operation of that bodega during the sixteenth century. The remains of a pre-1600 rectangular stone structure and clay floor were located below the surface in association with botija fragments, grapes, wheat, and other indigenous and local botanical and faunal remains. A partial bricklike exterior paving dates to the sixteenth century, as does a largely domestic assemblage whose only imported artifacts were Panamanian tin-enameled pottery. Kitchen artifacts included a few fragments of Cuy Plain pottery, a colono-ware that began to be produced in the sixteenth century. Industrial artifacts were also recovered from the Early component, including ceramics (botijas, tinajas, *mecheros* [large jars]) and lime. In all, archaeological data suggest that, at Locumbilla at least, material culture was primarily of Andean manufacture during the sixteenth century, with industrial elements of local manufacture and European design. With the exception of a single piece each of clear glass and iron, the only European elements recovered in pre-1600 contexts were plant and animal remains.

Middle-period deposits reflect the Andean production of tin-enameled and lead-glazed pottery as substitutions for imported wares. Two tin-enameled wares, Mas Allá Polychrome and Escapalaque Polychrome have been identified from the Moquegua assemblage (chapter 18), as well as Mojinete Glazed-and-Enameled pottery that combines two kinds of surface treatment. Lead glazing is also present in a variety of small bowls and in examples of Cuy Lead-Glazed pottery, a colono-ware that was sometimes glazed.

Cuy Plain pottery increases in frequency during both the Middle and Late periods and appears to have been the undecorated Colonial cooking ware of choice in this part of southern Peru. Some of the Cuy Lead-Glazed pottery appears to have been used in cooking as well. Decorated wares that seem to have fulfilled non-cooking functions, including red slipped, punctated, and incised coarse earthenwares, were relatively infrequent and appear to have been used primarily during the Middle period.

Painted coarse earthenware was recovered mainly from Early and Middle contexts, as seen most notably in polychrome painted Inka pottery recovered from Locumbilla. The presence of these luxury-quality wares is unusual because no Inka sites are known in Moquegua. The use of Inka pottery by high-status individuals is probable, be it by Spaniards or kurakas, and should be investigated in future research. During the late sixteenth and early seventeenth centuries, painted Inka pottery may have been used by Spaniards in Peru because they lack access to imported wares. This kind of substitution would have increased with distance from ports of entry. Because Lima was the primary point of entry, available quantities of imported ceramics were insufficient to meet the needs of high-status individuals and families in distant regions like Moquegua (Borah 1954; Lockhart 1968; Tschopik 1950).

The Moquegua ceramic assemblage as a whole reveals a number of interesting features with respect to similar assemblages from the more frequently researched settlements of Florida, Hispaniola, and Mexico, for example. In Peru, as elsewhere, locally made coarse earthenwares played an indispensable role in food preparation, frequently incorporating European formal elements (see chapter 6). Serving functions were most often met using tin-enameled and lead-glazed wares. In Moquegua, however, we see a glaring distinction in the dearth of imported Hispanic and European wares that were important social and utilitarian elements in Spanish Colonial material culture (Braudel 1973; Defourneax 1979).

Discussion

In response to the scarcity of imports, the Moquegua data show that, at least by the early seventeenth century, a Peruvian industry of tin-enameled and lead-glazed pottery production had begun. It is known that pottery factories were well established in Mexico in early Colonial times and were supervised by Spanish entrepreneurs who were either potters themselves or were at least familiar with Old World techniques. The same opportunities for ceramic production were present in Peru, given the already flourishing craft industries of the Andes and the large number of Spanish artisans known to have settled in Peru (Lockhart 1968; Tschopik 1950). From the inception of Colonial pottery production, indigenous laborers learned European techniques of glazing and the use of the potter's wheel. Through time, these laborers may have acquired a desire to use these new products.

Whether or not the creation and use of new products or the admixture of traits in Moquegua were matters of adaptation or acculturation is not clearly evident. As Reitz and Scarry (1985) have pointed out, the line between the two is difficult to draw, especially in places like the Colonial Andes, where concessions to environmental circumstances are necessary in many aspects of economic life. The successes of the Colonial period in Peru were the result of transculturation, with aspects of both economic and material life reflecting the combination of elements of both cultures. This appears to be especially the case during the Middle period, when the economic success of the wine industry in Moquegua was paralleled by the development of a largely internally produced domestic and industrial material inventory.

During the Early and Middle periods, the Spanish adapted to the scarcity of imported goods by using local products and by directing industries toward the manufacture of products suited more directly to their needs and desires. *Obrajes* (factories) for making both pottery and textiles provide two such examples. Also, Spaniards were acculturated to the successful adaptations developed during centuries of Andean civilization for efficient resource use in a harsh environment. The complex culture of the Andes, which had developed over the course of millennia, offered useful elements over which the Spanish took control. Andean culture offered infrastructural and technological elements that were similar to and, in some cases, more highly developed than those of Spain. This situation led the Spanish to incorporate non-European elements into the new Colonial culture.

With respect to the complexity of the indigenous culture and its contributions to Colonial culture, Peru shared a number of commonalities with Mexico. As Arnade (1960) pointed out, the level of cultural and infrastructural development of a contacted culture had much to do with Spanish success in an area and with the lasting effects of the culture which resulted from that contact. Indigenous adaptive strategies did not go unnoticed or untapped by the Spanish, for as Whitaker (1929:9) said, open-mindedness and conscious adaptation were much more frequent in the Spanish Colonial system than is commonly supposed.

In Peru, given the distance from Spain and the isolation of valleys like Moquegua, it may also be that a great deal of "Indian absorption" in the form of miscegenation took place, as discussed by Faron (1985). Opportunities for cultural interaction in Moquegua existed both within the context of the wine industry and with respect to intermarriage. Regardless of whether cultural mixture was biological in nature, the yanaconas who worked for Spanish estates experienced a cultural and legally defined transformation as part of the new Colonial economy in Peru. During the Middle period years in Moquegua, it may be that the Spanish were adapting or becoming acculturated through locational necessity, while the Indians and resultant mestizos were doing the same under a new economic system that held the potential for upward mobility. In both cases, need and opportunity appear to have combined in the formation of a Colonial culture born of a mixture of people and cultural elements.

The Late Colonial–period material culture of Moquegua illustrates a dramatic change that occurred in international trade and economics, again greatly altering artifact patterns in Peru. Imported pottery, which was mass produced in Europe and available worldwide at reasonable prices, appears in large quantities and begins to replace Andean-made pottery in Late proveniences within the bodega assemblages. Glass also became much more common, as did artifacts covering a wide range of domestic and industrially related categories. Articles of adornment, personal items, wooden barrels, lead baling seals, bricks, and various metal objects, to name a few, were brought in from Europe in large quantities. No longer isolated economically, the residents of Moquegua became independent of Spain during the nineteenth century and, as seen materially, became involved in and affected by the international influences of the Industrial Revolution.

Several authors (Arnade 1960; Dobyns and Doughty 1976; Mariátegui 1971; Wolf 1982) have pointed out the economic shortsightedness of Spanish policy with regard to its colonies. Spain supplied the colonies with priests, politicians, and nobles, while the colonies craved more practical things, among them economic opportunity and material wealth. At about the time of South American independence, the economic interests of the colonies and the capitalist West coincided (Mariátegui 1971:3–12), leading to the influx of material culture discussed above and to increased relations between Peru and England. The British supplied capital for railroads and industry in return for the guano and nitrates found along the coast. This trade launched Peru into yet another cultural transformation and toward the economic situation the country is in today.

Future Research

Historical archaeology is in a good position to further elucidate the cultural formations that grew out of the Spanish Colonial period in the Andes. Many potential contributions will be a long time coming, based on the scarce archaeological contexts available at this time and because of the nature of the questions most often put forth by historians and anthropologists working in the region. Many of these questions reveal a lack of information regarding the kurakas. What was the extent of their landholdings and which products from highland/lowland locations were under their control (Pease 1985:156)? How did the kurakas use resources, both for the benefit of the Spanish and to their own advantage? By studying these individuals, who were essentially economic and cultural middlemen, we may be able to learn more about how change under the Spanish was manifest in the thinking and behavior of indigenous communities that were adapting to changing economic conditions. Only a long-term, multidisciplinary search can accomplish these ends. Such a search will require the continuation of archaeological and historical studies of Colonial Peru.

A number of specific problems can be pursued archaeologically in Peru. First, more must be known about the Colonial artifacts in general and about the industries and people that produced the pottery, textiles, botijas, and tinajas of the Colonial period. Studies of craft specialization could reveal additional areas in which Andean and European technologies and products were developed. Studies by metallurgists could tell us something about the production of metal objects, whether of lead, copper, silver, gold, or iron. Amorphous fragments of iron were recovered from a few early contexts in Moquegua, and we can only speculate that some sort of metalworking was taking place in Peru, perhaps locally. A number of questions also remain with regard to the use of faunal and botanical resources in Peru, especially husbandry and cultivation practices, and the acquisition of such resources in relation to different elevational settings and communities.

Altitudinal differences must also be considered in assessing the degree of admixture, both cultural and biological, in different parts of the Andes (see chapter 16). The effects of hypoxia may have hindered the ability of Spaniards to reproduce at high altitudes, resulting in small criollo and mestizo populations in high-elevation settlements. The overall influence of Hispanic culture on highland communities is known to have been much less than that evidenced in the lowlands (Harris 1964; Morner 1967). Through future research, it may be possible to construct a scale of sorts relating cultural admixture in the Andes and relative altitude.

One scale useful in considering acculturative influences was proposed by Casagrande, Thompson, and Young (1964), who point out that distances between Spain and Colonial ports were compounded by restrictive international trade laws and environmental extremes and are necessary considerations when assessing and scaling the transmission of "Hispanicity" in the Americas (Skowronek 1989).

More data are needed from previously unstudied areas of Spanish Colonial settlement to understand adaptation/acculturation from a broader perspective which takes into account a number of factors, some of which may be interrelated. Miscegenation, for example, may be more common in remote valleys associated with industrial activities that entailed greater ethnic interaction. Through consideration of a wider variety of socioeconomic and environmental circumstances, it may be possible to identify additional and more general influences on cultural formation and to clarify the differences between acculturation and adaptation.

We need more specific information about the residents of Moquegua and their lifestyles. Not enough is known at this time about the status or ethnic identities of the inhabitants in general, or the bodegas in particular, to allow a comparative look at a range of behavior. If that were possible, we could look at archaeological data associated with Spaniards, kurakas, municipal leaders, indigenous laborers, and mestizo populations to investigate the patterns associated with each. With such a database, it would be possible to address specific research questions more concretely. Ideally, a comparative study of town life in Moquegua versus life at the bodegas might have revealed contrasts in material culture which would have allowed us to begin to distinguish between varying socioeconomic levels within the valley. Instead, the overall pattern that has emerged is that, in lieu of alternatives, the residents of the Moquegua Valley found that the mixture of elements from both European and Andean cultures was a successful adaptive feature of the Colonial period.

This research has addressed what Kubler (1946:363) called the most poorly studied aspect of Colonial life in the Andes—its material culture. In so doing, archaeological patterns in a previously uninvestigated area have been established, creating a better understanding of Spanish Colonial adaptations and acculturation in the Americas. A wide range of data is necessary if we are to generalize with regard to Latin America, a cultural entity so diverse that it cannot be reduced to any one of the distinctive cultural factors that contributed to its formation. In Peru, at least, the culture of today has its own distinct Euro-Andean personality, created from the realities of ecology, history, and the process of cultural hybridization.

Acknowledgments. This research was supported by grants to Prudence Rice and the Moquegua Bodegas Project from the National Endowment for the Humanities (No. RO-21477-87) and the National Geographic Society (Nos. 3566-8 and 4065-89). Additional support was provided at the University of Florida by the Division of Sponsored Research, the Department of Anthropology (John Goggin Fellowship), the Center for Latin American Studies (Vining Davis Field Research Grant), and the Florida Museum of Natural History. Thanks go to Pru Rice, who served as intellectual and spiritual leader during the conduct of this investigation.

✝ Chapter 18

Tin-Enameled Wares of Moquegua, Peru

Prudence M. Rice

Abstract

Excavations at wine haciendas in the Moquegua Valley of far southern Peru yielded quantities of "industrial" ceramics for making and transporting wine and brandy, as well as domestic pottery used in household cooking, serving, and storage activities. Among the latter are the tin-enameled wares, or *loza*, represented by 753 sherds; these are described in some detail. Most of this pottery has a red paste with green and black decoration and is believed to have been manufactured in southern Peru; only 12 percent or so of the tin-enameled sherds represent types produced in Panama, Mexico, Europe, or elsewhere in the Andes. Considered comparatively, two decorative traditions are evidenced in the loza, a green series and a blue series. These traditions are believed to represent distinct technological and stylistic spheres of tin-enameled ware production and exchange that may be related to geography, status, and/or origins of the potters.

Resumen

En las excavaciones de haciendas vinícolas del Valle de Moquegua en el extremo sur de Perú se han recuperado cantidades considerables de cerámica industrial para la producción y transporte de vino y brandy, al igual que alfarería doméstica empleada en las actividades de cocción, servicio, y almacenamiento desempeñadas en unidades residenciales. Entre esta última se incluyen las lozas con esmalte de estaño, representadas por 753 tiestos, mismos que se describen en este capítulo. La mayoría de esta cerámica tiene pasta roja con decoración en verde y negro, que se cree fue manufacturada en el sur de Perú; únicamente cerca del doce porcentaje de los tiestos con esmalte de estaño representan tipos producidos en Panamá, México, Europa, o en otras zonas de los Andes. En términos comparativos, son evidentes dos tradiciones en la loza, es decir una serie verde y una serie azul. Se piensa que estas tradiciones representan esferas tecnológicas y estilísticas distintas de la producción e intercambio de la loza con esmalte de estaño, que pueden relacionarse con la geografía, el estatus y/o los orígenes de los alfareros.

THE SPANISH COLONIAL WINE HACIENDAS of the Moquegua (Osmore) Valley, in the mountainous desert region of far southern Peru (figure 18.1), were the focus of archaeological survey, excavations, and analysis between 1985 and 1990 (deFrance 1993; Rice 1987; Rice and Smith 1989; Smith 1991; and chapter 17). During the course of this work, the Moquegua Bodegas Project identified the locations of 130 *bodegas* (wineries), situated along the edge of the narrow strip of arable land 29 km long in the middle reaches of the valley. These sites consisted of multi-roomed, cane-roofed structural complexes built of adobe. Spatially and functionally, the complexes can be described in terms of two sectors: an industrial area, where wine and brandy were made, and a residential sector, where estate personnel lived. In addition, many of the sites included large open courtyard areas presumed to have been used for storage or for corralling animals.

Three field seasons of excavations, from 1987 through 1989, resulted in the recovery of a wide range of artifactual materials (see chapter 17). This chapter provides a summary description of the ceramics from the bodegas, with particular attention to the tin-enameled wares. Like the sites, the ceramics represent two functional groups, industrial and domestic, differing not only in their uses but also in their places of manufacture.

Industrial Ceramics

Industrial ceramics are earthenwares used primarily in the production, storage, and transport of wine and brandy. All these wares are believed to have been manufactured in the Moquegua Valley rather than imported. Part of this reasoning is based on the sheer quantity, size, and weight of these vessels, making it inconvenient and uneconomical to bring

FIGURE 18.1 Southern Peru and Moquegua. *Drawing by Greg Charles Smith. Reprinted by permission of the* Society of Historical Archaeology

them in from elsewhere in this rugged terrain. In addition, twenty-six kilns were identified at bodega sites in the valley during field operations (see Rice 1994; Rice and Van Beck 1993; Van Beck 1991). Some or all of these kilns could have been used in firing these vessels. Industrial ceramics recovered from the bodegas include tinajas, botijas, mecheros, and setters:

- *Tinajas* are large unglazed earthenware jars used for the fermentation and storage of wine and brandy. Measuring up to 1.5 m or more in height and manufactured by coiling and paddle-and-anvil techniques, they were sunk into the ground in rows inside the large rooms of the industrial sector of the bodegas.

- *Botijas*, better known to archaeologists working in the Americas as "olive jars," are wheel-made, narrow-mouthed, conical-based vessels used for transporting wine and brandy. A buried kiln at Locumbilla bodega (see Rice 1994) was surrounded by enormous quantities of botija waster sherds, confirming the manufacture of these vessels at that site. A radiocarbon date on charcoal from the kiln indicated an early-seventeenth-century date of construction/use.

- *Mecheros* are large, deep, wide-mouthed jars or ollas with a small, flat base. These vessels were found only among the kiln wasters at Locumbilla, and many had a thick resinous material in the interior. Mecheros may have been used to heat the pine pitch that was applied to the interior of the botijas.

- *Setters* are wheel-thrown rings or collars of clay found among the Locumbilla wasters. Interpreted as kiln furniture, they are assumed to have been used in supporting botijas in the kiln during firing.

Domestic Ceramics

Domestic ceramics include vessels presumed to have been used primarily in cooking, serving, and storage. Five categories can be mentioned: pre-Hispanic ceramics, Colonial coarse earthenwares, European whitewares, porcelain, and tin-enameled wares (see chapters 12, 13). All or almost all these domestic wares were imported into the Moquegua Valley. Two of the categories, pre-Hispanic ceramics and Colonial coarse earthenwares, probably came from elsewhere in southern Peru (see chapter 17). European whitewares were found in abundance in Moquegua only in late deposits, presumably as a consequence of the opening of European trade that accompanied the late eighteenth century Bourbon reforms and the declaration of *comercio libre* (free trade). Oriental porcelains were recovered only as very tiny fragments.

Tin-Enameled Pottery

Of all the domestic pottery, the tin-enameled ware (*loza*) was of particular interest in this study. By analogy with other sites in Spanish America, loza is assumed to have been the fine tableware used in Colonial households. Comparison of the Moquegua pottery with ceramics recovered from sites elsewhere in Spanish Colonial America (see Deagan 1987; McEwan 1992) revealed distinct stylistic and technological differences, raising questions concerning their place of manufacture and the development of a ceramic industry in southern Peru. In New Spain, for example, tin-enameled ware manufacture began in the mid to late sixteenth century (Lister and Lister 1982a:13, 1982b:88). In the Andes, however, data regarding the beginnings of production of fine tablewares are sketchy and often contradictory. In southern Peru, loza of a quality ostensibly comparable to that of Talavera, Spain, was said to have been produced in the community of Pupuja, north of Lake Titicaca, by the late eighteenth century (Tschopik 1950:202). Most of the loza found at the Moquegua bodegas was probably manufactured in this general area, but it is definitely not comparable in quality to Talavera ceramics.

One of the difficulties in working with the ceramics from the bodegas is that archaeological excavations in southern Peru generally have not been directed toward the Colonial period. Consequently, descriptive analyses and periodization of Colonial ceramic assemblages from the Moquegua sites were carried out without the advantage of comparative collections from elsewhere in the region. In addition, it has been difficult to date these wares. Only two sherds were recovered from sixteenth-century contexts (that is, stratigraphically below a volcanic ash deposit dating to a February 1600 eruption): one fragment of Mas Allá Polychrome and one of Corregidor Polychrome. Most of the excavated sherds came from seventeenth century and later contexts. Fragments of nearly all these southern Peruvian types were also recovered from surface collections at the bodegas, suggesting that their manufacture may have continued into the twentieth century. Sherds of these types found at the bodegas, particularly Mas Allá Polychrome, closely resemble ceramics manufactured as recently as the early twentieth century in the southern highlands of Peru, in the area north of Lake Titicaca. Today, examples of this material can be seen in antiquities shops in Cusco and elsewhere in the highlands.

The tin-enameled ceramics from Moquegua were analyzed and described by means of the type-variety method of classification, a hierarchical procedure for defining successively more inclusive categories of similarity of pottery (Gifford 1960; Wheat, Clifford, and Wasley 1958). The units in the type-variety system are these:

- *Ware* is defined by shared features of surface treatment, manufacturing technology, and/or paste composition

- *Group* is identified within wares by shared surface treatment, often based on color

- *Type* is defined within ceramic groups on the basis of shared decorative technique

- *Variety* is the smallest unit of differentiation, one or more of which are identified within a type

The Moquegua ceramics were classified by a top-down procedure that begins by identifying wares in the collection and then dividing wares into groups, groups into types, and types into varieties.

Through this procedure, the tin-enameled loza from the Moquegua bodegas was grouped into two wares, Contisuyu Tin-enameled ware and Mojinete Glazed-and-Enameled ware. These wares, believed to have been manufactured in southern Peru (although not in Moquegua), share the same well-oxidized, reddish-brown, fine-grained, and dense paste.[1] Forms are generally the same in both wares, principally brimmed plates and simple bowls, both with foot rings; sometimes small cups are found. Other rare forms in Contisuyu ware include storage jars, a candlestick (in Mas Allá Polychrome), and a tile (of Escapalaque Polychrome). In addition to these two Peruvian wares, a number of other sherds of tin-enameled wares were recovered which represent other manufacturing centers: one group of sherds was classed as Panama ware, believed to have been produced in Panama Vieja; a very small number of sherds (not described here) may possibly represent Mexican products; and a larger group of sherds is probably from one or more as-yet-unidentified production centers in the Andes.

Contisuyu Tin-enameled Ware. Contisuyu Tin-enameled ware is represented by two types, Mas Allá Polychrome and Escapalaque Yellow Polychrome.

Mas Allá Polychrome features green and purple-to-black painted decoration on a light, opaque background enamel that varies in color from cream to pale bluish-green. Decoration is simple and informal, featuring repeated floral or leaflike motifs (figure 18.2). On plates, a green lip band and loosely interlocking black guilloches typically occur on the brim. Bowls may have a central design element executed in black and green.

Escapalaque Yellow Polychrome is similar to Mas Allá in having green and black decoration, but it differs by virtue of its rather garish greenish-yellow background. Escapalaque Polychrome usually has thicker and blacker pigment, often applied with finer line work. Plates are relatively rare, and rim decoration features diagonal lines and frondlike elements (figure 18.3).

On both types, the opaque enamel covers the entire interior and exterior surfaces of the vessels. The quality of the enamel is poor: coverage is often thin and uneven, and the coating may be dull and/or granular, indicating poor firing.

Mojinete Glazed-and-Enameled Ware. Unlike Contisuyu ware, which has tin enameling on both surfaces, Mojinete Glazed-and-Enameled ware combines tin enameling with lead glazing as surface treatments. The three types in this ware, Pasto Grande Plain, Mariscal Polychrome, and Corregidor Polychrome, subsume a great deal of variability.

Pasto Grande Plain type (figure 18.4a-c) has a thick, opaque, bright green glaze or enamel on one surface and a clear or brownish-green lead glaze on the other. Sherds of Mariscal Polychrome type (figure 18.4d,e) have the Pasto Grande type bright green glaze on one surface (usually the interior), while the other surface has the typical decoration of Mas Allá Polychrome: green and black painting on light green opaque enamel. The third type, Corregidor Polychrome (figure 18.5), has this same green-and-black polychrome enamel on one surface (usually the exterior) and a clear brown or green lead glaze on the interior.

Like the surface treatment of this ware, the paste is highly variable. Most common is the dense, brownish-red paste of Mas Allá and Escapalaque Polychromes, but sometimes the coarser pastes more typically seen in unglazed vessels were

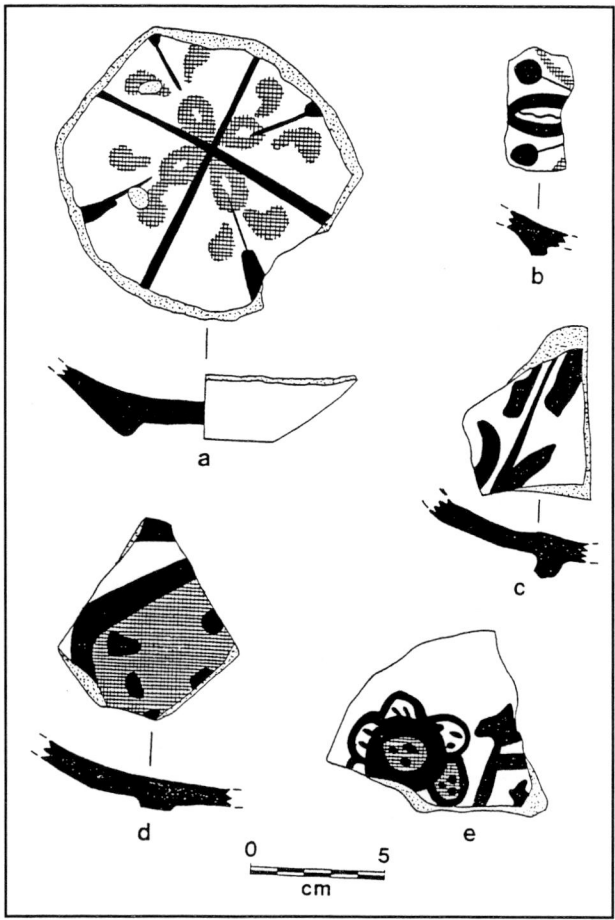

FIGURE 18.2 Mas Allá Polychrome bases and interiors of plates or bowls have green and purplish-black interior decoration over light green to cream enamel. *All illustrations by Prudence M. Rice*

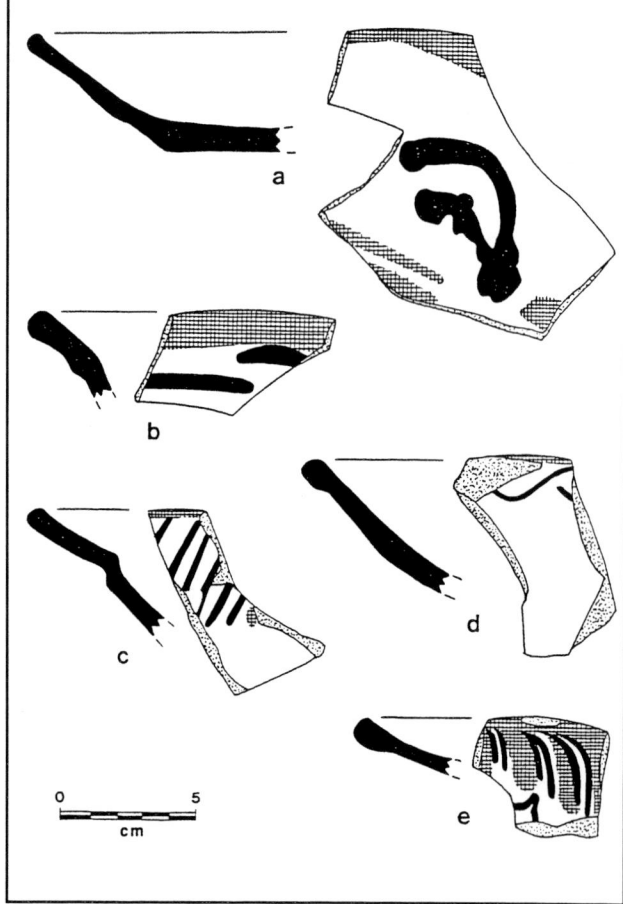

FIGURE 18.3 Escapalaque Polychrome plates and bowls have green and black interior decoration over yellow enamel.

used. A few sherds appear to be from vessels that were handbuilt rather than wheel-made.

Panama Ware

The tin-enameled pottery from the Moquegua bodegas that is believed to have been imported from Panama includes several types previously described in the literature, such as Panama Blue-on-White, Panama Plain, and Panama Polychrome (see Baker 1968; Deagan 1987; Goggin 1968; Long 1967). Panama Polychrome subsumes a great deal of variability in its decoration, and two varieties have been designated on the basis of style (Deagan 1987:91); of the two, Variety A is present in Moquegua.[2] In addition, a few sherds of Panama Plain were identified (Smith 1987) at the non-bodega Inka-Colonial site of Torata Alta, at higher elevations in the Osmore drainage; this type was not identified at the bodegas. Although the Panamanian sherds have a reddish-brown paste similar to ceramics made in southern Peru, they are easily distinguished from that material on the basis of surface treatment. Panamanian types feature an opaque white (sometimes very pale greenish) enamel with decoration primarily in blue or blue and brownish-black. Other colors such as green and yellow were occasionally used.

This pottery was produced in the Pacific port town of Panama Vieja, which was established in 1519 and handled the Pacific trade with both New Spain and Peru. One or more kilns on the edge of the town produced Blue-and-White (and other polychrome) tin-enameled ceramics from 1600 (or perhaps earlier) until January 1671, when the settlement was sacked by the English pirate Henry Morgan and subsequently abandoned (Baker 1968; Long 1967).

Panama-manufactured ceramics have been found at a number of places in Andean South America, including Lima and Ecuador, as well as in Costa Rica (de la Cruz de Lemos N.D.:461) and Ocelocalco in Pacific coastal Chiapas, Mexico (Gasco 1987:314–316). Unfortunately, lack of access to type descriptions and collections has sometimes made it difficult for Andean investigators to identify Panamanian types in their excavations. Although the sherds were acknowledged to be similar to known Panama ware types, they were not always directly attributed to this source and instead were thought to have been of local manufacture. Indeed, Goggin (1968:47–48, 165) is partly responsible for this because he claimed that the distribution of this material in northern Andean

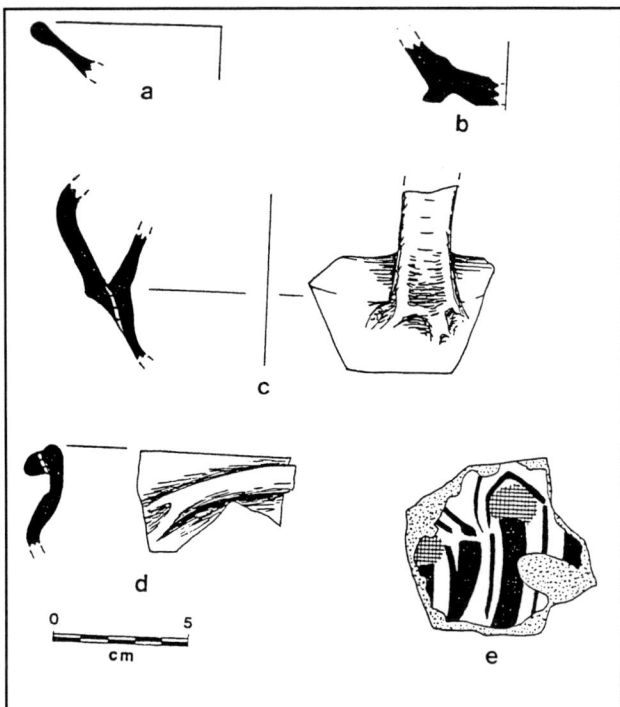

FIGURE 18.4 Pasto Grande Plain (*a-c*) and Mariscal Polychrome (*d, e*) *a*, green glazed interior and exterior; *b*, green exterior, brown interior; *c*, green interior and exterior; *d*, green and black exterior decoration over light green enamel; *e*, storage jar fragment.

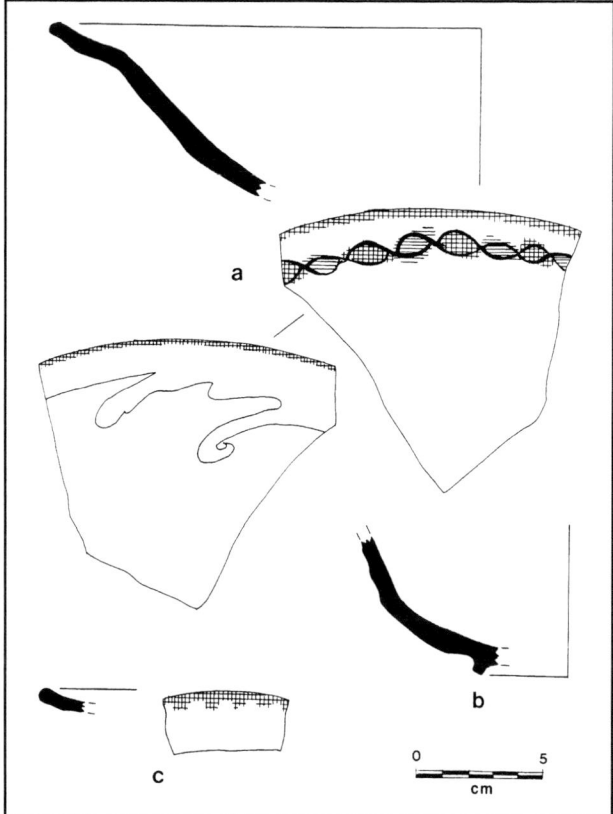

FIGURE 18.5 Corregidor Polychrome small cups or bowls

South America argued for an origin in Lima (see also Acevedo 1986). Cárdenas' (1971) work at Huaca Palomino, Peru, revealed sherds that in illustration seem identical to Panama Polychrome from Panama Vieja; excavations at Casa Osambela in Lima yielded sherds of a type designated L-3 (Flores, García Soto, and Huertas 1981:41, 51) which is surely Panama Blue-on-White. Similarly, tin-glazed sherds from Ecuador, thought to be locally made (Fournier-García 1989:63), are probably from Panama and include at least one example of Panama Polychrome (again, judging from illustrations only).

Source Unidentified

Besides these wares, three new types were named in the Moquegua collections. The initial working hypothesis was that these materials had a Panamanian origin, but very preliminary results of the characterization study[1] suggest that this may not be the case. Their reddish paste is similar to that of other Andean types, but stylistically they are different from published materials from the Panama Vieja kiln (Baker 1968; Long 1967), as well as from the southern Peruvian tin-enameled wares just described.

Two of the new types, Recua Polychrome (figure 18.6) and Cielo Blue Polychrome (figure 18.7b–d), are identified by a distinctive, well-made, glossy, robin's egg blue (that is, non-cobalt-based) tin-enameled ground. Decoration is highly variable, including purplish-black, green, and sometimes yellow-gold pigments; occasionally one surface has brown or green lead glazing. Sherds of Cielo Blue are very thin walled and too tiny to identify decoration; one sherd of Recua Polychrome displays a painted bird motif while another has a chain-like band on the brim.

The third new type, Cobre Green Polychrome (figure 18.7a), has black and green decoration over lime-green enamel. This type is rare in Moquegua; it was found primarily near the Locumbilla kiln (Rice 1994). Decoration includes bird and floral motifs.

Discussion

The presence of non-European tin-enameled wares at the Moquegua bodegas raises questions about the role of these wares in the Colonial economy. Some 753 sherds of tin-enameled ware were recovered from excavations at four bodega sites in Moquegua.[3] Of this total, approximately 88 percent is believed to have been manufactured in southern Peru and 12 percent imported from other areas. Of the imported material, Panama and Europe each contributed less than 3 percent, and less than 1 percent is from Mexico. The bulk (approximately 7 percent) is from an unknown source or sources probably elsewhere in Andean South America (see chapter 17).

Most existing descriptions of ceramics from Spanish Co-

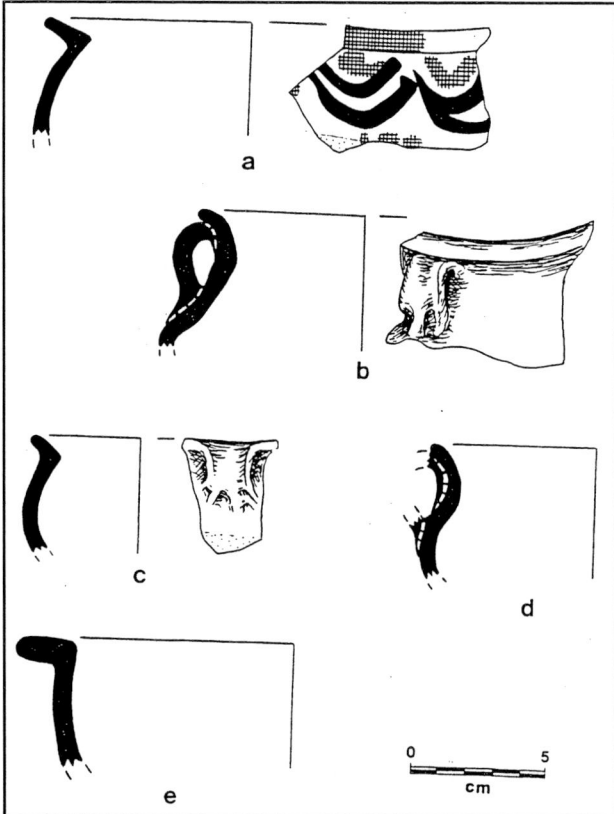

FIGURE 18.6 Recua Polychrome bowl has blue-green enameled interior and lead glazed exterior

lonial sites in the Americas are based on collections recovered from sites in the Atlantic portion or east-facing orbit of the empire, particularly New Spain and the greater Caribbean region. This area subsumes Mexico, the Caribbean islands, northern South America (Venezuela and the eastern part of Colombia), and the southeastern United States, including Florida. Pacific South America, by contrast, was a distant world within the Spanish Colonial economic sphere. For many types of goods, such as wine, the Andean region was a completely separate trading network. Access to Andean markets required not only the arduous journey across the Atlantic and Caribbean seas, but an overland trek through the steamy jungles of the Panamanian Isthmus, followed by another six weeks of ocean voyage fighting strong northerly currents southward along the Pacific coast of Ecuador and Peru. For bulky, heavy, and/or fragile goods, the costs of transport to Peru from Spain, or indeed from the Caribbean, may not have been worth the anticipated profits.

An effective and economic solution would have been to develop closer sources of supply within this distant Andean trading sphere for these classes of goods. It is not illogical, therefore, to suggest that sources of imported tin-enameled wares in the Andean region might have been developed within the viceroyalty and adjacent regions, such as Lima, Quito, or Panama, rather than Spain or Mexico. Such Pacific centers of the production to tin-enameled ware are not well known in the historical or archaeological literature yet, although the kilns of Panama were tested nearly 40 years ago.

One of the unusual and significant characteristics of the South American loza, both Peruvian made and imported (Panamanian and other Andean), is the ubiquity of green pigment. Most studies of majolica from Spain in particular and Europe in general, as well as New World tin-enameled wares found in the Atlantic trading region (sites in the Caribbean and the southeastern United States), have highlighted the importance of blue as a pigment. Blue is present as a ground color (for example, Ligurian Blue-on-Blue, formerly Ichtucknee Blue-on-Blue) and overwhelmingly present as a principal decorative pigment either alone or in combination with other colors. The emphasis on cobalt blue decoration is commonly traced to Ming and Ch'ing porcelains from China and their widespread popularity and imitation.

Green pigments, on the other hand, were seemingly little valued by the Spaniards. There may have been "a Spanish prejudice against green, possibly because it was a special color to the Muslims" (Lister and Lister 1982a:14), just as blue had special symbolism for Christians. Green and black decoration was especially common in Paterna in eastern Spain in the thirteenth and fourteenth centuries, with a history going back to the Arab world of Egypt, Persia, and Mesopotamia (Sánchez-Pacheco 1981:57–58; González Martí 1944:103–192). Similarly, the common green and brown decoration on the wares of Teruel, in the sixteenth century and later, are traced to earlier *mudéjar* (Arabic) influence (Alvaro Zamora 1978). Green became more widely acceptable by the seventeenth century and was employed in the decoration of several Mexican types.

In much of the Americas, green pigments seem to have had a much more prominent role than blue in the painted decoration. Many New World tin-enameled pottery types, as well as some of the Spanish material, had a background color that varied from pale greenish to an outright lime green. Some had a creamy white background color that varied to pale greenish (for example, Columbia Plain [Goggin 1968:118], Fig Springs Polychrome [Goggin 1968:152], and Panama Plain and Panama Polychrome [Deagan 1987:91–92; Long 1967:15]). A few others had a distinctively green surface (for example, Treasure Island Plain from Panama, characterized by "emerald green glaze" [Long 1967:42]). Still other types, among them the Moquegua material and some from the Panama Vieja kiln site, used green as a decorative pigment, usually in combination with brownish- or purplish-black manganese-based pigments.[2]

Except for Columbia Plain and Fig Springs Polychrome, most of these types, which we might refer to as the "green series," have a southern source of manufacture (in Panama and/or South America), as well as a southern distribution. In this same area, there is a relative de-emphasis of cobalt blue-

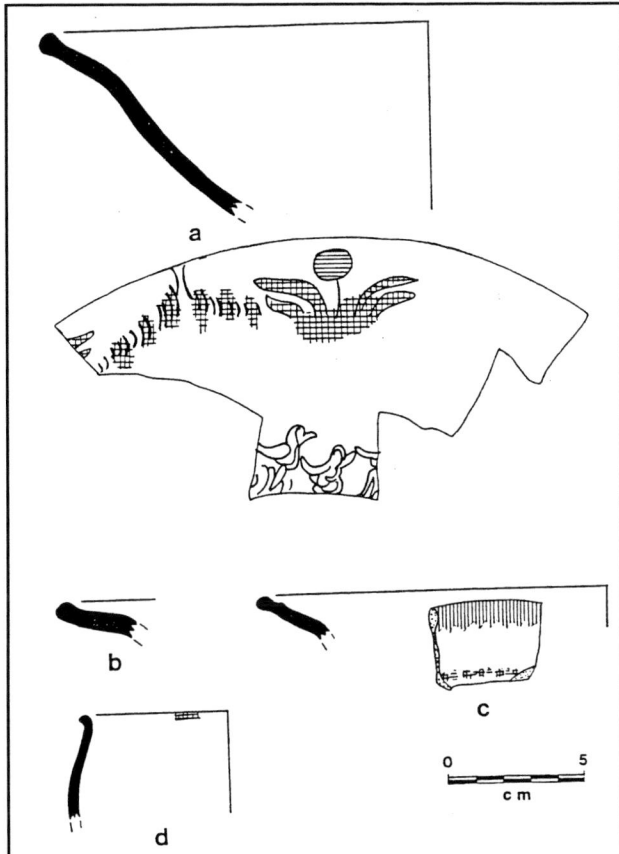

FIGURE 18.7 *a*, partly reconstructed Cobre Green Polychrome bowl with interior decoration over green interior and esteior enamel; *b-d*, Cielo Blue Polychrome with decoration over robin's egg blue enamel.

painted decoration (except for Panama Blue-on-White type), which is found more commonly in the northern sphere of Colonial interaction comprising the Caribbean and Mexico.

The geographical separation of blue series versus green series in both background and decoration of tin-enameled wares calls for some explanation. Two possible factors can be suggested. One possibility revolves around differences in the availability of blue pigment (such as cobalt) and the costs of importation (see Lister and Lister 1987:326n177 for data on processing cobalt), when comparing the northern or Caribbean sphere of trade and manufacture in the Americas with the more distant southern or Pacific sphere. Though lacking cobalt, the Andes are rich in copper minerals (sources of green pigments), and these could have been widely exchanged along with other goods circulating through the southern Colonial economic sphere. Perhaps for reasons of low cost, green seems to be the dominant color of second-grade loza in Colonial New World manufactures, particularly those circulating in the Pacific trade sphere.[4] For example, green and black were the dominant colors of the second-grade pottery recovered from Moquegua, and Green-on-White similarly seems to have been the dominant second-grade of loza in Quito (Buys 1992:16–17, 31–32; chap-

ter 12). In addition, several variants of Green-on-Cream (and Green- and "Brown"-on-Cream) wares were represented by 268 sherds found at Ocelocalco in Pacific coastal Mexico (Gasco 1987:307–318); most of these are second grade wares thought to have been manufactured in Mexico City. In Puebla, Mexico, potters' guild regulations specified that green was to be used only on "loza común" (Lister and Lister 1974:33).

A second possible explanation requires consideration of the geographical and cultural origin of the potters of the Pacific sphere, including Peru, Ecuador, and Panama, in an effort to understand why they shared a similar decorative vision and language. It has been suggested that the potters of Peru and Panama may have come from eastern Spain, where green and black pigments were an important part of the decorative style and vocabulary. Regarding the potters of Panama Vieja, the Listers (1974:44,45) suggest that they may have been from Granada and that they employed firing methods typical of Sevillian/Genoese potters. In addition, they note that

> the motifs...the habit of only partial glazing, the restricted use of green and brown with only a bit of yellow and virtually no blue—plus the earlier style of motifs noted at Panama—makes one suspect that the potters who got to the southern viceroyalty or their descendants had roots in the Spanish Levante or southeastern Castile, whereas those of New Spain were more firmly tied to the ceramic traditions of Andalusia or northwestern Castile. (Lister and Lister 1974:49)

Both the Listers (1974:48) and Stastny (1981:101) suggest that the Peruvian potters may have come from Teruel in Aragon, Spain because of the predominance of green and brown decoration in that region. Teruel pottery was manufactured in two series: one with blue decoration, inspired by oriental porcelains, the status ware; the other, a green and manganese brown ware representing continuities from the traditional wares of the area's mudéjar past (Alvaro Zamora 1978:90–96; González Martí 1944).[5] Decoration in the green and brown series manufactured after the Muslim expulsion in 1610 is simpler, featuring vegetal and floral motifs. A common central motif is a large bird with a long tail and sharp beak, posed on leafy vegetation.

Panama is of interest because it lies geographically between the two production and distribution of tin-enameled ware spheres, circum-Caribbean and Pacific. The source of supply of the enamel ingredients, tin and lead ores, for the Panama-made pottery could have been any of three regions: Spain, Mexico, and Peru. The pottery produced at the kilns at Panama Vieja is of further interest in light of these two geographical and decorative spheres of tin-enamel wares. Ceramics excavated from the site and surface collected in the vicinity of the two kilns (Baker 1968; Long 1967) share characteristics of each: some have blue-on-white decoration similar to material of the Caribbean periphery, while other material features greater emphasis on green (as background and also decoration) similar to ceramics from the Andes. The little-known Panamanian green-and-brown painted variant may have been stylistically related in some way to Mas Allá Polychrome in Peru; the colors and general style of decoration seem comparable.[6]

In sum, I suggest that two distinct technological and stylistic spheres of production and exchange of tin-enameled ware existed in Spanish Colonial America. One of these, which is much better known and investigated, includes Spain and Mexico. It is represented by ceramics found at Colonial sites in the circum-Caribbean region (including northern South America and Florida), and it was a heavy producer and consumer of cobalt-blue series wares. The other, established slightly later, is still little known archaeologically because of the paucity of investigations to date. It is a southern or Pacific sphere that includes Panama and the Andes and has a distinctive decorative language and technology oriented largely around green series wares which, by cultural definition and technological attributes, are second-quality wares. Panama, as a point of tangency between the two spheres, seems to have participated in both. The stylistic and technological relationships of the wares in this southern sphere, together with the cultural, religious, and ethnic origins of the region's potters, are important questions that will merit attention in the future.

Acknowledgments. The Moquegua Bodegas Project was supported by grants from the National Endowment for the Humanities (RO-21477-87) and from the National Geographic Society (3256-86, 3566-87, and 4065-89). I thank Greg Charles Smith, who supervised field and laboratory operations in Moquegua from 1987 to 1990.

Notes

1. Mineralogical and chemical characterization of the pastes and glazes of the Andean and Panamanian tin-enameled wares is currently under way under the direction of Jaqueline Olin and James Blackman of NIST (National Institute of Standards and Technology). Analyses have not been completed.
2. Within the Panama Polychrome type, sherds having green and brown/black decoration alone do not represent a named variant, although Long (1967:16) isolated 178 of these sherds as a decorative variant.
3. When shovel tests, surface collections, and kiln excavations are included, more than one thousand sherds of tin-enameled ware were recovered. This discussion, however, is restricted to material recovered from excavations at the four sites that were the focus of the Bodegas Project investigations: Locumbilla, Chincha, Yahuay, and Estopacaje. See Smith 1991: Tables 7.2, 7.5, 7.8, 7.11 for totals.
4. The vessels here classified as Cielo Blue Polychrome may have been a fine ware (*loza fina*) judging from the blue ground color and the technological characteristics (thin walls and well-fired glaze).
5. Pottery making in Spain, and particularly the manufacture of glazed pottery, was associated with Muslims or *moriscos* (Christianized Muslims), at least since the eleventh century (see Deagan 1987:26; Glick 1979:238–241; also Lister and Lister 1987:324 for arabisms in potters' vocabulary) and even following the Christian reconquest. It is tempting to associate blue colors (and Blue-and-White painted status wares) with Christian symbolism and growing Christian power in Spain, while green remained a symbol of its former Muslim sovereigns. This, together with the products of the Italian potters in Seville, would have established the status goods that were transferred to Spain's earliest colonies in the New World, the Caribbean and New Spain. The establishment of pottery (and tile) workshops in the Pacific colonies and in the Andes occurred somewhat later, in the late sixteenth and early seventeenth centuries, at the time when cultural pressures on non-Christians was increasing. Despite the Crown's efforts to control who was able to migrate to the New World colonies (in order to exclude non-Christians), there may be some relationship between Muslim expulsion and the predominance of green decoration in the pottery produced by the late-established workshops in the southern part of the Spanish Colonial world.
6. Stylistic analysis of these materials is the subject of a master's thesis in progress.

Glossary

adoratorios	shrines		in the bottom (in the Yucatán)
aguardiente	brandy	chacra	agricultural plots in the Andean region
albarradas	dry stone wall		
alcalde mayor	Spanish administrator of a district	chich pile	a circular or oval pile of crushed limestone
apaxtle	basin	cholo	person of mixed Indian and European ancestry
apílol	pitcher		
arco toral	main arch	coadjutor	assistant to a bishop
areba	cassava bread	comal	clay griddle, used to heat tortillas and other foods
aríbalo	Inka-style storage jar		
atrío	atrium	comercio libre	free trade
audiencia	high court of a region, and the region itself	commendador	commander
		congregación	Spanish colonial institution of forcible removable of native peoples from dispersed settlements into a centralized community
bacín	large, cylindrical chamber pot		
barrio	neighborhood or ward of a town		
bodega	winery		
bofedales	spring-fed marshes		
botija	earthenware vessel for storing wine, olives or water	conquistadores	a leader in the Spanish Conquest of America
bucaro	fountain	convento	convent or monastery
cabecera	head town or base mission	coro	choir
cabecera de doctrina	headquarters church	cofradía	religious co-fraternity
cabildo	The municipal council and offices of a town	criollo	in México, children of Spanish parents; elsewhere in Latin America, fussion of indigenous and Spanish elements
cacique	Indian chief, usually a hereditary leader (from Arawak)		
cajete	bowl	cure	priest
camote	sweet potato	doctrine	Indian parish; also Christian instruction
can tero	mason		
candelero	candlestick	doctrinero	friar or priest in charge of a doctrine and the Christian instruction of the Indians
capilla	chapel		
cargas	loads, approximately 50 pounds		
casa de burros	small stable	egei	wooden board used with a piece of quartz to grate manioc roots
caserio	small settlement		
caste	Colonial racial category used for individuals of mixed	ejido	community's communal lands
		el voto de sangre	vow of blood
cédula	decree and the paper upon which it is written	encomendero	individual who held an encomienda
cenote	sinkhole in limestone with a pool	encomienda	grant of Indians and their tribute

eras	to an individual Spaniard irrigation channels	planta	buildings and other facilities that form the core of an estate
escudo	Insignia, coat of arms	presidencia	a Mercedarian house having less than the required eight religious members to meet the daily obligations of Mass, not located within *encomienda* territory, independent of the authority of a *comendador* and directly under the jurisdiction of the governing body in Guatemala
estancia	cattle ranch		
finca	plantation or ranch		
fiscal	prosecutor; an Indian official charged with bringing Indians together for religious education		
gremio	guild		
hacendado	hacienda owner		
horno, hornilla	small mud oven		
huipil	Indian woman's blouse, woven on a backstrap loom	presidio	military fort
		principal	Indian noble
jornalero	day laborer	probanzas	investigations of an individual's conduct in office
kuraka	native chief (in the Andes)		
league	distance of approximately five km	pueblo	village or small town
lebrillo	large, steep-sided basin, usually for washing hands	pueblo de indios	An Indian town
		pueblo de españoles	Spanish town
limosna	alms, charity	puna	high plateau
lomas	environment where dense sea fog supports certain plant life (on the Pacific coastal desert of Andean region)	quinta	large, elaborately decorated, rectangular masonry houses; country house
		ramada	an open, pole and thatch structure intended to provide shade over a work area
loza	generic term for tin-enameled wares, but may include other glazed or unglazed earthenware or porcelain		
		reducción	see congregación
		rejollada	a sinkhole
luneros	day laborers	relación	account
mecapal	tumpline, a strap that wraps around the forehead and is attached to a burden carried on the back	repartimiento de efectos	forced sales of goods imposed on Indians by Colonial officials
		resplandor	resplendent image
		retablo	altarpiece of a church
mechero	large, deep, wide-mouthed jars	santo	image
merced	land grant	solar	house lot
mestizo	person of mixed European and Indian ancestry	talpetate	Consolidated or semiconsolidated volcanic ash, sometimes hard enough to be quarried for building material
mita	system of rotating forced Indian labor (in the Andes)		
molcajete	ceramic or stone mortar	tepetate	soil derived from volcanic tuff
mudéjar	Arabic	terreno baldío	vacant land
municipio	political division similar to a county	tianguis	market
		tienda	store
noria	pump well	tinaja	large earthenware vessel (sometimes used for fermenting wine)
obraje	textile factory or workshop		
oidor	judge for an audiencia	tlachiquero	person who scrapes agave and collects the sap
palomares	dovecotes		
paraje	disperse rural settlement	tributario	Indian tributary
partido	religious district	vaquero	cowboy
peñol	fort	vara	Castillian yard (about 33 inches)
pilas	small water tanks	vega	intermontane depression
pipas	water-storage vessels	vicaría	territory or parish administered

	by a vicar or priest; a Mercerdarian house having less than the required eight religious members to meet the daily obligations of Mass, usually located within *encomienda* territory and attached to a specific convent under the jurisdiction of the *comendador*	visita	auxiliary town; inspection
		visita general	inspection reports by the vicar general of the region
		visita provincial	inspection reports by the elected head of the province, the vicar provincial
		visitas pastorales	pastoral visits to a benefice made by a bishop or other curate to assess the status of the parish
vicario	office of vicar or priest	yanacona	sharecropper or serf; category of person in the Andes in the pre-Columbian period
villa	small Spanish town, smaller than a city		

Bibliography

Abdala, S.
1992 Arquitectura. Casa del Gral. Manuel Oribe. *Patrimonio cultural*, Año 1 (1):17–26. Comisión del Patrimonio Histórico, Artístico y Cultural de la Nación. Montevideo, Uruguay: Ministerio de Educación y Cultura.

Acevedo, S.
1986 Trayectoria de la cerámica vidriada en el Perú. *Catálogo, Exposición "Vidriados y Mayólica del Perú,"* 1–14. Lima: Museo de Arte y de Historia, Universidad Nacional Mayor de San Marcos.

Actas del Capítulo General
1979 *Boletín de la Orden de la Merced número extraordinario.* Roma: Tipografía Guanella.

Acuña, R. (ed.)
1985 *Relaciones Geográficas del siglo XVI: México. Tomo I.* México, D.F.: Universidad Nacional Autónoma de México.
1986a *Relaciones Geográficas del siglo XVI: México. Tomo II.* México, D.F.: Universidad Nacional Autónoma de México.
1986b *Relaciones Geográficas del siglo XVI: México. Tomo III.* México, D.F.: Universidad Nacional Autónoma de México.

Ajofrín, F. de
1986 *Diario del viaje a la Nueva España.* México, D.F.: Secretaría de Educación Pública, Cien de México.

Alvarado, P. de
1871 Repartimento de la ciudad de Gracias a Dios y su fundación por Pedro de Alvarado (1536). In *Colección de documentos inéditos relativos al descubrimiento, conquista y organización de las antiguas posesiones españoles de América y Oceanía* 15:5–20. Madrid: Imprenta Española.

Álvarez, S.
1987a Recuperación y defensa de territorio étnico: El caso de Chanduy en la costa del Ecuador. *Boletín de Antropología Americana* 15:105–121. Washington, DC: Instituto Panamericano de Geografía e Historia.
1987b Artesanías y tradición étnica en la Península de Santa Elena. *Artesanías de América* 25:45–120. Cuenca, Ecuador: Centro Interamericano de Artesanías y Artes Populares.

Álvarez-Kern, A.
1992a Les missions Jesuites des Guarani. *Les dossiers d'archeologie* 169:46–49. Paris.
1992b Descoberta e colonizaçao da América: Impactos e contatos entre las sociedades indígenas e européias. In *América 92. V séculos de história, 500 anos de luta*, 3–6. Porto Alegre, Brazil.

Alvaro Zamora, M. I.
1978 *Cerámica Aragonesa decorada, desde la expulsión de los moriscos a la extinción de los alfares (siglos XVII-fines XIX/Com.XX).* Zaragosa, Spain: Libros Portico.

Ambrose, S., and M. DeNiro
1986 The isotopic ecology of East African mammals. *Oecologia* 69:395–406.
1989 Climate and habitat reconstruction using stable carbon and nitrogen isotope ratios of collagen in prehistoric herbivore teeth from Kenya. *Quaternary Research* 31:407–422.

Andrews, A. P.
1981 Historical archaeology in Yucatan: A preliminary framework. *Historical Archaeology* 15(1):1–18.

Anguiano, R. de
1946 Visita hecha a los pueblos de Honduras, por el gobernador intendente Ramón de Anguiano (1801). *Boletín del Archivo General del Gobierno de Guatemala* 11:113–150.

Ángulo, J., and C. Ángulo
1979 *El museo de Cuauhnahuac en el Palacio de Cortés.* México, D.F.: Instituto Nacional de Antropología e Historia.

Annis, V. L.
1968 *La arquitectura de Antigua Guatemala 1543–1773.* Guatemala: Editorial Universitaria.

Arana, M.
1983 Montevideo y la defensa de su patrimonio arquitectónico. In *Una ciudad sin memoria.* Grupo de Estudios Urbanos, 5–6. Montevideo, Uruguay: Ediciones Banda Oriental.

Armstrong, D. V.
1990 *The old village and the great house: An archaeological and historical examination of Drake Hall Plantation, St. Ann's Bay, Jamaica.* Urbana: University of Illinois Press.

Arnade, C.
1960 The failure of Spanish Florida. *The Americas* 15 (3):271–281.

Aronson, M., and P. Fournier-García
1993 Models for technological innovation: An ethnoarchaeological project in Pino Suarez, Mexico. In *Ceramics and civilization*, Vol. 6. *The social and*

cultural contexts of new ceramic technologies, edited by W.D. Kingery, 33–74. Westerville, Ohio: The American Ceramic Society.

Arredondo, H.
1955 Santa Teresa y San Miguel. La restauración de las fortalezas la formación de sus parques. *Revista de la Sociedad Amigos de la Arqueología* 13:39–443. Montevideo, Uruguay.
1956 Santa Teresa y San Miguel. La restauración de las fortalezas, la formación de sus parques. *Revista de la Sociedad Amigos de la Arqueología* 14:5–304. Montevideo, Uruguay.

Ashmore, W.
1987 Cobble crossroads: Gualjoquito architecture and external elite ties. In *Prehistoric interaction in the southeast Mesoamerican periphery: Honduras and El Salvador*, edited by E. J. Robinson, 28–48. BAR International Series 327. Oxford: British Archaeological Reports.

Ashmore, W., E. M. Schortman, P. A. Urban, J. C. Benyo, J. M. Weeks, and S. M. Smith
1987 Ancient society in Santa Barbara, Honduras. *National Geographic Research* 3(2):232–254.

Ashmore, W., P. A. Urban, E. M. Schortman, and J. C. Benyo.
1986 Proyecto arqueológico Santa Bárbara: Temporada de 1984. *Mexicon* 8(4):77–81.

Austral, A., and A. M. Rocchietti
1981 El procesamiento de datos en arqueología. *Revista de la Facultad de Humanidades y Ciencias* 1(3). Serie Ciencias Antropológicas. Montevideo, Uruguay.

Baker, H.A.
1968 Archaeological excavations at Panama La Vieja, 1968. Master's thesis, Department of Anthropology, University of Florida, Gainesville.

Bárcena, R., and D. Schávelzon
1990 *El Cabildo de Mendoza, excavaciones arqueológicas para su preservación.* Mendoza, Argentina: Municipalidad de Mendoza.

Barnes, M. R. and R. V. May
1972 *Mexican majolica in northern New Spain.* Occasional Paper. Pacific Coast Archaeological Society.

Barrán, P.
1990 *Historia de la sensibilidad en el Uruguay.* 2 vols. Montevideo, Uruguay: Ediciones Banda Oriental.

Barrera Rubio, A.
1983 La conquista de Mérida y la fundación de Yucatán. *Boletín de la Escuela de Ciencias Antropológicas de la Universidad de Yucatán* 58:9–21. México.

Barriga, V. M., ed.
1951 *Los terremotos en Arequipa, 1582–1868.* Arequipa, Perú: La Colmena.

Bartra, R.
1984 *Campesinado y poder político en México.* México, D.F.: Editorial Era.

Bate, L.F.
1989 Notas sobre el materialismo histórico. *Boletín de Antropología Americana* 19:1–29. México.

Bausero, L.
1958 El aniquilamiento del Cabildo: Será una invención Colonial pero nunca veraz reproducción histórica. *Diario Acción*, 6 de mayo. Montevideo, Uruguay.
1959 La reconstrucción del Cuartel de Dragones de Maldonado. *Suplemento Dominical "El Día,"* Año XXVIII No. 1386, 9 de agosto. Montevideo, Uruguay.
1974 Índices. *Revista de la Sociedad Amigos de la Arqueología* 16:1–23. Montevideo, Uruguay.
1981 Urbanismo: más vale tarde que ... *Opinar*, semanario del 30 de diciembre, 23. Montevideo, Uruguay.

Bausero, L., and V. Bonino
1957 Informe sobre el traslado de la Puerta de la Ciudadela de Montevideo. *Revista de la Sociedad Amigos de la Arqueología* 15:445–462. Montevideo, Uruguay.

Beaucage, P.
1982 Exchanges, inégalités, guerre: Le cas des Caraibas insulaires (XVII et XVIII Siécles). *Recherches Amerindiennes au Quebec* 12(3):179–191.

Bell, E., Personal communication

Bell, E., and T. Long
1992 *Antigua Guatemala.* Guatemala: Antigua Tours.

Benavides, A., and A. P. Andrews, eds.
1985 Arqueología histórica en el área Maya. *Revista Mexicana de Estudios Antropológicos* 31. Sociedad Mexicana de Antropología, México.

Benítez, J., and T. Chinchilla
1990 Análisis tipológico preliminar de la cerámica micácea. In Reconocimiento de los Municipios de Alotenango y Sumpango, Sacatepéquez. Informe final del Proyecto Encuesta Arqueológica Kaqchikel, on file at the Centro de Investigaciones Regionales de Mesoamérica, Antigua, Guatemala.

Benyo, J. C., and T. L. Melchionne
1987 Settlement patterns in the Tencoa Valley, Honduras: An application of the coevolutionary systems model. In *Prehistoric interaction in the southeast Mesoamerican periphery: Honduras and El Salvador*, edited by E. J. Robinson, 49–64. International Series 327. Oxford: British Archaeological Reports.

Bermann, M.
1993 Continuity and change in household life at Lukurmata. In *Domestic architecture, ethnicity, and complementarity in the south-central Andes*, edited by M. Aldenderfer, 114–135. Iowa City: University of Iowa Press.

Bernard-Bosch, L., V. Blanco-Conde, and A. Rives-Pantoja
1985 *La Manuela. Arqueología de un cafetal habanero.* La Habana, Cuba: Editorial de Ciencias Sociales.

Besio Moreno, N.
1934 *Buenos Aires, puerto del Río de la Plata, capital de la Argentina: Estudio crítico de su población (1536–1936).* Buenos Aires: Edición del autor.

Besso-Oberto, H.
1977 Arqueología histórica (un paradigma de investigación). Master's thesis, Escuela Nacional de Antropología e Historia, México.

Black, N. J.
1989 Transformation of a frontier mission province: The Order of Our Lady of Mercy in Western Honduras. Ph.D. dissertation, Department of Anthropology, State University of New York at Albany.

Boger, L. A.
1971 *The dictionary of world pottery and porcelain.* New York: Charles Scribner's Sons.

Bibliography

Bolaños, M., and O. Manosalvas
1989 Arqueología histórica. Caso Capilla del Robo, Quito. Informe Técnico. Ms. Instituto Nacional del Patrimonio Cultural, Quito, Ecuador.

Bolland, N. and A. Shoman
1977 Land in Belize 1765–1871. Mona, Jamaica: Institute of Social and Economic Research.

Borah, W.
1954 Early colonial trade and navigation between Mexico and Peru. *Ibero Americana* 38:1–170.

Borges Morán, P.
1977 *El envío de misioneros a América durante la época española*. Salamanca, Spain: Universidad Pontificia.

Borhegyi, S. F.
1950 Estudio arqueológico en la falda norte del Volcán de Agua. *Antropología e historia de Guatemala* 1:3–22.
1965 Settlement patterns of the Guatemalan highlands. *Handbook of Middle American Indians*, vol. 2, edited by G. Willey, 3–58. Austin: University of Texas Press.

Borstel, C., G. Conrad, and K. Jacobi
1989 Analysis of exposed architecture at San Antonio: Foundation for an excavation strategy. In *Ecology, settlement and history in the Osmore Drainage, Peru*, edited by D. Rice, C. Stanish, and P. Scarr, 371–394. Oxford: International Series 545. British Archaeological Reports.

Boutton, T., A. Harrison, and B. Smith
1980 Distribution of biomass of species differing in photosynthetic pathway in southeastern Wyoming grassland. *Oecologia* 45:287–298.

Bracamonte y Sosa, P.
1984 Haciendas, ranchos y pueblos en Yucatán (1821–1847). *Boletín de la Escuela de Ciencias Antropológicas de la Universidad de Yucatán* 11(66):3–21.
1985 Sirvientes y ganado en las haciendas Yucatecas (1821–1847). *Boletín de la Escuela de Ciencias Antropológicas de la Universidad de Yucatán* 12(70):3–15.
1988 Haciendas y ganado en el noroeste de Yucatan, 1800-1850. *Historia Mexicana* 37(4):613–639.
1989 Amos y servientes: Las haciendas de Yucatán 1800–1860. Master's thesis, Facultad de Ciencias Antropológicas, Universidad Autónoma de Yucatán, Mérida.
1990 Sociedades de sirvientes y uso del espacio en las haciendas de Yucatán: 1800–1860. *Historia Mexicana* 40(1):53–77.

Brading, D.A.
1975 *Mineros y comerciantes en el México borbónico (1763–1810)*. México, D.F.: Fondo de Cultura Económica.
1987 Bourbon Spain and its American empire. In *Colonial Spanish America*, edited by L. Bethell, 112–162. Cambridge: Cambridge University Press.

Braniff, B.
1992 *La frontera protohistórica Pima-Opata de Sonora*. Colección Científica 241. México, D.F.: Instituto Nacional de Antropología e Historia.

Braudel, F.
1973 *Capitalism and material life, 1400–1800*. New York: Harper and Row.

Brockington, L. G.
1989 *The leverage of labor: Managing the Cortés haciendas in Tehuantepec, 1588–1688*. Durham: Duke Univ Press.

Broda, J.
1979 Las comunidades indígenas y las formas de extracción del excedente: Época prehispánica y colonial. In *Ensayos sobre el desarrollo ecónomico de México y América Latina (1500–1975)*, edited by E. Florescano, 54–92. México, D.F.: Fondo de Cultura Económica.

Brown, M. J.
1990 Investigations at the Vollrath Blacksmith Shop (41 BX 786), San Antonio, Bexar County. Texas. Archaeological Survey Report, 188. Center for Archaeological Research, The University of Texas at San Antonio.

Brush, S.
1977 *Mountain, field, and family: The economy and human ecology of an Andean Valley*. Philadelphia: University of Pennsylvania Press.

Burger, R. L.
1989 An overview of Peruvian archaeology (1976–1986). *Annual Review of Anthropology* 18:37–69.

Burgoa, F. de
1989 *Geográfica descripción*, vol. 2 [1674]. México, D.F.: Editorial Porrúa.

Bushnell, G.H.
1951 *The archaeology of the Santa Elena Peninsula in south west Ecuador*. Occasional Publications of the Cambridge University Museum of Archaeology and Ethnology, 1. Cambridge: Cambridge University Press.

Buys, J.
1989 Hacia una interpretación de la historia constructiva del Convento de Santo Domingo de Quito. In *La preservación y promoción del patrimonio cultural del Ecuador*. Proyecto de Cooperación Técnica Ecuatoriana-Belga, 2. Quito.
1990 Cerámica Colonial y arqueología historica: El Convento de Santo Domingo (Quito). In *Cerámica Colonial y vida cotidiana*, 61–72. Cuenca, Ecuador: Fundación Paul Rivet.
1992 La alfarería Colonial. In *Historia de la cerámica en el Ecuador (síntesis)*, edited by S. Moreno y J. Peña, 33–36. Cuenca, Ecuador: Fundación Paul Rivet.

Buys, J., and B. Camino
1991 Reporte de las excavaciones arqueológicas en el Refectorio, Convento de Santo Domingo, Quito. Ms. Proyecto de Cooperación Técnica Ecuatoriana-Belga, Quito, Ecuador.

Buys, J., and V. Domínguez
1988 Excavaciones arqueológicas en el Museo Fray Pedro Bedón, Convento de Santo Domingo, Quito. Segunda fase. Ms. Proyecto de Cooperación Técnica Ecuatoriana-Belga, Quito, Ecuador.

Buys, J., V. Domínguez, and C. Andrade
1988 La investigación arqueológica en el Museo Fray Pedro Bedón, Convento de Santo Domingo. In *La Preservación y Promoción Cultural del Ecuador*. Proyecto de Cooperación Técnica Ecuatoriana-Belga, 1, Quito.

Calderón de la Barca, Marquesa de
1976 *La vida en México*. México, D.F.: Editorial Porrúa, S.A.

Canessa de Sanguinetti, M.
1976 *La ciudad vieja de Montevideo*. Montevideo, Uruguay: Ediciones AS.

Capurro, F.
1928 La Colonia del Sacramento. *Revista de la Sociedad*

Amigos de la Arqueología 2:63–254. Montevideo, Uruguay.

Cárdenas M., M.
1971 Huaca Palomino (Valle de Rimac): Fragmentaria vidriada fina con decoración en colores. *Arqueología PUC* 10:61–67. Boletín del Seminario de Arqueología. Lima: Instituto Riva-Aguero, Pontificia Universidad Católica del Perú.

Carias, M.
1985 La cristianidad centroamericana: La evangelización de Honduras. In *Historia general de la iglesia en América Latina*, edited by E. Dussel, 61–69. Salamanca, Spain: Ediciones Sígueme.

Carlson, D. L.
1983 Computer analysis of dated ceramics: Estimating dates and occupational ranges. *Southeastern Archaeology* 2(1):8–20.
1985 CERAMDATE. Department of Anthropology, Texas A & M University, College Station.

Carmack, R. M.
1973 *Quichean civilization: The ethnohistoric, ethnographic, and archaeological sources*. Berkeley: University of California Press.
1986 Ethnohistory of the Guatemalan Colonial Indian. In *Handbook of Middle American Indians*, supplement 4, edited by R. Spores, 55–70. Austin: University of Texas Press.

Carmagnani, M.
1988 *El regreso de los dioses: El proceso de reconstitución de la identidad étnica en Oaxaca, siglos XVII y XVIII*. México, D.F.: Fondo de Cultura Económica.

Carrera Stampa, M.
1959 Las ferias novohispanas. In *Las ferias comerciales de Nueva España*. México, D.F.: Reedición del Instituto Mexicano del Comercio Exterior.

Carvajal, Agustín and Daniel Valencia
1989 La casa de Talavera. *Notas mesoamericanas* 11:229-245

Casagrande, J., S.I. Thompson, and P.D. Young
1964 Colonization as a research frontier: The Ecuadorian case. In *Process and pattern in culture*, edited by R.A. Manners, 281–325. Chicago: Aldine Publishing Co.

Castellanos, A.
1974 *Uruguay, monumentos históricos y arqueológicos*. México, D.F.: Instituto Panamericano de Geografía e Historia.

Castillo F., V. M.
1978 Matrícula de tributos. In *Historia de México*, 3:523–588. México, D.F.: Salvat Mexicana de Ediciones.

Castro G., F.
1986 *La extinción de la artesanía gremial*. México, D.F.: Universidad Nacional Autónoma de México.

Castro Seaone, J.
1943 La expansión de la merced de la América Colonial. *Revista de Indias* 4:405–440.

Ceruti, C. N.
1983 Evidencias del contacto hispano-indígena en la cerámica de San Fé la vieja (Cayastá). *Presencia Hispánica en la Arqueología Argentina* 2:487–519.

Chamberlain, R. S.
1948 *The conquest and colonization of Yucatan, 1517–1550*. Publication 582. Washington, DC: Carnegie Institution of Washington.
1953 *The conquest and colonization of Honduras, 1502–1550*. Publication 598. Washington, DC: Carnegie Institution of Washington.

Chance, J. K.
1986 Colonial ethnohistory of Oaxaca. In *Handbook of Middle American Indians*, supplement 4, edited by R. Spores, 165–189. Austin: University of Texas Press.

Chapman, A. M.
1978 *Los lencas de Honduras en el siglo XVI*. Tegucigalpa: Instituto Hondureño de Antropología e Historia.
1985 *Los hijos del copal y candela*. México, D.F.: Universidad Nacional Autónoma de México.

Charlton, T. H.
1972 *Post-conquest developments in the Teotihuacan Valley, Mexico. Part 1: Excavations*. Report 5, Office of State Archaeologist, Iowa City.
1986 Socioeconomic dimensions of urban-rural relations in the Colonial period Basin of Mexico. In *Handbook of Middle American Indians*, supplement 4, edited by R. Spores, 123–133. Austin: University of Texas Press.

Charlton, T. H., and P. Fournier-García
1993 Urban and rural dimensions of the contact period. Central Mexico, 1521–1620. In *Ethnohistory and archaeology: Approaches to postcontact change in the Americas*, edited by J.D. Rogers and S.M. Wilson, 201–220. New York: Plenum Press.

Charlton, T.H., P. Fournier-García, J. Hernández, and C. Otis-Charlton
1987 El palacio de Cortés, Cuernavaca: Estudios de materiales arqueológicos del período histórico. Ms. Informe presentado al Consejo de Arqueología. Archivo de la Dirección de Arqueología del Instituto Nacional de Antropología e Historia, México.

Cheek, C., and N. González
1986 Black Carib settlement patterns in early 18th century Honduras: The search for a livelihood. In *Ethnohistory: A researcher's guide*. Studies in Third World Societies 35:403–429.

Cheek, C. D., T. L. Struthers, K. Jacobs, and M. Alonso
1987 Archeological and architectural investigations of public, residential, and hydrological features at the mid-nineteenth century Quintana Baths, Ponce, Puerto Rico. Prepared for the Jacksonville District, US Army Corps of Engineers. John Milner Associates, West Chester, Pennsylvania.

Chevalier, F.
1952 *La formation des grands domaines au Mexique: Terre et societé aux XVIᵉ-XVIIᵉ siècles*. Paris: Institut d'Ethnologie.

Ciudad Real, Antonio de
1976 *Tratado curioso y docto de las grandezas de la Nueva España*. Instituto de Investigaciones Históricas. México, D.F.: Universidad Nacional Autónoma de México.

Clendinnen, I.
1987 *Ambivalent conquests: Maya and Spaniard in Yucatan, 1517–1570*. Cambridge: Cambridge University Press.

Cline, H. F.
1950 Related studies in early nineteenth century Yucatecan social history. Microfilm Collection of Manuscripts on Middle American Cultural Anthropology 32. University of Chicago Library, Chicago, Illinois.

Bibliography

Códice Chimalpopoca
1975 *Anales de Cuauhtitlan y leyenda de los soles.* México, D.F.: UniversidadNacional Autónoma de México.

Collins, A. C.
1977 The maestros cantores in Yucatan. In *Anthropology and History in Yucatan*, edited by G. D. Jones, 233–247. Austin: University of Texas Press.
1980 Colonial Jacaltenango, Guatemala: The formation of a corporate community. Ph.D. dissertation, Department of Anthropology, Tulane University, New Orleans.

Comisión Oficial del IVo. Centenario
1941 *Documentos históricos y geográficos relativos a la conquista y colonización rioplatense.* 5 vols. Buenos Aires: Municipalidad de la Ciudad de Buenos Aires, Argentina.

Comisión del Patrimonio Histórico, Artístico y Cultural de la Nación
1971 Su creación, Ley 14.040. *Diario Oficial*, 27 de octubre (24):189–191. Uruguay.

Conlazo, D.
1990 *Los indios de Buenos Aires, siglo XVI y XVII.* Buenos Aires: Busqueda-Yuchán.

Conrad, G.
1991 Personal communication

Conrad, G., and A. Webster
1989 Household unit patterning at San Antonio. In *Ecology, settlement and history in the Osmore Drainage, Peru*, edited by D. Rice, C. Stanish, and P. Scarr, 395–414. International Series 545. Oxford: British Archaeological Reports.

Contreras Guevara, A.
1946 Relación hecha a Su Majestad por el gobernador de Honduras, de todos los pueblos de dicha provincia (1582). *Boletín del Archivo General del Gobierno de Guatemala* 11:5–19.

Cook, N. D.
1981 *Demographic collapse: Indian Peru, 1520–1620.* Cambridge: Cambridge University Press.

Cortés, E.
1972 *San Simón de la Laguna.* México, D.F.: Instituto Nacional Indigenista.

Crawford, M. H., ed.
1984 *Current developments in anthropological genetics*, Vol. 3. *Black Caribs: A case study in biocultural adaptation.* New York: Plenum Press.

Cruz Reyes, V. C., S. Palacios, J. Aguilar, and O. Maldonado de Vasquez
1986 La labor misionera de la Orden de la Merced en la Alcaldía Mayor de Tegucigalpa (Fundación del Convento de Las Minas). Paper presented at La Conmemoración del V Centenario del Descubrimiento de América, Costa Rica.

Culebro, C. A.
1975 *Monografía histórica de Chiapas: La zona costera de Soconusco a través de su historia.* Huixtla, Chiapas, Mexico: Editorial Culebro.

Curbelo, C., and L. Cabrera
1993 Arqueología histórica en Isla Gorriti. Proyecto de recuperación y puesta en valor de los bienes histórico-culturales de la Bahía de Maldonado. *Patrimonio Cultural* Año 2(2). Ministerio de Educación y Cultura. Comisión del Patrimonio Histórico, Artístico y Cultural de la Nación. Montevideo, Uruguay.

Custred, G.
1974 Llameros y comercio interregional. In *Reciprocidad e intercambio en los Andes peruanos*, edited by G. Alberti and E. Mayer, 252–289. Lima: Instituto de Estudios Peruanos.

D'Altroy, T. N., and R. L. Bishop
1990 The provincial organization of Inka ceramic production. *American Antiquity* 55(1):120–138.

Davidson, G.
1984 The Garifuna in Central America: Ethnohistorical and geographical foundations. In *Current developments in anthropological genetics*, Vol. 3. *Black Caribs: A case study in biocultural adaptations*, edited by M. H. Crawford, 13–36. New York: Plenum Press.

Davies, K.
1984 *Landowners in Colonial Peru.* Austin: University of Texas Press.

Deagan, K.
1982 Avenues of inquiry in historical archaeology. In *Advances in archaeological method and theory*, vol. 5, edited by M. B. Schiffer, 151–177. New York: Academic Press.
1983 *Spanish St. Augustine: The archaeology of a Colonial creole community.* New York: Academic Press.
1984 Consultant's Report on the Second Seminar in Historical Archaeology. Instituto Nacional de Cultura, UNESCO and OAS. Manuscript in possession of the author and on file at Florida Museum of Natural History, Gainesville.
1987 *Artifacts of the Spanish colonies of Florida and the Caribbean, 1500–1800.* Vol. 1. *Ceramics, Glassware and Beads.* Washington, DC: Smithsonian Institution Press.

Deetz, J.
1991 Introduction: Archaeological evidence of sixteenth- and seventeenth-century encounters. In *Historical archaeology in global perspective*, edited by L. Falk, 1–9. Washington, DC: Smithsonian Institution Press.

Defourneaux, M.
1979 *Daily life in Spain in the Golden Age.* Stanford: Stanford University Press.

deFrance, S. D.
1993 Ecological imperialism in the south-central Andes: Faunal data from Spanish Colonial settlements in the Moquegua and Torata Valleys. Ph.D. dissertation, Department of Anthropology, University of Florida, Gainesville.
1991 Personal communication

de la Cruz de Lemos, V.
s.f. *Historia general de Costa Rica.* Euroamericana de Ediciones Costa Rica, S.A. Personal communication.

DeNiro, M.
1987 Stable isotopy and archaeology. *American Scientist* 75:182–191.
1988 Marine food sources for prehistoric coastal Peruvian camelids: Isotopic evidence and implications. In *Economic prehistory of the Andes*, edited by E. Wing and J. Wheeler, 119–130. International Series 427.

Diario El País
1977 Isla Gorriti: Cobra interés proyecto turístico. 23 de octubre. Montevideo, Uruguay.

Diaz del Castillo, B.
1912 *The true history of the conquest of New Spain.* London: Hakluyt Society.

Diez de San Miguel, G.
1964 *Visita hecha a la provincia de Chucuito por Garci Diez de San Miguel en el año 1567.* Lima: Casa de la Cultura Peruana.

Dobyns, H. F., and P. L. Doughty
1976 *Peru: A cultural history.* New York: Oxford University Press.

Domínguez, L.
1978 La transculturación en Cuba (s. XVI-XVII). In *Cuba Arqueológica,* 1:33-50. Santiago de Cuba: Editorial Oriente.
1980 Presencia de porcelana oriental en algunos sitios coloniales de La Habana. In *Cuba Arqueológica* 2:27–37. Santiago de Cuba: Editorial Oriente.
1984 *Arqueología colonial cubana. Dos estudios.* Habana, Cuba: Editorial de Ciencias Sociales.
1989 La cerámica del sitio arqueológico El Yayal, Holguín. *Revista de Historia,* Año 3, 1(90):93–102. Holguín, Cuba.

Douglas, M., and B. Isherwood
1979 *The world of goods.* New York: Basic Books.

Dow, J. W.
1974 *Santos y supervivencias: Funciones de la religión en una comunidad otomí, México.* México, D.F.: Instituto Nacional Indigenista, México.

Dumond, C. S., and D. E. Dumond, eds.
1982 *Demography and parish affairs in Yucatan 1797–1897.* University of Oregon Anthropological Paper 27. Portland: University of Oregon.

Farnsworth, P. and J. S. Williams, eds.
1992 The archaeology of the Spanish Colonial and Mexican Republican periods. *Historical Archaeology* 26(1).

Faron, L. C.
1985 *From conquest to agrarian reform: Ethnicity, ecology, and economy in the Chancay Valley, Peru: 1533–1964.* Pittsburgh: University of Pittsburgh.

Farriss, N. M.
1968 *Crown and clergy in Colonial Mexico 1759–1821: The crisis of ecclesiastical privilege.* London: Athlone Press.
1984 *Maya society under Colonial rule: The collective enterprise of survival.* Princeton: Princeton University Press.
1986 Indians in Colonial northern Yucatan. In *Handbook of Middle American Indians,* supplement 4, edited by R. Spores, 88–102. Austin: University of Texas Press.

Feldman, L., and A. G. Mastache
1990 *Indice de documentos sobre el centro de México y cartografía antigua del área de Tula.* Colección Fuentes. México, D.F.: Instituto Nacional de Antropología e Historia.

Felton, D. L., and P. D. Schulz
1983 The Diaz Collection: Material culture and social change in mid-nineteenth century Monterrey. California Archeological Reports 23. Resources Protection Division, Cultural Resource Management Unit, Department of Parks and Recreation, Sacramento, California.

Ferguson, L. G.
1978 Looking for the "Afro-" in Colono-Indian pottery. *Conference on historic site archaeology* 12:68–86. Columbia, SC: Institute of Archaeology and Anthropology, University of South Carolina.

Fernández, J.
1982 *Historia de la arqueología argentina.* Mendoza, Argentina: Asociación Cuyana de Antropología.

Finney, K. V.
1985 Honduras. In *Research guide to Central America and the Caribbean,* edited by K. J. Grieb, 44–53. Madison: University of Wisconsin Press.

Fliert, L. V. de
1988 *El otomí en busca de la vida.* Querétero, México: Universidad Autónoma de Querétaro.

Flores Espinosa, I., R. García Soto, and L. Huertas V.
1981 Investigación arqueológica-histórica de la Casa Osambela (o de Oquendo), Lima. Lima: Instituto Nacional de Cultura.

Floyd, T. S.
1967 *The Anglo-Spanish struggle for Central America.* Albuquerque: University of New Mexico Press.

Fonseca Martel, C.
1972 La economía "vertical" y la economía de mercado en las comunidades altenas del Perú. In *Visita de la Provincia de León de Huánuco en 1562,* vol. 2, edited by John Murra, 317–338. Facultad de Letras y Ciencias, Universidad Nacional Hermilio Valdizan.

Fortunato, A.M.
1982 The Redemption as the fourth vow in the Mercedarian Order. Master's thesis, John Carroll University, University Heights, Ohio.

Fossari, T. D., ed.
1992 A pesquisa arqueológica do sítio histórico São José da Ponta Grossa. *Annais do Museu de Antropologia,* Ano 19, E. 20(19):35–103. Universidade Federal de Santa Catarina, Brasil.

Fournier-García, P.
1985a Arqueología histórica en la Ciudad de México. *Boletín de Antropología Americana* 11:27-31. Instituto Panamericano de Geografía e Historia, México.
1985b Evidencias arqueológicas de la importación de cerámica en México con base en los materiales del ex-convento de San Jerónimo. Tesis de Licenciatura en Arqueología, Escuela Nacional de Antropología e Historia, México.
1989 Veinte tiestos de mayólica procedentes de Ecuador. In *Tres estudios sobre cerámica histórica,* edited by P. Fournier, M. de Lourdes Fournier, and E. Silva, 62–66. México, D.F.: Instituto Nacional de Antropología e Historia.
1990 *Evidencias arqueológicas de la importación de cerámica en México, con base en los materiales del exconvento de San Jerónimo.* Colección Científica 213. México, D.F.: Instituto Nacional de Antropología e Historia.
1991 Etnoarqueología cerámica otomí. *Revista Mexicana de estudios antropológicos* 36:129–137. Sociedad Mexicana de Antropología, México.

1993a   Arqueología del colonialismo de España y Portugal: Imperios contrastantes en el Nuevo Mundo. Unpublished paper presented at the Conference Arqueología Histórica Americana. Colonia del Sacramento, Uruguay.

1993b   Alfarería y continuidad histórica entre los hñähñü del Valle del Mezquital, Hidalgo, México. Unpublished paper presented at the XIII Congreso Internacional de Ciencias Antropológicas y Etnológicas, México, D.F.

Fournier-García, P., ed.

1993c   Etnoarqueología cerámica otomí. Ms. Informe presentado a la Dirección Adjunta de Investigación Científica del Consejo Nacional de Ciencia y Tecnología, México.

Fournier-García, P., and J. Cedeño

1993   In the land of agave: Pulque and Otomí ethnic identification in Central Mexico. Unpublished paper presented at the XIII Congreso Internacional de Ciencias Antropológicas y Etnológicas, México, D.F.

Fournier-García, P. and T. H. Charlton

1993   Las colecciones de mayólica procedentes del Templo Mayor. Unpublished preliminary report submitted to Dr. Eduardo Matos Moctezuma. Archivo del Proyecto Templo Mayor del Instituto Nacional de Antropología e Historia, México.

Fournier-García, P., T. H. Charlton, and M. Aronson

1993   Análisis tecnoestilístico de la tradición de mayolica Colonial en Nueva España. Unpublished paper presented at the XIII Congreso Internacional de Ciencias Antropológicas y Etnológicas, México, D.F.

Fournier-García, P., and L. Fournier

1992   Catalogación y periodificación de materiales históricos de Sonora. In *La frontera Protohistórica Pima-Opata en Sonora, México*, vol. 3, edited by B. Braniff, 923–962. Colección Científica 241. México, D.F.: Instituto Nacional de Antropología e Historia.

Fournier-García, P., and F. A. Miranda-Flores

1992   Historic sites archaeology in Mexico. *Historical Archaeology* 26:75–83.

Frank, A. G.

1979   *La acumulación mundial, 1492–1789*. Madrid: Siglo Veintiuno de España Editores.

Fuentes y Guzmán, F. A. de

1933   *Recordación Florida: Discurso historial y demostración natural, militar y política del Reyno de Guatemala* (c.1675). Guatemala: Tipografía Nacional.

Funari, P. A.

1992   La arqueología en Brasil: Política y academia en una encrucijada. In *Arqueología en América Latina hoy*, edited by Gustavo Politis, 57–69. Biblioteca Banco Popular, Bogotá, Colombia.

Fusco Zambetogliris, N.

1990   Colonia del Sacramento: Un relevamiento sistemático en la zona urbana. *Boletín de Arqueología*, Año 2. 2:31–37. Montevideo, Uruguay.

1993   Arqueología urbana en la Colonia del Sacramento. Ponencia presentada en la VII Reunião Científica da Sociedade de Arqueologia Brasileira. João Pessoa, Paraiba, Brasil.

1995   Arqueología histórica. Ejemplos para el análisis de la interdisciplinariedad en el Uruguay. *Revista de Estudios Iberoamericanos*. Porto Alegre, Brasil.

Fusco Zambetogliris, N., L. Cabrera, C. Curbelo, and E. Martínez

1987   Investigaciones arqueológicas en Isla Gorriti (Dpto. de Maldonado). In *Primeras jornadas de ciencias antropológicas en el Uruguay*, 105–110. Ministerio de Educación y Cultura. Museo Nacional de Antropología, Montevideo, Uruguay.

Fusco Zambetogliris, N., and J. López Mazz

1992   La arqueología de los episodios Coloniales del Río de la Plata. *Patrimonio Cultural*, Año 1, 1:7–16. Ministerio de Educación y Cultura. Comisión del Patrimonio Histórico, Artístico y Cultural de la Nación. Montevideo, Uruguay.

Gade, D., and M. Escobar

1982   Village settlement and the Colonial legacy in southern Peru. *Geographic Review* 72:430–49.

Galinier, J.

1976   Oratoires Otomis de la región de Tulancingo. *Actas del XLI Congreso Internacional de Americanistas*. 3:158–171. México.

1990   *La mitad del mundo: Cuerpo y cosmos en los rituales otomíes*. México, D.F.: Universidad Nacional Autónoma de México, Centro de Estudios Mexicanos y Centroamericanos, Instituto Nacional Indigenista, México.

Gall, F., ed.

1978-1983   *Diccionario geográfico de Guatemala*. 4 vols. Guatemala: Tipografía Nacional, Instituto Geográfico Nacional.

García, V.

1991   Personal communication.

García, V., Hill R., and Shook, E.

1991   Personal communication

Garrow, P. H.

1987   The use of converging lines of evidence for determining socioeconomic status. In *Consumer choice in historical archaeology*, edited by S. Spencer-Wood, 217–231. New York: Plenum Press.

Gasco, J. L.

1987   *Cacao and the economic integration of native society in Colonial Soconusco, New Spain*. Ann Arbor: University Microfilms International.

1989a   The Colonial economy in the Province of Soconusco. In *Ancient trade and tribute: Economies of the Soconusco region of Mesoamerica*, edited by B. Voorhies, 287–303. Salt Lake City: University of Utah Press.

1989b   Economic history of Ocelocalco, a Colonial Soconusco town. In *Ancient trade and tribute: Economies of the Soconusco region of Mesoamerica*, edited by B. Voorhies, 304–325. Salt Lake City: University of Utah Press.

1989c   Una visión de conjunto de la historia demográfica y económica del Soconusco Colonial. *Mesoamérica* 18:371–399.

1990   Reconocimiento de pueblos Coloniales en la Provincia del Soconusco. *Boletín del Consejo de Arqueología*, 124–126.

1991   Indian survival and ladinoization in Colonial Soconusco. In *Columbian consequences*, vol. 3, edited by David H. Thomas, 301–318. Washington, DC: Smithsonian Institution Press.

1992   Material culture and Colonial Indian society in southern Mesoamerica: The view from coastal Chiapas, Mexico. In *The archaeology of the Spanish*

Colonial and Mexican Republican periods, edited by P. Farnsworth and J. S. Williams. *Historical Archaeology* 26(1):67–74.

1993 Socioeconomic change within Native society in Colonial Soconusco, New Spain. In *Ethnohistory and archaeology: Approaches to postcontact change in the Americas*, edited by J. D. Rogers and S. M. Wilsson, 163–180. New York: Plenum Press.

Gaston, M. F.
1990 *Blue Willow: An identification and value guide*. Paducah, Kentucky: Collector Books.

Geertz, C.
1963 *Agricultural involution: The process of ecological change in Indonesia*. Berkeley: University of California Press.

Geranio, S.
1928 Edilicia colonial. La Puerta de la Ciudadela y la Casa de los Ejercicios. *Revista de la Sociedad Amigos de la Arqueología* 2:317–330. Montevideo, Uruguay.

Gerhard, P.
1986 *Geografía histórica de la Nueva España, 1519–1821*. México, D.F.: Universidad Nacional Autónoma de México.
1993 *The southeast frontier of New Spain*. Rev. ed. Norman: University of Oklahoma Press.

Gibson, C.
1964 *The Aztecs under Spanish rule: A history of the Indians of the Valley of Mexico, 1519–1810*. Stanford: Stanford University Press.
1966 *Spain in America*. New York: Harper and Row.
1980 *Los aztecas bajo el dominio español, 1519–1810*. México, D.F.: Siglo Veintiuno Editores.

Gifford, J.C.
1960 The type-variety method of ceramic classification as an indicator of cultural phenomena. *American Antiquity* 25(3):341–347.

Glick, T. F.
1979 *Islamic and Christian Spain in the Early Middle Ages*. Princeton: Princeton University Press.

Goggin, J. M.
1960 *The Spanish olive jar: An introductory study*. Yale University Publications in Anthropology 62. New Haven: Yale University.
1968 *Spanish majolica in the New World*. Yale University Publications in Anthropology 72. New Haven: Yale University.

Goldstein, P.
1993 House, community, and state in the earliest Tiwanaku colony: Domestic patterns and state integration at Omo M12, Moquegua. In *Domestic architecture, ethnicity, and complementarity in the south-central Andes*, edited by M. Aldenderfer, 25–41. Iowa City: University of Iowa Press.

Gonçalves de Lima, Oswaldo
1986 *El maguey y el pulque en los códices mexicanos*. México, D.F.: Fondo de Cultura Económica.

González, N. L.
1988 *Sojourners of the Caribbean: Ethnogenesis and ethnohistory of the Garifuna*. Urbana: University of Illinois Press.

González Martí, M.
1944 *Cerámica del levante español, siglos medievales. Loza*. Barcelona: Editorial Labor.

González Obregón, L.
1983 *Las calles de México*. México, D.F.: Promociones Editoriales Mexicanas.

González Quintero, L.
1968 *Tipos de vegetación del Valle del Mezquital, Hidalgo*. Serie Paleoecología 2. México, D.F.: Instituto Nacional de Antropología e Historia.

Graham, E.
1991 Archaeological insights into Colonial period Maya life at Tipu, Belize. In *Colombian Consequences*, vol. 3, edited by D. H. Thomas, 319–335. Washington, DC: Smithsonian Institution Press.

Graham, E., D. M. Pendergast, and G. D. Jones
1989 On the fringes of conquest: Maya-Spanish contact in Colonial Belize. *Science* 246:1254–1259.

Granado Baeza, B.
1845 Informe dado por el cura de Yaxcaba. In *Registro Yucateco*, vol. 1. Colección Alfredo Barrera Vásquez, Centro Regional de Yucatán, Instituto Nacional de Antropología e Historia, Merida, Yucatán.

Grieshaber, E. P.
1979 Hacienda-Indian community relations and Indian acculturation: An historiographical essay. *Latin American Research Review* 14(3):107–128.

Grijalva, Fray J. de
1985 *Crónica de la Orden de nuestro padre San Agustín en las provincias de la Nueva España: En cuatro edades desde el año de 1533 hasta el de 1592*. México, D.F.: Editorial Porrúa.

Guerrero, R.
1983 *Los otomíes del Valle del Mezquital*. México, D.F.: Gobierno del Estado de Hidalgo. Instituto Nacional de Antropología e Historia.
1985 *El pulque*. Contrapuntos. México, D.F.: Instituto Nacional de Antropología e Historia.

Guíbovich, P.
1984 Índice del primer libro notarial de Moquegua. In *Contribuciones a los estudios de los Andes centrales*, edited by S. Masuda, 174–405. Tokyo: University of Tokyo.

Guillemin, J.
1977 Urbanism and hierarchy at Iximche. In *Social process in Maya prehistory*, edited by N. Hammond, 227–264. New York: Academic Press.

Hamerly, M. T.
1973 *Historia social y económica de la antigua Provincia de Guayaquil, 1763–1842*. Guayaquil, Ecuador: Publicaciones del Archivo Histórico del Guayas.

Harris, M.
1964 *Patterns of race in the Americas*. New York: Norton.

Hatch, M. P.
1987 La importancia de la cerámica utilitaria en arqueología con observaciones sobre la prehistoria de Guatemala. *Anales de la Academia de Geografía e Historia de Guatemala* 61:151–183.

Healy, P. F.
1984 The archaeology of Honduras. In *The archaeology of lower Central America*, edited by D.Z. Stone and F.W. Lange, 113–161. Albuquerque: University of New Mexico Press.

Heberling, S. D.
1985 "All earthenware plain and flowered": Socio-economic

Bibliography

    status and consumer choice in ceramics on early nineteenth-century historic sites. Master's thesis, University of Massachusetts, Boston.

Helbig, C.
1964   *El Soconusco y su zona cafetalera en Chiapas*. Tuxtla Gutiérrez, Chiapas, México: Instituto de Ciencias y Artes de Chiapas.

Helms, M. W.
1976   Introduction. In *Frontier adaptations in lower Central America*, edited by M. W. Helms and F. O. Lovejoy, 1–22. Philadelphia: Institute for the Study of Human Issues.

Hernández A., J.
1980   Catálogo de vidrio. Exconvento de San Jerónimo. Ms. Informe inédito. Dirección de Monumentos Históricos del Instituto Nacional de Antropología e Historia, México.
1992   Comunicación personal

Herrera Canales, I.
1977   *El comercio exterior de México, 1821–1975*. México, D.F.: El Colegio de México.

Herrera y Tordesillas, A. de
1726-1730   *The general history of the vast continent and islands of America, commonly called the West Indies*. London: J. Batley.

Hill, R.
1991   Personal communication

Hodder, I.
1984   Survey 2: Ideology and power--the archaeological debate. *Society and space* 2:347–353.

Holm, O.
1968   Ignacia, la alfarera de Cerro Alto (Ecuador). *Cuadernos de Historia y Arqueología* 33:240–282. Guayaquil: Casa de la Cultura Ecuatoriana, Núcleo del Guayas.
1971   La cerámica Colonial del Ecuador. *Boletín de la Academia Nacional de Historia* 116:265–278. Quito.

Hunt, M. Espejo-Ponce
1974   Colonial Yucatan: Town and region in the seventeenth century. Ph.D. dissertation, Department of History, University of California, Los Angeles.
1976   The processes of the development of Yucatan, 1600–1700. In *Provinces of early Mexico: Variants of Spanish American regional evolution*, vol. 36, edited by I. Altman and J. Lockhart, 33–62. Los Angeles: UCLA Latin American Center Publications.

Hyslop, J.
1990   *Inka settlement planning*. Austin: University of Texas Press.

Idrovo Uriguen, J.
1990   Siglos XVI y XVII: La desarticulación del mundo andino y sus efectos en la alfarería indígena del austro ecuatoriano. In *Cerámica Colonial y vida cotidiana*, 21–38. Cuenca, Ecuador: Fundación Paul Rivet.

Inamura, T.
1981   Adaptación ambiental de los pastores altoandinos en el sur del Perú. In *Estudios etnográficos del Perú meridional*, edited by S. Masuda, 65–83. Tokyo: University of Tokyo Press.

Instituto Histórico de la Orden de la Merced
1986   *La Orden de la Merced Espíritu y Vida*. Rome: Tipografía Guanella.

Israel, J.A.
1980   *Razas, clases sociales y vida política en el México Colonial, 1610–1670*. México, D.F.: Fondo de Cultura Económica.

Johnson, K.
1982   Resource-use knowledge among the Otomí Indians of the Mezquital, México. *National Geographic Society Research Reports*, vol. 14, edited by P.H. Oehser, J.S. Lea, and N.L. Powars, 315–324. Washington, DC: National Geographic Society.

Jones, D. M.
1980   The archaeology of nineteenth century haciendas and ranchos of Otumba and Apan, Basin of Mexico. Post-conquest developments in the Teotihuacan Valley, Mexico, part 5. In *Mesoamerican research colloquium research report 2*: Department of Anthropology, University of Iowa, Iowa City.

Joseph, J. W., and S. C. Byrne
1992   Socio-economics and trade in Viejo San Juan, Puerto Rico: Observations from the Ballajá Archeological Project. In *The archaeology of the Spanish Colonial and Mexican Republican periods*, edited by P. Farnsworth and J. S. Williams, 45–58. Historical Archaeology 26(1).

Julien, C.
1983   *Hatunqolla: A view of Inca rule from the Lake Titicaca region*. University of California Publications in Anthropology 15. Berkeley: Univ of California Press.
1985   Guano and resource control in sixteenth-century Arequipa. In *Andean ecology and civilization*, edited by S. Masuda, I. Shimada, and C. Morris, 185–231. Tokyo: University of Tokyo Press.

Kelemen, P.
1967   *Baroque and rococo in Latin America*. New York: Dover Publications.

Kennedy T., A.
1989   Historia artística y arquitectónica del Convento de Santo Domingo de Quito. Ms. Informe Parcial, vol. 1. Proyecto de Cooperación Técnica Ecuatoriana–Belga. Quito.
1990   Apuntes sobre arquitectura en tierra y cerámica en la Colonia. In *Cerámica Colonial y vida cotidiana*, 39–60. Cuenca, Ecuador: Fundación Paul Rivet.

Kolonitz, P.
1984   *Un viaje a México en 1864*. México, D.F.: Secretaría de Educación Pública.

Konrad, H. W.
1980   *A Jesuit hacienda in Colonial Mexico: Santa Lucia, 1576–1767*. Stanford: Stanford University Press.

Kramer, W.
1988   The politics of encomienda distribution in early Spanish Guatemala 1524–1544. Ph.D. dissertation, University of Warwick, England.

Kubler, G.
1946   The Quechua in the Colonial world. In *Handbook of South American Indians*, vol. 2, edited by Julian H. Steward, 331–410, Washington, DC: Smithsonian Institution.
1990   *Arquitectura mexicana del siglo XVI*. México, D.F.: Fondo de Cultura Económica.

Lanning, E. P.
1967   Archaeological investigations on the Santa Elena

Peninsula, Ecuador. Unpublished report to the National Science Foundation on research carried out under Grant GS-402, 1964–1965.

Lara Pinto, G.
1980 Beitrage zur indianischen Ethnographie von Honduras in der 1. halfte des 16. Jahrhunderts unter besonderer Berucksichtigung der historischen Demographie. Ph.D. dissertation, University of Hamburg.
1982 La región de El Cajón en la etnohistoria de Honduras. *Yaxkin* 5(1):37–50.
1985 Apuntes sobre la afiliación cultural de los pobladores indígenas de los valles de Comayagua y Sulaco, siglo XVI. *Mesoamérica* 9:45–52.
1991 Change for survival: The case of the sixteenth century indigenous populations of northeast and mideast Honduras. In *Columbian Consequences*, vol. 3, edited by D. H. Thomas, 227–243. Washington, DC: Smithsonian Institution Press.

La Salvia, F., and J. Bracho
1989 *Cerámica Guarani*. Porto Alegre, Brasil: Posenato Arte y Cultura.

Lechuga, M. del C., and F. Rivas
1989 La arqueología del pulque. Tesis de Licenciatura en Arqueología, Escuela Nacional de Antropología e Historia, México.

LeeDecker, C. H., T. Klein, C. A. Holt, and A. Friedlander
1987 Nineteenth-century households and consumer behavior in Wilmington, Delaware. In *Consumer choice in historical archaeology*, edited by S. M. Spencer-Wood, 233–259. New York: Plenum Press.

Lerdo de Tejada, M.
1967 *Comercio exterior de México desde la conquista hasta hoy*. Facsimilar de la edición de 1853. México, D.F.: Banco Nacional de Comercio Exterior.

Libro de las tasaciones de pueblos de la Nueva España. Siglo XVI
1952 Prólogo de Francisco González de Cossío. México, D.F.: Archivo General de la Nación.

Lindao Quimí, R. and K. Stothert
1994 *El uso vernáculo de los árboles y plantas en la Península de Santa Elena*. Guayaquil: Fundación Pro-Pueblo, La Cemento Nacional y Subdirección Programas Culturales, Banco Central del Ecuador.
1995 *Así fue mi crianza: Recuerdos de un nativo de la Parroquia Chanduy*. Guayaquil: Fundación Pro-Pueblo, La Cemento Nacional.

Lister, F. C., and R. H. Lister
1974 Maiolica in Colonial Spanish America. *Historical Archaeology* 8:17–52.
1978 The First Mexican Maiolicas: Imported and locally produced. *Historical Archaeology* 12:1-24
1982a *Sixteenth century maiolica pottery in the Valley of Mexico*. Anthropological Papers, 39. Tucson: University of Arizona Press.
1982b The potter's quarter of Colonial Puebla, Mexico. *Historical Archaeology* 18:87–102.
1987 *Andalusian ceramics in Spain and New Spain. A cultural register from the third century B.C. to 1700*. Tucson: University of Arizona Press.

Livingstone, D., and W. Clayton
1980 An altitudinal cline in tropical African grass floras and its paleoecological significance. *Quaternary Research* 13:392–402.

Lockhart, J.
1968 *Spanish Peru, 1532–1560: A Colonial society*. Madison: University of Wisconsin Press.

Long, G. A.
1967 Archaeological excavations at Panama Vieja. Master's thesis, Department of Anthropology, University of Florida, Gainesville.

López, L. and L. Huertas
1990 Relación de viñas y bodegas de Moquegua, siglos XVI y XVII. *Trabajos arqueológicos en Moquegua, Perú*, vol. 3, edited by L.K. Watanabe, M.E. Moseley, and F. Cabieses, 255–258. Lima: Museo Peruano de Ciencias de la Salud and Southern Peru Copper Corporation.

López Águilar, F., and P. Fournier-García
1991 Estudios de cultura material en "pueblos sin historia": Las investigaciones sobre los hñähñü del Valle del Mezquital. *Cuicuilco* 27:7–14. Escuela Nacional de Antropología e Historia, México.
1992 Proyecto Valle del Mezquital. *Boletín del Consejo de Arqueología*, 1991, 173–175. Consejo Nacional para la Cultura y las Artes-Instituto Nacional de Antropología e Historia.

López Águilar, F., P. Fournier-García, and C. Paz
1988 Contextos arqueológicos y contextos momento. El caso de la alfarería otomí del Valle del Mezquital. *Boletín de Antropología Americana* 18:99–131.

López Coda
Comunicación personal

Lovell, W. G.
1985 *Conquest and survival in Colonial Guatemala: A historical geography of the Cuchumatán Highlands, 1500–1821*. Kingston: McGill–Queen's University Press.

Luján Muñoz, J.
1988 *Agricultura y sociedad en el Corregimiento del Valle de Guatemala, 1670–80*. Cuaderno de Investigación 2-88. Dirección General de Investigación, Guatemala: Universidad de San Carlos de Guatemala.

Luján Muñoz, L.
1972 *Síntesis de la arquitectura en Guatemala*. Guatemala: Universidad de San Carlos de Guatemala.
1974 Legislación protectora de los bienes culturales de Guatemala. Consejo Nacional para la Protección de los Bienes Culturales de Guatemala, 1974.
1977 *Fuentes de Antigua Guatemala*. Consejo Nacional para la Protección de Antigua Guatemala. Guatemala: Editorial José Pineda Ibarra.
1981 Algo sobre la arqueología en Antigua Guatemala. Carta suplemento Carta Informativa. Consejo Nacional para la Protección de Antigua, Guatemala, mayo-junio 1981.
1982a *El Arquitecto Mayor Diego de Porres 1677-1741*. Guatemala: Editorial Universitaria.
1982b Arqueología histórica en Antigua Guatemala. In *Historia y antropología. Ensayos en honor a J. Daniel Contreras R.* Guatemala: Facultad de Humanidades Universidad de San Carlos.

Lutz, C.
1981 Historia de la población de la Parroquia de San Miguel Dueñas, Guatemala: 1530–1770. *Mesoamérica* 2:64–82.

1984   *Historia sociodemográfica de Santiago de Guatemala 1541–1773.* Guatemala: Centro de Investigaciones Regionales de Mesoamérica.

MacLeod, M. J.
1973   *Spanish Central America: A socioeconomic history, 1520–1720.* Berkeley: University of California Press.
1983   Ethnic relations and Indian society in the Province of Guatemala, ca. 1620–1800. In *Spaniards and Indians in southeastern Mesoamerica, Essays on the history of ethnic relations,* edited by M. J. MacLeod and R. Wasserstrom, 189–214. Lincoln: University of Nebraska Press.
1985   Indian family size in seventeenth century Honduras: Some implications for Colonial demographic history. In *Estudios del reino de Guatemala: Homanaje al Profesor S.D. Markman,* edited by D. Kinkead, 101–116. Sevilla: Escuela de Estudios Hispano Americanos.

Mariátegui, J. C.
1971   *Seven interpretive essays on Peruvian reality.* Austin: University of Texas Press.

Markman, Sidney D.
1966   *Colonial architecture of Antigua Guatemala.* Philadelphia: The American Philosophical Society.
1984   *Architecture and urbanization in Colonial Chiapas, México.* American Philosophical Society Memoir 153. Philadelphia: American Philosophical Society.

Martínez Compañon, B.
1985   *Trujillo del Perú.* Madrid: Ediciones Cultura Hispánica.

Martínez Sarasola, C.
1992   *Nuestros paisanos los indios.* Buenos Aires: Emecé.

Marx, C.
1974a   *Contribución a la crítica de la economía política.* México, D.F.: Ediciones de Cultura Popular.
1974b   *El Capital. Crítica de la economía política,* vol. 1. México, D.F.: Fondo de Cultura Económica.

Marx, C., and F. Engels
s.f.   *Obras escogidas.* Moscú: Editorial Progreso.

Marzal, M. M.
1981   *Historia de la antropología indigenista: México y Perú.* Lima: Fondo Editorial de la Pontificia Universidad Católica del Perú.
1983   *La transformación religiosa peruana.* Lima: Fondo Editorial de la Pontificia Universidad Católica del Perú.

Mendizabal, M. O. de
1947   Evolución económica y social del Valle del Mezquital. In *Obras completas* 6:7–258. México, D.F.: Talleres Gráficos de la Nación.

Mentz-Ribeiro, P. A., C. Torrano-Ribeiro, and I. da Silveira
1988   Arqueología e história da Aldeia de São Nicolau do Rio Pardo, RS, Brasil. *Revista do CEPA* 15(18):5–92. Facultades Integradas de Santa Cruz do Sul, Brasil.

McEwan, B.G.
1992   The role of ceramics in Spain and Spanish America during the 16th century. In *The archaeology of the Spanish Colonial and Mexican Republican periods,* edited by P. Farnsworth and J. S. Williams, 92–108. *Historical Archaeology* 26(1).

Miller, G. L.
1980   Classification and economic scaling of 19th century ceramics. *Historical Archaeology* 14:1–40.
1986   Of fish and sherds: A model for estimating vessel populations from minimal vessel counts. *Historical Archaeology* 20:59–85.
1987   Origins of Josiah Wedgwood's "Pearlware." *Northeast Historical Archaeology* 16:83–95.

Moir, R.
    Personal communication

Mondragón, L., and N. Noguera
1992   Las fuentes documentales y la evidencia arqueológica. Ponencia presentada en el XIV Encuentro Nacional de Estudiantes de Historia, Monterrey, Nuevo León, México.

Mondragón, L., N. Noguera, and P. Fournier-García
1991   Cultura material de los hñähñü de Santa María del Pino, Hidalgo: La arquitectura religiosa. *Revista mexicana de Estudios Antropológicos* 36:119–127. Sociedad Mexicana de Antropología.

Montejo, F. de
1864   Carta del adelantado don Francisco de Montejo sobre el estado y accidentes de la provincia de Guatemala (1539). In *Colección de documentos inéditos relativos al descubrimiento, conquista y organización de las antiguas posesiones españoles de América y Oceania* 24: 250–297. Madrid: Imprenta Español.

Moreno, H., ed.
1985   *Los agustinos, aquellos misioneros hacendados: Historia de la Provincia de San Nicolás de Tolentino de Michoacán, escrita por Fray Diego de Basalenque.* México, D.F.: Secretaría de Educación Pública/Cultura.

Moreno Toscano, A.
1976   El siglo de la conquista. In *Historia general de* 2:1–81. México, D.F.: El Colegio de México.

Morner, M.
1967   *Race mixture in the history of the Americas.* Boston: Little, Brown and Company.
1975   La hacienda hispanoamericana: Examen de las investigaciones y debates recientes. In *Haciendas, latifundios, y plantaciones en América Latina,* edited by E. Florescano, 15–48. México D.F.: Siglo veintiuno Editores.

Mujica, E.J., M. A. Rivera, and T. F. Lynch
1983   Proyecto de estudio sobre la complementariedad económica tiwanaku en los valles occidentales de centro-sur andino. *Revista Chungara* 11.

Murra, J.
1964   Una apreciación etnológica de la visita. In *Visita hecha a la provincia de Chucuito por Garci Diez de San Miguel en el año 1567,* 421–442. Lima: Casa de la Cultura Peruana.
1972   El "control vertical" de un máximo de pisos ecológicos en la economía de las sociedades andinas. In *Visita de la provincia de Huánuco, por Inigo Ortiz de Zuniga* 2:427–476. Huánuco, Perú: Universidad Hermilio Valdizan.
1985   The limits and limitations of the "vertical archipelago" in the Andes. In *Andean ecology and civilization: An interdisciplinary perspective on Andean ecological complimentarity,* edited by S. Masuda, I. Shimada, and C. Morris, 14–20. Tokyo: University of Tokyo.

Navarrete, C.
1978   The prehispanic system of communication between Chiapas and Tabasco. In *Mesoamerican communication*

routes and cultural contacts, edited by T. A. Lee, Jr. and C. Navarrete, 75–106. Papers of the New World Archaeological Foundation 40. Provo: Brigham Young University Press.
1994 Personal communication

Newson, L.
1986 *The cost of conquest: Indian decline in Honduras under Spanish rule.* Boulder, Colorado: Westview Press.

Núñez Henríquez, P.
1984 La antigua aldea de San Lorenzo de Tarapaca, Norte de Chile. *Revista Chungara* 13:53–65.

Obregón, G.
s.f. La mesa mexicana. *Artes de México* 107(1):60–63. México.

Odriozola, M. A.
1970 La antigua Colonia del Sacramento. *Los Departamentos: Colonia* 14:45–49. Ediciones Nuestra Tierra, Montevideo, Uruguay.

Onega, E., M. Caporale, and V. Mata
1991 Análisis de los materiales cerámicos del área "Casa del Gobernador." Ponencia presentada en la VI Reunião Científica da Sociedade de Arqueología Brasileira. Río de Janeiro.

Otto, J. S.
1977 Artifacts and status differences: A comparison from planter, overseer, and slave sites on an antebellum plantation. In *Research strategies in historical archaeology*, edited by Stanley South, 91–118. New York: Academic Press.

Pahl, G. W.
1988 The survey and excavation of La Canteada, Copán, Honduras: Preliminary report, 1975 season. In *The periphery of the southeastern Classic Maya realm*, edited by G. W. Pahl, 227–261. Los Angeles: UCLA Latin American Center Publications.

Palacios, S.
1987 *Las iglesias Coloniales de la ciudad de Comayagua.* Tegucigalpa: Instituto Hondureño de Antropología e Historia.

Palerm, A.
1979 Sobre la formación del sistema Colonial: Apuntes para una discusión. In *Ensayos sobre el desarrollo ecónomico de México y América Latina (1500–1975)*, edited by E. Florescano, 93–127. México, D.F: Fondo de Cultura Económica.

Parker, J., and K. Stothert
1983 Weaving a cotton saddlebag on a two-bar vertical loom on the Santa Elena Peninsula, Ecuador. *The Textile Museum Journal* 22:19–32.

Parsons, J. R.
1971 *Prehistoric settlement patterns in the Texcoco region, Mexico.* Museum of Anthropology Memoir 3. Ann Arbor: University of Michigan.

Paso y Troncoso, F. del
1905 Descripción del Arzobispado de México. *Papeles de Nueva España*, vol. 3. Sucesores de Rivadeneyra. Madrid: Imprenta de la Real Casa.
1979 *Colección de Mendoza o Códice Mendocino.* Introducción, textos y comentarios de Jesús Galindo y Villa. México, D.F: Editorial Cosmos.

Patch, R.
1979 *A Colonial regime: Maya and Spaniard in Yucatán.* Ann Arbor: University Microfilms International.
1985 Agrarian change in eighteenth-century Yucatán. *Hispanic American Historical Review* 65(1):21–49.
1988 Personal communication
1993 *Maya and Spaniard in Yucatan, 1648–1812.* Stanford: Stanford University Press.

Pease, F.G.Y.
1982 The formation of Tawantinsuyu: Mechanisms of colonization and relationship with ethnic groups. In *The Inca and Aztec states, 1400–1800: Anthropology and history*, edited by G. Collier, R. Rosaldo, and J. Wirth, 173–198. New York: Academic Press.
1985 Cases and variations of verticality in the southern Andes. In *Andean ecology and civilization: An interdisciplinary perspective on Andean ecological complementarity*, edited by S. Masuda, I. Shimada, and C. Morris, 141–160. Tokyo: Tokyo University Press.

Pendergast, D.
1991 The Southern Maya Lowlands contact experience: The view from Lamanai, Belize. In *Colombian Consequences*, vol 3, edited by D. H. Thomas, 337–355. Washington, DC: Smithsonian Institution Press.

Pendergast, D., G. D. Jones, and E. Graham
1993 Locating Maya Lowlands Spanish Colonial towns: A case study from Belize. *Latin American Antiquity* 4:59–73.

Peniche, R.
1983 *Nueva relación de Mérida.* México, D.F: Maldonado Editores.

Peña, S. de la
1979 *La formación del capitalismo en México.* México, D.F: Siglo Veintiuno Editores.

Pérez Rodríguez, P. N.
1966 *Historia de las misiones mercedarios en América.* Madrid: Revista Estudios.

Pinto Soria, J.
1988 *El Valle Central de Guatemala (1524–1821): Un análisis acerca del origen histórico del regionalismo en Centroamérica.* Guatemala: Editorial Universitaria.

Placer-López, G.
1968–1983 *Bibliografía Mercedaria.* 3 vols. Madrid: Monasterio de Poyo.

Pollan, S. D.
1992 Nineteenth century transfer-printed whitewares from the Tambo River, southwest coast of Ecuador. Unpublished manuscript in author's possession.

Polo Sifontes, F.
1981 Título de Alotenango: Clave para ubicar geográficamente la Antigua Itzcuintepec Pipil. *Antropología e Historia de Guatemala* 3:109–125.
1986 *Los Cakchiqueles en la conquista de Guatemala.* Guatemala: Editorial José de Pineda Ibarra.

Porras, P.
1974 *Historia y arqueología de la ciudad española Baeza de los Quijos.* Quito: Centro de Publicaciones de la Pontificia Universidad Católica del Ecuador.

Pratt-Puig, F.
1980 *Significado de un conjunto cerámico hispano del siglo XVI de Santiago de Cuba.* Santiago de Cuba: Editorial Oriente.

Ramos, J., and D. Schávelzon
1992 Historia y arqueología de Palermo de San Benito;

aspecto de su planeamiento ambiental. *Anales del Instituto de Artes Americano e Investigaciones Estéticas* 27(8):74–92. Buenos Aires.

Rands, R., and R. Smith
1965 Pottery of the Guatemalan Highlands. *Handbook of Middle American Indians*, vol. 2, edited by R. Wauchope and G. Willey, 95–145. Austin: University of Texas Press.

Raymond, L.
1984 *Spindle whorls in archaeology*. Museum of Anthropology Occasional Papers in Anthropology 30 Greely: University of Northern Colorado.

Reed, N.
1964 *The caste war of Yucatan*. Stanford: Stanford University Press.

Reina, R. E., and R. M. Hill II
1978 *The traditional pottery of Guatemala*. Austin: University of Texas Press.

Reina Valenzuela, J.
1983 *Historia eclesiástica de Honduras, 1502–1600*. Tegucigalpa: Tipografía Nacional.

Reiner, R., and F. Bryant
1986 Botanical composition and nutritional quality of alpaca diets in two Andean rangeland communities. *Journal of Range Management* 39(5):424–427.

Reitz, E.
1989 Vertebrate fauna from El Azúcar, Ecuador. Unpublished manuscript in possession of author and on file at the Museum of Natural History, University of Georgia, Athens.

Reitz, E., and M. Scarry
1985 *Reconstructing historic subsistence with an example from sixteenth-century Spanish Florida*. Society for Historical Archaeology Special Publication 3. Glassboro, NJ: Society for Historical Archaeology.

Rejón, C. A. G.
1846 *Memoria leida ante el Augusto Congreso Extraordinario de Yucatan por el Secretario General de Gobierno*. El dia 18 de septiembre de 1846. S.P.I.
1862 *Memoria del Secretario General de Gobierno del Estado de Yucatán*. Septiembre de 1862. Mérida: Imprenta José Dolores Espinosa. S.P.I.

Remesal, A. de
1932–33 *Historia general de las Indias Occidentales y particular de la gobernación de Chiapa y Guatemala*, vol. 2. Guatemala: Tipografía Nacional.
1966 *Historia general de las Indias occidentales y particular de la gobernación de Chiapas y Guatemala*, vol. 4. Guatemala: Ministerio de Educación.

Ricard, R.
1966 *The spiritual conquest of Mexico: An essay on the apostolate and the evangelizing method of the mendicant orders in New Spain: 1523–1572*. Berkeley: University of California Press.
1986 *La conquista espiritual de México*. México, D.F: Fondo de Cultura Económica.

Rice, P.M.
1987 The Moquegua Bodegas Survey. *National Geographic Research* 3(2):136–138.
1994 The kilns of Moquegua, Peru: Technology, excavations, and functions. *Journal of Field Archaeology* 21(3):325–344.

Rice, P. M. and D.L. Ruhl
1989 Archaeological survey of the Moquegua bodegas. In *Ecology, settlement, and history in the Osmore Drainage*, edited by D.S. Rice, C. Stanish, and P. Scarr, 479–501. International Series 545. Oxford: British Archaeological Reports.

Rice P.M., and G.C. Smith
1989 The Spanish Colonial wine industry of Moquegua, Peru. *Historical Archaeology* 23(2):41–49.

Rice, P.M., and S.L. Van Beck
1993 The Spanish Colonial kiln tradition of Moquegua, Peru. *Historical Archaeology* 27(4):65–81.

Richter, E.
1971 Untersuchungen zum "Lenca" Problem. Ph.D. dissertation, University of Tubingen.

Rippy, J.F.
1946 The dawn of manufacture in Peru. *Pacific Historical Review* 3:147–157.

Rives, A., L. Domínguez, and M. Pérez
1991 Los documentos históricos sobre las encomiendas y las experiencias indias de Cuba y las evidencias arqueológicas del proceso de contacto indohispano. *Estudios Arqueológicos* 1989. La Habana, Cuba: Editorial Academia.

Robacker, E.F., and A.F. Robacker
1978 *Spatterware and sponge, hardy perennials of ceramics*. New Jersey: A.S. Barnes and Company.

Robinson, E. J.
1990 Reconocimiento de los Municipios de Alotenango y Sumpango, Sacatepequez. Informe Final del Proyecto Encuesta Arqueológica Kaqchikel. Manuscript in author's possession.
1993a Chitak Tzak, Un centro regional Postclásico Tardío de los mayas Kaqchikel. Paper presented at the VII Simposio de Arqueología Guatemalteca. Museo de Arqueología y Etnología, Guatemala.
1993b Chitak Tzak, a Late Postclassic regional center of the Kaqchikel Maya. Paper presented at the American Anthropological Association Meeting, Washington, DC.

Rojas, P.
1981 *Historia general del arte mexicano: época Colonial*. vol. 1. México, D.F: Editorial Hermes.

Romero Frizzi, M. de los A.
1990 *Economía y vida de los españoles en la Mixteca Alta: 1519–1720*. México, D.F: Instituto Nacional de Antropología e Historia.
1991 Personal conversation with J. F. Zeitlin, Instituto Nacional de Antropología e Historia, Centro Regional de Oaxaca.

Rousseau, A.
1989 Excavaciones arqueológicas en el Hospital San Juan de Dios, Quito. Ms. Informe Técnico, Instituto Ecuatoriano de Obras Sanitarias. Quito.
1990 *Proyecto arqueológico Plaza Santo Domingo*. Folleto Informativo: Investigación Arqueológica 1. Municipio de Quito, Dirección de Planificación, Unidad de Apoyo Técnico. Agencia Española de Cooperación Internacional. Sociedad Estatal Quinto Centenario.
1990 Comunicación personal
1991 Comunicación personal

Rowe, J.
1982 Inca policies and institutions relating to the cultural

Roys, R. L.
1939 *The Titles of Ebtun*. Carnegie Institution of Washington Publication 505. Washington, DC.

Rubio Sánchez, M.
1989 *Historia del añil o xiquilite en Centro América*, vols. 1–2. El Salvador: Ministerio de Educación.

Rundel, P.
1980 The ecological distribution of C_4 and C_3 grasses in the Hawaiian Islands. *Oecologia* 45:354–359.

Ruthsatz, T., and U. Hoffmann
1984 Die Verbreitung von C_4-Pflanzen in den semiariden Anden NW-Argentiniens. *Phytocoenologia* 12(2–3):219–249.

Rydén, S.
1947 Archaeological *researches in the Highlands of Bolivia*. Göteborg: Elanders Boktryekeri Aktiebolog.

Sahagún, Fray B. de
1989 *Historia general de las cosas de Nueva España*. México, D.F: Dirección General de Publicaciones del Consejo Nacional para la Cultura y las Artes.

Salomon, F.
1980 *Los señores étnicos de Quito en la época de los incas*. Colección Pendoneros 10. Otavalo, Ecuador: Instituto Otavaleño de Antropología.

Salwen, B., and S. T. Bridges
1977 Cultural differences and the interpretation of archaeological evidence: Problems with dates. *Researches and Transactions of the New York State Archaeological Association* 17(1):165–173.

Samayoa Guevara, H.
1957 Historia del establecimiento de la Orden Mercedaria en el reino de Guatemala, desde el año de 1537 hasta 1653. *Antropología e Historia de Guatemala* 9:30–43.

San Martin, F.
1987 Comparative forage selectivity and nutrition of South American camelids and sheep. Ph.D. dissertation, Texas Technological University, Lubbock.

Sánchez Mosquera, A. M.
1991 Fauna vertebrada de un sitio Colonial en la Península de Santa Elena, Provincia del Guayas, Ecuador. Unpublished paper in author's possession.

Sánchez-Pacheco, T.
1981 Paterna y manises. In *Cerámica esmaltada española*, 53–72. Barcelona: Editorial Labor.

Schaedel, R. P.
1992 The archaeology of the Spanish Colonial experience in South America. *Antiquity* 66:216–242.

Schávelzon, D.
1987 *Tipología de recipientes de gres cerámico para la arqueología histórica de Buenos Aires*. Buenos Aires: Centro de Arqueología Urbana.
1988 *Tipología de loza arqueológica de Buenos Aires*. Buenos Aires: Centro de Arqueología Urbana.
1991 *Arqueología histórica de Buenos Aires: La cultura material porteña de los siglos XVIII y XIX*. Buenos Aires: Editorial Corregidor.
1992a *La arqueología urbana en la Argentina*. Buenos Aires: Centro Editor de América Latina.
1992b *Arqueología histórica de Buenos Aires: Túneles y construcciones subterráneas*. Buenos Aires: Editorial Corregidor.
1994 *Arqueología e historia de la Imprenta Coni, Buenos Aires*. Historical Archaeology in Latin America, vol. 1. Columbia: South Carolina Institute of Archaeology and Anthropology, University of South Carolina.
1995 *Arqueología e historia del Cabildo de Buenos Aires: Informe de las excavaciones 1991–1992*. Historical Archaeology in Latin America, vol. 8. Columbia: South Carolina Institute of Archaeology and Anthropology, University of South Carolina.

Schávelzon, D., and J. Ramos
1991 Excavaciones arqueológicas en el Caserón de Rosas en Palermo, informe de la 2a. temporada (1988). *Revista del Instituto de Investigaciones Históricas Juan Manuel de Rosas* 26:71–92. Buenos Aires.

Schortman, E. M., and P. A. Urban
1987 Survey within the Gualjoquito hinterland: An introduction to the investigations of the Santa Barbara Archaeological Project. In *Prehistoric interaction in the southeast Mesoamerican periphery: Honduras and El Salvador*, edited by E. J. Robinson, 5–27. International Series 327. Oxford: British Archaeological Reports.

Schortman, E. M., P. A. Urban, and W. Ashmore
1984 Reconstrucción de historia cultural e interacción intercultural en Gualjoquito, Santa Bárbara, oeste-central de Honduras. *Mexicon* 6(3):34–38.

Schortman, E., P. Urban, W. Ashmore, and J. C. Benyo
1986 Interregional interaction in the SE Maya periphery: The Santa Barbara Archaeological Project, 1983–1984 seasons. *Journal of Field Archaeology* 13:259–272.

Schuetz, M.
1969 *The history and archaeoloqy of Mission San Juan Capistrano, San Antonio, Texas*. Austin: State Building Commission Archaeological Publication 1.

Schwaller, J. F.
1985 *Origins of church wealth in Mexico: Ecclesiatical revenues and church finances, 1523–1600*. Albuquerque: University of New Mexico Press.
1987 *The church and clergy in sixteenth-century Mexico*. Albuquerque: University of New Mexico Press.

Sebastian, L., J. de Mesa, and T. Gisbert de Mesa
1985 *Summa Artis. Historia general del arte*, vol. 18. Madrid: Espasa-Calpe.

Seifert, D. J.
1977 *Archaeological majolicas of the rural Teotihuacan Valley, Mexico*. Ann Arbor: University Microfilms International.

Semo, Enrique
1981 Historia mexicana, economía y lucha de clases. Ediciones Era, S.A., México.

Sharer, R., W. Ashmore, and R. Hill
1970 The pottery of Antigua Guatemala. A report of the collections recovered by the Hispanic American Research Project 1969–1970. Manuscript in author's possession.

Shephard, S. J.
1983 The Spanish criollo majority in colonial St. Augustine. In *Spanish St. Augustine: The archaeology of a colonial creole community*, edited by K. Deagan, 65–97. New York: Academic Press.

Bibliography

    1987   Status variation in antebellum Alexandria: An archaeological study of ceramic tableware. In *Consumer choice in historical archaeology*, edited by S. Spencer-Wood, 163–198. New York: Plenum Press.

Sherman, W. L.
    1971   Indian slavery and the Cerrato reforms. *Hispanic American Historical Review* 51:25–50.

Shimada, I., and M. Shimada
    1985   Prehistoric llama breeding and herding on the north coast of Peru. *American Antiquity* 50(1):3–26.

Shook, E.
    1952   Lugares arqueológicos del Altiplano meridional central de Guatemala. *Antropología e Historia de Guatemala* 4(2):3–40.
    1991   Personal communication
    1993   Personal communication

Siller, J. A., and J. Abundis
    1984   La casa del adelantado Francisco de Montejo en Mérida. *Cuadernos de Arquitectura Virreinal* 1:25–45. Universidad Nacional Autónoma de México.

Skowronek, R. K.
    1989   A New Europe in the New World: Hierarchy, continuity, and change in the Spanish sixteenth century colonization of Hispaniola and Florida. Ph.D. dissertation, Department of Anthropology, Michigan State University.

Smith, G. C.
    1987   Personal communication
    1991   *Heard it through the grapevine: Andean and European contributions to Spanish Colonial culture and viticulture in Moquegua, Peru.* Ann Arbor: University Microfilms

Smith, Kimball
    1991   Personal communication to Karen Stothert

Smith, R. K., and B. Westbury
    1985   Preliminary report on the 1985 Atahualpa/Punta Pelada Pipeline Corridor Archaeological Mitigation Project. Unpublished report, Department of Anthropology, Southern Methodist University, Dallas.

Smith, R., J. Ramírez Flores,, and L. Pasquel
    1976   *Los consulados de comerciantes en Nueva España.* Instituto Mexicano del Comercio Exterior.

Soustelle, J.
    1937   *La famille Otomi-Pame du Mexique Central.* Institut d'Ethnologie. Travaux et Memoires 26. University de Paris.

South, S.
    1972   Evolution and horizon as revealed in ceramic analysis in historical archaeology. *The Conference on Historic Site Archaeology Papers* 6:71–116.
    1977   *Method and theory in historical archaeology.* New York: Academic Press.
    1990   From thermodynamics to a status artifact model: Spanish Santa Elena. In *Columbian Consequences*, vol. 2, edited by D. H. Thomas, 329–341. Washington, DC: Smithsonian Institution Press.

Spalding, K.
    1970   Social climbers: Changing patterns of mobility among the Indians of Colonial Peru. *Hispanic American Historical Review* 50:645–664.
    1973   Kurakas and commerce: A chapter in the evolution of Andean society. *Hispanic American Historical Review* 53(4):581–599.
    1982   Exploitation as an economic system: The state and the extraction of surplus in Colonial Peru. In *The Inca and Aztec states, 1400–1800*, edited by G. Collier, R. Rosaldo, and J. Wirth, 321–342. New York: Academic Press.
    1984   *Huarochirí: An Andean Society Under Inca and Spanish Rule.* Stanford, California: Stanford University Press.

Spencer-Wood, S., and S. D. Heberling
    1983   Ceramics and socioeconomic status of the Green family, Windsor, Vermont. *Northeast Historical Archaeology* 13:33–52.

Spores, R.
    1984   *The Mixtecs in ancient and Colonial times.* Norman: University of Oklahoma Press.

Stanish, C.
    1985   Post-Tiwanaku regional economies in the Otora Valley, Southern Peru. Ph.D. dissertation, Department of Anthropology, University of Chicago.
    1989a   Household archaeology: Testing models of zonal complementarity in the south central Andes. *American Anthropologist* 91(1):7–24.
    1989b   An archaeological evaluation of an ethnohistorical model. In *Ecology, settlement and history in the Osmore Drainage*, edited by D. Rice, C. Stanish, and P. Scarr, 303–320. International Series 545. Oxford: British Archaeological Reports.
    1992   *Ancient Andean political economy.* Austin: University of Texas Press.

Stanish, C. and I. Pritzker
    1983   Archaeological Reconnaissance in Southern Peru. *Field Museum of Natural History Bulletin* 54:6-17.

Starn, O.
    1991   Missing the revolution: Anthropologists and the war in Peru. *Cultural Anthropology* 6(1):63–91.

Stastny, F.
    1981   *Las artes populares del Perú.* Madrid: Ediciones Edubanco.

Stern, S.
    1982   *Peru's Indian peoples and the challenge of the Spanish conquest: Huamanga to 1640.* Madison: University of Wisconsin Press.

Steward, J.
    1943   Acculturation studies in Latin America: Some needs and problems. *American Anthropologist* 45:198–204.

Stone, D. Z.
    1948   The Northern highland tribes: The Lenca. *Handbook of South American Indians*, vol. 4, edited by J. H. Steward, 205–217. Washington, DC: Bureau of American Ethnology.

Stothert, K. E.
    1993   *Un sitio de Guangala Temprano en el suroeste del Ecuador.* Guayaquil: National Museum of Natural History, Smithsonian Institution, and Museo Antropológico, Banco Central del Ecuador.
    1994   Early petroleum extraction and the archaeology of tar boiling in coastal Ecuador. In *In quest of mineral wealth: Aboriginal and colonial mining and metallurgy in Spanish America*, edited by A. Craig and R. West, 343–354. *Geoscience and Man* 33. Baton Rouge: Louisiana State University.

Stothert, K. E., and J. Parker
    1985   El tejido de una alforja en la Península de Santa

Elena. *Miscelánea Antropológica Ecuatoriana* 4(4):141–160. Guayaquil: Boletín de los Museos del Banco Central del Ecuador.

Strickon, A.
1965 Hacienda and plantation in Yucatan: An historical-ecological consideration of the folk-urban continuum in Yucatan. *América Indígena* 25:35–65.

Sussman, L.
1977 Changes in pearlware dinnerware, 1780–1830. *Historical Archaeology* 11:105–111.
1979 Spode/Copeland transfer-printed patterns found at 20 Hudson's Bay Company sites. Canadian Historic Sites: Occasional Papers in Archaeology and History 22. Ottawa: Parks Canada, National Historic Parks and Sites Branch.

Szeczy, J.
1953 *Santiago de los Caballeros de Goathemala en Almolonga.* Guatemala: Ministerio de Educación de Guatemala.

Taylor, W. B.
1972 *Landlord and peasant in Colonial Oaxaca.* Stanford: Stanford University Press.

Teeri, J.
1979 The climatology of the C_4 photosynthetic pathway. In *Topics in plant population biology*, edited by O. Solbrig, S. Jain, G. Johnson and P. Raven, 356–374. New York: Columbia University Press.

Teeri, J., and L. Stowe
1976 Climatic patterns and the distribution of C_4 grasses in North America. *Oecologia* 23:1–12.

Terán Najas, R.
1991 Investigación sobre la historia artística y arquitectónica del Convento Santo Domingo de Quito, siglos XVI–XVIII. Informe Final. Ms. Proyecto de Cooperación Tecnica Ecuatoriano-Belga, Quito.

Terán de Rodríguez, P.
1989 *Investigaciones arqueológicas y estudio de cerámica Colonial. Convento de San Francisco de Quito. Sitio: OPQSF-2.* V Centenario del Descubrimiento de América. Quito: Instituto de Patrimonio Cultural del Ecuador, Instituto de Cooperación Iberoaméricano de España.
1991 Comunicación personal

Thomas, D. H., ed.
1991 *Colombian consequences* Vol. 3. Washington, DC: Smithsonian Institution Press.

Tieszen, L., D. Hein, S. Qvortrup, J. Troughton, and S. Imbamba
1979a Use of ^{13}C values to determine vegetation selectivity in East African herbivores. *Oecologia* 37:351–359.

Tieszen, L., M. Senyimba, S. Imbamba, and J. Troughton
1979b The distribution of C_3 and C_4 grasses and carbon isotope discrimination along an altitudinal and moisture gradient in Kenya. *Oecologia* 37:337–350.

Tojeira, J. M.
1986 *Panorama histórico de la iglesia en Honduras.* Tegucigalpa: Centro de Documentación de Honduras.

Tranfo, L.
1974 *Vida y magia en un pueblo otomí del Mezquital.* México, D.F.: Secretaría de Educación Pública—Instituto Nacional Indigenista 34.

Treacy, J.
1982 The ceramics industry of Samborondon. Unpublished manuscript, Department of Anthropology, University of Wisconsin, Madison.

Toussaint, M.
1974 *Arte colonial en México.* México, D.F.: Imprenta Universitaria, Universidad Nacional Autónoma de México.

Tschopik, H., Jr.
1950 An Andean ceramic tradition in historical perspective. *American Antiquity* 15(3):196–218.

Tschopik, M.
1946 *Some notes on the archaeology of the Department of Puno, Peru.* Papers of the Peabody Museum of American Archaeology and Ethnology 27(3). Cambridge: Harvard University.

Tutino, J. M.
1976 Provincial Spaniards, Indian towns, and haciendas: Interrelated sectors of agrarian society in the valleys of Mexico and Toluca, 1750–1810. In *Provinces of early Mexico: Variants of Spanish American regional evolution*, edited by I. Altman and J. Lockhart, 36:176–194. Los Angeles: UCLA Latin American Center Publications.

UNESCO
1979 Convention concerning the protection of the World Culture and Natural Heritage, United Nations. UNESCO, Paris.

Urban, P.
1993 Central Santa Bárbara region. In *Pottery of prehistoric Honduras: Regional classification and analysis*, edited by J. S. Henderson and M. Beaudry-Corbett, 137–170. Monograph 35. Institute of Archaeology, University of California, Los Angeles.

Urban, P. A., and S. M. Smith.
1987 The incensarios and candeleros of central Santa Barbara: distributional and functional studies. In *Prehistoric interaction in the southeast Mesoamerican periphery: Honduras and El Salvador*, edited by E.J. Robinson, 267–279. International Series 327. Oxford: British Archaeological Reports.

Valencia, M.
1991 Introducción a la arqueología y cerámica del Convento de Santo Domingo, Antigua, Guatemala. Paper presented at V Simposio de Arqueología Guatemalteca, Museo Nacional de Arqueología y Etnología, Guatemala.

Valero de García Lascuráin, R.
1991 *Solares y conquistadores. Orígenes de la propiedad en la Ciudad de México.* México, D.F.: Instituto Nacional de Antropología e Historia.

Van Beck, S. L.
1991 Spanish Colonial kilns of Moquegua, Peru. Master's thesis, Department of Anthropology, University of Florida, Gainesville.

Van Buren, M., P. Bürgi, and P. Rice
1993 Torata Alta: A late highland settlement in the Osmore Drainage. In *Domestic architecture, ethnicity, and complementarity in the south-central Andes*, edited by M. Aldenderfer, 136–146. Iowa City: University of Iowa Press.

Van Buren, M.
1993 Community and empire in southern Peru: The site of

Torata Alta under Spanish rule. Ph.D. dissertation, Department of Anthropology, University of Arizona.

Van Oss, A. C.
1984 Pueblos y parroquias en Suchitepéquez Colonial. *Mesoamérica* 7:161–179.
1986 *Catholic colonialism: A parish history of Guatemala, 1524–1821.* Cambridge: Cambridge University Press.

Van Young, E.
1983 Mexican rural history since Chevalier: The historiography of the Colonial hacienda. *Latin American Research Review* 18(3):5–61.

Vargas, J.M.
1967 *Patrimonio artístico ecuatoriano.* Quito: Imprenta Santo Domingo.
1986 *Historia de la Provincia Dominicana del Ecuador, siglos XVI y XVII.* Quito: Editorial Royal.

Vázquez, F.
1937–1944 *Crónica de la Provincia del Santísimo Nombre de Jesus de Guatemala de la Orden de N. Seráfico Padre San Francisco en el reino de la Nueva Espana* (1714). Guatemala: Tipografía Nacional.

Vásquez Núñez, G.
1931 La conquista de los indios americanos por los primeros misioneros. *Biblioteca Hispana Missionum* 1:190–213. Barcelona.
1968 *La Orden de La Merced en Hispanoamérica.* Madrid: Edita Revista Estudios.

Vetancurt, Fray A. de
1971 *Teatro mexicano: Descripción breve de los sucesos ejemplares históricos y religiosos del Nuevo Mundo de las indias, crónica de la Provincia del Santo Evangelio de México.* Biblioteca Porrúa 45. México, D.F: Editorial Porrúa.

Villacorta, J. A.
1942 *Historia de la capitanía general de Guatemala.* Guatemala: Tipografía Nacional.

Villavicencio, M.
1984 *Geografía de la República del Ecuador.* Quito: Corporación Editora Nacional.

Viqueira, C., and J.I. Urquiola
1990 *Los obrajes en la Nueva España, 1530–1630.* México, D.F: Dirección General del Consejo Nacional para la Cultura y las Artes.

Wallerstein, I.
1979 *El moderno sistema mundial: La agricultura capitalista y los orígenes de la economía-mundo europea en el siglo XVI.* México, D.F: Siglo Veintiuno Editores.

Wasserstrom, A.
1983 *Class and society in central Chiapas.* Berkeley: University of California Press.

Wauchope, R.
1949 Las edades de Utatlan e Iximche. *Antropología e Historia de Guatemala* 1(1).

Weberbauer, A.
1945 *Mundo vegetal de los Andes peruanos.* Lima: Ministerio de Agricultura.

Webre, S.
1990 Water and society in a Spanish American city: Santiago de Guatemala, 1555–1773. *Hispanic American Historical Review* 70:1.

Webster, S.
1973 Native pastoralism in the South Andes. *Ethnology* 12:115–133.

Weeks, J. M., and N. J. Black
1987 Investigaciones sobre el periodo Postclásico en el Valle de Tencoa, Departamento de Santa Bárbara, Honduras. *Yaxkin* 10(2):135–150.
1991 Mercedarian missionaries and the transformation of Lenca Indian society in western Honduras, 1550–1700. In *Columbian Consequences*, vol. 3, edited by D. H. Thomas, 245–261, Washington, DC: Smithsonian Institution Press.

Weeks, J. M., N. J. Black, and J. S. Speaker
1987 Postclassic and colonial occupation in Santa Barbara, Honduras. In *Prehistoric interaction in the southeast Mesoamerican periphery: Honduras and El Salvador*, edited by E. J. Robinson, 65–94. International Series 327. Oxford: British Archaeological Reports.

Wentworth, T.
1985 Distributions of C_4 plants along environmental and compositional gradients in southeastern Arizona. In *Plant Community Ecology: Papers in Honor of Robert H. Whittaker*, edited by R.K. Peet, 111–131.

Westbury, B.
1984 Appendix E: The historic materials. In The Atahualpa/Playas Pipeline Corridor Survey (July 1984): Report of sites and recommendations, by R. K. Smith, A. E. Marks, and M. Masucci. Unpublished report, Department of Anthropology, Southern Methodist University, Dallas.

Wetherington, R., ed.
1978 *The ceramics of Kaminaljuyu, Guatemala.* Monograph Series on Kaminaljuyu. University Park: Pennsylvania State University.

Wheat, J.B., J.C. Clifford, and W.W. Wasley
1958 Ceramic variety, type cluster, and ceramic system in Southwestern pottery analysis. *American Antiquity* 24(1):34–47.

Wheaton, T. R., and P. H. Garrow
1985 Acculturation and the archaeological record in the Carolina Low Country. In *The archaeology of slavery and plantation life*, edited by Theresa Singleton, 239–60. New York: Academic Press.

Whitaker, A. P.
1929 The Spanish contribution to American agriculture. *Agricultural History* 3(1):1–14.

Whiter, L.
1970 *Spode: A history of the family, factory, and wares from 1733 to 1833.* London: Barrie and Jenkins.

Williams, P., and M. R. Weber
1986 *Staffordshire II: Romantic transfer patterns cup plates and early Victorian china.* Jeffersontown, Kentucky: Fountain House East.

Wobeser, G. von
1983 *La formación de la hacienda en la época Colonial.* México, D.F: Universidad Nacional Autónoma de México.

Wolf, E.
1982 *Europe and the people without history.* Berkeley: University of California Press.

Ximénez, F.
1929–31 *Historia de la Provincia de San Vicente de Chiapa y Guatemala de la Orden de Predicadores.* 3 vols. Guatemala: Tipografía Nacional.

Yentsch, A.
1991 Engendering visible and invisible ceramic artifacts, especially dairy vessels. *Historical Archaeology* 25(4):132–155.

Young, T.
1847 *Narrative of a residence on the Mosquito shore.* London: Elder and Co.

Zaportes Pallares, J.
1983 *Vida eclesial en Guatemala a fines del siglo XVII, 1683–1701.* Guatemala: CENALTEX.

Zavala, S.
1984 *El servicio personal de los indios de la Nueva España-I: 1521–1550.* México, D.F.: El Colegio de México.

Zeitlin, J. F.
1978 *Community distribution and local economy on the southern Isthmus of Tehuantepec: An archaeological and ethnohistorical investigation.* Ann Arbor: University Microfilms International.

1989 Ranchers and Indians on the southern Isthmus of Tehuantepec: Economic change and indigenous survival in Colonial Mexico. *Hispanic American Historical Review* 69(1): 23–60.

1994 Precolumbian barrio organization in Tehuantepec, Mexico. In *Caciques and their people*, edited by J. Marcus and J. F. Zeitlin, 275–300. Anthropological Papers of the Museum of Anthropology 89. University of Michigan, Ann Arbor.

Zeitlin, R. N.
1993 Pacific coastal Laguna Zope: A regional center in the Terminal Formative hinterlands of Monte Alban. *Ancient Mesoamérica* 4:85–101.

Zilbermann de Luján, C.
1987 *Aspectos socioeconómicos del traslado de la ciudad de Guatemala, 1773–1783.* Guatemala: Academia de Geografía e Historia de Guatemala.

Zúñiga Corres, I.
1968 El origen de la Orden de La Merced en Guatemala. *Anales de la Sociedad de Geografía e Historia de Guatemala* 41:432–542.